Second Language Teacher Education

International Perspectives

Second Language Teacher Education

International Perspectives

Edited by

Diane J. Tedick
University of Minnesota

LEA LAWRENCE ERLBAUM ASSOCIATES, PUBLISHERS
2005 Mahwah, New Jersey London

Lawrence Erlbaum Associates, Inc., Publishers
10 Industrial Avenue
Mahwah, New Jersey 07430

Cover design by Kathryn Houghtaling Lacey

Library of Congress Cataloging-in-Publication Data

Second language teacher education : international perspectives / edited by Diane J. Tedick.
p. cm.
Includes bibliographical references and index.
ISBN 0-8058-4879-7 (cloth : alk. paper)
ISBN 0-8058-4880-0 (pbk. : alk. paper)
1. Language teachers—Training of. 2. Second language acquisition. I. Tedick, Diane J.

P53.85.S434 2004
418'.0071—dc22 2004053339
CIP

Books published by Lawrence Erlbaum Associates are printed on acid-free paper, and their bindings are chosen for strength and durability.

Printed in the United States of America
10 9 8 7 6 5 4 3 2

This volume is dedicated to teachers around the world who devote their professional lives to helping others learn languages.

Contents

Contributors

Dick Allwright, Lancaster University, Lancaster, England
Martha Bigelow, University of Minnesota, Minneapolis, Minnesota
Heidi Byrnes, Georgetown University, Washington, DC
Nancy Cloud, Rhode Island College, Providence, Rhode Island
Sharon Cormany, Patrick Henry High School, Minneapolis, Minnesota
Nancy E. Dubetz, Lehman College, City University of New York, Bronx, New York
Julian Edge, Aston University, Birmingham, England
Tony Erben, University of South Florida, Tampa, Florida
Tara W. Fortune, University of Minnesota, Minneapolis, Minnesota
Donald Freeman, School for International Training, Brattleboro, Vermont
Sachiko Hiramatsu, State University of New York at Buffalo, Buffalo, New York
Karen E. Johnson, The Pennsylvania State University, University Park, Pennsylvania
Bill Johnston, Indiana University, Bloomington, Indiana
Julie Kalnin, University of Minnesota, Minneapolis, Minnesota
Rebecca Mahan-Taylor, Indiana University, Bloomington, Indiana
Christina Maynor, Patrick Henry High School, Minneapolis, Minnesota
Faridah Pawan, Indiana University, Bloomington, Indiana
Leslie Poynor, University of New Mexico, Albuquerque, New Mexico
Susan Ranney, University of Minnesota, Minneapolis, Minnesota
Angela Scarino, University of South Australia, Adelaide, South Australia
Elana Shohamy, Tel Aviv University, Tel Aviv, Israel
Lorraine C. Smith, Adelphi University, Garden City, New York

Marguerite Ann Snow, California State University, Los Angeles, California
Elaine Tarone, University of Minnesota, Minneapolis, Minnesota
Diane J. Tedick, University of Minnesota, Minneapolis, Minnesota
Constance L. Walker, University of Minnesota, Minneapolis, Minnesota

Foreword

Sarah J. Hudelson
Arizona State University

I came into the field of second language teaching in 1966 as a VISTA Volunteer in South Texas. The small home that my roommate and I rented in a Mexican-American barrio became a kind of community center, and every weekday morning our living room became an *escuelita*, a preschool, for 3- and 4-year-old neighborhood children who did not speak English. The idea was that my roommate and I, neither of whom had any formal background in early childhood education, elementary education, or education related to teaching a second language, would be English teachers. We spoke English; therefore we would teach English. That first teaching experience (in which I believe that I learned more Spanish than the children in the *escuelita* learned English) sent me, at the end of VISTA service, back to graduate school. I was seeking elementary education teaching certification, but I was also looking for a knowledge base that would assist me in teaching English and school content to non-English-speaking children. That ongoing search has led me to a career in education.

More than 35 years later, I would characterize myself currently as a bilingual/second language teacher educator, with a special and abiding interest in children's first and second language literacy development. As an elementary school classroom teacher, a graduate teaching assistant, a curriculum writer, and a teacher educator, I have worked mainly in Spanish–English bilingual education and in English as a second language (ESL) teaching settings around the United States and, to a much lesser extent, in English as a foreign language (EFL) education in South America, Europe, and North Africa. It is from this set of experiences, and particularly from my career as a teacher educator, that I come to Diane Tedick's volume, *Second Language Teacher Education: International Perspectives.*

The work that Tedick has collected and organized here brings together perspectives of teacher educators and teachers in a variety of second language settings around the world. Some work in ESL or EFL education, others in foreign language education, and still others in bilingual or immersion education contexts. The settings vary from elementary schools to secondary and postsecondary classrooms. Some of the contributors describe projects carried out with preservice and novice teachers. Others chronicle the professional growth and renewal of experienced educators. Fully one fourth of the chapters feature second language teaching and teacher education outside the United States.

My own experience has been that professional sharing most often is limited to others in one's own specialization: ESL educators, for example, communicating mostly with other ESL (and perhaps EFL) professionals in forums such as conferences and publications of professional organizations (e.g., Teachers of English to Speakers of Other Language—TESOL). Although there is talk about collaboration and cross-fertilization, this talk does not always lead to action. One of the outstanding features of this collection is that it does bring together the voices of professionals from related areas of second language teacher education to share their expertise and their challenges. In this volume, Tedick set out intentionally to represent the diversity in what she terms "the world of second language teacher education ..." and to "... contribute to meaningful professional dialogue among teacher educators across languages, levels, settings, and geographic and second language contexts" (Preface, this volume, p. xvii).

The contributions have been placed into one of four themes. Each theme addresses a broad question: What should second language teachers know and be able to do? What kinds of contexts do second language teachers and teacher educators live and work in? How might teachers and teacher educators collaborate in second language teaching and learning settings? Given the knowledge base, varying contexts, and multiple possibilities for collaboration, what are some examples of effective second language teacher education in action? Although the specific responses to these questions vary, all of the contributions share certain stances with regard to teachers and teacher education, and the chapters articulate the ways that second language teacher educators around the world are struggling to make these visions reality.

The first stance is that teachers are professionals, not technicians. This is true regardless of whether teacher educators are working with preservice or inservice teachers and regardless of the age of the students taught. The second stance is that teachers must construct their own knowledge rather than have someone else transmit it to them. The third stance is that knowledge construction necessarily involves collaboration. In the case of educators, the collaborators must include teachers themselves and often others from outside the classroom, such as university and school district colleagues, who join together to form a learning community. Collaborative work must stem from a belief in the equality of all participants in the collaboration. The fourth stance is that teachers need to be at the center of their own professional development. Teachers need to ask their own questions and seek to answer them, even as they collaborate with others.

This volume has impressed me for several reasons. The first is, as already mentioned, its international perspective, combined with the inclusion of scholars from a number of second language teaching and scholarly communities. It is stimulating to read about innovative approaches to second language education and to second language teacher education in other contexts. The chapters serve to stimulate and energize those of us who may develop tunnel vision because we are so involved in our own local circumstances. The volume also impresses me because it includes contributions from well-established, internationally known scholars acknowledged as leaders in their respective fields and from young, up-and-coming scholars who represent the future of these fields. To me, this variety sends the message that valuable contributions to the dialogue about second language teacher education come from a variety of sources and that the dialogue is alive and well and will continue. Finally, the volume impresses me because of the contributions of practicing teachers. The inclusion of teacher authors sends a message that practitioners' voices matter.

As she concludes the preface to this book, Diane Tedick writes that "this volume is purposefully about second language teacher education specifically. It is by and for second language teacher educators around the world" (p. xxii). I applaud Tedick's determination to focus on this particular audience, in all its variety and complexity, and I applaud the result of her efforts. I am confident that this volume will stimulate further conversations and collaborations among those of us whose passion is the teaching and learning of second languages.

Preface

The world of second language teacher education is a complex one, encompassing a wide range of second language contexts, national and international contexts, and instructional and institutional settings. From English as a second language (ESL) to English as a foreign language (EFL) to foreign language education, bilingual education, language immersion education, and from Pre-K–12 settings, to community colleges and four year institutions, to adult language instructional settings, second language education and teacher education takes place in numerous contexts across the globe. Our world is also a fragmented one. Rarely do teacher educators from different second language and instructional contexts have an opportunity to engage in professional dialogue, despite the fact that ultimately, we are all working toward the same goal—the preparation and continuing professional development of second language teachers so that their students might communicate across linguistic and cultural boundaries. This edited volume serves as one attempt to address this fragmentation. In it, I aim to bring together research, theory, and best practices from a variety of second language teacher education contexts and to contribute to meaningful professional dialogue among teacher educators across languages, levels, settings, and geographic and second language contexts.

The genesis for this volume was the Second International Conference on Language Teacher Education held in May 2001. Many of the chapters in this book were originally presented at the conference but have evolved considerably since then. Other chapters share work that was not presented at the conference but that contributes to the dialogue across contexts. The conference continues to be held every other year at the

University of Minnesota[1] and it serves as a stimulus for collaboration among teacher educators representing this wide range of second language contexts. It is my hope that this volume will also serve as a similar stimulus to spark collaboration and professional dialogue across areas. We have much to learn from and with each other.

THE ORGANIZATION OF THE VOLUME

This volume is comprised of 18 chapters. It is divided into four sections that are thematically conceptualized as follows:

1. The knowledge base of second language teacher education.
2. The contexts of second language teacher education.
3. Collaborations in second language teacher education.
4. Second language teacher education in practice.

The "knowledge base" refers to what it is that second language teachers need to know and understand to be effective teachers and how that knowledge is incorporated into second language teacher education. The knowledge base is a broad theme and encompasses research and perspectives on, for example, knowledge and experiences, beliefs and attitudes, teacher socialization and learning, teacher cognition, teacher identity, reflective teaching, and values and ethical dispositions. Quite recently, a number of professional organizations have attempted to define the knowledge base through the creation of standards for second language teacher education.

"Contexts" also represents a broad theme, which touches on the contexts in which second language teacher education takes place and second language contexts themselves (ESL, EFL, foreign language, immersion, bilingual education) as well as different geographic, social, cultural, political, and institutional contexts. Context is, in a word, *key* in second language teacher education.

The third theme, "collaborations," speaks to the importance of cooperation and collaborative relationships in the work of second language teacher education. It includes institutional collaboration between schools and colleges of teacher education as well as the collaborative relationships that are formed among second language teachers or teacher

---

[1]This biennial conference is sponsored by the University of Minnesota's College of Education and Human Development and College of Liberal Arts in partnership with the Center for Advanced Research on Language Acquisition (CARLA), a U.S. Department of Education Title VI Language Resource Center. More information can be found at the CARLA Web site: http://www.carla.umn.edu/

educators themselves, including examples of action research that results from collaborative relationships.

Finally, "second language teacher education in practice" focuses on how the work of second language teacher education is accomplished. This theme showcases program models and underlying philosophies and provides examples of how the other three themes—knowledge base, contexts, and collaborations—are embedded in actual programs.

Each of these themes is very broad. Several books could be written about each theme itself—indeed, many such books have already contributed to the profession. The intention of this volume is not to provide a thorough examination of each theme but rather to offer a sample of perspectives on and examples of how each of the themes manifests itself in second language teacher education in various countries around the world. These four themes are also interrelated, and this interrelation can be seen throughout the chapters that comprise the book. At the same time, each theme can be considered in turn. The chapters in the first section, for example, all emphasize aspects related to the knowledge base even though they also reflect issues related to contexts or practices. Table P.1 presents an overview of the chapters organized by theme and identifies the contexts that are represented—that is, the context of the work presented, the second language and institutional context, and whether the chapter focuses on preservice and/or inservice teacher education.

Some of the chapters in the volume reflect all four themes yet are placed in a particular section because they present especially strong examples of that theme. For example, Nancy Dubetz's chapter (chap. 13, this volume) appears in the section on Collaborations, yet it reflects each of the four themes. Dubetz's chapter focuses on the collaboration that occurs in a study group in the context of an urban elementary school that has been designated as a Professional Development School (PDS), which involves a collaborative relation between a teacher education program in a nearby college and the school. Of particular importance to the study group and the PDS is a priority goal of supporting the English language development and content learning of the ESL learners enrolled in the school's bilingual program (context). Throughout the year that the study takes place, study group participants share their knowledge, beliefs, and teaching strategies (knowledge base and practices) with each other and in so doing, transform their own theories of practice, which "reflects a teacher's negotiation of multiple sources of *knowledge* [italics added], including personal beliefs and values, pedagogical and content knowledge, knowledge of children, and the expectations of the school culture where she or he works" (Dubetz, chap. 13, this volume, p. 235). Yet because the study

TABLE P.1

Overview of Second Language Teacher Education Contexts Represented in Chapters

Chapter and Author(s)	*Research (R), Theory (T), and/or Practice (P)*	*Work Context*	*Language Setting Represented (ESL, EFL, FL, Bilingual Immersion)*	*Inservice and/or Preservice Teacher Education*	*Instructional Setting Represented (Elementary, Secondary, Postsecondary)*
Theme I: Knowledge Base					
1. Tarone & Allwright	T	General[a]	General	General	General
2. Freeman & Johnson	T	General	General	General	General
3. Scarino	R	Australia	FL	Inservice	Secondary
4. Johnston, Pawan, & Mahan-Taylor	R	Japan	EFL/ESL	Inservice	Postsecondary
5. Freeman & Johnson	T & R	General	General (FL)	General	General
Theme II: Contexts					
6. Shohamy	T	General	General	General	General
7. Hiramatsu	R	Japan	EFL	Inservice	Secondary
8. Byrnes	T & P	United States	FL (TAs)	Preservice and inservice	Postsecondary
9. Poynor	R	United States	Bilingual and ESL	Preservice and year 1	Elementary

		Theme III: Collaborations			
10. Edge	T & P	United Kingdom	General (teacher educators)	Inservice	Postsecondary
11. Smith	R	United States	ESL	Inservice (adjunct)	Postsecondary
12. Cormany, Maynor, & Kalnin	R & P	United States	FL & ESL	Inservice	Secondary
13. Dubetz	R	United States	Bilingual & ESL	Inservice	Elementary
		Theme IV: Practices			
14. Snow	P & T	United States	ESL	Preservice	All
15. Cloud	P & T	United States	Bilingual & Immersion	Preservice and inservice	Elementary and secondary
16. Erben	P & T	Australia	Immersion	Preservice	Postsecondary
17. Bigelow & Tedick	P & T	United States	All	Preservice and inservice	K–12 (or all)
18. Walker, Ranney, & Fortune	P & T	United States	Grade level and content area	Preservice	K–12

Note. ESL = English as a second language, EFL= English as a foreign language, FL = Foreign language, K–12 = Kindergarten through 12th grade.[a]General = no specific context is highlighted.

reported by Dubetz has as its center the collaborative relationship that emerges in the PDS study group, the chapter offers a particularly strong example of the theme of collaborations.

Similarly, chapter 7 (this volume), by Sachiko Hiramatsu, is located in the section on Contexts and presents a case study of EFL teaching in Japan. Hiramatsu explores the impact that two national reform initiatives have had in one high school, in particular the Japanese Exchange and Teaching program, which brings in native English speakers as assistant language teachers to collaborate and team teach with Japanese teachers of English, and the revision of the English curriculum, which requires a course in oral communication. As Hiramatsu presents the results of her study through the voices of teachers, we get a glimpse of the knowledge base that informs their thinking, of the practices in which they engage, and of the challenges the participants face as they struggle to collaborate in the teaching of new oral communication classes. The context of EFL teaching in Japan in light of these two reform initiatives is absolutely central to the study and thus explains the chapter's placement in the section on Contexts.

Each of the four sections of the book begins with a brief introduction to situate the chapters within the section's theme. The chapters are also briefly summarized so that readers are able to see how the theme is embedded in the various contributions that comprise that section.

Although this book represents an attempt to bring together a wide range of contexts and instructional and institutional settings in which second language teacher education occurs, it does not account for all of the different contexts of second language teacher education. Nor does it offer inclusion of native language teacher education—language arts education in elementary schools, English education for the secondary level, and composition and literature instruction in postsecondary contexts. Second language teacher educators are very aware that there are similar debates and efforts in the world of first language education, and indeed, much of the work that we do in second language teaching and teacher education draws in part on the important developments that emerge in first language contexts. The reference lists that accompany each of the chapters serve as a testament to this fact. Nevertheless, this volume is purposefully about second language teacher education specifically. It is by and for second language teacher educators around the world.

ACKNOWLEDGMENTS

I am deeply grateful to many individuals who have helped to bring this volume to fruition. First, I would like to thank the contributors to the book, all valued colleagues who share my interest in language teacher education. I appreciate their wonderful work and the patience they have shown throughout the process.

A number of teacher educators participated in a blind review of the manuscripts that were submitted for consideration for this volume. Their thoughtful reactions and insights greatly improved the quality of the contributions to this volume. Sincere thanks to the following individuals for their careful reading and valuable suggestions:

Elizabeth Bernhardt	Director, Language Center Professor, German Studies Stanford University
Diane Birckbichler	Professor, Department of French and Italian Director, Foreign Language Center The Ohio State University
Barbara A. Campbell	Program Director, English Language Institute, State University of New York at Buffalo
Carmen Coballes-Vega	Dean of the College of Professional Studies Metropolitan State University, St. Paul, Minnesota
JoAnn Crandall	Professor, Department of Education Director, Doctoral Program in Language, Literacy, and Culture University of Maryland Baltimore County
Helena Curtain	Associate Professor, Department of Curriculum and Instruction, University of Wisconsin Milwaukee
Diane Ging	Teaching Specialist, Language, Literacy and Culture, The Ohio State University
JoAnn Hammadou Sullivan	Professor, French and Foreign Language Education, University of Rhode Island
L. Kathy Heilenman	Associate Professor, Foreign Languages and ESL Education, University of Iowa
Suzanne Irujo	Professor Emerita of Education Boston University
Gilbert Jarvis	Chairperson Professor Emeritus, School of Teaching and Learning The Ohio State University
Pam McCollum	Senior Education Consultant, Intercultural Development Research Association, San Antonio Texas
Irma Josefina O'Neill	Senior Program Officer, New Visions for Public Schools, New York

Charlene Polio	Associate Professor, Linguistics and Languages, Michigan State University
Dorothy Rissel	Associate Professor, Department of Learning and Instruction, State University of New York at Buffalo
Keiko Samimy	Associate Professor, Language, Literacy and Culture, The Ohio State University
José E. Vega	Professor, Department of Teacher Education, University of Wisconsin-River Falls

The two reviewers of the manuscript as a whole, Loretta S. Verplaetse and Sarah J. Hudelson, offered extremely valuable feedback and insightful questions that helped in important ways to shape the volume. Special thanks also to Sarah for graciously agreeing to write the foreword to the volume.

The staff at Lawrence Erlbaum Associates has been very supportive. Sara Scudder and Lori Hawver had tremendous patience with me throughout the process of preparing the manuscript for publication. I am also grateful to Naomi Silverman, my editor, for believing in the book from the beginning and for her guidance along the way.

I would also like to thank Cathy Zemke in the department of Curriculum and Instruction at the University of Minnesota for her help in preparing the manuscript and Jessie Eastman for additional help and moral support.

Heartfelt thanks also to Michael Lind for giving me the time, support, and much needed distractions during the time that the book was coming together.

Finally, I would like to express my sincere appreciation to the language teachers with whom I work. Their commitment to language teaching inspires me every day, and their insights and challenging questions help me grow as a language teacher educator.

—Diane J. Tedick

Theme I

THE KNOWLEDGE BASE OF SECOND LANGUAGE TEACHER EDUCATION

A central issue in teacher education is the question of what constitutes the knowledge base of teaching and how it relates to the content and practice of teacher education. What do teachers need to know and how is that knowledge embedded in teacher education in both preparation programs and ongoing professional development for teachers? As described in the general teacher education literature and in the second language teacher education literature, the knowledge base is seen as a broad construct and includes, for example, research and theory on teachers' knowledge and beliefs, teacher cognition, teacher learning in formal and informal contexts, teachers' ways of knowing, teacher socialization, reflective teaching, teacher identity, values and ethical dispositions, and the nature of disciplinary knowledge. In addition, the knowledge base has most recently been operationalized as standards for second language teacher education that have been developed by various professional organizations. The chapters in this first section of the book explore some of the issues that encompass the knowledge base.

In 1998, Donald Freeman and Karen E. Johnson served as guest editors of a special-topic issue of the *TESOL Quarterly*, which focused on research and practice in English as a second language teacher education. The lead article was authored by Freeman and Johnson (1998) and has since become quite important in the field. It is cited often (indeed, in a number of chapters in this volume), yet it has not been without controversy. This section of the book opens with a critique of the

Freeman and Johnson article in chapter 1 by Elaine Tarone and Dick Allwright. Their chapter raises a number of key questions and points about the stance that Freeman and Johnson took; most notably, Tarone and Allwright argue that second language teacher education is different from teacher education for other disciplines. They further claim that whereas it should draw on research in general teacher education, second language teacher education needs also to build research that is unique to second language contexts. Tarone and Allwright also argue for the role of the second language learner in a model of the knowledge base of second language teacher education and make a strong case for the key role that second language acquisition (SLA) research must play in language teacher education.

In the spirit of encouraging continued debate and dialogue in the field, chapter 2 presents a response by Donald Freeman and Karen E. Johnson to the critiques raised about their 1998 article by Tarone and Allwright in chapter 1. Freeman and Johnson's response helps to clarify a number of the points they made in 1998. They continue to argue that the subject matter of language does not differentiate second language teacher education from teacher education in general and conclude that they and their colleagues, Tarone and Allwright, will need to "agree to disagree" on their respective views. They further point out what they believe to be misinterpretations about their 1998 work, importantly emphasizing the value they place in SLA research and its role in teacher education, for example.

In reading the first two chapters (Tarone & Allright, chap. 1; Freeman & Johnson, chap.2), readers are left to ponder their own beliefs about and experiences with second language teacher education. Clearly, there is no one "truth" when it comes to discussion about what constitutes the knowledge base in second language teacher education.

Chapter 3 (Scarino) brings home the complexity and breadth of the knowledge base of second language teacher education with its focus on values and ethical dispositions as critical components of the knowledge base. Offering a description of a research study that was conducted with foreign language teachers in the Australian context, Angela Scarino shows how introspection and restrospection can be used as powerful research tools for uncovering teachers' implicit knowledge, values, and ethical dispositions. Throughout her chapter, Scarino weaves in the voices of teachers to show what drives their judgments of student writing in French. In so doing, Scarino makes a strong argument for the importance of attending to "ethical knowing" in second language teacher education programs.

The construct of the knowledge base is expanded further in chapter 4, in which Bill Johnston, Faridah Pawan, and Rebecca Mahan-

Taylor report on a portion of a larger study that focuses on teacher knowledge from the perspective of continued professional development. The teacher showcased in this chapter was teaching English as a foreign language at the university level in Japan. Johnston, Pawan, and Mahan-Taylor focus on teacher identity (specifically, two aspects of identity that they refer to as cultural and professional identity) and teacher knowledge and beliefs. Within these two broad areas related to the knowledge base (identity and knowledge/beliefs), Johnston, Pawan, and Mahan-Taylor point to tensions that emerge in the teacher's discourse, tensions that are in part framed by what the authors refer to as "personal agendas and cultural baggage" (p. 68) but which may be compared to values and ethical dispositions as described in the previous chapter by Scarino (chap. 3).

The final chapter in this section of the book returns us to Donald Freeman and Karen E. Johnson. In chapter 5, Freeman and Johnson further their conceptualization of the knowledge base of language teacher education by focusing on the relation between teacher knowledge and student learning. Like the two chapters before it, this chapter also brings in the voice of the teacher yet this time with student voices as well. Freeman and Johnson first describe the "actions, activity, and tools" of teaching; they then explore the relation between teaching and learning (and the role that activity and tools play) by examining three conceptual frames that have been used to describe this relation. Finally, they draw on data collected in the Teacher Knowledge Project at the School for International Training to illustrate the third conceptual frame, which is one of influence, that is, how professional development influences teachers' teaching and how that teaching influences student learning.

Together, these five chapters offer the field a window into various aspects of the knowledge base of second language teacher education. They explore questions such as, Is second language teacher education different from other kinds of teacher education? In what ways? What values and ethical dispositions underlie the knowledge that teachers use? What constitutes teacher identity and how do knowledge and beliefs interact with that identity? How does the work that language teachers do intersect with the work that language learners do? What is the relation between what teachers know and believe, how they act, and how students are influenced by those actions?

REFERENCES

Freeman, D., & Johnson, D. (1998). Reconceptualizing the knowledge-base of language teacher education. *TESOL Quarterly, 32,* 397–418.

Chapter **1**

Second Language Teacher Learning and Student Second Language Learning: Shaping the Knowledge Base

Elaine Tarone
University of Minnesota

Dick Allwright
Lancaster University

INTRODUCTION

As the editors of a special issue of *TESOL Quarterly* devoted to language teacher education, Freeman and Johnson (1998) make a significant contribution to the debate with their key article titled "Reconceptualizing the Knowledge-Base of Teacher Education." In this article they set out the need as they see it for a reconceptualization of the knowledge base of language teacher education, and then they suggest what the reconceptualized knowledge base would need to look like. We consider each of these points in turn, first the need to reconceptualize the knowledge base and second the postulated content of the knowledge base.

THE NEED TO RECONCEPTUALIZE THE KNOWLEDGE-BASE OF LANGUAGE TEACHER EDUCATION

The argument made by Freeman and Johnson (1998) in favor of a reconceptualization of the knowledge base for language teacher education appears to us to rest essentially on two major charges that they make against language teacher education as it is currently practiced. First, they argue that people designing language teacher education programs typically fail to take into account, at the level of curriculum design, what we know about general teacher learning; second, they argue that language teacher education programs also typically fail to deal with the social context of schools and schooling. We believe these two charges warrant further examination. Our purpose in writing this chapter is therefore to offer this further examination of Freeman and Johnson's arguments and to draw what we now see as the appropriate conclusions for the design of language teacher education programs and therefore for the design of appropriate research programs.

We know that in doing so, we probably run the risk of appearing to want to undermine what we in fact see as the most important point made by Freeman and Johnson (1998), namely, that the design of second language teacher education programs should in principle be centrally based on what is known about second language teacher learning. It is precisely because we want to give that point the strongest possible support, however, that we see it as necessary and helpful to analyze in some detail the case made by Freeman and Johnson. In brief, we fear, as we hope to show below, that because of the structure of their argument, their article risks antagonizing the very people they will most certainly need on their side.

As background to our further examination, we first comment that unlike Freeman and Johnson (1998), who throughout their article deal with teacher learning and teacher education as largely undifferentiated unitary concepts, we see a need from the outset to focus specifically on second language teacher learning and second language teacher education programs. A very important contribution made by Freeman and Johnson has been to point to the large amount of research that has been done on teacher learning in general. As they point out, research on teacher learning has expanded exponentially in recent years and that research must be relevant to language teacher education. However, we differ from Freeman and Johnson in our unwillingness to assume that we know precisely how that research on general teacher learning bears on second-language teacher learning and therefore on second-language teacher education. To put it in a nutshell, we believe that teachers of different subject areas must learn different things and may have to learn those things in different ways. For example, learning to pay attention to the linguistic forms produced by our students while simultaneously processing the content of their utterances is something that is not required of a biology teacher or a ballet teacher. It is not clear how and when a second-language teacher must learn to do this. Consequently, we feel strongly that in addition to research on general teacher learning, which has generated good information for us to begin with, research is also needed specifically on second-language teacher learning. We believe that we have important allies in this regard: For example, Brice Heath (2000, p. 34) points to the need in our field for education researchers to have a grounding in linguistics and other disciplines related to understanding the context of language use. The goal, Brice Heath says, is to bring qualitative research findings to bear on the transformation of coursework in second-language teacher education.

In thinking about second language teacher education, we believe we should distinguish at least between preservice courses and those offered to teachers with classroom experience (i.e., between preservice and inservice programs). In fact, we see a need to go further and to differentiate both conceptually and practically between teacher training, teacher education, and teacher development for our purposes here. Whereas others (such as Crandall, 2000, p. 36) have pointed to the traditional balance in language teacher education between education and training, we add a third dimension, namely teacher development. Conceptually we see training as being concerned with skills (such as being able to write legibly on the blackboard or being able to speak up so that a whole roomful of children can hear everything you say to them). Education is concerned with knowledge (such as being aware of all the different uses to which a blackboard could be put or knowing something about the English article system). Development is concerned with understanding (such as understanding why children, especially teenage children, may find it difficult to perform their best in a foreign language classroom).

By understanding, we are referring to something beyond merely having a particular skill or having a certain piece of knowledge. Understanding is whatever helps us to use our skill and knowledge appropriately. Knowing how to get learners to work in groups (a pedagogic skill) and knowing that it could help their linguistic development (pedagogic knowledge) does not in itself mean we are not going perhaps to make unwise decisions about the use of group work in our lessons. Understanding may also be what helps us to feel we know what we are doing and why so that we may be able to feel at ease with what we are doing with our skill and our knowledge.

In practice, we see that all three notions are relevant all the time to all the stages of a teacher's career but that the balance between them may vary importantly over time. For example, to take the simplest set of possibilities, a novice language teacher may first and foremost need the practical skills to survive initial teaching experiences. However, later on, once survival is assured, that same teacher may wish to know a lot more about the background to language teaching. Later still, that teacher may also wish, against a background of skilled competence and wide knowledge, to develop a deeper understanding of factors affecting second language learning and use in his or her classroom. At this stage, the understanding may be sought more for the sake of increased job satisfaction than for the sake of improved classroom performance. We believe these distinctions are very important in designing second language teacher education programs and thus *a fortiori* for designing a satisfactory research program for second language teacher learning.

The Two Charges and the Relationship Between Them

Essentially, we believe that Freeman and Johnson (1998) weaken their overall argument for a reconceptualization of the knowledge base for language teacher education by taking teacher education as a unitary concept in itself and then by raising two charges against current practice in language teacher education as if both were equally important and not in need of separate treatment. They weaken their argument because by putting their two charges together, they risk losing everything if either one of the charges does not stand up successfully to further scrutiny. In this regard, it is important that both of the charges are about the status quo in teacher education programs and about the historical tradition that underlies the current situation. In this sense, they are matters of fact rather than matters of value judgment. In other words, although we would be happy to agree with Freeman and Johnson that if their charges accurately describe the status quo then the situation for language teacher education is indeed currently highly regrettable, we feel we should at least pause first to ask ourselves if the situation is quite as bad as they suggest with regard to both of their charges.

Charge One. Language teacher education programs currently fail to take what we know about teacher learning properly into account as a part of the knowledge base for the design of language teacher education programs.

Certainly there is an increasing awareness of the importance of teachers' prior learning experiences in shaping their beliefs and practices and the need to get teacher learners to reflect on that prior experience (cf. Crandall, 2000, p. 35). However, is it true that current second language teacher education programs do not take this into account? This charge is a descriptive one, not restricted geographically within the Freeman and Johnson (1998) article. Therefore it will stand or fall depending on our knowledge of teacher education practices around the world. It is obviously difficult to have an authoritative view on this matter though if it is truly intended as a global claim put forward as descriptively true of all (or even only most) teacher education programs everywhere for teachers at all stages of their careers. We can, however, accept that Freeman and Johnson may perhaps have more of a right to an opinion on the matter than most given their established positions in the field. Yet we should probably also hold on to the thought that the issue at hand is in principle a matter of fact, an empirical matter. In the absence of a presentation of the empirical evidence, Freeman and Johnson's position is necessarily an opinion, a professional judgment, and as such, we would not wish to take issue with them here.

If we provisionally accept the charge as stated, then, and also accept that it calls attention to an undesirable state of affairs, then we can also accept the proposition that the field needs to give thought to the role of what we know about teacher learning in general and about second language teacher learning in particular as part of the knowledge base that should inform second language teacher education program design. It is in this specific area that we hope that our chapter will contribute to the debate.

Charge Two. Current second language teacher education programs fail to include coverage of social context as an issue.

We have just seen that the first charge was essentially a matter of fact for which we had to, and were willing to, rely on authoritative opinion. This second charge is also a matter of fact about current language teacher education practices globally. It is also a matter of judgment, presumably because what constitutes coverage of social context could be a matter of unending (although possibly also endlessly stimulating) debate. We might therefore expect legitimate discussion as to whether any given language teacher education program does or does not represent social context considerations satisfactorily.

In fact, we do see this particular charge as contentious and its presentation in Freeman and Johnson's (1998) article as unhelpful both to their position and to the field in general. It would have been more helpful to the field, we suggest, to acknowledge the good practice (in Freeman and Johnson's terms) that we believe does exist and to show how to build on it rather than to risk appearing to wish to deny that it exists at all. We do not believe that it would be at all difficult to find current practical examples of language teacher education programs that do in fact pay considerable attention to social context in the ways suggested as important by Freeman and Johnson. Yet such programs may not conform to Freeman and Johnson's first criterion: that what is known about teacher learning has actually formed a significant part of the knowledge base on which the overall language teacher education program had been designed.

We believe that confounding the two importantly different issues involved in the two charges does not serve well Freeman and Johnson's (1998) overall purpose, as we see it at least, of recruiting supporters for a campaign of radical change in second language teacher education.

We believe that Freeman and Johnson(1998) would have been more persuasive if they had adopted as their unique proposition the eminently defensible claim that the most important issue facing language education programs currently is how to use our developing understanding of teacher learning to inform the design and conduct of second language teacher education programs. It is to this issue itself that we now turn.

MAPPING OUT A RESEARCH PROGRAM

What is our developing understanding of teacher learning? We may have certain understandings about the nature of language teacher learning, but as Freeman and Johnson (1998) point out,[1] there is little research in our journals on teacher preparation to directly support or contradict many of those understandings. Although we agree with Freeman and Johnson that there is an established body of research on general teacher learning, we also believe, with such scholars as Crandall (2000), that more research on second language teacher learning—research such as that in Freeman and Richards (1996) and Johnston and Irujo (2001)—is urgently needed. Similarly, however, it would be deeply damaging to any such research program if it were based on an idea that we find constantly alluded to throughout the Freeman and Johnson article,[2] the contention that the only context that really matters for lan-

[1]Specifically Freeman and Johnson (1998) note, "A search of the *TESOL Quarterly* cumulative indexes from 1980 to 1997 reveals that only 9% of the featured articles are listed under the topic *teacher preparation*" (pp. 397–398).

[2]Note Freeman and Johnson's (1998) claim that "the bulk of this research argues that what teachers know about teaching is largely socially constructed out of the experiences and classrooms from which teachers have come" (p. 400). Also, "Learning to teach is a long-term complex developmental process that operates through participation in the social practices and contexts associated with learning and teaching" (Freeman and Johnson, 1998, p. 402; not, apparently, through participation in the social practices and contexts associated with teacher learning).

guage teacher learning is that of the actual second-language classroom. We also believe that it would be deeply damaging if the research program failed to reflect, as we suggested at the outset of this chapter, the potentially very different modes of learning that might be optimal for language teachers at different stages of their careers.

We need longitudinal studies documenting both the contexts and ways in which novice (preservice) and experienced (inservice) language teachers learn to teach languages. Such studies should examine separately the experience of the preservice teacher and the inservice teacher because these teacher learners, as we have noted, may in fact learn in different contexts and ways from one another. Such longitudinal studies should examine second language teacher learning as it takes place in contexts such as these: in the language classroom, in hallways in conversations with colleagues, in university courses, in university practicum experiences; at professional conferences and at home reading professional publications such as this one. Such studies should also examine the various ways in which this teacher learning takes place: through imitation of mentor teachers, through observation of all kinds of second language (L2) classrooms, through challenges to one's system of beliefs about the way languages are learned encountered in academic classrooms and readings, through observation of second language learners in classroom contexts, through quiet reflection on one's own teaching (and learning) practice, and through discussions with colleagues and peers. Our understanding of second language teacher learning will surely develop more quickly and more precisely as results from such studies come in.

Redesigning Language Teacher Education Programs

Next, we need to find ways for our developing understanding of language teacher learning to inform our design and conduct of second language teacher education programs. Our understanding cannot, as we have just seen, be informed at present by much research on language teacher learning. The lack of direct research on language teacher learning certainly presents us with an immediate and very practical problem. How can we presume to start altering the overall design of language teacher education programs when only a handful of studies on language teacher learning have been done? Freeman and Johnson (1998) point to the large body of general teacher-learning research and argue that research on general teacher learning might for the present impact our design and conduct of language teacher education programs. Indeed, it appears that many of us have already started in this direction, altering our programs in ways we later describe. First, however, we feel we should look more closely at what it might mean to allow the design and conduct of second language teacher education programs to be directly influenced by what we know about general teacher learning.

The Academic Fallacy. We believe that two possible shapes of future second language teacher education programs can already be ruled out. The first of these is what we might call "the academic fallacy": the belief that a novice can become an effective second language teacher merely by taking a set of content courses on teaching, learning, and language structure and so developing a body of declarative knowledge about what language teaching and learning involve. This, for example, is the belief that a graduate student who learns the rules for the formation of passive sentences and who understands the function of the passive in English discourse will then be well prepared to teach English as a second language (ESL) students how to use the passive voice. Or a methods teacher might believe that the best way to train student teachers to respond to student errors is to show them examples of various methods of providing corrective feedback. It is this fallacy that Freeman and Johnson (1998) appear to be battling against most explicitly in their article, as when they say, "teachers are not empty vessels waiting to be filled with theoretical and pedagogical skills" (p. 401). The discontinuity between these academic content courses and the language classroom appears to set up a gap that cannot be bridged by beginning teacher learners. The content of these academic content courses either is or appears to novice language teachers to be irrelevant to the process of learning to teach languages more effectively to real students in real classrooms. Alternatively, it may be content that, however relevant in principle and in the long term, cannot yet be used by novice teachers in the context of their own teaching. In this sense, the content of academic courses is effectively decontextualized. Even worse, perhaps, the mere fact that content is being presented academically in academic courses may lead novice teachers who share the commonly held lay view that the only place for learning to teach is in the classroom to assume that declarative knowledge of such content is not going to be of any value to them.

The Noninterface Fallacy. However, there is a second (converse) fallacy of language teacher education, and this is what we would call the "noninterface fallacy," the fallacy of doing away with academic content courses and trying instead to make the teacher learning situation identical to the target teaching situation. This fallacy asserts that language teachers can only acquire the ability to teach languages in the context of the language classroom itself; no teacher learning can take place outside that context. This fallacy is similar to claims made about second-language acquisition (SLA) by Krashen (1982), namely, claims that consciously learned information about language can have no beneficial impact on the process of acquisition of that language. By analogy, language teachers might be assumed to learn best by being put into a language classroom, possibly under the guidance of a mentor teacher, and told to teach. This essentially noninterface position would suggest that things consciously learned in academic content courses can have no impact on actual language teaching. It is a kind of learning by doing approach. However, one needs more than the ability to speak a language fluently and to manage a classroom if one is to be an effective second-language teacher: One must be able to think analytically both about the structure of the language itself and about the learning processes of the students to make decisions about course content that meets student needs. For example, this fallacy might assume that any native speaker who spends a bit of time in a classroom will be able to answer student questions effectively. However, is it true that anyone who has taught ESL in a sixth-grade classroom can also explain to college-level international students exactly why they can say "He looked carefully at the picture" but not "He looked carefully up the word?" (Yule, 1998, p. 155). The danger of the learn-by-doing approach is that when an individual's only teacher education consists of being put into a language classroom and asked to learn to teach by teaching, even with the guidance of a mentor those individuals are unlikely to emerge with the flexibility to cope with teaching contexts different from those in which they have been apprenticed.[3] Mentors engaged in teaching their own classes often have very little time to spend with novice teachers, imparting, beyond skills, a body of knowledge and a framework of understanding; many may in fact may even find it very difficult to articulate for novices the rationale for their actions in the classroom. In fact, individuals who have been placed in language classrooms with no previous preparation are precisely those who typically apply to our teacher education programs as in-service teachers seeking a better knowledge base and understanding of the process of language teaching and language learning in the halls of academe. Second language teacher learners, like second-language learners, seem to need some conscious learning of information, and experienced teacher learners seem to hold to an "interface" position, believing that things they consciously learn in a content course can eventually have an impact on their actual language teaching performance.

---

[3]In Britain, this approach to industrial training (known as "sitting with Nellie") was abandoned many years ago as entirely unsuited to the complexity of modern industrial working practices.

We worry that Freeman and Johnson (1998) may risk appearing to fall into the noninterface fallacy when for example they claim that in traditional language teacher education programs, "the true locus of teacher learning lay in on-the-job initiation into the practices of teaching and not in the processes of professional teacher education" (p. 399).

Reconsidering the Complexity of the Teacher Learner Population

The research on general teacher learning that Freeman and Johnson (1998) brought to our attention appears to suggest that second language teacher education programs should provide some better integrated way of presenting the (now reconceptualized) knowledge base of language teaching so that its content can be more immediately accessible to, and useful for, language teachers in the process of classroom teaching. This suggests that more and better bridges must be built between learning a body of knowledge and using that body of knowledge in teaching language in the classroom.

Yet will research show this to be true of all language teacher education? The heterogeneity of the second language teacher learners we deal with is surely a central question. For example, the need for integration in the presentation of the knowledge base in teacher education programs might be essential for novice teachers but less so for experienced ones.

Distinguishing earlier between training, education, and development, we argued that although all include some focus on skills, knowledge, and understanding, they can be distinguished because they emphasize these three kinds of knowledge to different degrees. Novice teachers may require more teacher training than experienced ones because they are likely to need relatively more learning of concrete teaching skills. At the same time but to a lesser degree, they need to begin to form a base of knowledge and to acquire enough understanding to begin to construct a framework within which they can make informed decisions about the use of their newly acquired (or learned) skills or new knowledge. However, for them the integrated presentation of knowledge and skills within a coherent framework of understanding may be essential. They may not yet know why they will eventually find it helpful to know about phonetics or morphology or second language acquisition. They may need guidance in understanding why certain kinds of knowledge are needed or when certain skills and bits of knowledge should be exercised in their classrooms. Such questions can only be answered in an integrated presentation of the knowledge base. Research may show that it is beginning teachers without a well-developed framework of understanding who may need the most integrated presentation of the knowledge base.

Of course, some lack of integration in language teacher education, even for novices, may be unavoidable. Research may show that novice language teachers need to learn a lot that is narrowly about second language teaching and learning, information that may not have any immediate use but that they may find they need later. Then, when confronted, for example, by a student question about verb aspect, it may be helpful for them to remember that they were taught something about syntax, that they did learn it, or at least they still know where to look for an answer. That may give them the confidence to promise to return to the matter in a subsequent lesson when they have done their own homework instead of fudging the issue in class. In other words, although novice teachers may be found to benefit from language teacher education programs that are highly integrated, there may be some aspects of such programs that really need not be fully integrated.

Conversely, inservice teachers who already engage in best practices in their classrooms are more likely to need teacher education or teacher development: more emphasis on the declarative knowledge base or on understanding than on the acquisition of skills. They are also more likely to feel comfortable with a less integrated presentation. Indeed, experienced inservice teachers are often people who return to teacher education programs for an in-depth understanding of theory to support their current classroom practice or for very specific, decontextualized coursework: courses on grammar, for example, or courses on phonetics or technology training. They are also likely to read research articles to improve their understanding. As a consequence, they might possibly change or fine-tune their teaching practices at the level of teaching skill. For example, an anonymous reviewer of this chapter shared with us the experience of reading a research article by Laufer and Hulstijn (2001) that stimulated a personal rethinking of pedagogical practices in teaching vocabulary. Other experienced teachers might read the same article and find justification for continuing their current pedagogical practices. Such teachers may want an in-depth understanding to make their life's work more coherent and smooth running, to reexamine and justify for themselves their most basic orientation to second language teaching. Similarly, experienced teachers who already have worked out a framework of knowledge and understanding within which to make informed teaching choices may be the people most likely to seek out specific bodies of knowledge that fill identified gaps in their framework (e.g., for technology training or structure of language). They may be able to contextualize these pieces of the knowledge base themselves. A real-world example of a popular ESL teacher education program set up precisely for these sorts of experienced teachers seeking specialized inservice coursework focusing on content is described in Mabbott and Heinze (2001).

Of course, research may find that some experienced inservice teachers—those who have not thought about their framework of knowledge and understanding for some time and who may need to reconstruct that framework—may benefit from an integrated presentation of the knowledge base in their inservice training just as preservice teachers do. They may need to be asked to reexamine their classroom practice in light of evidence from research findings that conflicts with assumptions in their framework of understanding or in light of new possibilities for the delivery of instruction via technology. For example, language teachers who rely on "recasts" (i.e., correct paraphrases) when providing feedback in response to student errors may be led to reflect on this when they read studies such as Lyster and Ranta's (1997), which show that using recasts is likely to lead to less student correction than other forms of teacher feedback. Such teachers may need to add new skills in light of changes in their framework of understanding. Resistance to change on the part of such teachers may be very high, and it may take an integrated approach to convince them that their framework of understanding needs development.

Crucially, then, the diversity of the population of second language teacher learners means that both the need for more or less focus on skills versus knowledge versus understanding in the knowledge base and for a more or less integrated presentation can be expected to vary. We must therefore be cautious in making generalizations about the way second language teacher learning in general takes place.

We have not even begun to take into account the usual individual differences among learners (age, gender, aptitude, intelligence, motivation, learning style, first language and L2 linguistic proficiency, etc., etc.), which we might also expect to impact on teacher learning just as they are presumed to do on all other sorts of learning. Of course, we have not yet mentioned culture as a possible variable. Do we not have reason to expect people to learn to be teachers differently in different cultures?

Summary: Reconceptualizing the Knowledge Base

We have reviewed two reasons why Freeman and Johnson (1998) feel that the knowledge base of language teacher education needs to be reconceptualized: that the knowledge base does not include either what we know about teacher learning or what we know about the social context of schools and schooling. We suggested that the first reason, which seems much stronger, could be separated from the second. Indeed, we strongly supported the idea that research on second language teacher learning should be done to build on existing research on general teacher learning, suggesting the need for longitudinal studies documenting both the contexts and ways in which novice (preservice) and experienced (inservice) language teachers learn to teach languages. We considered what it might mean to allow the design and conduct of language teacher education programs to be directly influenced in the absence of much of this kind of specific research by what we know from research conducted on general teacher learning, urging that we try to avoid both the academic fallacy and the noninterface fallacy and aim for a more integrated approach. We urged that a distinction be maintained among teacher training, teacher education, and teacher development in meeting the needs of a range of different types of teacher learners who might need differential focus on skills, knowledge, and understanding and who also might need varying degrees of integration in the presentation of these kinds of knowledge.

Having considered the rationale for reconceptualizing the knowledge base for language teacher education and the ways in which such a reconceptualized knowledge base might affect the design of second language teacher education programs, we turn now to examine the content of the knowledge base itself, as outlined by Freeman and Johnson (1998).

WHAT THE RECONCEPTUALIZED KNOWLEDGE BASE WOULD NEED TO LOOK LIKE

Freeman and Johnson (1998) provide a model in Figure 1 of their article (see p. X in Freedman & Johnson, chap. 2, this volume) that delineates the content of the reconceptualized knowledge base of language teacher education. That knowledge base does include an explicit recognition of the knowledge that the language teacher learners themselves bring to the table, and we have already discussed the difficulty of specifying, in the absence of research specifically on language teacher learning, exactly what that knowledge consists of. However, aside from this important area, it is not clear to us from this model how else the content of the knowledge base would differ from the present knowledge base—aside from one important area. Our most fundamental difficulty with the content of this knowledge base has to do with what is not there: the second language learner.

On the Role of the Second Language Learner

The "activity of teaching/knowledge base" framework in Freeman and Johnson (1998) Figure 1 (p. 406), indicates who does the activity of teaching, where, and how. Clearly for Freeman and Johnson, the who in the activity of teaching is simply the teacher. However, *teach* is not an intransitive verb; it is not an activity one does by oneself. One has to teach something to someone. It is disturbing that Freeman and Johnson barely mention students or second language learners in their discussion of language teacher education. Indeed, the omission is deliberate, as Freeman and Johnson (1998) say, "language teacher education is primarily concerned with teachers as learners of language teaching rather than with students as learners of language. Thus teacher education focuses on teacher-learners (Kennedy, 1991) as distinct from language learners" (p. 407).

We find the lack of a clear role for the learner in this framework very troubling. One cannot teach in a vacuum; one always teaches someone (and learns from them in the process too); it is our view that teaching/learning must always be negotiated (cf. Allwright, 2001). Indeed, as both Barcelos (2001) and Kiely (2001) illustrate, the relationship between learner and teacher beliefs is itself a fertile area for research and exploration. Kiely (2001), for example, presents ethnographic and interview evidence showing how student feedback and evaluation create a cycle of teacher resistance, reflection, and finally innovation: a context for teacher change and development. The framework for the knowledge base in our view should include a clear understanding of learners, who they are, why they learn, what they need to learn, what motivates them, and how a teacher goes about negotiating the teaching/learning activities with them. The management of learning (cf. Allwright, 2001) can only be accomplished by the learners and the teacher together.

Reasons for Leaving Out the Language Learner in the Knowledge Base

Freeman and Johnson (1998) explicitly address the absence of the learner from their conceptualizations as follows:

> Language learners and language learning/acquisition seem to be noticeably absent from our exposition of the knowledge-base. Although it is clearly critical for teacher-learners to know and understand something of how individuals learn languages both inside and outside the classroom, it is also important to recognize the relative place of this knowledge vis a vis successful teaching. (p. 411)

Yet in fact, Freeman and Johnson (1998) do not tell us what they mean by successful teaching, nor ultimately what the relative importance of a teacher's knowledge about SLA is in their model of language teacher learning—they merely assert that teacher learners should understand something of how individuals learn languages. Then they turn aside from the issue of what teachers should know about the way students learn second languages, to make three points about the field of SLA research from the perspective of language teacher education. It is implied that because the field of SLA research can be criticized in certain ways, language teachers do not need to familiarize themselves with the results of that research.

Three Points About SLA Research From a Language Teacher Education Perspective

We review the points made by Freeman and Johnson (1998) here and suggest that they do not provide an adequate set of reasons for leaving out the learner in their construct of language teacher education. Freeman and Johnson (1998) state first that the field of SLA has viewed L2 learners from an individualist perspective, in which a social constructivist view of SLA would "seem to interface more directly with the nature of classroom language learning" (p. 411). Which approach—individualist or social constructivist—would be more descriptive of classroom learning we cannot say; in fact, we think it would be hard to prove. However, we need to point out that both approaches are currently being used in SLA research, and both have produced useful insights for language teachers. Lightbown and Spada (1998) review very concrete research findings, many descriptive of classroom learning, which they show to be relevant for classroom teaching. Many of the studies they cite might be called "individualist" (they are certainly not social constructivist), yet these studies have clear implications for teaching. Liu (1991) examines in detail the progress of a Chinese boy learning English L2 in and out of classrooms; he does not use a social constructivist approach, but his findings are directly relevant for classroom teachers. Of course, much current SLA research is social constructivist; Swain and Lapkin (1998) analyze processes of SLA within a Vygotskyian framework and show how learners and those around them coconstruct utterances and support the processes of SLA. In a study that might be relevant for research on language teacher learning, Platt and Troudi (1997) use a social constructivist approach to demonstrate how a teacher's "theory" of SLA results in her failure to promote the acquisition of L2 literacy by an English language learner in her class. Thus, we do not feel it is accurate to label all of SLA research as either individualist or constructivist or to claim the unprovable: that one of these approaches is better suited to classroom acquisition processes.

The second point made about SLA research is that its results do not articulate well with classroom practice and so are not usable by teachers. We are sure that this is true of some but certainly not all or even most of the results of SLA research. Studies such as that by Yule and Macdonald (1990) have very clear implications for teachers interested in setting up pair-work activities that foster productive student interaction in second language classrooms: The authors show in very concrete terms why teachers must consider the learners' relative proficiency and interactive role in setting up pair work or else watch the activity fail. We have cited other studies on topics such as vocabulary acquisition (Laufer & Hulstijn, 2001) and teacher response to student error (Lyster & Ranta, 1997), studies whose findings have direct relevance for, and should influence, language teacher practice. It is certainly true that SLA researchers themselves do not claim to restrict all their research only to that which produces results that are usable by teachers; much study of SLA is done as pure research, not for purposes of application. In spite of this, as we have argued previously, there is a great deal of SLA research that is directly relevant to classroom processes of SLA and that should be familiar to classroom teachers because it can directly affect choices they make in their classrooms, which can affect the success or failure of their students.

Finally, Freeman and Johnson (1998) suggest that teachers must understand their own beliefs and knowledge about learning and teaching and how those impact their students. We agree. Yet of course, this does not mean that teachers' own beliefs and knowledge about learning and teaching should never be challenged in light of research findings or in light of the impact they have on their students. Widdowson (1992, p. 271) cautions that language teacher education programs should always allow for the possibility of change and suggests that ideas from outside the classroom may be essential for that purpose. We have mentioned previously the study by Platt and Troudi (1997) in which a teacher's beliefs about SLA caused her to treat one of her students in such a way that that student failed to learn; that teacher was completely unaware of the way in which her beliefs impacted that student because the student used good strategies for hiding her failure to learn. In fact, instructively enough, it was the research study itself that made the teacher aware of the problem. We think that SLA research has an important role to play in helping teachers evaluate their beliefs and knowledge about SLA and to decide to change these if they are not productive of learning on the part of their students or themselves.

Teachers, researchers, and students need to work together to understand the process of SLA and the way in which all of their beliefs and understandings about language learning affect the learning outcomes of students. To us, this implies a fundamental shift in the way in which SLA research is presented to and used by teachers: It should be presented not as a product—a set of results of studies conducted by experts—but as a process that can be used by teachers as well as researchers, a set of procedures for examining the progress of second-language learners. In other words, teacher learners should not just be informed of the basic findings of SLA; they should be invited to employ useful research techniques themselves to join in gathering information about the language learners in their classes. This information gathering can take the form of modest, focused, practitioner-designed research projects within the Exploratory Practice framework (Allwright, 2001), which are complementary to the normal professional activity of classroom language teachers (Wallace, 1996). It is this orientation that is encouraged, for example, in Tarone and Yule (1989): Teachers are urged to gather data themselves as a part of regular ongoing needs analysis at the local level, on what the learners in their classrooms know, what they need to know, and what their perspective on learning is. Such research by teachers should be very useful to them. Of course, it should also be of great interest to researchers who need new perspectives and new questions from the classroom.

Summary: The Content of the Knowledge Base

In sum, the new knowledge base outlined for us by Freeman and Johnson (1998) appears to be rather sparsely specified. It appears that a new addition is an account of what it is that second language teacher learners already know about language learning and teaching at various stages of their learning but that the precise outlines of this knowledge are still to be specified in an important but just beginning research program. It also appears that something important has been left out of this new knowledge base, namely, the second language learner. We have pointed out the dangers of omitting the area of SLA research altogether and suggested that this area should be included in language teacher education programs in such a way that teacher learners are not viewed as simply consumers of the results of this research but rather as partners in an ongoing research effort aimed at identifying the knowledge and needs of second language learners at the local level in language classrooms.[4]

CONCLUSION

We applaud the continuing[5] evaluation of what it is that we offer in second language teacher education programs and the way in which we of-

[4]See Brumfit (1995) for a description of a research program of this sort.

[5]There is a long history in our field of reflection on the nature of applied linguistics, the relation between theory and application, and the sort of graduate preparation we provide our teacher learners. We have refrained throughout this chapter from pointing out that many of the issues we consider here have been seriously discussed in the literature for many decades, but lest we be accused of ahistoricity (cf. Thomas, 1998), we must refer to at least some of them as foundational and worthy of rereading in light of this discussion. These include the papers in Alatis, Stern, and Strevens, 1983; Mackey, 1965; Widdowson, 1990, and so forth.

fer it. Such continual rethinking of our educational efforts is essential to ensure the continuing vitality of our programs. We agree with Freeman and Johnson (1998) that there is a need for a longitudinal research program focused on the way in which second-language teachers learn their craft, but we urge caution in making premature assumptions about the outcomes of such a research program. We believe that second-language teacher learners at different stages in their careers and functioning in different contexts may have very different learning needs. We also urge that in our enthusiasm for this new research effort, focused on the language teacher learner, we not omit an ongoing focus on the second-language learner and the ways in which the language learner and the language teacher learn together in the second-language classroom. We are very positive as to the outcomes of this new orientation and research effort, and we applaud Freeman and Johnson for their work in initiating it.

REFERENCES

Alatis, J. E., Stern, H. H., & Strevens, P. (Eds.). (1983). *Applied linguistics and the preparation of second language teachers: Towards a rationale.* Washington, DC: Georgetown University Press.

Allwright, R. (2001). Three major processes of teacher development and the appropriate design criteria for developing and using them. In B. Johnston & S. Irujo (Eds.), *Research and practice in language teacher education: Voices from the field* (CARLA Working Paper No. 19, pp. 115–134). Minneapolis, MN: Center for Advanced Research on Language Acquisition.

Barcelos, A. M. F. (2001). The interaction between students' beliefs and teacher's beliefs and dilemmas. In B. Johnston & S. Irujo (Eds.), *Research and practice in language teacher education: Voices from the field* (CARLA Working Paper No. 19, pp. 77–97). Minneapolis, MN: Center for Advanced Research on Language Acquisition.

Brice Heath, S. (2000). Linguistics in the study of language in education. In B. M. Brizuela, J. P. Stewart, R. C. Carrillo, & J. B. Berger (Eds.), *Acts of inquiry in qualitative research* (Reprint Series No. 34, pp. 27–36). Cambridge, MA: Harvard Educational Review.

Brumfit, C. (1995). Teacher professionalism and research. In G. Cook & B. Seidlhofer (Eds.), *Principle and practice in applied linguistics* (pp. 27–41). New York: Oxford University Press.

Crandall, J. A. (2000). Language teacher education. *Annual Review of Applied Linguistics, 20,* 34–55.

Freeman, D., & Johnson, D. (1998). Reconceptualizing the knowledge-base of language teacher education. *TESOL Quarterly, 32,* 397–418.

Freeman, D., & Richards, J. C. (Eds.). (1996). *Teacher learning in language teaching.* Cambridge, England: Cambridge University Press.

Johnston, B., & Irujo, S. (Eds.). (2001). *Research and practice in language teacher education: Voices from the field.* Minneapolis, MN: Center for Advanced Research on Language Acquisition.

Kennedy, M. (1991). *An agenda for research on teacher learning* (National Center for Research on Teacher Learning Special Report SR Spring 91). East Lansing: Michigan State University.

Kiely, R. (2001). Classroom evaluation—Values, interests and teacher development. *Language Teaching Research, 5,* 241–261.

Krashen, S. (1982). *Principles and practice in second language acquisition.* New York: Pergamon.

Laufer, B., & Hulstijn, J. (2001). Incidental vocabulary acquisition in a second language: The construct of task-induced involvement. *Applied Linguistics, 22,* 1–26.

Lightbown, P., & Spada, N. (1998). *How languages are learned* (2nd ed.). New York: Oxford University Press.

Liu, G. (1991). *Interaction and second language acquisition: A case study of a Chinese child's acquisition of English as a second language.* Unpublished doctoral dissertation, La Trobe University, Melbourne, Australia.

Lyster, R., & Ranta, L. (1997). Corrective feedback and learner uptake: Negotiation of form in communicative classrooms. *Studies in Second Language Acquisition, 19,* 37–66.

Mabbott, A., & Heinze, K. (2001, May). *Reconceptualizing ESL public school teacher education.* Paper presented at the Second International Conference on Language Teacher Education: Building on Our Strengths, Minneapolis, MN.

Mackey, W. F. (1965). *Language teaching analysis.* London: Longman.

Platt, E., & Troudi, S. (1997). Mary and her teachers: A Grebo-speaking child's place in the mainstream classroom. *Modern Language Journal, 78,* 497–511.

Swain, M., & Lapkin, S. (1998). Interaction and second language learning: Two adolescent French immersion students working together. *Modern Language Journal, 82,* 320–337.

Tarone, E., & Yule, G. (1989). *Focus on the language learner.* New York: Oxford University Press.

Thomas, M. (1998). Programmatic ahistoricity in second language acquisition theory. *Studies in Second Language Acquisition, 20,* 387–405.

Wallace, M. (1996). Structured reflection: The role of the professional project in training ESL teachers. In D. Freeman & J. C. Richards (Eds.), *Teacher learning in language teaching* (pp. 281–294). Cambridge, England: Cambridge University Press.

Widdowson, H. G. (1990). *Aspects of language teaching.* New York: Oxford University Press.

Widdowson, H. G. (1992). Innovation in teacher development. *Annual Review of Applied Linguistics, 13,* 260–275.

Yule, G. (1998). *Explaining English grammar.* New York: Oxford University Press.

Yule, G., & Macdonald, D. (1990). Resolving referential conflicts in L2 interaction: The effect of proficiency and interactive role. *Language Learning, 40,* 539–556.

Chapter **2**

Response to Tarone and Allwright

Donald Freeman
School for International Training

Karen E. Johnson
The Pennsylvania State University

We welcome the opportunity to engage with our colleagues Tarone and Allwright (chap. 1, this volume) in the ongoing professional conversation in this critical area of how people learn to teach second languages. Their input is not only most welcome but also greatly needed. Clearly, having more interlocutors who share these concerns will only strengthen the discussion. Thus, we are heartened that Tarone and Allwright, with their career-long concerns with how teachers and learners work in classrooms, bring that stature and background to these issues.

As is often the case with any critique, our first response to Tarone and Allwright (chap. 1, this volume) was to be a bit defensive. It is difficult to read others' interpretations of your words and ideas, especially when it feels as though you have been misunderstood or partially understood. Indeed, it brings to mind the famous disclaimer of T. S. Eliot's J. Alfred Prufrock (p. 163), "That is not what I meant at all. That is not it, at all." However, believing that such interactions are critical in building a field, it is important to go beyond our first reactions. So we propose to structure our response as we would a good conversation, that is first to "hear" the points of critique and second to respond to them. In our response, we further distinguish between what we see as the "common ground" between us and what we believe are areas for further discussion and research.

HEARING

Tarone and Allwright (chap. 1, this volume) find that we do not distinguish between teacher learning and teacher education as general, or what they term "unitary concepts," and those concepts as they are applied—or perhaps better put, instantiated—in the learning and education of language teachers:

> We differ from Freeman and Johnson in our unwillingness to assume that we know precisely how that research on general teacher learning bears on second language teacher learning and therefore on second language teacher education. To put it in a nutshell, we believe that teachers of different subject areas must learn different things and may have to learn those things in different ways.

Setting this as the backdrop, Tarone and Allwright (chap. 1, this volume) focus on their understanding of two aspects of our analysis: first, "that people designing language teacher education programs typically fail to take into account, at the level of curriculum design, what we know about general teacher learning," and second, such language teacher education (LTE) programs "also typically fail to deal with the social context of schools and schooling" (p. 6).

RESPONDING

We begin by agreeing with Tarone and Allwright (chap. 1, this volume). We do hold the understanding that there are certain fundamental processes, or perhaps Chomskyan deep structures, in how people learn to teach through formal and nonformal means. In fact, we say the following. "We argue that learning to teach is an a priori process with which teacher education must articulate. We contend that the field must better document and understand teacher learning for teacher education to be more effective" (Freeman & Johnson, 1998, p. 402). So if by "largely undifferentiated unitary concepts" Tarone and Allwright (chap. 1, this volume, p.) mean, as they seem to do, that we do not distinguish, at one level, among different sorts of teacher learning and teacher education based on subject matter, we would accept that critique.

The argument seems to us an ontological one: namely, that somehow the subject matter of language uniquely changes or differentiates language teachers as teachers from teachers of other subject matters. This seems to us a nonresearchable proposition for two reasons. First, it is based on a belief in a fundamental difference in ontology between teachers and language teachers just as our view is based in a belief in the basic commonality on a foundational level of professional learning across subject matters. So in a research-based examination—were it even feasible—our two positions would be mirror images of one another. Our "null hypothesis" would be Tarone and Allwright's (chap. 1, this volume) view cited previously, "that teachers of different subject areas must learn different things and may have to learn them in different ways" (p. 7). Their null hypothesis would be our view, also cited previously, that "learning to teach is an a priori process" (Freeman & Johnson, 1998, p. 402).

In the final analysis, we may have to agree to disagree on our respective views here. We would, however, suggest that there is a substantial body of work that supports the view that there are fundamental processes in teacher learning (e.g., Ball, 2000; Darling-Hammond, 1998; Darling-Hammond & Sykes, 2000). This work has been aggregated from research on teacher learning across various subject matters including teaching foreign/second languages; thus, it is hardly generic in either data or analyses but rather amasses patterns of findings that suggest such fundamental professional learning processes. Brice Heath (2000), whom Tarone and Allwright (chap. 1, this volume) mention, does not seem, in our reading, to contradict any of the previously cited research. Instead, Brice Heath's (2000) goal seems quite different as she writes, "My goal here is to ask what we know about linguistics and its contributions to qualitative research about language in education" (p. 27). Interestingly, at the end of that paper, Brice Heath (2000) seems to echo the more broad-based view of teacher learning when she writes, "Qualitative research has an extensive future, primarily because it has the potential to answer previously unaddressed questions of language in education. Advancements in theory will come through work that stays tightly connected to the central concern in education—learning" (p.34).

That said, however, as LTE researchers we would very much agree with Tarone and Allwright that too little research has been undertaken with people who are learning to teach second languages as subject matter, and this was precisely the major thrust of our argument, one point on which we all seem to agree.

We move, then, to the first of the two "charges": that we contend that most LTE programs do not account for what is known about teacher learning broadly. Here we agree with Tarone and Allwright (chap. 1, this volume) that this statement is an assertion based on our experience of and exposure to LTE programs in many countries and contexts around the world. It is indeed, as they say, a "professional judgment" and not an empirical finding. Nonetheless, we would stand behind the statement that, we believe can be substantiated for teacher education programs generally from many international studies[1] as well as in the United States (e.g., Wilson, Floden, & Ferrini-Mundy, 2001). Again, we agree that specific data on LTE programs is sorely lacking;[2] however, there seems to be no reason to believe, given the educational structures and mechanisms that provide it, that LTE programs would differ from other forms of teacher education.

The second charge—that Tarone and Allwright (chap. 1, this volume) summarize us as saying that LTE programs "also typically fail to deal with social context of schools and schooling" (p. 6)—is to us perhaps the most interesting and useful point of discussion. It is here that we feel we have been misread, for Tarone and Allwright (chap. 1, this volume) mention as a gloss that we are criticizing "what constitutes coverage of social context" (p. 9) in LTE programs. Actually, the point we make about social context of schools and schooling is not about how the various and diverse topics that come under this heading are treated in LTE programs. We would readily acknowledge—as Tarone and Allwright (chap. 1, this volume) suggest we do—that it would not "be at all difficult to find current practical examples of language teacher education programs that do in fact pay considerable attention to social context" (p. 10). There are clearly many LTE programs that teach about diverse aspects of social context, as, for example, the articles by Stein (1998), by Bailey et al. (1998), and by Samuel (1998) in the 1998 special topic *TESOL Quarterly* volume demonstrate.

These examples, and many other excellent examples like them, focus primarily on teaching potential teachers about the important place of schools and schooling as social contexts for student learning. However, our point is a slightly different one. We argue that LTE programs as they are currently designed generally do not address schools and schooling as a critical social context for teacher learning. We wrote, "This domain [in our framework, see Fig. 2.1] argues that an understanding of schools and schooling as the social and cultural context for *teacher learning* [italics added] is critical to establishing an effective knowledge-base" (Freeman & Johnson, 1998, p. 408). We then expanded on what we meant by schools as sociocultural settings and schooling as a sociocultural process. Here again, other articles in the 1998 special topic *TESOL Quar-*

[1]We refer, for example, to studies by the World Bank (2000), the Organization for Economic Cooperation and Development (2002), and the Third International Mathematics and Science Study (1996).

[2]This is one of the major goals of the newly formed TESOL International Research Foundation; see Duff and Bailey (2001).

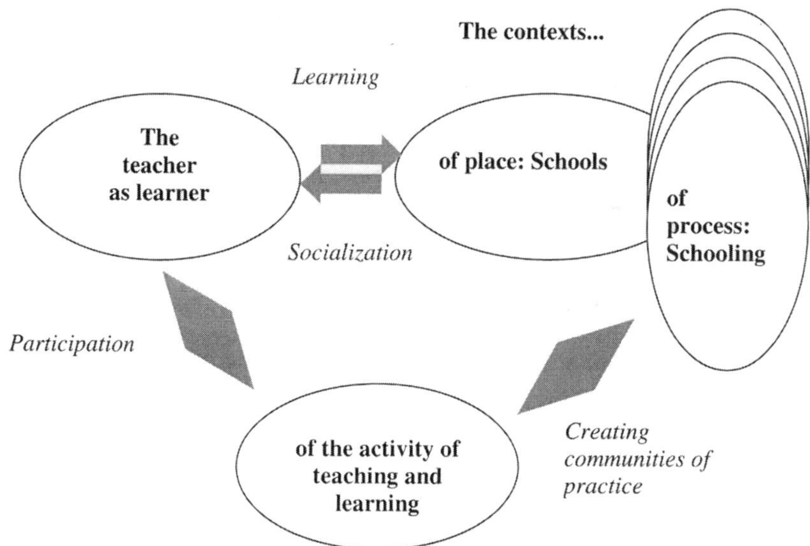

FIG. 2.1 Framework for the knowledge base of language teacher education. Domains are in boldface; processes are in italics.
Note. From "Reconceptualizing the Knowledge-Base of Language Teacher Education," By D. Freeman and K. E. Johnson, 1998, *TESOL Quarterly, 32,* p. 406. Copyright 1998 by Teachers of English to Speakers of Other Languages, Inc. Reprinted with permission.

terly volume by Clair (1998), by Gebhard (1998), and by Clarke, Davis, Rhodes, and DeLott Baker (1998) offer promising counterexamples to what we see as the status quo in LTE programs. This status quo, we contend, generally does not address how schools socialize both potential and practicing teachers when they are students as well as when they are teaching themselves.

FROM HERE: THE "TEACH IS NOT AN INTRANSITIVE VERB" ISSUE

Tarone and Allwright (chap. 1, this volume) then turn to a discussion of what they believe is the state of a "'developing understanding of teacher learning'" (p. 10). From this point onward in their chapter, we find some to agree with, some to question, but most to welcome as further useful grist for the theoretical mill of these conversations. Time and space are too limited, nor would it be particularly useful we think to pick apart the differences and to argue about some points, as Prufrock might have done (p. 163): "That is not what I meant at all. That is not it, at all." Instead, we close this response by engaging a central issue that seems to have led some to a bitter critique of our work. We might call this issue, borrowing from Tarone and Allwright (chap. 1, this volume) we hope in their spirit, the "*teach* is not an intransitive verb" (p. 17) issue, or as they quite accurately explain, "[teaching] is not an activity one does by oneself" (p. 18).

We have been strongly criticized by some, and certainly without the care and accuracy of the present critique, that we disparage second language acquisition (SLA) research and do not include the language learner directly in our framework (Fig. 2.1). We wish to take this occasion to state clearly that we do indeed value research in SLA and have always held that such knowledge needs to inform the work of language teachers. We state, as Tarone and Allwright (chap. 1, this volume) cite us as saying that "it is clearly critical for teacher-learners to know and understand something about how individuals learn languages both inside and outside the classroom," and we continue that it is a matter of emphasis: "it is also important to recognize the relative place of this knowledge vis-a-vis successful teaching" (Freeman & Johnson, 1998, p. 411). Some might criticize us for not holding SLA as the sine qua non of language teacher knowledge, and some might argue that we ought to focus more explicitly in the framework on what language teachers need to know about language learners. However, it cannot be said that we reject the value to language teachers of knowledge about language and how people learn and use it.

Thus we do need to challenge Tarone and Allwright's (chap. 1, this volume) one interpretative statement that "It is implied that because the field of SLA research can be criticized in certain ways, language teachers do not need to familiarize themselves with the results of that research" (p. 19). That has never been our intent nor our implication; rather, we do affirm the value of such knowledge. The fact that we speak of "understand[ing] something of how individuals learn languages" (Tarone & Allwright, chap. 1, this volume, p. 18) seems to reflect fairly accurately the current movement in systems that we are trying to educate a broader spectrum of teachers in language education issues; the Crosscultural, Language, and Academic Development (CLAD) and Bilingual, Crosscultural, Language, and Academic Development (BCLAD)[3] endorsements now required of

[3]The CLAD and the BCLAD are endorsements required of those who want to teach with linguistically and culturally diverse students in California public schools. California mandates that teachers must have this endorsement coupled with valid teaching credentials to work with English language learners. The CLAD endorsement authorizes the holder to teach in settings where the instruction is primarily in English; the BCLAD permits the holder to teach in bilingual settings in the language of emphasis and in English.

teachers in California or the *Progetto Lingue* (Ministero della Pubblica Istruzione, 2001) in Italy are two disparate examples.[4]

In summary, we would agree with Tarone and Allwright (chap. 1, this volume) that teach is a transitive verb, and that who the learners in classrooms are, what and how they learn (or don't learn), and under what circumstances and conditions matters critically to the professional learning of their teachers. Furthermore, concern for and understanding of language both as the medium of instruction and as subject matter fit squarely in transitive space between teacher and learner. The fact that the core of our concern is the teacher and teacher professional learning over time should not alter these common points of reference. Our intent in writing about the knowledge base as a framework has been to introduce a different map of what for many seems to be well known and perhaps even overly familiar territory. We know very well, as the saying goes, that the map is not the territory but rather a way of looking at it. So if this way of looking stimulates good discussion, it can only have served its purpose. As Eliot's Prufrock says at another point (p. 164), "Oh do not ask what is it? Let us go and make our visit."

REFERENCES

Bailey, F., Hawkins, M., Irujo, S., Larsen-Freeman, D., Rintell, E., & Willett, J. (1998). Language teacher educators collaborative conversations. *TESOL Quarterly, 32,* 536–545.

Ball, D. L. (2000). Bridging practices: Intertwining content and pedagogy in teaching and learning to teach. *Journal of Teacher Education, 51*(3), 241–247.

Brice Heath, S. (2000). Linguistics in the study of language in education. In B. M. Brizuela, J. P. Stewart, R. C. Carrillo, & J. B. Berger (Eds.), *Acts of inquiry in qualitative research* (Reprint Series No. 34, pp. 27–36). Cambridge, MA: Harvard Educational Review.

Clair, N. (1998). Teacher study groups: Persistent questions in a promising approach. *TESOL Quarterly, 32,* 465–492.

Clarke, M. A., Davis, A., Rhodes, L. K., & DeLott Baker, E. (1998). Principles of collaboration in school-university partnerships. *TESOL Quarterly, 32,* 592–600.

Council of Europe. (1998). *Plurilingual and multicultural competence.* Strasbourg, France: Author.

Darling-Hammond, L. (1998). Teachers and teaching: Testing policy hypotheses from a National Commission Report. *Educational Researcher, 27*(1), 5–15.

Darling-Hammond, L., & Sykes, G. (Eds.). (2000). *Teaching as a learning profession: Handbook of policy and practice.* San Francisco: Jossey-Bass.

---

[4]First launched in 1999, the *Progetto Lingue 2000* is an initiative of the Italian Ministry of Education (Ministero della Pubblica Istruzione, 2001) to strengthen second language instruction in Italian schools as part of integration of educational systems in the European Union according to the principles of the Council of Europe (1998) Common European Framework of Reference for Modern Languages.

Duff, P., & Bailey, K. (2001). Identifying research priorities: Themes and directions for the TESOL international research foundation. *TESOL Quarterly, 35,* 595–616.

Eliot, T. S. (Thomas Stearns, Ed) 1888-1965. (1998). *Eliot: Poems and prose.* New York: A. A. Knopf.

Freeman, D., & Johnson, K. E. (1998). Reconceptualizing the knowledge-base of language teacher education. *TESOL Quarterly, 32,* 397–417.

Gebhard, M. (1998). A case for professional development schools. *TESOL Quarterly, 32,* 501–510.

Ministero della Pubblica Istruzione. (2001). *Progetto Lingue 2000: Atti dei seminari per i nuovi formatori di lingue straniere* [Language program 2000: An outline for courses for the formation of foreign language]. Rome: Author.

Organization for Economic Cooperation and Development. (2002). *Attracting, developing, and retaining, effective teachers.* Paris: Author.

Samuel, M. (1998). Changing lives in changing times: Preservice teacher education in postapartheid South Africa. *TESOL Quarterly, 32,* 576–583.

Stein, P. (1998). Reconfiguring the past and the present: Performing literacy histories in a Johannesburg classroom. *TESOL Quarterly, 32,* 517–528.

Third International Mathematics and Science Study. (1996). *Trends in mathematics and science achievement around the world.* Boston: International Evaluation Agency.

Wilson, S., Floden, R., & Ferrini-Mundy, J. (2001). *Teacher preparation research: Current knowledge, gaps, and recommendations.* Seattle: Center for the Study of Teaching and Policy, University of Washington.

World Bank. (2000). *Education sector strategy.* Washington, DC: Author.

Chapter **3**

Introspection and Retrospection as Windows on Teacher Knowledge, Values, and Ethical Dispositions

Angela Scarino
University of South Australia

INTRODUCTION

My interest in teacher knowledge is first in its nature as comprising formal, theoretical, and practical knowledge (see Clandinin & Connelly, 1987; Clark & Peterson, 1986; Connelly & Clandinin, 1985; Elbaz, 1983, 1991; Shulman, 1986, 1987, 1992) and ethical knowing; second, my interest is in its construction and use in the act of teaching. The coinage of the phrase "ethical knowing" (in the present continuous) is intended to highlight that the ever-evolving act of knowing, that is, constructing, using, reflecting on knowledge and its responsible use is inseparable on the one hand from the values and beliefs that comprise the ethical system that individuals develop through their ongoing processes of enculturation and on the other hand from its linguistic representation. Teacher knowledge is characterised in the literature as formal, theoretical, practical, and contextual (among other descriptors) in relation to realms of knowledge and their interrelation and in relation to knowledge acquisition and learning. This kind of characterisation, however, excludes values and ethics, for example, knowing about ways of acting and interacting with responsibility to others and ways of making knowledge (i.e., people's knowing) of value to the world in which we live. It also excludes metaknowledge, that is, the capability to reflect on the construction and the power of knowledge.

Teaching involves constantly making judgments that are shaped by teachers' frameworks of knowledge, values, and ethical dispositions. It calls for doing justice to the learning of each individual student and for considering notions of equity, fairness, and consequences of judgments of students' learning and progress. My specific focus for investigation is the area of school-based assessment, a site where judgments for learning, which draw on teachers' knowledge, values, and ethical dispositions, are centre stage.

In considering teachers' ethical knowing in action, I am concerned with both its possibilities and potential limits. The possibilities reside in "getting inside" teachers' knowing and understanding the complex, contextualised, knowledge-values-and-ethics laden act of teaching and, in my work specifically, the act of assessing. Although the role of teachers is frequently described as being focussed on practice, research on teacher knowledge suggests that beyond being a mirror of practice, teachers' work is a mirror of their conceptual thinking: constructing, applying, organising, and evaluating their framework of knowing within a system of values and ethical dispositions. These influence the way they interpret and judge reality in their everyday work and express it through their own language, which, in its turn, impacts on student learning within the culture of their particular context.

The potential limits of teacher knowledge reside in the extendedness and depth of the culturally learned conceptions that shape teachers' interpretations and judgments. As Bourdieu (1984) stated in relation to the judgment of taste:

> One can say that the capacity to see *(voir)* is a function of the knowledge *(savoir)*, or concepts, that is, the words, that are available to name visible things, and which are, as it were, programmes for perception. A work ... has meaning and interest only for someone who possesses the cultural competence, that is, the code, into which it is encoded. (p. 2)

Teachers' judgments are bounded by their socialisation and enculturation. Limits also reside in the knowledge claims and their justification by both teachers and researchers in their respective work. As discussed by Fenstermacher (1994), "The challenge for teacher knowledge research is not simply one of showing that teachers think, believe, or have opinions but that they know. And even more important that they know that they know" (p. 51).

Teachers and researchers need to be aware of their own and others' formal, theoretical, and practical orientations, their internal and often implicit frameworks of knowledge, values, and ethical dispositions and to be able to explain and justify the interpretive stances, actions, and judgments they make constantly in their work. They need to recognise the multiple interpretive frames and different worldviews and theories within which experiences and actions reside and use these multiple understandings to act knowingly and ethically.

In this chapter, I draw on data from a longitudinal study of three experienced senior secondary teachers of French as a foreign language in South Australia judging their students' second language writing performance. The data provide a window on the nature of teachers' knowledge, values, and ethical dispositions and the way these are activated in making judgments. In discussing the data, I highlight the interplay of knowledge, values, and ethical dispositions in teachers' work as well as the bounded nature of that knowledge. Finally, I draw some general implications for teacher education.

RESEARCH METHOD

Over a 2-year period, the teachers designed eight common writing tasks that were completed by their students, a group of 30 students in total. The writing tasks included text types such as description, narrative, letter, and a commentary on a literary text.

After each assessment episode, each of the teachers met individually with the researcher to assess his or her students' writing. Using introspection, they rated each episode, and each verbal report was audio-recorded. They also compared episodes of students' writing across the following pairs or groups of tasks: 1–2, 2–3, 3–4, 1–4, and 1–8, and these verbal reports were also audio-recorded.

For the 1st year of the study (i.e., for Tasks 1–4), the teachers returned individually 1 week after each initial rating session to participate in retrospection. This involved listening to the tape recording of their initial rating, stopping the recording at any point where they wished to make further comment. These retrospection sessions were also audio-recorded. In addition, teacher histories captured in individual interviews were also audio-recorded, as were end-of-year group discussions with the three teachers.

All audio recordings were fully transcribed. The data set was supplemented by analysis of published documents of the Senior Secondary Assessment Board of South Australia (SSABSA), including policies, syllabuses, and examiners' reports.

The Teacher's Profile

For the purposes of this chapter, the data are confined to one of the teachers, Rose, as she judges the performance of two of her students, Rosie and Edwina. Rose is a highly experienced teacher of French who has been involved extensively in the external examination process for exit from secondary school in the South Australian state educational landscape, including a period of 6 years as the state assessment authority's Chief Examiner for French. As an experienced teacher, Rose has a long history of inside-the-classroom teaching and assessing experiences of French (Sadler, 1985, 1987) in two private schools for girls in South Australia as well as a history of outside-the-classroom experience with the world, with language, and with norms of culture (Purves & Purves, 1986, p. 178).

Rose's judgments are embedded within and bounded by her personal framework of knowledge, values, and ethical dispositions and are expressed in her own distinctive language through a series of recurring words and metaphors (such as *sophistication, consciousness, excitement, life*). She has been an active constructor of the culture of senior secondary French in South Australia through the SSABSA,[1] a culture in which she acts comfortably and that she communicates to her students and colleagues. At the same time, although she knows the culture of senior secondary French intimately, it remains a discrete sphere of involvement, which is limited to one language in one assessment authority system in one state.

The Teacher's Framework of Knowledge, Values, and Ethical Dispositions

From an analysis of the verbal report data for Rose, I highlight two positionings. The first is an intellectual positioning derived on one hand from her orientation to the text and specific features of performance that include criteria and standards and a set of expectations about what students should be able to produce in response to the assessment task; on the other hand, Rose's intellectual positioning derives from the ultimate purpose of the exit examination for senior secondary students, which includes certification and selection for ter-

---

[1]See SSABSA (1990) for a manifestation of the culture of French Studies at senior secondary level.

tiary study based on academic performance. The second is a social and ethical positioning derived, among other dimensions, from her orientation to long-term, human, affective relationships in teaching and learning, nurturing individual student's learning and their progress, and recognising her own and others' expectations of her as a teacher. In the act of judging performance, she is confronted, albeit intuitively or subconsciously, with the responsibility of determining how to use her knowledge of criteria and standards and, simultaneously, how also to consider her students as young, sentient beings, her relationship with them, the consequences of her actions and judgments, and ethical concerns that pertain. She has to seek to find "equilibrium among justice, caring and truthfulness" (Oser, 1994, p. 104) as she judges their work.

I consider the two positionings simultaneously rather than separately to respect the holistic nature of judging. The process of judging involves describing (i.e., identifying and classifying), analysing (i.e., examining the relation among parts, integrating a range of particulars), and interpreting and evaluating (i.e., attaching meaning to the work as a whole).

Interpreting involves multiple layers and influences as presented in Figure 3.1. Using McNamara's (1996, p. 86) schematic representation of the interactional nature of performance assessment as a starting point, the figure presents the extent to which interpretation comes to the fore in judging performance. These interpretations are influenced by the teacher's knowledge, values, and ethical dispositions and the various roles he or she plays, often simultaneously.

From an overall content analysis of the data set for the three teachers in this study, specific dimensions of knowledge that emerge include the teacher's personal, cultural, and professional history; his or her philosophy of language, languages education, and how languages and cultures are learned and assessed; his or her internal system of criteria and standards and those of others; his or her understanding of students (as persons, as learners, as developing language learners, and as language users) with diverse interests, motivations, and capabilities; general pedagogy; curriculum, including planning, resources, assessing, and evaluating; the educational context, including social and power structures of school communities and cultures as places that create and sustain meanings and values; and the economic, cultural, and political contexts that constitute the professional landscape. These dimensions are all integrated within the teacher's framework of knowledge, values, and ethical dispositions and embedded in their personal constructs.

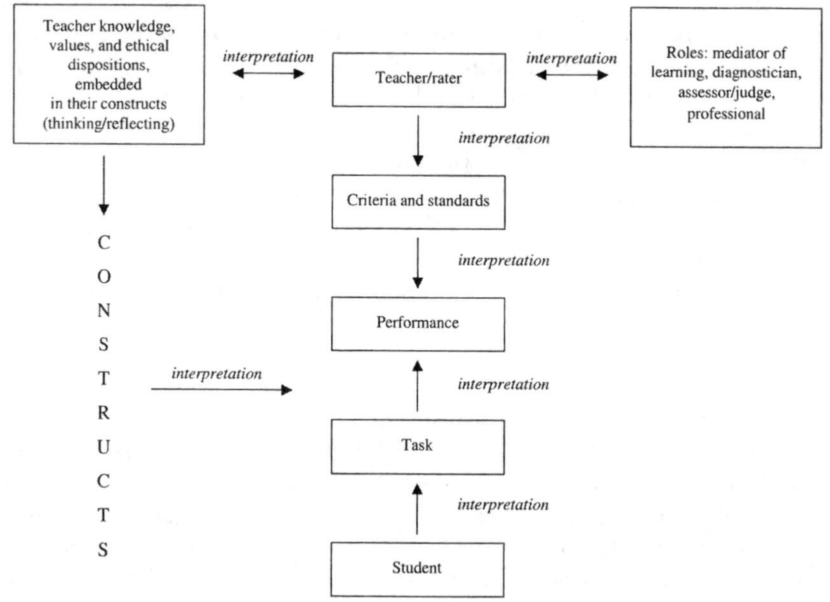

FIG. 3.1. Influences and layers of interpretation in judging student performance. From Fig. 3.9 in "Proficiency and its relation to performance,"*Measuring second language performance* by T. F. McNamara, 1996, Upper Saddle River, NJ: Pearson Education, Inc. Copyright © 1996 by Pearson Education, Inc. Adapted with permission

This is the judgment Rose, the teacher, makes of Rosie, her student on the first task:

> And Rosie starts off by writing her date in French[2] and Rosie, you know I don't like the date in French.
>
> Now Rosie's an interesting person. Rosie's got everybody's back up since she was in about Grade 2. She's always been a difficult child; she's now in year 11. She's very good at saying ... her father died of cancer, very, very quickly, in a matter of 3 months; and tragic, really tragic; ... er ..., 18 months ago. She thinks she's very very bright; she has actually got a few brains but, ... er ..., because she talks so much in class she misses out on an awful lot of the, the very detailed stuff that you need in French; I mean you have to listen; you have to get that little ... those nitty gritty bits that, you know, make it sophisticated, make it ... top notch. (Task 1 Introspection)

Rose begins by focussing on the date, notices an error, and addresses the student directly. Although the student is not physically present, Rose makes comments about her as if they were in conversation. This

[2]The teacher actually means English, but in the verbal report, she says French.

feature occurs frequently and is a marker of the relationship Rose has with her students. Rose's knowledge is embedded in these relationships with her students. The direct interaction triggers a description of the student as a person, her home background, as a student of French, and the recurring vignette of Rosie talking too much, all of which are meshed with the teacher's view of learning French: "the very detailed stuff that you need in French"—"those nitty gritty bits"—and the contrast between the student's behaviour and the teacher's perception of what is needed for success. Rose also describes her relationship with Rosie: "She and I get on quite well together. God knows why!" She cannot consider the student's text without first situating the student. Then she turns to the text:

> *Cette person est mon amie*; and she has got *personne* written in English; *mon amie* is right in the "ie" and she has got the *mon* in front of it which you don't always get either. *Elle s'appelle Jackie. Elle a dix huit ans, elle est plus vielle que moi.* Now then she's got a spelling mistake with *vieille*; they find it very hard at this stage to differentiate between *vieille* and *âgée*, as far as they're concerned *vieille* is old and old is old, and it's got nothing to do with sort of older in age but old, old age. *Jackie est assez grand*, no agreement; *elle a cheveux longs*; the *les* is missing; *elle a les cheveux longs et blonds; elle a les yeux bleu aussi*; no "s" on the *bleu*. Now that is typical of Rosie; she knows it; she has not listened; the attention to detail is missing; and she's really got to get on top of that if she wants to get herself the mark that she really wants, Rosie, cause Rosie is quite ambitious. *Dans la photo elle porte un jean*, good, *et une noir chemise*; oh, there we go; that's typical, the adjective going before; thinking in English; she knows very well they're ... they're written up on the board on the side of the wall the adjectives that go before, and *noir* is certainly not one of them; and there is no agreement either; she's got a big mistake there.
>
> ... Again that's a common ... that takes a long time to come that *que* infused in the subordinate clause; they think again in ... er ... and I think she is very pretty, and they just translate it straight through without the *que* to introduce it; *très jolie*, the *jolie* has got the agreement, which is good. (Task 1 Introspection)

Her judgment is contextualised in relation to the psychological development of the particular student, of students in general, in relation to language teaching, learning, pedagogy and assessment, and the social relationships in teaching and learning. It involves placing the text within the context of the person's history (for both the assessed and the assessor) and the context of the situation in which it is located. These contextual dimensions form frames of reference, which the teacher draws on as she reads, interprets, and judges student performance.

In the feature-by-feature description, each observation that Rose makes within the intellectual positioning is accompanied by an evaluative comment that expands on the judgment through the social and ethical positioning. For example, in relation to the accurate rendition of *mon amie*, Rose observes that Rosie "has got the *mon* in front of it which you don't always get either," indicating a positive valuing of that form. The next error is explained in terms of, "they find it very hard at this stage to differentiate ...," with this explanation suggesting that the teacher is likely to weigh the error less severely because of its difficulty at this particular stage in the trajectory of teaching and learning. Rose proceeds to note a lack of adjectival agreements and relates this to the student's regular pattern of behaviour and this student's expectations ("Rosie is quite ambitious."). In response to a correct sentence, the teacher adds the comment "good" and then a disciplinary tone in relation to a further error that she judges to have been avoidable. The tone and choice of language reflect the manner in which Rose speaks to her students in class. The comment, "she's got a big mistake there" indicates that she rates that particular error more severely than others.

Rose concludes her judgment as follows:

> She's written a fair bit ... the content is OK; she has structured it into paragraphs; she has actually given me, ... er ..., what that last sentence could be taken as ... er ... a conclusion, though I would have preferred it to have been written as separately. Er ..., a lot of those mistakes are sheer carelessness; you couldn't possibly give it an A standard because there are too many mistakes in it. And honestly, I don't think it's worth more than 15½; she won't be happy with that, but that's what it is worth as it is in fact even 15 probably, but I do, I'll give her the 15½ to keep her happy; and that half is a charity mark. There is potential there, if she gets herself, ... er ..., I'll have to impress it on her again, she really needs to get her head stuck into it, because she has got the ability to do it; there's a certain flow to that which is quite nice ... er ..., the sentences are not short, static, little things; they're nice little sub clauses, subordinate clauses there, and, ... er ... she gives a little story; ah, it's interesting but it needs a lot of spit and polish to get it up to standard. (Task 1 Introspection)

Here Rose proceeds to summarise and score the student's performance, that is, to shape a variety of judgments into a single interpretation or decision. After briefly summarising a range of criteria she has considered (i.e., length of text, content, structure of text, accuracy), she begins by contemplating the highest score, always wanting to see her students' performance in the best light possible, ("you couldn't possibly give it an A standard"). She judges the errors as being avoidable ("sheer carelessness"). In assigning a score, she immediately considers the consequences; she anticipates her student's response ("she won't be happy"). She considers the feedback she is going to give and recognises from the outset with this first task what becomes the key word for her judgments of Rosie, namely "flow," and one of the criteria to which she attaches a great deal of value, namely, the use of coordination and subordination. There is a constant interweaving of the intellectual and social/ethical dimensions throughout her judgment.

The retrospection process allows the teacher to reflect on her previous judgment; she states:

> She's got the ideas. There's no doubt about it. She's got a certain flow. That's what Rosie thrives on, is the flow. She just loves ... and she just writes it, and it almost comes spontaneously. And she couldn't give a stuff about grammar because she writes to speak the language. And, and she will. She'll probably tell me the French make more mistakes than she does anyway. Now, she's going to come back, in February, and she will be speaking fluently. She will have learnt every swear word under the sun, and she will try to use every bit of slang that she possibly can, the whole way through. You know, I'll spend the year beating it out of her. But there is, a life to her writing. And, you, you've got to appreciate that. Some of the other is technically correct, beautiful, technical language, scientific language. But this one, has got it, it oozes ... er ... atmosphere, I don't know, it's Rosie. I mean, you, you need to know Rosie, to see ... That girl is alive! Her writing is also alive. It's not correct, but, it gives you, it gives you entertainment. It's interesting. She, she tries to get you a little story, and she's got enough vocabulary, to actually get it across to you. Mind you, she's also ambitious. Rosie wants 20 next year. Rosie hasn't got a hope in ... of getting a 20. Even with her 3 months in France, she hasn't got a hope in ... She gets up to a 17, ... er ..., I'll try and tell her: Oh dear, 17, 18, Rosie is the very most, but I know Rosie doesn't listen to you either. Mother has very selective hearing. You tell mother that, you know, she's missed far too much grammar. Well she might surprise us all yet, and she might be top of the state. Oh, dear God. So, with Rosie

> and her mother like that ... no, I must say that I do like Rosie. (Task 3 Retrospection)

Through retrospection, a certain distance can be achieved when the teacher stands back from the student's text and reconsiders her judgment of it. Again, as with the initial introspection, it reflects the hybrid mix of the intellectual, social, and ethical dimensions of Rose's judgments. The process of explanation and justification is at once part of the evidence and an essential feature of the act of appreciation. Using very short sentences, Rose highlights the idea of "flow," which comes to characterise Rosie's writing over the 2 years. Describing Rosie's texts cannot be separated from Rosie, the person. Rose appreciates the intellectual, what she describes in this text as "technically correct, beautiful, technical language, scientific language" but also the social, affective value, the feeling of intensity about "flow" and "life" that characterise Rose's construction of Rosie.

The account concludes with a qualification to Rose's enthusiasm about Rosie. The teacher considers the student to be ambitious in aiming for a perfect score in French in the final, external, public examination and sets an expectation of a mark of 17 or 18 out of 20.[3] She also reflects on parental expectations. Rose comments in a negative tone about the mother's expectations given the fact that she judges them to be unrealistic; but then she immediately turns to a personal and positive conclusion about the student.

This retrospective text also demonstrates the comparative and contrastive dimension of making judgments. The contrast between the "technically correct" and the "flow" becomes a leitmotif as Rose compares and contrasts Rosie's writing with that of a third student in the class, Manuela (whose work is not discussed in this chapter). Manuela is the student whose performance Rose generally uses as a benchmark. Rose is oriented toward the structure and accuracy of the language ("technically correct" in Rose's words) but also a sense of text, style, vitality, and a sense of being ("flow" in Rose's words).

The distancing effect created by the longitudinal comparative and retrospective processes also brings a sense of holism within and across judgments. This holism relates to the process of discovering patterns and relationships, considering and reconsidering the evidence, the teacher's own previous judgments, and connecting these to a historical perspective, that is, the student's past, present, and future perfor-

---

[3]This is, in fact, the only case in which Rose underestimates the student's performance. Rosie does score a perfect score of 20 in the final examination.

mances and the teacher's past and present judgments. In short, Rose is making sense of the texts before her and turning observations to evidence. The comparative and retrospective processes also highlight the dynamic nature of students' progress and teacher judgments in relation to the progression or regression in students' performance. For example, the student Rosie becomes for the teacher a case study of ongoing improvement, whereas Manuela becomes a case study of regression, and Edwina becomes a case study of slow progress and distance travelled. What is not evident, despite the opportunity created by the distancing effect, is self-awareness about herself as assessor and judge.

The verbal reports of Rose's judgments, taken as a whole, demonstrate the way in which knowledge of criteria and standards for assessing student performance is meshed with the range of dimensions that comprise the teacher's interpretive framework of knowledge, values, and ethical dispositions. A summary of the criteria to which Rose ascribes value within the intellectual positioning is provided in the extract that follows:

> They have been told that if they want an A they have to have a subjunctive in there, they have to have an *après avoir* ... er ... I will be looking probably for a relative pronoun or a demonstrative pronoun, I will be looking for little adverbial introductions to sentences, and probably transition, good transition, good transition words or whatever you want to call them, or introducing a new paragraph; I will be looking for some sort of coherence from one paragraph to the next and I will definitely be looking for a bit of paragraphing, which in this day and age is not easy to get. You get slabs of concrete and one big long paragraph from beginning to end, and I will be looking for a conclusion. (Tasks 1–2 Comparative)

Rose, however, makes no analytic statement without immediately providing an affective, evaluative overlay. The evaluative remarks constitute a process of qualifying, explaining, or justifying, which are part of establishing, weighing, and generalising the evidence while at the same time considering short- and long-term consequences, albeit perhaps at a subconscious level. Despite the availability of published criteria for judging performance in the SSABSA (1990) syllabus for French and Rose's active role in their development, there is no match between these and the actual criteria that she uses in the act of judging her student's work.

Although on the surface, Rose's precise, analytic criteria (e.g., use of an *après avoir*, sequence of tenses, subjunctives, etc.) reveal what could be seen as a conservative focus on grammatical accuracy, they are also markers of complexity of thought and language, her intellectual positioning or "sophistication," to use her own word. When students use these structures, they necessarily draw connections among ideas, or relate events in time, or add an emotional overlay to a particular idea. For Rose, it is these features that are emblematic of the kind of abstract thinking ("consciousness") that she values in students and that marks senior secondary education for her.

Edwina's performance stands in contrast to Rosie's and provides an example of how the teacher's judgment adjusts, that is, how she uses her framework of knowledge, values, and ethical dispositions flexibly to take account of the individual student.

Rose begins her judgment in Task 1 with a profile of Edwina:

> Edwina Porter is another interesting character here. Edwina came into me last year, having done the first.... Edwina has been at ... [school] since about Grade 3 or 4, in other words, she's been doing French throughout the junior school. She keeps telling me she's never learnt anything, and mind you looking at her French, sometimes I wonder if she isn't telling me the truth; ... er ... she came into me last year; she wanted to do French; she had very little confidence in herself;
>
> ...
>
> ... er ... I don't know what she's like in any other subjects but she really is, and I suppose you shouldn't categorise students, but she's very much a B student. She ... she's very willing, she tries ... right, well here comes Edwina. (Task 1 Introspection)

Following the profile of the student,[4] to contextualise the judgment, Rose alludes to the problem of categorisation of students and no doubt the ethicality of her own categorisation of the student.

After a feature by feature analysis, the teacher makes a summary judgment:

> This is a very weak essay Edwina. You have to try and be positive when you are doing these things; if I tell her it's a lot of crap she might just scrunch it up and throw it in the bin and never listen to me again and she'll be doing economics next week. So, one

[4]Although it is likely that the profile is provided for the benefit of the researcher, nonetheless, the teacher feels obliged to contextualise the judgment she makes.

> has got to be positive in these situations; so I'll tell her that there is potential for some good sentences in there but she's got to start thinking in French. (She writes in the comments.) And I will put it down to nerves this time and hope that by the next time she will have developed a little bit more sense of the French language.
>
> ... Now I'm sure you will do far better next time. I'm not at all sure of it, never mind! You can live in hope! It will be interesting to see what improvement there is. I can't fail it which is what it is worth, so I'm going to give her a 12; it is not worth 12; 12 is not a good mark anyway but, she has got to be given some sort of, ... er ..., encouragement mark. Now this is the way marking has gone today; now this is the unfortunate thing about marking because, you cannot mark them on the value anymore; you'll have no students left. Unfortunately we live in a society where they're given credit ... er ... for an absence of ability, to try and keep them in the thing, and this goes, I think, right through almost every phase of life, it is not just here, but particularly in language which is an extremely difficult subject. If you want to have any students at all, you've got to sort of, reward any little bit in there that is correct, any little bit; I mean this is really worth probably 8 in straight language. There's very little to recommend it to be quite honest, but if I give 8 to that student, next week she'll be gone. There is a chance that if I keep her throughout the year, and if she does listen and she does, actually I can bet you that if she does matric[5] next year, she will probably get a 15 and 16. So, they're the games we play. I don't know how ethical they are, to be quite honest, but that's the kind of a world that we live in today. The same with my Manuela. Manuela will not be happy with 17. Manuela doesn't want anything under 19. However it is an A; I've given her an A. I'd say myself it's worth probably 16, but Manuela would just die if she got 16. Er ..., she is capable of bringing better effort to her work and I'm sure she will make mid year exams; she would do better than that because she rises to the occasion. This one would actually collapse; she would collapse in a heap if I failed her. (Text 1 Introspection)

This text brings into relief again the way in which judgment is mediated by the teacher's framework of knowledge, values, and ethical dispositions. Rose uses her professional knowledge, considers social aspects of teaching and learning, and considers the political dimension of student numbers in her senior class; she considers the long-term conse-

[5]Matric is an abbreviation of the term *matriculation* (i.e., Year 12, the final year of secondary school education in South Australia.

quences of her actions and judgments and above all, the ethical questions. She knows that judgment requires thoughtful anticipation of consequences. Her views of society in general are also incorporated in the judging process. As part of the retrospection in relation to this episode, Rose recounts her conversation with Edwina's parents as a direct consequence of her judgment:

> Perfectly true, and I might add that the aftermath of that was that Edwina collapsed in a heap and the first thing she said was, I am not doing French next year, I'm definitely giving it up. I had mother and father up to see me, both of them; normally only mother comes on parent/teacher night, but I had both and we had a very long discussion about Edwina's ability in French, etc., etc. I did tell them that, probably, Edwina would get a B, but definitely not to think that she could get any better; that we would reassess the situation at the end of the year, and to ... er ... compare it with the other subjects, and we would see how she would go. I also stressed the point that if she is enjoying ... if she gets some satisfaction out of the subject and gets on with the teacher, and there is a small class, there is a certain advantage to doing it, rather than jumping into another subject that she hasn't done, where she is not "comfortable," and insecure. She will, actually, I would say, if she does do it next year, she probably will get a B, and that in itself would be a miracle as well, because you work them up to a B, you prepare them, you give them skills, but that is not to say that later on at University, she is going to be in your top students; but these students are getting into Uni. Her strong point is that she is a very good worker, she will listen to you, she writes everything down, she will give you back everything you give her. She has not got that spark of intelligence to work on her own, she is a follower. And I might add that I have had students like her, no, slightly better, doing PhDs today; so who am I to judge what Edwina might become? In five or ten years time Edwina might be doing a PhD too, but at this stage, Edwina, to me is ... good God ... anyway ... a very nice girl! (Task 1 Retrospection)

Later texts in the series of eight provide examples of the progress as reflected in the judgments made over time. Rose judges Edwina in her own terms in relation to the distance she has travelled as well as in relation to the requirements established through the exteral examinations process.

> I mean, she's the one who has travelled the longest journey in this. Rosie has travelled too but in a completely different way. But this one, I mean this is without any props at all; normally she collapses in a heap if she hasn't got the dictionary. Dictionary sort of, you know ... I, I think it's good. I'm, I'm probably going to over mark but I'm going to give her a 14 because I'm going to give her a bottom B and she will be so thrilled with that, that it will be sort of an encouragement for her because she's never got more than 10 or 11. And I'm going to put, "This shows great promise, Edwina. There is huge improvement from last year." And there's still huge to go, mind you, but we won't say that just yet. She needs every bit of encouragement and she will just work and work and work. Actually I'm quite pleased with what she's written there. I'm amazed at what she's written. I mean, apart from me writing over there, it's nowhere near what it was last year. No, that's, that's really good. (Task 5 Introspection)

Finally, in judging Edwina's performance on the last task, which was undertaken as part of the external examination, Rose comments:

> My friend Edwina. I'm looking forward to seeing what Edwina wrote *Chère Cécile;* the *chère* has got the accent going the right way and it is feminine. Wonderful. *Chère* in there is masculine
>
> ...
>
> ... er ... another year or two, you know and a bit of the spit and polish would start to pay off here; *je voudrais aller à l'Université d'Adelaide; pour,* in order to, too hard; *étudier;* the infinitive is enough; *le commerce ... er ... mais avant ça je voudrais;* I don't know why on earth there's a full-stop there; *rester avec ma famille à Victor pour les vacances de Noël. Ma <u>mere</u>;* accent missing; *a voulu;* with an *-ou-; que j'aille en France,* wow, wow, wow! ... *pour un ou deux mois rester avec une famille <u>français</u>;* no agreement; *pour,* she had the *pour* in and then crossed it out ... er ... thinking should it or shouldn't it? should it or shouldn't it and then of course she got it out and it should have stayed; *apprendre la langue pendant que je m'occupe des enf-,* les enfants, *des enfants. Mais je <u>preferai</u>,* and of course with all these -r-s we can't possibly get the tenses right and the accents.
>
> ...

> Do you know something? That's not a bad letter. I bet you she would have got a 16 for that. If not, me, no, I don't.... Would there be enough to give it a 17? Er ... I would say 16½ but they[6] don't give halves so I'll say 16 and I will be quite interested to see. I'll know in a couple of months' time what these kids have actually got in those, what they would have been given; ... er ... depending on where the batch came up because she's got some good points in there. I know she's made some booboos. She's made some ... but when you compare this with what she did at the beginning of last year, I'll tell you what. And it goes to show that if she's really got, you know, ... er ... well *un peu de confiance* in them, they do rise to the occasion. They can actually learn something! Now she's not a polyglot and she's not a *bi-lingue* and she's none of those things, but believe you me she has come an awful long way. (Task 8 Introspection)

The phrase "my friend Edwina" captures here the relationship between the teacher and student. Rose is surprised to find the use of the subjunctive mood, one of her markers of progress. She places herself in the mind of the student trying to recall or apply a particular grammatical concept. In assigning a score, the teacher recognises that for the external assessor considering this script, the final mark would depend on the pattern of assessing prior to assessing Edwina's script ("depending on where in the batch came up"). Finally, she reflects on her student's progress and the importance of having demonstrated confidence in her.

DISCUSSION AND IMPLICATIONS

Consideration of the data demonstrates the interrelated and dynamic nature of the teacher's framework of knowledge, values, and ethical dispositions and how these are activated in making judgments in teaching and in assessing student performance. It extends beyond the kinds of characterisations that portray teacher knowledge as practical or formal or contextual. With Rose, there is evidence of the continuous interplay of the intellectual, the social, and ethical positionings that characterise the teacher's ethical knowing. There is also evidence of her recognition of the consequences and the ethics of judgments. The substance of her teaching, the qualities she seeks in her students' performances, and the rewards for her students are all manifestations of her "culture" of teaching, which in turn influences her students' con-

---

[6]This refers to assessors who mark the external examination scripts.

struction of their own dynamic framework of knowledge, values, and dispositions developed through the social and discursive relationships in their classroom. Using features of the teacher's process of activating her framework of knowledge, values, and ethical dispositions, it is possible to draw out some principles of ethical knowing that have implications for teacher education.

Introspection provides a means of drawing out the teacher's implicit knowledge, conceptions, assumptions, values, and ethical dispositions. Her judgments, as revealed in the verbal reports of each of the introspective, retrospective, and comparative assessment episodes gathered over the 2-year period, are based on her own internal criteria, her own frames of reference, and the knowledge, values, and ethical dispositions she has formed through her own history of experiences. The principle here is that ethical knowing involves the active construction of knowledge by the individual, in interaction with others and with technologies, in mediating and interpreting experience; it involves making explicit the implicit conceptions that shape people's thinking in fundamental ways (Resnick, 1989). It also involves constantly developing and using connections among various kinds of knowledge: formal and informal, discipline-based and generic, internal and private, external and public (Resnick, 1987) and recognising that knowledge, values, and ethics are interwoven in complex ways.

The culture of the classroom as a place where social relations are played out, the social relationships and interactions with students past and present and the culture of the external examinations are ever present in the teacher's judgments. The principle of ethical knowing here is that knowing is diverse and situated, shaped by the context of use, that is, the situational and social interactional circumstances (Brown, Collins, & Duguid, 1989; Bruner, 1986; Lave, 1988).

The teacher's own distinctive language is a product of her own formal education in England and in Australia as well as her teaching experience, which mirrors and mediates her knowledge, values, and ethical dispositions in her daily human reality. The principle of ethical knowing is that it involves developing and using language and other forms of symbolic representations of ideas, events, actions, concepts, and procedures.

Finally, the teacher's judgments always include an evaluative and affective stance. The principle of ethical knowing is that it extends beyond the knowledge base or disciplines and capabilities to include values and dispositions of the person (Bereiter & Scardamalia, 1989). It includes awareness that judgments are relative to an individual's own cultural makeup, what matters to him or her as an educator and ultimately as a human being. It responds to Fenstermacher's (1994) challenge that teachers should "know that they know" (p. 51).

Ethical knowing, then, requires self understanding on the part of teachers and teacher educators of (a) their own ever-evolving, dynamic framework of knowledge and their capability to generate new knowledge; (b) the deeply social and ethical nature of knowledge and its activation in teaching; (c) the process of "enculturation," both their own and that of their students; (d) the wider complex political, social, and cultural context of education and the way in which it impacts on their work; (e) their own judgments and how they are shaped by their own values and ethical dispositions; and (f) being able to articulate the consequences of their judgments and actions.

Implementing these principles in the curriculum for teacher education cannot be achieved through a single course or project, but rather they constitute an orientation for the curriculum as a whole so that ethical knowing becomes a reflexive way of thinking and doing. This is captured in Cochran-Smith and Lytle's (1999) notion of "stance" combined with Pennycook's (2001) notion of restively "problematising givens." It involves continuously providing opportunities in all courses for students to develop their judgment; to become aware of their own assumptions, motivations, knowledge, and values and those of others; to become aware of their own ways of thinking, knowing, and doing and those of others; to become aware of their own language, images, and metaphors and those of others; and to become aware of how all these develop and change over time. By awareness here, I do not intend a vague notion of generalised understanding but rather an ongoing active and critical process of interpreting and interrogating their own practices, theories, and research and those of others.

The challenge for teacher education, both preservice and inservice, is to give primacy to the ever-evolving dynamic and interrelated framework of knowledge, values, and ethical dispositions that intending and practising teachers bring to their work and to constantly build on and challenge their implicit conceptions. It involves developing ways of thinking and doing, continuously integrating thought and action rooted in the interrelation of knowledge, values, and ethics. Teacher education requires ongoing questioning and reflection: How do I know what I know? What don't I know? Why do I do what I do? How do I know the reasons for what I do and ask my students to know and do? What are the consequences of what I do? In this way, epistemological and ethical inquiry becomes an integral way of thinking and doing education in all its diversity.

REFERENCES

Bereiter, C., & Scardamalia, M. (1989). Intentional learning as a goal of instruction. In L. B. Resnick (Ed.), *Knowing, learning, and instruction: Essays in honor of Robert Glaser* (pp. 361–392). Hillsdale, NJ: Lawrence Erlbaum Associates.

Bourdieu, P. (1984). *Distinction. A social critique of the judgment of taste* (R. Nice, Trans.). London: Routledge & Kegan Paul. (Original work published 1979)

Brown, J. S., Collins, A., & Duguid, P. (1989). Situated cognition and the culture of learning. *Educational Researcher, 18* (1), 32–42.

Bruner, J. (1986). *Actual minds, Possible worlds*. Cambridge, MA: Harvard University Press.

Clandinin, D. J., & Connelly, F. M. (1987). Teachers' personal knowledge. What counts as personal in studies of the personal. *Journal of Curriculum Studies, 19,* 487–500.

Clark, C. M., & Peterson, L. (1986). Teachers' thought processes. In M. Wittrock (Ed.), *Handbook of research on teaching* (3rd ed., pp. 255–295). New York: Macmillan.

Cochran-Smith, M., & Lytle, S. (1999). Relationship of knowledge and practice. Teacher learning in communities. In A. Iran-Nejad & C. D. Pearson (Eds.), *Review of research in education* (Vol. 24, pp. 249–306). Washington, DC: American Educational Research Association.

Connelly, F. M., & Clandinin, D. J. (1985). Personal practical knowledge and the modes of knowing: Relevance for teaching and learning. In E. Eisner (Ed.), *Learning and teaching and the ways of knowing. Eighty-fourth Yearbook of the National Society for the Study of Education, Part II* (pp. 174–198). Chicago: University of Chicago Press.

Elbaz, F. (1983). *Teacher thinking: A study of practical knowledge*. London: Croom Helm.

Elbaz, F. (1991). Research on teacher's knowledge: The evolution of a discourse. *Journal of Curriculum Studies, 23,* 1–19.

Fenstermacher, G. D. (1994). The knower and the known. The nature of knowledge in research on teaching. In L. Darling-Hammond (Ed.), *Review of research in education* (pp. 3–56). Washington, DC: American Educational Research Association.

Lave, J. (1988). *Cognition in practice. Mind, mathematics, and culture in everyday life*. New York: Cambridge University Press.

McNamara, T. F. (1996). *Measuring second language performance*. London: Longman.

Oser, F. K. (1994). Moral perspectives on teaching. In L. Darling-Hammond (Eds.), *Review of research in education* (pp. 57–127). Washington, DC: American Educational Research Association.

Pennycook, A. (2001). *Critical applied linguistics*. Mahwah, NJ: Lawrence Erlbaum Associates.

Purves, A. C., & Purves, W. C. (1986). Viewpoints: Cultures, text models, and the activity of writing. *Research in the Teaching of English, 20,* 174–197.

Resnick, L. B. (1987). *Education and learning to think*. Washington, DC: National Academy Press.

Resnick, L. G. (Ed.). (1989). *Knowing, learning and instruction*. Hillsdale, NJ: Lawrence Erlbaum Associates.

Sadler, D. R. (1985). The origin and functions of evaluative criteria. *Educational Theory, 35,* 285–297.

Sadler, D. R. (1987). Specifying and promulgating achievement standards. *Oxford Review of Education, 13,* 191–209.

Senior Secondary Assessment Board of South Australia (SSABSA). (1990). *French extended course. Year 12 detailed syllabus statement.* Adelaide, South Australia, Australia: Author.

Shulman, L. (1986). Paradigms and research programs in the study of teaching. In M. Wittrock (Ed.), *Handbook of research on teaching* (3rd ed., pp. 3–36). New York: Macmillan.

Shulman, L. (1987). Knowledge and teaching. Foundations of the new reform. *Harvard Educational Review, 56,* 1–22.

Shulman, L. (1992). Toward a pedagogy of cases. In J. Shulman (Ed.), *Case methods in teacher education* (pp. 1–29). New York: Teachers College Press.

Chapter **4**

The Professional Development of Working ESL/EFL Teachers: A Pilot Study

Bill Johnston
Faridah Pawan
Rebecca Mahan-Taylor
Indiana University

INTRODUCTION

The research described in this chapter constitutes the first step in a large-scale study of the professional development of working English as a second language and/or English as a foreign language (ESL/EFL) teachers after graduation from a U.S. masters program. The larger study will examine the lives of 12 graduates from a U.S. masters program over a period of approximately 5 years.

In this chapter, we describe the first interview of the study, which we decided to treat as a kind of pilot (although we had piloted the protocol on each other before beginning the study). We interviewed Bea, an experienced American teacher teaching ESL at a Japanese university. In the chapter, we analyze data from this interview with a view to the continuation of the study.

The chapter follows the thrust of much recent research in teacher education in seeking to portray teacher knowledge not as an isolated set of cognitive abilities but as fundamentally linked to matters such as teacher identity and teacher development. In this study, teacher knowledge is seen in relation to teachers' lives and the contexts in which they work.

Theoretical Framework and Principal Research Questions

The principal research questions in our study are as follows: (a) What happens to teachers after the master of arts (MA)? and (b) How do the careers and professional development of working teachers match up with our assumptions about such teachers' needs, interests, and concerns?

The theoretical framework employed in this study is grounded in the existing literature on teacher professional development both in general education and in TESOL. Four clear focuses can be identified in this literature:

Teacher Life Stories. The TESOL literature has begun to follow the lead of research in general education (e.g., Goodson, 1992; MacLure, 1993) in investigating the ways in which teachers tell their life stories and how these stories relate to their professional development. Teacher narratives are starting to be used in teacher education (Bailey et al., 1996), and there are also the beginnings of research on the stories told by experienced teachers (Johnson & Golombek, 2002; Johnston, 1997).

Professional Development. An aspect of teacher life stories that is of great interest to us are stories concerning growth as a teacher. There are now an increasing number of studies looking at how experienced teachers continue to grow professionally by extending their understanding of their work, whether through action research (Edge, 2001; Edge & Richards, 1993; McNiff, 1993) or in other ways (e.g., Clair, 1998; Johnson & Golombek, 2002); there is, further, a common agreement that continued professional development is a need felt by all teachers regardless of their level of expertise and experience.

Teacher Beliefs and Knowledge. A crucial part of what it is to be a teacher and of one's professional development as a teacher are the beliefs one holds about teaching and the knowledge one has. Although the exact nature of this knowledge remains subject to lively debate, it is widely accepted that teacher professional development cannot be understood without reference to the assumptions teachers bring to their work and their complex understandings of that work and of their own part in it (Borg, 1998; Clandinin & Connelly, 1995; Golombek, 1998; Johnston & Goettsch, 2000; Woods, 1996).

Teacher Identity. Finally, there is a newly emerging literature that looks at language teacher identity. This includes ways in which teachers negotiate identities across cultural boundaries, for example, in the case of expatriate teachers (Duff & Uchida, 1997; Johnston, 1999); how identities are developed in teacher education contexts (Varghese, 2001); the identities of nonnative speaker teachers of EFL and ESL (Braine, 1999; Liu, 1999); and the question of whether teachers are professionals (Edstam, 2001; Moran, 1996).

Our contention is that these four focuses are not separate, freestanding elements but rather represent important parts of a whole. Specifically, each is related to the others, and taken together they comprise a detailed picture of the professional growth and development of teachers. This relation is portrayed in Fig. 4.1, which presents the theoretical framework graphically.

Two other key features of the framework must be pointed out. First, we see each of these focuses to be related to the others; indeed, throughout our analysis, we emphasize their interrelatedness and stress the fact that more than anything else, these are conceptual categories for analytic convenience. The interrelatedness of the focuses is represented by the lines joining each box to every other box. By the same token, we

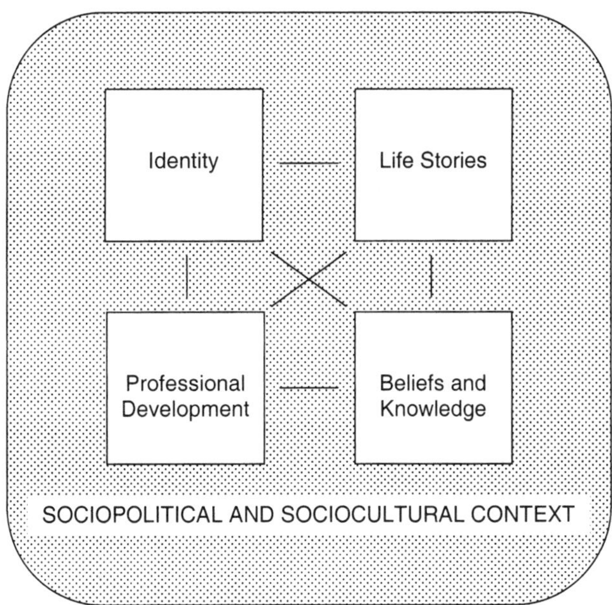

FIG. 4.1. Teacher professional development.

stress that no linear sequence exists among the boxes, and no particular progression or narrative is implied in their arrangement.

Second, the entire model—that is, the teacher's professional development as a whole—is permeated with the particular qualities and characteristics of the sociocultural and sociopolitical environment or environments in which it takes place. No element of life story, professional development, beliefs and knowledge, or teacher identity can be properly understood without taking into account the complex social, cultural, and political context in which it occurs. The shaded background, labeled "Sociopolitical and Sociocultural Context," is intended to convey this notion.

The principal research questions driving the study were mentioned previously, and are repeated here for convenience: What happens to teachers after the MA? How do the careers and professional development of working teachers match up with our assumptions about such teachers' needs, interests, and concerns?

More specific questions arise from the different components of the theoretical framework:

1. How do teachers tell their life stories? What discourses do they draw on in constructing these stories? Is it possible to speak of the "careers" of ESL teachers?
2. What forms of professional growth and professional development do MA teachers choose for themselves? What are their greatest perceived needs?
3. What kinds of linguistic and other knowledge do teachers draw on in their work?
4. What form or forms of identity do teachers claim, acknowledge, or resist? How are these identities expressed or conveyed?
5. What features of the sociopolitical context in which teachers work are significant in the answers to the other questions posed in this study? What issues of power and culture are central in their professional development?

RESEARCH DESIGN

Data Collection

As mentioned previously, the broader study for which this chapter constitutes a beginning is a long-term, 5-year project looking at the lives and professional development of working ESL/EFL teachers. Data are to come from extensive semistructured interviews with 12 working teachers who graduated from one U.S.-based MA in TESOL program from 3 to 10 years prior to the commencement of the study. Participants will be selected to be representative of the overall demographics of the program in terms of gender and national origin and also to reflect a range of different national and institutional working contexts. Given that the program primarily focuses on preparing teachers to work with adult learners, most of the teaching contexts represented will be in this domain.

The principal source of data will be transcripts of extensive semi-structured interviews conducted annually with each of the participants. The Appendix contains the interview protocol, although in the present case this was used more as an informal checklist than a structured series of questions. The interview with Bea on which this chapter is based took place in March 2001 and lasted about 90 min. In the broader study, additional data will come from other sources, including follow-up e-mail exchanges, found data such as resumes, and where possible, classroom observations.

Data Analysis

The data analysis was initially conducted independently by each of the three authors, whose analyses were then compared and compiled.

The analysis of the data in this study has four basic qualities. First, it is qualitative: That is to say, it primarily involves the interpretive analysis of text. Beyond a fairly rudimentary content analysis and the extraction of basic biographical and other factual information, we have concentrated on close, attentive readings of the text that are sensitive not just to what Bea says but to the ways in which she says it. By the same token, we have eschewed the use of automated electronic data analysis procedures, relying rather on our sensibilities as readers. This lends the analysis something of the quality of literary analysis (Coffey & Atkinson, 1996; Silverman, 1993). Such an approach is respectful of the text yet seeks to look beneath it to understand it better.

Second, the analysis is discourse based. This means that rather than necessarily regarding the interview transcripts as exact records of "what is," we see them as being to an important degree an example of self-presentation through discursive means. In other words, we are interested in how teachers create identity, life stories, and so on through language as much as "objective" features of professional life such as where they work, when and why they change jobs, and so on (Johnston, 1997).

Third, the analysis is postmodern or poststructural in nature (Riessman, 1993). The particular feature of the postmodern that we are referring to here is the notion that rather than searching for singular and coherent understandings, we are prepared to find and acknowledge multiple, perhaps contradictory and conflicting discursive accounts of, for example, life choices or features of teacher identity within any given interview.

This leads to the fourth and perhaps most salient feature of the analysis. With particular reference to the previous quality, that of the postmodern, we have chosen in our analysis to focus on *tensions* in the transcript. By this we refer to understandings, choices, and decisions that involve conflicting or opposing values and beliefs and that constitute the living dynamics of the teacher's professional development. As we demonstrate, in light of the qualities of analysis outlined previously, we have found this approach to yield particularly rich understandings of Bea's professional life and professional development.

PILOT STUDY: BEA

Bea, an American from the Midwest, is an experienced teacher in her late 40s. At the time of the interview, she was teaching EFL in a private university in Japan. Bea's educational background is as varied as her professional experiences. She has had extensive training in fine arts, English literature, and teaching ESL. She graduated from the MA program in 1999. Bea was an administrator in several small colleges and in nonprofit organizations. She has also had 20 years of experience teaching academic reading and writing in traditional and nontraditional contexts in tertiary and professional institutions.

Bea was interviewed during a visit to the United States. The interview was conducted by the three authors of this chapter; it was tape-recorded and subsequently transcribed. As described previously in the section on research design, the interview was semistructured using the interview protocol given in the Appendix.

In considering what to present in this chapter, we decided to focus in detail on only certain elements of the theoretical framework, rather than attempt comprehensive coverage. We chose what seemed to us the two most interesting aspects of the framework to emerge from the interview: the question of teacher identity and Bea's knowledge and beliefs as a teacher.

Teacher Identity

Current understandings within many branches of the social sciences see identity as involving at least three related qualities (Gergen, 1991; Norton, 1997; Sarup, 1996). First, identity is complex and contradictory, comprising multiple, often conflicting allegiances and belongings. Second, identity is crucially dependent on social, cultural, and political context. Third, identity is to a significant extent established, negotiated, and developed through discourse. All these qualities mean that identity is not stable or fixed but is rather dynamic and subject to change over time.

These qualities are especially striking in second language teachers. Certain areas in particular have been identified in the research as constituting contested aspects of language teacher identity. In this section, we focus on two of these. The first is the expatriate EFL teacher's role as de facto representative of her home culture, and more broadly her relationship to and with the host culture (Duff & Uchida, 1997; Johnston, 1999); we refer to this as *cultural identity*. The second is the contested notion of professionalism and the teacher's identity as professional (Edstam, 2001; Johnston, 1997); this we call *professional identity*. Both areas, as the reader will see, raise the question of *marginality* that is omnipresent in the field of ESL and EFL teaching.

Cultural Identity

One fundamental tension underlying the work of expatriate EFL teachers is that, although many consider themselves to be atypical, unusual representatives of their home country, the people of the host culture regard them as typical exemplars of Americans, British, and so forth. Bea certainly exemplifies this tension. She says: "Whether I like it or not, I'm a representative of Western culture there, [laughs] often, you know, a notable one, [laughs] you know, 'ooh, you're from America!'" She adds further that, "I feel very American in Japan, way more than I do here [in the United States]"; and she says that this feeling of "being American" intensifies as she continues to live and work in Japan. "I've talked to other people and we've all shared this sense of, the longer we're there, the more American we feel or the more Canadian or, you know, wherever you're from."

This tension—between her own view of herself as not typically American and her role in Japan as exemplar of "American culture"—is mirrored in another central tension for Bea. It is also true that the longer she is in Japan, the better she understands the host culture; this represents a transformation of her own cultural identity, and also of her professional identity as an effective, expert teacher and individual in the Japanese university context. Of the Japanese attitude toward her, she says, "It's like they're grateful when we know enough of the etiquette and the social, you know, to sort of—not fit in, but—not horrify anybody." Yet as she continues to live and work in Japan and her own familiarity with the host culture increases, Bea reports that the Japanese perception of her value declines, rendering her less professionally desirable to the institution she works for:

> Because the Japanese historically have always had this perception of, you bring foreigners, when you bring them in, for some reason, some technical skill, something that you can get from them, and then when you've got it, you send them home. There's never any sense that you become Japanese. Um, I mean, you can't. You are an outsider—period. [laughs] It doesn't matter how long you're there. And that gets translated institutionally into these ideas of, like, 2-year contracts at certain schools or, um, what we call "fresh," you know, people who have been working in Japan for 10 or 15 years find it very difficult to keep getting jobs because they're perceived of as being old in the sense of not fresh anymore. They're, like, not American enough anymore. They've been here too long. And I find that really ironic.

Bea's cultural identity in Japan, then, is, as Norton Peirce (1995) put it, "a site of struggle" (p. 9). On one hand, in opposition to her own view of herself, she is seen as a representative of her country, a role she acknowledges while admitting it is determined by her sociocultural context. On the other hand, her increasing comfort in Japanese cultural settings is offset in her view by the Japanese perception of her as no longer having to offer what they originally wanted from her. In both cases, we suggest that the tensions of identity are partly derived from clashes between external and internal identities—that is, between *assigned* or *perceived* identities (those identities attributed to her by other people, especially those in the host society) and *felt* or *claimed* identities (those identities that Bea herself acknowledges or wishes to take for herself).

We further suggest, though, that to a significant extent these tensions of identity exist within Bea herself. She says that she herself feels "way more" American in Japan than at home in the United States; although she does not say so, it seems apparent from the way she both presents the view of herself as "not fresh enough" and simultaneously resists it that this tension too is one that is present within her. Thus, the tensions of identity are not merely clashes between external and internal views of the self but are part of Bea's own internal, dynamic, evolving set of identities.

The element of marginalization must also be pointed out here. Bea uses the term "outsider" to describe (her account of) the Japanese attitude toward her; marginality can also be read in other comments, including her description of her growing competence in meeting

Japanese cultural expectations: "We know enough of the etiquette and the social, you know, to sort of—*not fit in, but*—not horrify anybody" (italics added). Bea is careful to exclude "fitting in" as an option she has at her disposal in her dealings with members of her host culture. Throughout the interview, it is clear that Bea is not only conscious of her marginalized position in both cultural and professional contexts, but that to a large extent she accepts it; it might even be suggested that Bea and other expatriate teachers actively embrace marginality (Johnston, 1999).

Finally, in all of this there is a powerful discursive element. As mentioned previously, identity is not a set of decontextualized, neutral labels but is constructed and reconstructed anew through language at every moment. Bea's discursive construction of herself as teacher and as expatriate American in Japan, and of Japanese attitudes toward her, is just that—a presentation through language in a particular context, that of a research interview with three TESOL colleagues. Furthermore, we wish to draw attention to the fact that at many moments, the interview takes on a hall-of-mirrors quality as Bea represents not only her own point of view but the views and words of other expatriates, of her students, and of other Japanese. All these voices are filtered in Bakhtinian fashion (Bakhtin, 1981; Johnston, 1997) through her own, and are thus part of her own discourse; in this way too, the external tensions of perceived versus felt or claimed identity become internalized through discourse, and the speaker becomes the nexus at which competing discourses of cultural identity "fight it out" (Bakhtin, 1981, p. 327) in the speech of the individual.

Professional Identity

There has been endless debate in the field over whether TESOL is a profession and whether teachers are professionals. Where this debate has been taken up in empirical research (e.g., Edstam, 2001; Johnston, 1997), an important aspect of it has been phenomenological in nature, looking at how teachers themselves perceive their work and their field. We posed such a question to Bea; we cite her response at length here:

Interviewer: Do you see yourself as a professional and, if so, how do you understand that term?

Bea: Yeah, militantly so. [laughs] Never used to be, but after going through the wars of being adjunct composition faculty—that, you know, the sort of lowest on the ladder, never tenured, never secure—and then adjunct at several other schools, even, I mean, even when I worked as

> an administrator in a university setting, I was still considered adjunct faculty, so it never goes away. And now working abroad, um, I don't even entertain any notions of tenure in Japan. I mean, it's just a concept that there's so much resistance to and so few foreigners have ever been given tenure in university systems. Um, and there are so many ways for them not to give you tenure that it would be really stupid to think, "oh, but, I'm going to be different. I'm going to be the one that ..." No. Not even thinking it. This is purely adjunct for me. But, because of all that, it also makes me much more aware of having to really work to continue to see myself and do things to see myself as a professional, in order to kind of, I hope gently, force other people to see me as a professional, because, institutionally, it's not there. Um, I think if you're, you know, given the title, given the tenure, given the office, you know, whatever the trappings are, the retirement plan [laughs], the golden retirement plan, you know, it may be easier to just sort of assume you're a professional, and you don't have to think about it. But the systems I've worked in have always marginalized folks—me and folks that have done my job. So, I mean, if *I* don't do things to see myself as a professional, nobody else is going to.

Bea's comments on her own professionalism reveal a set of interrelated tensions underpinning her professional identity. The most powerful and central of these is a tension between perceptions of the work of teachers from outside and their own view of their work and worth. This tension can be conceptualized as a clash between perceived identity and claimed identity, as mentioned previously. In this case, the disjuncture between perceived and claimed identity may be seen as a prime source of the marginalization that Bea explicitly mentions.

Yet the situation is more complex than this. Although marginalization seems to cross national and institutional boundaries, the particular forms it takes are specific to certain contexts. In Bea's case, professional acknowledgment seems bound up with the cultural identity we discussed earlier; the impossibility of securing a tenured position is due not to characteristics of the teaching occupation itself, nor to TESOL, but to Bea's identity as a non-Japanese. Although at one level this actually mitigates the marginalization of the field, for Bea and others like her it constitutes one more obstacle in the path of professional recognition.

It is not accurate, though, to say that this tension is a purely external versus internal one. As with issues of cultural identity, the really interesting aspect of the tension is that it exists within Bea's own discourse. She admits openly that her own view of herself as professional is not natural or easy but constitutes a continual, ongoing struggle—that she has to "really work" at seeing herself as a professional. The battle to convince the outside world of one's professional worth is at all times paralleled by a battle to persuade *oneself* of this identity. Thus, as with the contradictory view of cultural identity, opposing visions of teacher professional identity meet within the discourse of the individual teacher.

To conclude this section, the interview with Bea reveals several fundamental tensions regarding teacher identity, including dynamics of both cultural identity and professional identity. All these tensions show the complex, dynamic, and changing nature of teacher identity; all are rooted firmly in particular sociocultural and political contexts; and all are reflected in the complex and multivoiced discourse of the teacher.

Beliefs and Knowledge

We were interested in Bea's beliefs about teaching and learning and how she as a practicing teacher is able to integrate into her teaching the linguistic and educational knowledge she has acquired. To that end, we asked Bea questions about the degree to which the education she received at the master's level prepared her for the work that she is currently engaged in; what she has learned since then, formally and informally; and what she feels she "knows" about teaching at the present time. Her responses to the questions provided information about Bea's formal teacher preparation in ESL teaching in a TESOL program at a large research university in the Midwest; the role and function of the various teaching experiences she has had; and finally, a cross-cultural perspective on what she knows now as an American teacher abroad.

From the information that Bea shared with us, we noticed tensions emerging within her beliefs about teaching and how she integrates knowledge acquired from formal preparation and from experience into her work. These tensions are contradictory forces that pull Bea in different, often opposing directions.

Formal Preparation in TESOL. Despite the many years of on-the-job preparation that Bea has had, she was required by the profession to obtain formal preparation and certification in the field. Information from Bea's interview revealed tensions she experiences with regards to the formal preparation that she undertook in the TESOL program. On the one hand, Bea accepts the necessity of the formal preparation in teaching, as it would give her better access to jobs she desires. However, she struggles with the limited degree to which the preparation prepared her for real-life teaching. When asked about what prepared her the most for teaching in those positions, Bea had the following to say:

> I'll tell you though, what prepared me had nothing to do with TESOL. I mean that's probably not the politically correct answer, but it had nothing to do with TESOL training. It had to do with my previous experiences teaching ... because I mean, I taught in the basic skills area as well as ... general knowledge. You know, you get faced with everything [laughs], you name it. I mean, bring in a guy, literally guards bringing in the guy, a student, and shackling him to the desk, you know, 'cause he's on work release [from prison] to attend class. You know, students who are functionally illiterate and hiding it, um, Vietnam vets with serious posttraumatic stress, you know, problems. And I was just faced with so much stuff ... that demanded flexibility that I think *that* was the best preparation.

It is clear here that Bea believes the flexibility she has acquired from her numerous experiences as a teacher is most useful and defines her teaching. However, without a piece of paper that attests to her qualifications, she would not have been able to proceed to do what she already knows how to do well. Bea experiences tension emerging from having to acknowledge the utility of her formal preparation to get a job while at the same time being unable to give credit to the preparation to help her do what the job actually requires.

Bea was focused on her own goals and purposes while pursuing the masters in TESOL. Such a situation created tension in terms of the quality of education she perceives she obtained from the program. The quote following is illustrative:

> During the MA.... Um, most useful, probably the broad overview of the literature, SLA [second language acquisition] literature, I would say ... to have a sense of where the field's been, what's being looked at, what isn't being looked at, how people develop their perspectives as researchers which [is] very different from my own orientation. Um, I mean, in English, we are expected to do original research. That was just a given.... And then I come into this program, and I am specifically told, "do not do original research," by my professors! You mean, I'm supposed to repeat someone else's work? What's the point of that? [laughs]

Bea acknowledged that she found the program enlightening in that it gave her a broad overview of the field. On the other hand, however, it was constraining in that professorial requirements in the preparation kept her from pursuing undertakings of her choice in school. The previous quote highlights a clash between the autonomy she knew as a professional and expectations levied on her by her professors while she was in school. Such a situation created a tension of the kind mentioned earlier and colored her perception about the contributions the program has had on her profession.

Teaching Experiences

One of the major tensions emerging from the data centers on Bea's extensive experience in teaching and the function it has in her knowledge and beliefs about teaching. The experiences that Bea has had as teacher provide her with a very strong foundation that she uses as a basis for judgment and evaluation. However, the experiences may also have discouraged her from exploring alternative approaches:

> But everything I came across, I looked at through the perspective of what I'd already experienced, which is good, I think, because it means, although I had a huge filter and a lot of things I threw away, frankly [laughs] because they didn't bear out with my experience, at least I had some touchstone to analyze this stuff. On the other hand, it made me pretty ruthless about throwing things out, and if I hadn't had that experience, maybe I would have taken in and tried more than I did. Um, I didn't have a lot of patience for things that I just felt were nonsense.

Bea's tension at this point is between the reliability of her background experience as a schema to help her evaluate new ideas and approaches, in contrast to it being a "ruthless" filter that makes her judgmental and impatient about new information. This is a tension that many veteran teachers have but rarely acknowledge.

The tension, however, has not prevented Bea from keeping up with current trends in theory and research as part of her efforts to incorporate the latest ideas and practices into her teaching. She reads professional journals, attends conferences, and writes. Bea's interest in incorporating sustained content into her ESL teaching, for example, demonstrates an awareness of current issues. However, Bea's desire to be at the forefront of knowledge is tempered by the realization that new approaches do not always speak to what she is experiencing in the classroom. This is another source of tension for Bea, as can be seen in the following quote:

> I keep reading in the pedagogy about making students comfortable, which I don't really have any problem with ... but I do think it's been interpreted, then, in the literature of teacher training to mean the teachers need to be entertainers, the teachers need to be therapists, the teachers need to sacrifice everything in favor of making students comfortable. Well, I mean, I think it's nonsense. I think discomfort is motivation [laughs], you know, I think dissatisfaction is a motivation, I think realism plays a role in this, and, yeah, I think part of being a professional is learning to assess what is, like, momentary discomfort that will lead to a gain versus discomfort that's paralyzing and overwhelming and will alienate.... Um, if I hadn't had the experiences I'd had that have shown me with varying levels and types of students that comfort just isn't the issue, you know, maybe I would have been more patient with that and that would have gone into my pedagogy.

As can be seen here, the applicability of information to her teaching experiences and individual context is of importance to Bea. Nevertheless, she keeps up with current information and makes it a part of her professional knowledge, regardless of whether or not it relates directly to her particular experience.

"American Knowledge"

For financial and employability reasons, Bea is now teaching abroad. As an American teacher, Bea relies on the information and knowledge she gained in the United States as bases not only for classroom teaching but also for other professional endeavors in her current country of employment. There, Bea is pleasantly surprised and puzzled at the same time to find interest in knowledge she considers outdated. Although Bea finds the interest reenergizing, she is frustrated at the same time because she is unable to go beyond the knowledge she already has and take it one step further:

> And now I go abroad, and, at least in Japan, um, they're just thirsty for this stuff [sustained content]. And I find certain people who are doing the same sorts of things and feeling the same frustration, like, why is this novel to these people? Where have they been for 20 years?

> ... I am not a revolutionary! I am revisiting research from 25-30 years ago! This isn't new stuff.

Bea's tension stems from having to spend most of her time revisiting the same information, although she has been rewarded with attention for the endeavor. Bea struggles with the need to experience intellectual growth that seems to contradict the pleasure she experiences from renewed interest in ideas that have been part of her knowledge for quite some time.

Bea has firm beliefs that ideas she brings to the classroom in the foreign country are what the students need to learn and accept. However, she also understands that the cultural expectations in the country have the ability to override her efforts to have students adopt those ideas. Such a realization again creates a tension, as is evident in the following quote:

> I mean, ultimately, it [shyness] is a cultural behavior, and I will accept that in [this culture's] classroom, it may be a functional behavior. I don't know that, but I'll accept that it may be. It's not functional in an English classroom, and these folks are studying comparative cultures, they want to go abroad, they want to be functional—they need to get over it!

The tension here is one that many American teachers may encounter when they teach in another country. What they believe is necessary and what the people in the culture consider most important does not always agree. Teachers, then, have an important responsibility of finding ways to work with the two so that students are not caught in the middle, finding themselves unable to fulfill either the expectations of their American teachers or those of their home culture.

Although numerous, the tensions that emerged from Bea's beliefs and conceptions of teacher knowledge are common to and reflect the reality of the profession. The more experience they gain and the longer they remain in the field, the more teachers see value in the work that they do in the classroom and the more they trust their instincts derived from real-life engagement with students to guide their teaching (see Kubota, 1998). Formal preparation and knowledge obtained from it is relegated to a secondary position. However, to play the "professional game," experienced teachers, exemplified by Bea, keep up with current theoretical thinking in the field regardless of any disjuncture they perceive between theory and their own practice in the classroom. The current movement in teacher preparation to develop reflective practitioners through action research (Freeman, 1998) emerged to redress the disjuncture by acknowledging the primacy of teachers' own experiences in the classroom.

Finally, Bea's tensions with her need for intellectual growth and her perception of culturally appropriate student behavior remind us all that teachers are individuals with personal agendas and cultural baggage. As teachers, we are part of the equation and our objectives, goals, and sense of well-being need to be sufficiently addressed if the job of educating is to be done well.

CONCLUSIONS

In seeking to place teacher knowledge in the context of teachers' lives and work, in this study we posed two principal questions. The first of these was, What happens to teachers once they leave the MA program? Because this chapter focuses on two parts in particular of the model of teacher professional development presented previously—identity, and knowledge and beliefs—we might rephrase this question for our present purposes as follows: Who do teachers become after their MA?, And, what do they come to know after their masters program is over?

It is clear from the analysis of Bea's interview that teacher identity continues to develop and change as the teacher moves through her or his professional life. For expatriate teachers, cultural identity emerges dialogically and dynamically through encounters with the sociocultural and political context—encounters, moreover, that change both sides. In Bea's case, her identity can only be understood in relation to the Japanese context in which she was working. Professional identity too is shaped both by contextual features—how identity is assigned by others—and by the agency of the teacher herself. Both types of identity evolve dynamically, the result of often competing forces both outside and within the individual teacher. For this reason, the notion of tensions of professional development has been a particularly fruitful one in this study. Similarly, our emphasis on the discursive construction of reality and of teacher knowledge reveals how much of professional development takes place through the far from transparent medium of language and discourse.

The second question we posed at the beginning was, How do the realities of teacher professional development jibe with our preexisting notions of their needs, concerns, and interests? Insofar as such preexisting notions are embedded in the structure, content, and discourse of MA programs, which are intended to prepare teachers for a career in teaching, it seems plain that some features of these programs are more successful than others in carrying out this intention. In Bea's case, the knowledge base that she draws on is considerably wider than that represented by her MA program of study, thus creating one major tension in the development of her professional knowledge and beliefs; furthermore, we saw that experience, as well as having an enriching effect, can also have a limiting influence on receptivity to new ideas. Returning to the topic of identity, it would seem that this was not addressed in Bea's MA program and generally does not figure highly in our conceptualizations of teachers' professional development needs; yet in Bea's case identity, and more specifically tensions of identity, obviously form a major part of her growth and change as a teacher.

This pilot study suggests that the professional development needs of experienced teachers, although different from those of beginning teachers, are no less complex and conflict ridden. Teacher development takes place amid competing values, forces, and impulses; furthermore, it is centered around contested uses of language (such as competing designations of "professionalism"). Thus, in this study, by treating the data not as a straightforward record of what is but rather as Bea's own discursive presentation of her situation, we have been able to reveal how both identity and knowledge and beliefs are important discursive constructions in Bea's evolving "story of the self."

Of course, many questions have still gone unanswered. It remains to be seen how Bea's actual professional future will develop. Likewise, subsequent analysis of the life stories told by Bea will need to examine how the tensions of identity and knowledge impact the career and life choices she makes. Both these issues will assume greater prominence as the study moves through the coming years.

Last, it must be emphasized that Bea is only one graduate from only one master's program. It is an empirical question whether Bea's assessment of the value of her graduate studies is shared by others from her program, and also to what extent this program is similar to other programs. Given the paucity of previous research on this topic, we can only acknowledge the limitations of this study and call for further research that looks at other graduates from other programs, asking how their MA work aligns (or fails to align) with their subsequent professional experiences as teachers. Such research is urgently needed if we wish to have an informed knowledge base from which to develop the content and structure of our MA programs.

REFERENCES

Bailey, K. M., Bergthold, B., Braunstein, B., Fleischman, N. J., Holbrook, M. P., Tuman, J., Waissbluth, X., & Zambo, L. J. (1996). The language learner's autobiography: Examining the "apprenticeship of observation." In D. Freeman & J. C. Richards (Eds.), *Teacher learning in language teaching* (pp. 11–29). New York: Cambridge University Press.

Bakhtin, M. M. (1981). *The dialogic imagination* (C. Emerson & M. Holquist, Trans.). Austin: University of Texas Press.

Borg, S. (1998). Teachers' pedagogical systems and grammar teaching: A qualitative study. *TESOL Quarterly, 32,* 9–38.

Braine, G. (Ed.). (1999). *Non-native educators in English language teaching*. Mahwah, NJ: Lawrence Erlbaum Associates, Inc.

Clair, N. (1998). Teacher study groups: Persistent questions in a promising approach. *TESOL Quarterly, 32,* 465–492.

Clandinin, D. J., & Connelly, F. M. (1995). *Teachers' professional knowledge landscapes*. New York: Teachers College Press.

Coffey, A., & Atkinson, P. (1996). *Making sense of qualitative data. Complementary research strategies*. Thousand Oaks, CA: Sage.

Duff, P. A., & Uchida, Y. (1997). The negotiation of teachers' sociocultural identities and practices in postsecondary EFL classrooms. *TESOL Quarterly, 31,* 451–486.

Edge, J. (Ed.). (2001). *Action research*. Alexandria, VA: TESOL.

Edge, J., & Richards, K. (Eds.). (1993). *Teachers develop teachers research*. Portsmouth, NH: Heinemann.

Edstam, T. S. (2001). Perceptions of professionalism among elementary school ESL teachers. In B. Johnston & S. Irujo (Eds.), *Research and practice in language teacher education: Voices from the field* (pp. 233–249). Minneapolis: University of Minnesota, Center for Advanced Research in Second Language Acquisition.

Freeman, D. (1998). *Doing teacher-research: From inquiry to understanding*. Pacific Grove, CA: Heinle & Heinle.

Gergen, K. J. (1991). *The saturated self: Dilemmas of identity in everyday life*. New York: Basic Books.

Golombek, P. R. (1998). A study of teachers' personal practical knowledge. *TESOL Quarterly, 32,* 447–464.

Goodson, I. F. (Ed.). (1992). *Studying teachers' lives*. New York: Teachers College Press.

Johnson, K. E., & Golombek, P. R. (Eds.). (2002). *Teachers' ways of knowing: Narrative inquiry as professional development*. Cambridge, England: Cambridge University Press.

Johnston, B. (1997). Do EFL teachers have careers? *TESOL Quarterly, 31,* 681–712.

Johnston, B. (1999). The expatriate teacher as postmodern paladin. *Research in the Teaching of English, 34,* 255–280.

Johnston, B., & Goettsch, K. (2000). In search of the knowledge base of language teaching: Explanations by experienced teachers. *Canadian Modern Language Review, 56,* 437–468.

Kubota, R. (1998). Voices from the margin: Second and foreign language teaching approaches from minority perspectives. *Canadian Modern Language Review, 54,* 394–412.

Liu, D. (1999). Nonnative-English-speaking professionals in TESOL. *TESOL Quarterly, 33,* 85–102.

MacLure, M. (1993). Arguing for your self: Identity as an organizing principle in teachers' jobs and lives. *British Educational Research Journal, 19,* 311–322.

McNiff, J. (1993). *Teaching as learning. An action research approach*. London: Routledge.

Moran, P. R. (1996). "I'm not typical": Stories of becoming a Spanish teacher. In D. Freeman & J. C. Richards (Eds.), *Teacher learning in language teaching* (pp. 125–153). New York: Cambridge University Press.

Norton, B. (1997). Language, identity, and the ownership of English. *TESOL Quarterly, 31,* 409–429.
Norton Peirce, B. (1995). Social identity, investment, and language learning. *TESOL Quarterly, 29,* 9–31.
Riessman, C. S. (1993). Narrative analysis (*Qualitative Research Methods Series*, Vol. 30). Beverly Hills, CA: Sage.
Sarup, M. (1996). *Identity, culture, and the postmodern world.* Athens: University of Georgia Press.
Silverman, D. (1993). *Interpreting qualitative data. Methods for analyzing talk, text and interaction.* London: Sage.
Varghese, M. (2001). Professional development as a site for the conceptualization and negotiation of bilingual teacher identities. In B. Johnston & S. Irujo (Eds.), *Research and practice in language teacher education: Voices from the field* (pp. 213–232). Minneapolis: University of Minnesota, Center for Advanced Research in Second Language Acquisition.
Woods, D. (1996). *Teacher cognition in language teaching: Beliefs, decision-making, and classroom practice.* New York: Cambridge University Press.

APPENDIX

Interview Protocol

1. Life stories.

What did you do in life before you took the MA?

Tell us about your life since the MA. What jobs have you held? What significant events have taken place in your personal life? What led you to change jobs and/or places of residence?

What have been the most important turning points in your professional and personal life?

How do you see the next 5 years of your life, both professionally and personally? What are your goals?

2. Teacher knowledge.

To what extent did your MA prepare you for the work you have done since you graduated? What should have been covered that wasn't? What were the most useful components of your training?

What have you learned since, either formally or informally?

How would you describe "what you know" about teaching at present?

3. Teacher development.

What forms of professional development have you found most useful in the period since your graduated? Tell us about your experiences of professional development.

What are your goals for learning and for professional development for the future?

4. Identity.

How do you identify yourself? What identity or identities are most important to you?

Do you see yourself as a teacher?

Do you see yourself as a professional?

5. Sociopolitical context.

What social and political contexts have you worked in or been involved with since you graduated? What do you have to say about these contexts? How have they impacted your work, your life story, your knowledge, your identity?

Chapter 5

Toward Linking Teacher Knowledge and Student Learning

Donald Freeman
The School for International Training

Karen E. Johnson
The Pennsylvania State University

INTRODUCTION

Walk into any language classroom,[1] no matter where it is in the world, and you will see things going on, and you will hear language being used. Teachers will be saying and doing things, and students will be saying and doing things. Even if the participants are not physically moving around the classroom, even if the rows of desks are fixed, even if it is completely silent, there is activity going on. There is language being used (and not used) in the classroom. The people who use (or don't use) it verbally or in writing and when and how they use it all constitute the activity of language teaching and learning. In this chapter, we probe that activity. We examine the question of what all

[1]To simplify things, we use the term *language* classroom to refer to classrooms in which languages are taught and learned as foreign or second languages. However, we recognize that in essence, all classrooms are—to a greater or lesser degree—language classrooms because most content in them is presented in and through language. We believe that the arguments we advance in this chapter apply to classrooms in this larger sense as well.

these comings and goings—all this activity—adds up to. How do the work called *teaching*, the actions of the teacher, and the work called *learning*, the actions, in the broadest sense, of the students, connect? Because classrooms are predicated on this connection, the assumed link between what teachers know and do and what, through their teaching, their students come to know and be able to do is arguably the most fundamental relationship in education. In this chapter, we reexamine how this basic equation relates teaching to learning. Our intent is to move beyond the prevalent notions of causality that dominate thinking and rhetoric about this connection to reframe it as a "relationship of influence" between teacher learning and student learning. In so doing, we argue that a more sophisticated and sensitive way of conceptualizing this relationship is needed to capture and more fully understand the work in the language classroom.

This chapter is organized in three parts. In the first part, we introduce the notions of activity, how tools are used in activities, and how these notions apply to the second language classroom. In the second part, we offer a series of conceptual frames that map the relationship between teaching and learning. These frames serve to orient the specific analysis of activity and tools that follows. To illustrate this conceptualization in the third part, we draw from research in the Teacher Knowledge Project based at the Center for Teacher Education, Training, and Research at the School for International Training.[2]

We contend that examining the nature of activity in language teaching and learning and specifically how tools are used in language classrooms will refocus attention on the link between what teachers know and what their students learn and do not learn. Further, such analysis allows us to look closely at how teachers' professional learning can alter the nature of activity in language classrooms through the tools that are used to create and mediate that activity, and thus, we can probe the relationship between what teachers know and what, through their teaching, their students come to know and are able to do.

ACTIONS, ACTIVITY, AND TOOLS

We begin by defining our key terms, specifically *actions, activity,* and *tools*. Actions refer to what individuals do, in this case in language classrooms. Actions are behaviors such as standing, walking, pointing, the physical sides of talking or writing, waiting for someone else to talk, and

[2]The Teacher Knowledge Project was initiated in 1998 with funding from the Fund for the Improvement of Post-Secondary Education, U.S. Department of Education. For further information, please see http://www.sit.edu/tkp

so on. Activity is usually seen as an aggregate of many actions. Yet in fact, this common notion is inadequate. If you think of a soccer game, for example, the actions of the individual players—passing, trapping, or shooting the ball, attacking and defending, running, standing still—all make up the game. However, as an activity, the game is more than these distinct actions. It has an ebb and flow, a strategy and a history of its own. It is a whole that is greater than the sum of its individual parts.[3]

What does this distinction between actions and activity gain us? In the case of teacher education, the relation between actions and activity elaborates a clear disjuncture between teacher training and classroom practice. Teachers are trained to take actions, to do things that they control in their classrooms. However, these actions—such as doing a jigsaw activity, giving a dictation, doing pair work or role plays, for example—land in classrooms in which other people, namely, students, are also taking actions, some which may contravene what the teacher intends. Thus the teacher's actions plus the students' actions do not add up to the activity in the language classroom. Rather, just as with the soccer game, it is the interplay among the actions of participants that creates the metalevel of activity that is a language class in itself.

This leads to the term *tool*. A tool is something that is used to do a particular job. An individual has a purpose—something that he or she needs or wants to do, an action that he or she wants to undertake—that gets the person into the activity. Through the activity, the person uses the tool or tools to accomplish that purpose. So tools are often the sites, both physical and virtual, around which activity happens or is organized. To anchor this discussion in the particular, we focus in what follows on a tool that is very common in the language classroom: the overhead projector (OHP). If asked about the OHPs and how they are used in the language classroom, teachers may say such things as

1. "I usually use the OHP to present information to students."
2. "When I use the overhead, it helps my students pay attention to what's important in the lesson."
3. "I often will put students' homework on the overhead so that they can see their mistakes."
4. "I use the OHP to gather information from my students. I ask a question and then write up what they say."

Each of these statements is about the same tool, the OHP. Yet each one suggests a different type of activity. Gathering information from

---

[3]This parallel is more articulately explained in Fleck (1935/1979).

students is quite different, for example, from presenting information to them. In the former, the OHP is used to collect knowledge and information; in the latter, it is used to introduce knowledge. Thus, the purpose of the activity[4] shapes how the tool is actually used by participants. This purpose can play itself out on many levels. There is, for example, a purpose that is immediate to that time and place, as in "I'm using the overhead to present the dialogue in chapter 3." This purpose is akin to the objective of the lesson. There is also a broader purpose, more akin to a philosophy or pedagogical approach, of how teaching and learning are organized in relation to one another, as in "teaching inductively by gathering participants knowledge versus teaching deductively by explaining knowledge to them." These levels of purpose interact and mutually inform one another in the use of the tool. So tools are framed by the purposes for which they are used, and purposes flow from and flow into activity to shape actions of the participants. In the case of education broadly and in language classrooms in particular, the purposes of teaching flow from larger social views[5] of how teaching and learning connect, which we turn to now.

THREE CONCEPTUAL FRAMES

The following is a very brief history of thinking about how the connection between teaching and learning has been conceived. We organize the history around three key conceptions of the relationship, each of which forms the basic map that relates what teachers know and do to what their students come to know and be able to do in the language classroom. How these two forms—known respectively as teaching and learning—are mapped in relation to one another is likewise central to the work of teacher education because, in theory at least, teachers learn to teach in ways that cause, direct, or influence their students' learning. Thus, for teacher educators, the connection between teacher learning and student learning as it passes through what teachers know and are able to do, and this passage from teacher professional learning to teacher knowledge to student learning is a central concern of teacher education and of classroom teaching.

The First Frame: Causal Conditionality

Arguably the central and enduring theoretical conception of teaching in relation to learning is to contend that *Teaching→ leads to→ student*

[4]In some analyses of activity, *purpose* is referred to as the object of the activity system; see, for example, Engeström, Miettinen, and Punamäki (1999).

[5]These larger social views are similar to what Gee (1990) called *discourses*, the social constructions that give meaning to the actions of individual participants in an activity.

learning. This frame, which permeates the field of education and dominates public discourse, presents an essentially behavioral or causal view of teaching in relation to student learning. In this frame, *student learning* is generally defined as "student performance" that is assessed by standardized measures such as tests. With its theoretical roots in the product–product research paradigm of the 1960s (Dunkin & Biddle, 1974) and its popular, commonsense appeal, this causal view of the teaching–learning relationship is essentially the default option in public policy and general thinking about education. Usually this frame is expressed in a causal conditional statement that exhorts the teacher: "If you teach it well, students will learn it." Thus, the syllogism follows that "If students don't learn it, then you didn't teach it adequately." The formulation is on its face brutally simplistic; however, it belies the complexity of people's experiences as students and as teachers. Nonetheless, it continues to hold tremendous sway in the public discourse about education and school reform. For example, current moves in U.S. education to evaluate teachers and schools based on students' standardized test scores appeals to this notion that teachers can be directly and causally accountable for their students' performance.[6]

Returning to the example of the OHP in the theoretical frame that "teaching causes student learning," when the OHP is conceptualized as a tool to present information to students, the roles of the teacher and the students are organized in particular ways. The basic "chalk and talk" discourse patterns in classrooms (Cazden, 1988; Johnson, 1995) instantiate these roles in which teachers give information and students receive it and store it away in what Paulo Freire (1970) referred to as the banking metaphor of education. It is important to recognize, however, that the OHP as the tool does not itself make these roles happen. Rather, it is the purpose of the activity as the participants see it that organizes the classroom in this way, and this purpose can be framed in a larger sense by this causal-conditional conception of teaching in relation to learning.

The Second Frame: Reasoned Causality

The basic problem with the causal-conditional frame is that it does not correspond to reality or experience. Logically, if teaching did cause learning, then education would be successful all—or at least most—of the time. Textbooks could "teach" students; The lesson taught last week would work again this week and would "work" exactly in the same way.

---

[6]For an excellent critical discussion, pro and con, of this causal-conditional view, see Meier (2002).

Classrooms would be a veritable educational Eden or perhaps an Orwellian (1949) pedagogical *1984*. Beyond this obvious inaccuracy, for the last two decades, the central critique of the causal-conditional frame of the teaching–learning relationship has been that it does not account for teacher education and how teachers learn (or come to do) new and different things in their classrooms (Freeman & Johnson, 1998). It is an article of faith that teacher education matters, one which recently has been substantiated in various ways by different research measures (e.g., Wilson, Floden, & Ferrini-Mundy, 2001). This second theoretical frame connects teacher education to teaching and student learning by arguing that *Teacher training→leads to→good teaching*.

Underlying this frame is the idea that human thinking drives human actions, which is found in a cognitive research paradigm and more specifically in an information-processing view of teacher thinking (e.g., Freeman, 1996; Johnson, 1999). A classic instance of this view is the work of Shavelson and Stern (1981) in which teacher thinking is represented as a flow chart, in essence depicting teachers' instructional decisions as rational, linear, unitary, and easily defined. In this information-processing view, definitions of action are expanded to include the teacher's thoughts or cognitive actions. Thus, the focus shifts from what teachers are doing to what is going on in their heads. This reasoning can be shaped or caused to improve through input of new ideas and practices. So the reasoned causality frame is captured in the assumption that the better we train teachers through the information we give them about theory and successful classroom routines, the better they will teach.

A quintessential example of this view of the teaching–learning relationship is captured in the work of the 1980s teacher supervision guru, Madeline Hunter. In the Introduction to the 34th printing of her book *Mastery Teaching*, which first appeared in 1982, Hunter clearly argues for this view of reasoned causality; she writes the following:

> In this book, and the accompanying set of *Mastery Teaching Videotapes,* you will find described many teaching techniques you are already using. We learned these techniques from watching effective teachers teach. We have labeled these techniques and explained the psychological theory behind why they work. As a result, from now on you will know what you are doing when you teach, why you are doing what you do, and do that consciously and deliberately to increase your students' learning. (p. ix)

The essential elements are evident. There are techniques assembled from watching effective teachers teach, and there is theory behind why they (the techniques) work. Thus, technique plus theory adds up to a form of what we call "reasoned causality," a sort of "teach it based on good theory and they will learn" approach to teaching and learning.

Applying this second view of teaching–learning to the OHP example, the frame of reasoned causality suggests that teachers may use the OHP according to the theory they have been taught and/or the practices they have mastered. Because the theory is true and the practices are solid, teachers will, to gloss Hunter, "know what they are doing when they teach, why they are doing what they do." Therefore, because their teaching is informed with this reasoning, their students will learn through the use of the OHP. Thus, the role of the teacher has changed in this frame; she or he is now a thoughtful decision maker, a user of informed technique, but nothing has changed from the students' perspective. As in the causal-conditional frame, the focus remains squarely on the teacher. Better training in how to use the tools of the trade should result in better student outcomes. To borrow Hunter's words (1982), using the overhead projector "consciously and deliberately" will "increase your students' learning (p. ix)."

The Third Frame: A Relationship of Influence

The second frame introduces the notion that Herbert Walberg referred to in 1972 as "teachers' mental lives;" however, it actually does little to encompass the interrelation between teaching and learning. In fact, the first two frames create a sort of developmental continuum in which one does not replace the other, but rather the second adds reasoning as an element to elaborate on or extend the first. Using the terms of *action* and *activity* and *tool*, in the first two frames, the emphasis is on the teacher's actions and on physical tools such as the OHP in the example. Activity, seen as the game and not the individual moves, is absent, as is the notion that tools can be concepts as well as physical things.

The third frame integrates these two missing elements of the lesson as activity and of the teacher's work as using conceptual tools. In this way, the focus shifts subtly to how teachers learn to organize lessons and to use both physical and conceptual tools in teaching. Thus, it addresses how their professional learning influences their teaching and in turn, how that teaching influences their students' learning. We use the verb *influence* deliberately because although teaching does not cause learning, neither is it entirely irrelevant to or disconnected from it. In fact, the challenge is to uncover how this relationship of influence between teaching and learning unfolds. We contend that the relationship is organized primarily by means of physical and conceptual tools. These tools enable the activity of the language classroom; they are how the work gets done.

Thus, in essence the third frame argues that *Teacher Learning→Classroom Activity→Student Learning*.

Consider the example of a soccer game mentioned previously: The players' use of the physical tools—the soccer ball, their feet, and the goal posts—as well as their actions with these tools is guided by conceptual tools: Who shall I pass the ball to? Who is forward, off sides, and who is backfield? These questions in the minds of the players guide their play. So the use or blending of the physical and conceptual tools with the players' actions creates the activity of the game in which each player's action is shaped by the conditions of play. This is a relationship of influence at work in the unfolding of the game. As in the classroom, it is the constantly shifting perspectives of the participants that drive the activity.

In terms of the language classroom, this third frame shifts from a static view of what is going on in the teacher's head—reasons guiding actions and techniques—to a dynamic view of teacher learning in relation to student learning, which always exists in a context (as the soccer game in our example), which is socially situated (as between the two players), and which develops over time and through practice. Thus, to create a shorthand, we argue that this relationship of influence is contextual, socially situated, and developmental (Freeman, 1994). The relationship of influence combines three levels: teacher learning, classroom activity, and student learning. On the level of teacher learning, it raises the question, "How do these conceptual tools arise and how are they developed over time and through practice?" On the level of classroom activity, there is the related question, "How do teachers blend physical and conceptual tools into activity?" And on the level of student learning, there is the question, "How do students see and experience these tools?" To address these questions, we turn in the third part of this chapter to examine activity in one particular language classroom and specifically, the role of one specific tool, the OHP in that activity.

ACTIVITY IN A LANGUAGE CLASSROOM

To elaborate this third frame, we focus on a high school French class at a regional, rural high school to examine the nature of activity that goes on there. In particular, we focus on how one physical tool—the OHP—is used by this teacher in creating language learning activity. We probe the teacher's understanding of the physical tool, how it is influenced by other conceptual tools, and how it shapes classroom activity that leads to student learning.

The data in the following analysis are drawn from the research program of the Teacher Knowledge Project at the School for International Training. The Teacher Knowledge Project offers reflective professional development to classroom teachers of all subjects and grade levels at sites in Vermont and around the United States.[7] Through professional development seminars in classroom inquiry and new teacher mentoring and support, the Project offers teachers a disciplined way to think about their teaching in relationship to their students' learning. The following data is taken from the classroom and work of Maggie Brown Cassidy, a 30-year teacher of French at Brattleboro Union High School in southeastern Vermont. Cassidy is a long-time member of the Project and now serves as its Associate Director.

Maggie Cassidy's Classroom

To set the instructional scene, unlike in most high school foreign language classes in the United States, Cassidy and her colleagues do not use textbooks. The language content is not written down ahead of time; rather it evolves within a proficiency-based framework from the students themselves. Cassidy says, "For many years, I used a textbook, or I should say, on the surface my teaching was linked to a textbook. But now I don't. I've come to realize that it is much too easy for students to leave the language within the covers of the book."

In a collaborative study, Freeman (1992) documented how Cassidy's classroom functions to construct new foreign language content through a carefully scripted group of procedures that include brainstorming, investigation and negotiation of form and meaning, and enactment. Through these interactions, the students in effect create the language that they then learn to use. By design, every French class that Cassidy teaches and indeed all foreign language classes at the high school include students at 3 different proficiency levels. These groupings enable students to learn from each other, but, as Cassidy points out, "In many ways every student in the class is working from a different language base." The content of each level—labeled as "novice," "intermediate," and "advanced" according to the American Council on Teaching Foreign Languages (1986) guidelines—has a particular theme. At the novice level, students focus on their immediate lives. As Cassidy describes it, "It's all about me, me, me. They talk about themselves, their school, their friends, their hobbies, their homes, their community. It's all about them." At the intermediate level, the theme is life history, which Cassidy describes as "focusing on their lives past, present, and future, and some survival French, say ordering in a restaurant, a visit to the doctor, and so on." At the advanced level, the theme focuses on Francophone history

[7] For further information on the Teacher Knowledge Project, please see http://www.sit.edu/tkp

and literature. Although, as Cassidy explains, students "read a novel, poems, a play, and work with dialogue from French films," the class is not a conventional arts and literature survey. Cassidy says, "Most of our attention is on what generalizations we can make about humans and human behavior. So while I set these general themes, the stuff that fills up those themes comes from them."

Mapping the activity in the classroom, there are three principal phases of activity in Cassidy's classes. These phases do not take place in a linear progression but overlap, often occurring and reoccurring many times within one lesson as well as over the course of several weeks. In the first phase, the students generate the new language through brainstorming activities with help from the teacher. Cassidy sets the topic and the students brainstorm the specific content in a mixture of French and English, which she notes down generally on the OHP. Cassidy intervenes as necessary to help with content or to direct the activity, but overall, the control is shared with students in this phase as they participate in developing the content.

In the second phase, students assume the major role in developing their understanding of the language by rehearsing the French content with their peers and reviewing explanations that Cassidy has originally introduced. The form of the language and explanations for it are investigated, negotiated, and ultimately agreed on in peer work and directly with the teacher. The collective aspect of learning in this phase is apparent when, for example, sentences in French that have been individually created become the collective texts when they are written up on the OHP. As students examine this content, think about it, and learn to express and explain to each other the mechanics of French grammar and lexicon, they build a shared understanding of the language. Peer interaction is critical in this phase because the explanations that they create are social, tested through interactions with other students and with the teacher.

In the third phase, the French that has been sorted out through social interaction becomes a ritual performance bringing form, meaning, and metalinguistic explanation together. As they use French in short interactions, tasks, and role plays, students will often refer to text on the OHP as they work together to rehearse the common explanations for what they are doing. This phase is highly impromptu, with Cassidy triggering the performances. There is a fourth phase—which could be called *mastery*—which is largely unnoticed, as students use French appropriately so that it blends into the ongoing activity of the class.

To an outsider, the flow of activity in Cassidy's lessons—from brainstorming, to rehearsing content and explanation, to ritualized performance, to mastery—appears seamless and even disorganized. Indeed, because there is no textbook and no familiarly recognizable methodology, there are few conventional markers of the classroom. So how is this soccer game played? What are the tools that get this activity done? To look closely at the activity, we need to understand the role of the central physical tool in this activity: the OHP.

The OHP as a Physical Tool: "We All See It, But We All See It Together." In an interview, Cassidy describes how she creates content from student participation through the three phases of the cyclical process just described. Unprompted, Cassidy identifies the OHP as the locus of activity, the central physical tool, in this production:

> The OHP is where this happens, it is where they come together. With the *intermediare*, working on describing past events, I might announce a theme, say World War II, and ask them to come to class with any vocabulary they know, in English or French, and we put it on the OHP. This tells me what they know and don't know. It enables me to "see" what my students know. I don't assume anything and I don't bore them either. So, the OHP can be a powerful diagnostic.

Cassidy views the OHP as a tool that can be used to find out the state of her students' knowledge; it enables her to build on what they know and to identify where there are gaps in their knowledge both of French language and of the world that may need to be filled in. The OHP also creates common content out of individual experience. Cassidy says, "The material comes from them; it's their lives. It gets put up on the overhead projector and then it becomes common." Cassidy goes on to say, "The OHP is like holding up a mirror that everyone can see. I can see and they can see, and they bounce their knowledge off the mirror. We all see it, but we all see it together. And we all create it together."

Besides uncovering what her students know and don't know and creating common knowledge, Cassidy also views the OHP as a tool that promotes flexibility and fluidity in her teaching:

> For me the, OHP is not static, it allows my teaching to be fluid because if a kid gives me a word and I begin to write, I might pause halfway through and say, "Now does this [word] need an *x* or not?" and they argue about that for awhile, and we figure it out, and we go on. In a textbook, the words are already there and they're all right. Who cares about that? But when it comes from them, it's alive and they care about it. They want to get it right, because it's theirs. And it gets created right in front of their eyes.

Although the OHP is prominent in Maggie's classroom, in some ways it also has an invisible quality. Cassidy says

> We use the OHP to play with language. It is sort of like badminton, where we volley back and forth and the OHP is the net. We attend to the net all the time but that's not what we are focusing on, we're focusing on the language, not the OHP. So, as we are using the language to do something, I'll stop and think, "Oh, they need this now" or "They knew all these words but they couldn't pronounce any of them, so that's what I'll do next." When the language evolves this way, I see their learning, I see what they need, I can respond to what they need, right then, not after we finish an exercise in a book, but right in that instant.

The OHP evidently plays multiple roles in Cassidy's classroom. It serves as a locus of the French content, as a diagnostic device to cull the new from the known, as a site of metalinguistic discussions (as in "Now does this [word] need an *x* or not?"), and as a repository for their evolving command over the new language.

Seeing, Fluidity, and Reflection: From the Conceptual Tool to Its Operational Use. These multiple roles do not come about on their own, unaided. Rather, they are animated by a group of conceptual tools, evidence of which we can find embedded in how Cassidy describes her use of the OHP in her teaching. We argue, after Vygotsky (1978) and other socioculturalists, that this evidence occurs in two parts: what we call the conceptual tools themselves and what we call their operational uses. The tools come about in professional development, whereas their operational uses emerge in how Cassidy applies these concepts/tools to the physical tool to shape the activity in her day-to-day teaching. To build this analysis, we begin with the operational use of the conceptual tool and then follow it back to the conceptual tools. To focus this analysis, we single out three operational uses. The first is the idea of seeing, as when Cassidy says (as cited previously)

> We put it [content] on the OHP. This tells me what they know and don't know. It enables me to *see* what my students know. [...] The OHP is like holding up a mirror that everyone can see. I can see and they can see, and they bounce their knowledge off the mirror. *We all see it, but we all see it together.* (italics added)

The second use is caught in the idea of fluidity in practice, as when Cassidy says, "[the] OHP is not static, it allows my teaching to be fluid.

[...] When it [the content] comes from them, it's alive and they care about it." The third use focuses on the practice of reflection, specifically what Schön (1983) called *reflection-in-action*, which Cassidy shows when she says, "So, as we are using the language to do something, I'll stop and think, 'Oh, they need this now,' or 'They knew all these words but they couldn't pronounce any of them, so that's what I'll do next.'" This third use is, in effect, a meta-use of the other two, a point to which we will return later in this discussion.

We refer to these as three operational uses because they provide the scripts that blend the conceptual tools acquired in professional development with the physical tool, the OHP, as it is used in the activity of teaching–learning French in Cassidy's classroom. The question we pursue is how do the three conceptual tools arise? What in Cassidy's recent experiences in professional development as a learner of teaching influenced the development of these three tools: seeing, fluidity in practice, and reflection-in-action? So we turn now to the teacher learning side of the equation and to the professional development in reflective practice offered by the Teacher Knowledge Project in which Cassidy has taken part as a participant, a facilitator, and a trainer.

Professional Development in Reflective Practice

The following is Cassidy's own description of the professional development in the Project:

> The Inquiry Seminars [in the Teacher Knowledge Project] provide you with time to talk about your teaching and hear about the teaching of others and this in itself becomes confidence inducing. You know, you think stuff about your teaching all the time, but when you talk about it in public, with people who know you and where you are coming from, it becomes real. Through this talk, we know what we are doing, we know why we are doing it, we know how we do what we do, and we can tell others why we are doing it.

Cassidy says of her participation as a teacher learner in the Inquiry Seminars

> Teaching is so much "right in the moment" and reflective teaching enables me to take a step back, to turn on a dime, and know that when I turned and how I turned all were for sound reasons. Reflection enables me to name what I do, this is what we do in

> the Inquiry Seminars, we name what we do, and once you name it, you can do all sorts of things with it.

Through the seminar discussions in which teachers describe and analyze aspects of student learning in their classrooms using a Deweyan (Dewey, 1938) framework of reflective description and analysis of classroom practices (Rodgers, 2002), ideas surface and develop as shared analyses. As Cassidy puts it, "This is what we do in the Inquiry Seminars: We name what we do, and once you name it, you can do all sorts of things with it." In our analysis, we call these levers *conceptual tools.*

One tool is what seminar participants call "unsolicited feedback from students," which Cassidy describes as follows:

> *Feedback from students*, it's coming at me all the time, like a stream of information; their body language, their accents, their fluency, all the content, all the stuff around the content but also all the information that is telling me about their affect, their affective relationship to what we're doing. It's just always coming at me and that's what I work with to be able to make decisions as I go along.

Through her work in the Inquiry Seminars, Cassidy feels she has developed an ability to take in the unsolicited feedback that she is getting constantly from her students and to use it to make thoughtful decisions about what and how she will teach. Feedback combines with a second tool, which Cassidy calls "stepping back." Cassidy says this enables her to gain perspective and balance in her moment-to-moment interactions with her students:

> Reflective teaching requires that I *step back,* that I be less impulsive, that I read students, so that I know when to engage with them and when to leave them alone. Sometimes it's just that tiny *stepping back,* when I think to myself, "How can I make the most of this moment?"

As we trace the relationship of influence, we can map Cassidy's encounter in the Inquiry Seminar with these two conceptual tools—unsolicited feedback and stepping back—as she uses them operationally in the classroom activity. In the classroom, unsolicited feedback and stepping back become seeing and fluidity. To operationalize the conceptual tool of unsolicited feedback from students, the teacher needs to see it. Similarly, as she steps back and repositions herself affectively and cognitively in relation to her students and the content, the teacher can more fluidly manage the intricacies of instruction. This is where the meta-use of reflective teaching enters in. Overall reflective practice invites teachers to consider how changing the operations through which an action is carried out can ultimately change the activity in which the action is embedded. The Inquiry Seminar supplies tools as concepts that allow and indeed encourage that consideration to happen. As Cassidy steps back, reads students, reflects in action, and makes thoughtful decisions about what to do and say, we begin to see how she blends physical and conceptual tools into activity.

This leads to the third question about student learning: How do Cassidy's students see and experience these physical and conceptual tools? Or in terms of the third frame, what is the relationship of influence that connects teacher learning, in this case of reflective teaching, to student learning or the learning of French?

Linking Teacher Learning to Student Learning

Research in the Teacher Knowledge Project seeks to document the ways in which reflective professional development influences teachers' work and their students' learning. Thus, data of all sorts are collected that can help uncover the complexities of this dynamic process. One type of holistic data includes students' drawings of their own learning. In the case of Cassidy's high school French class, the students were asked to draw and then narrate in writing "a moment in their classroom when something that the teacher did helped them learn French." These drawings are very telling, especially given what we have said about the actions, activity, and tools embedded in Cassidy's French classes.

The following data include five drawings that were gathered by Cassidy according to the preceding prompt. They are accompanied by the student's description of the drawing shown in Figs. 5.1 through 5.5.[8]

The OHP seems to figure prominently in the learning for each of these students. In fact, in the last two drawings, the teacher is not even visible. The analysis that we propose argues that the physical tool, the OHP, and the teacher's and students' actions with that tool are guided by the teacher's operational use of conceptual tools. The OHP is a physical tool used to step back and see what students know and to reflect on and use student feedback so as to be flexible and fluid while teaching. Thus, these conceptual tools create operational scripts for

[8]The Teacher Knowledge Project is indebted to Drawing on Education, a research project at Boston College School of Education, for their early consultation in the development of this methodology.

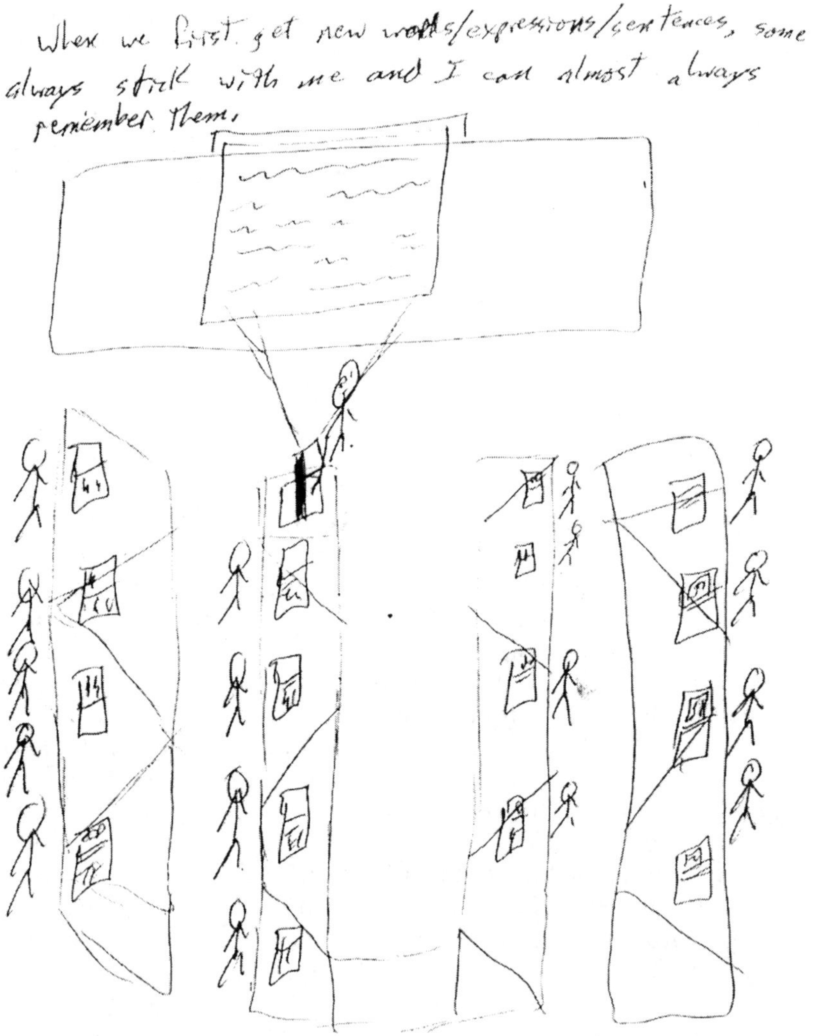

FIG. 5.1. Student drawing Number 1. "When we first get new words/expressions/sentences, some always stick with me and I can almost always remember them."

When Madam Cassidy is writing new words on th
the overhead and explaing them, it really helps.
When she gives examples of words in context,
it helps me with the grammar and also the
spelling, and helps me know which form of
the word to use. Taking notes from
the overhead helps with spelling, and when
Madam pronounces
the words & we repeat them, it helps
with pronunciation

FIG. 5.2. Student drawing Number 2. "When Madame Cassidy is writing new words on the overhead and explaining them, it really helps. When she gives examples of words in context, it helps me with the grammar and also the spelling, and helps me know which form of the word to use. Taking notes from the overhead helps with spelling and when Madame pronounces the words, and we repeat them it helps with pronunciation."

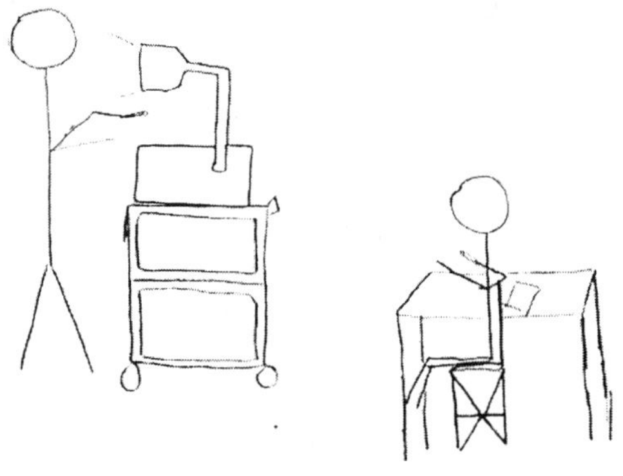

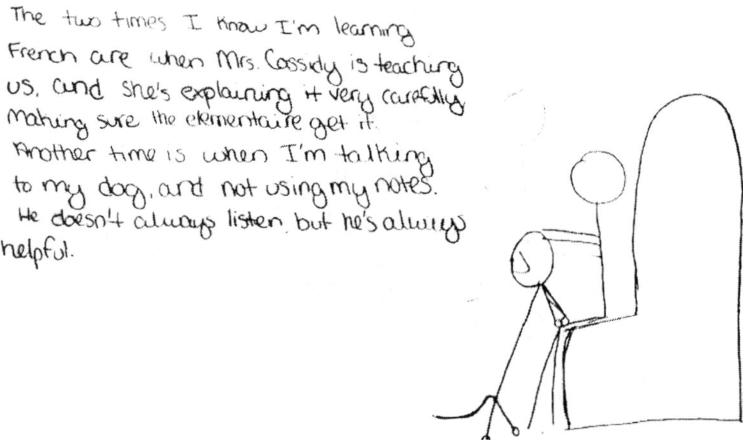
The two times I know I'm learning
French are when Mrs. Cassidy is teaching
us, and she's explaining it very carefully
making sure the elementaire get it.
Another time is when I'm talking
to my dog, and not using my notes.
He doesn't always listen but he's always
helpful.

FIG. 5.3. Student drawing Number 3. "The two times I know I'm learning French are when Mrs. Cassidy is teaching us and she's explaining it very carefully, making sure the *elementaire* get it. Another time is when I'm talking to my dog, and not using my notes. He doesn't always listen, but he's always helpful."

how the physical tool, the OHP, is used in the activity of teaching and learning French.

However, what of the influence on student learning? Cassidy talks of the OHP as a badminton net: "We use the OHP to play with language.... We attend to the net all the time but that's not what we are focusing on, we're focusing on the language, not the OHP." Indeed, Cassidy's stu-

corrections

After we do an activity in class, or for
homework, we go over it on the overhe
and make corrections. This helps me
a lot, because it shows me what
I do wrong, and what I do right,
also I am able to correct my
mistakes. After doing this, I usually
don't make the mistakes I had
over again.

FIG. 5.4. Student drawing Number 4. "After we do an activity in class or for homework, we go over it on the overhead and make corrections. This helps me a lot, because it shows me what I do wrong and what I do right, also I am able to correct my mistakes. After doing this, I usually don't make the mistakes I had over again."

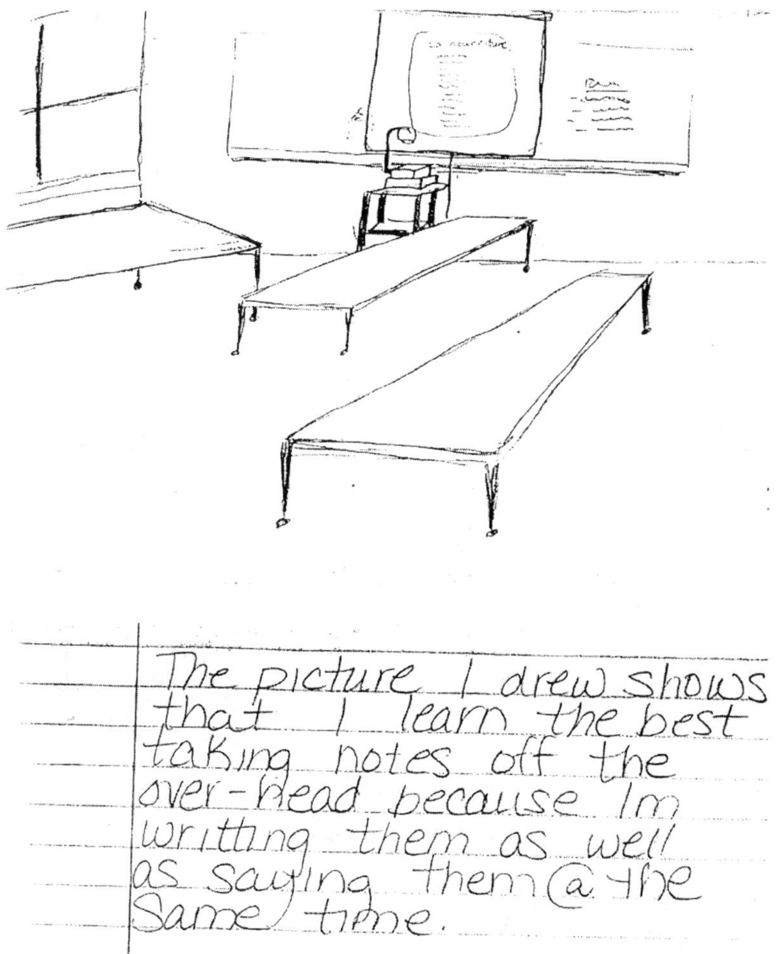

FIG. 5.5. Student drawing Number 5. "The picture I drew shows that I learn the best taking notes off the over-head because I'm writing them as well as saying them at the same time."

dents seem to see their own learning of French as mediated by how this particular physical tool, the OHP, is used to create activity in the classroom. This is how the game is played, how the work of teaching and learning French gets done in her classroom, and it hints at the relationship of influence between teacher knowledge and student learning. As we pursue this connection, it is important to examine not only what the students learn but how they understand and experience that learning. Thus, in probing this relation of influence, we are examining not only the content or what is learned but the process or how it is learned, for one cannot exist without the other.

CONCLUSION

All of this suggests that just as we are broadening our ideas about teaching to see it as more than simple classroom behavior, we need likewise to broaden and make more sophisticated our conceptions of student learning. The conventional measures of learning as student performance—test scores, homework assignments, and the like—may tell us how many French vocabulary words these students know or if they have mastered the *passé composé*, but these are what Ayers (1993) calls "the least interesting and least significant aspects of learning" (p. 116). These measures are artifacts of a causal-conditional view of teaching in relation to learning; they serve to underscore only the most technicist views of student learning in classrooms, and they serve to reenforce the most deskilled approaches to teacher learning, teacher education, and professional development (see Meier, 2002).

Conventional evidence of student learning fails to tell us how students experience the activity of teaching and learning, which, according to Vygotsky (1978), is where true learning takes place. "Internalization," in Vygotsky's (1978) words, should not be narrowly defined as

> The learning of material or symbolic artifacts such as a language. Rather, the concept embraces the internalization of the broader human cognitive and symbolic artifacts, such as social values and beliefs, the cumulative knowledge of one's culture, and scientifically expanded concepts of reality. (p. 126)

When Cassidy's students learn French, they are not only learning to speak, read, and write the language, but they are also internalizing her values and beliefs about the language and about how to learn and even to teach it. These are things that Cassidy, in turn, has internalized from her own experiences as a learner and teacher of French over the past 30 years. Learning French like any classroom content is not only an internal, individual process; it is an activity with its origins in social settings where that content happens.

We are most interested in how teacher knowledge influences student learning. To map this territory, we need to look beyond what we can see, the behaviors and measurable performances of teachers and students that make up most of the day-to-day studies of classrooms. We have to examine how teachers and students think in and about the activity of teaching and learning. In this thicket of teachers' and students' thinking, we move beyond simple causality to unearth the relation of influence that sometimes leads teaching to learning. In an article on teacher learning in the context of school reform, Charles Thompson and John Zueli (1999), the former a university professor and the latter a high school teacher, draw the following analogy that captures the heart of our argument:

> Thinking is to a student's knowledge as photosynthesis is to a plant's food. Plants do not get food from the soil. They make it through photosynthesis, using water and nutrients from the soil and energy from sunlight. No photosynthesis, no food. Students do not get knowledge from teachers, or books, or experience with hands-on materials. They make it by thinking, using information, and experience. No thinking, no learning. (p. 346)

REFERENCES

American Council on the Teaching of Foreign Languages. (1986). *ACTFL proficiency guidelines.* Yonkers, NY: Author.

Ayers, W. (1993). *To teach: The journey of a teacher.* New York: Teachers College Press.

Cazden, C. (1988). *Classroom discourse: The language of teaching and learning.* Portsmouth, NH. Heinemann.

Dewey, J. (1938). *Experience and education.* New York: Macmillan.

Dunkin, M., & Biddle, B. (1974). *The study of teaching.* New York: Holt, Rinehart & Winston.

Engeström, Y., Miettinen, R., & Punamäki, R. L. (Eds.). (1999). *Perspectives on activity theory.* New York: Cambridge University Press.

Fleck, L. (1979). *The social construction of scientific thought.* Chicago: University of Chicago Press. (Original work published 1935)

Freeman, D. (1992). Collaboration: Constructing shared understandings in a second language classroom. In D. Nunan (Ed.), *Collaborative language learning and teaching* (pp. 56–80). Cambridge, England: Cambridge University Press.

Freeman, D. (1994). InterTeaching and the development of teachers' knowledge. *Perspectives: A Journal of TESOL-Italy, 20*(1), 5–16.

Freeman, D. (1996). The "unstudied problem: Research on teacher learning in language teaching." In D. Freeman & J. C. Richards (Eds.), *Teacher learning in language teaching* (pp. 351–378). New York: Cambridge University Press.

Freeman, D., & Johnson, K. E. (1998). Reconceptualizing the knowledge-base of language teacher education. *TESOL Quarterly, 32,* 397–417.

Freire, P. (1970). *Pedagogy of the oppressed.* New York: Continuum.

Gee, J. (1990.) *Social linguistics and literacies: Ideology in discourses.* New York: Falmer.

Hunter, M. (1982). (34th Ed) *Mastery teaching.* CA: El Sequrdo Publications.

Johnson, K. E. (1995). *Understanding communication in second language classrooms*. New York: Cambridge University Press.

Johnson, K. E. (1999). *Understanding language teaching: Reasoning in action*. Boston: Heinle & Heinle.

Meier, D. (2002). *Will standards save public education?* Boston: Beacon.

Orwell, G. (1949). *Nineteen Eighty-four: A novel*. NY: Harcourt Brace.

Rodgers, C. (2002). Seeing student learning: Teacher change and the role of reflection. *Harvard Educational Review, 72,* 230–253.

Schön, D. (1983). *The reflective practitioner*. San Francisco: Jossey-Bass.

Shavelson, R. J., & Stern, P. (1981). Research on teachers' pedagogical thoughts, judgments, decisions, and behavior. *Review of Educational Research, 51,* 455–498.

Thompson, C., & Zueli, J. (1999). The frame and the tapestry: Standards-based reform and professional development. In L. Darling-Hammond & G. Sykes (Eds.), *Teaching as a learning profession* (pp. 341–375). San Francisco: Jossey-Bass.

Walberg, H. (1972). Decision and perception: New constructs in research on teaching effects. *Cambridge Journal of Education,* 7(1), 12–20.

Wilson, S., Floden, R., & Ferrini-Mundy, J. (2001). *Teacher preparation research: Current knowledge, gaps, and recommendations*. Seattle: Center for the Study of Teaching and Policy, University of Washington.

Vygotsky, L. S. (1978). *Mind and society: The development of higher psychological processes*. Cambridge, MA: Harvard University Press.

Theme **II**

CONTEXTS OF SECOND LANGUAGE TEACHER EDUCATION

Second language teacher education takes place in multiple contexts and with diverse populations, in which language, culture, and identity are intricately bound together. These contexts are often impacted by actions taken by formal and informal decision-making bodies, which may or may not involve the participation of teacher educators. This section of the book explores issues related to this theme. Like the theme of knowledge base, the theme of contexts is a broad one. It includes second language contexts themselves (English as a second language [ESL], English as a foreign language [EFL], foreign language, immersion, bilingual education) as well as different geographic, social, cultural, political, and institutional contexts. It also encompasses analytical perspectives on the contexts in which second language teacher education takes place as well as contextual factors related to the larger society and culture that impact teacher education such as issues related to policy or advocacy. Contextual factors are fundamental to second language teacher education.

The chapters in this section come at the theme of contexts from a number of different perspectives. Chapter 6 (Shohamy) offers a policy perspective that has important implications for language teacher educators; chapter 7 (Hiramatsu) also addresses policy but from the standpoint of reform efforts in English teaching in Japan; chapter 8 (Byrnes) explores language teacher education in the context of a university-level foreign language department with a focus on the professional development of graduate teaching assistants; and chapter 9 (Poynor) the final chapter of the section, moves to elementary-level ESL and bilingual teacher education, focusing on the context of the teacher education program, and explores how the teacher education experience influences student teachers' practice.

The first chapter (Shohamy) in this section touches on an important policy issue affecting all language programs and thus being an important issue for language teacher education, that is, tests and the impact they have on language education. In chapter 6 Elana Shohamy explores the power that tests can have over teachers—the ways tests can influence curriculum and instruction in the language classroom when teachers are pressured by the school and societal contexts to "teach to the test." Shohamy argues that teachers need to take control and not allow the power of tests to mandate what they do in classrooms; rather, they need to become strong advocates for "use-oriented" testing and to become critical users of tests. In so doing, teachers can be perceived as professionals rather than "servants of the system." The role of teacher education in this process is clear. How do teacher educators help both beginning and veteran teachers understand the misuses of tests? How do they help them explore the myth of objectivity in testing? In contexts all over the world (and increasingly in the United States where accountability is the mantra), high-stakes tests that impact students' lives are a reality. How do teacher educators help to empower second language teachers to become responsible and involved leaders and advocates for their students?

The impact of high-stakes testing as described in Shohamy's chapter (chap. 6) as well as top-down policy reform are illustrated in the next chapter in this section. In chapter 7 Sachiko Hiramatsu takes us to Japan where EFL education has seen major reforms in the past 15 years. Through the voices of the teachers, Hiramatsu explores the impact of two reforms—the Japan Exchange and Teaching program and the revision of the English curriculum—in one high school in Japan. The Japan Exchange and Teaching program invites college graduates who are native English speakers from all over the world to engage in assisting and team teaching with Japanese teachers of English in high schools. The revision of the English curriculum, a more recent reform that went into effect in 1996, requires courses in oral communication. These reforms have had an important impact in schools where teachers have traditionally taught English in Japanese. At the same time, Japan's continued emphasis on high-stakes university entrance examinations in English, which focus on grammar and reading comprehension, has made movement toward communicative language teaching difficult for some teachers. Hiramatsu observed classes and interviewed both Japanese teachers of English as well as the native English-speaking assistant. In this chapter, Hiramatsu reports on what she learned and identifies a number of implications if these reform efforts are to have major impact on EFL teaching in Japan.

Chapter 8 (Byrnes) moves to the context of foreign language teaching at the university level in the United States. Specifically, Heidi Byrnes explores the professional preparation of graduate teaching assistants (TAs) for teaching within foreign language departments. Byrnes begins with an overview of the problems that characterize the socialization of TAs into the field of foreign language education and then proposes a reconceptualization of TA education. The reconceptualization is framed in three ways: by *contents* (the need to link teaching and research as well as the content of a TA program itself), *commitments* (an exploration of the new roles and responsibilities all faculty have to take on as they educate the department's TAs), and *structures* (an analysis of programmatic and administrative consequences in accepting such a reconceptualization). Byrnes then illustrates each of these in the context of the German Department at Georgetown University where major curriculum reform has been at the forefront of the department's efforts over the past 4 years. She describes a content-oriented, task-based curriculum reform project called "Developing Multiple Literacies," which challenged the traditional split between language and content that plagues the majority of university language departments in the United States and which brought about the reconceptualization of TA education. Chapter 8 comes to a close with mention of some of the challenges brought about by these changes as well as the professional growth for faculty and TAs alike that emerged in the process.

The context of the final chapter (Poynor, chap. 9) in this section is that of ESL and bilingual education at the elementary level. Drawing on her own experience as a beginning teacher 10 years earlier, Leslie Poynor explores in chapter 9 the influence that an ESL/Bilingual reading and language arts methods course has on the practice of teachers in their 1st year of teaching. In particular, Poynor's aim is to explore the impact that a "transaction" methods course might have on beginning teachers' practices when they find themselves in the context of a traditional school. Poynor explains transactional teaching practices as those that "(a) accept all social, cultural, and linguistic background knowledge and experience as valuable; (b) include those experiences in the explicit curriculum; and (c) regard all children, including culturally, linguistically, and economically marginalized children, as capable and developing human beings" (pp. 160–161). To explore this issue, Poynor uses a phenomenological approach, weaving into three collective texts the stories of Paul and Carmen (the two beginning teacher participants in the study) with her own stories of early teaching in rural Alabama. Poynor concludes that the choices they made as beginning teachers of language minority learners were indeed influenced by their cultural and historical contexts, including their transaction methods courses. Poynor faces the difficult questions that plague progressive teacher educators and teachers—how do teachers take what they learn in progressive teacher education programs to the real context of traditional schools? Poynor finds that it is through the collective texts themselves that teachers and teacher educators can find some answers.

The chapters in this section of the book highlight the complexity and importance of context in language teacher education. They speak to the socially situated nature of language and learning. How might teacher educators embed in their programs challenges to the status quo? How do challenges to the status quo get played out in traditional contexts be they in Japan, a university foreign language department, or elementary ESL and bilingual classrooms in the United States?

Chapter **6**

The Power of Tests Over Teachers: The Power of Teachers Over Tests

Elana Shohamy
Tel Aviv University

INTRODUCTION

The act of language testing is not neutral; although not explicitly stated, language tests are often used in a "top-down" manner as tools for defining language knowledge, implementing policies, and gatekeeping unwanted groups (Shohamy, 2001). As part of this process, teachers become the agents through whom such power and control are being exercised, as teachers are often responsible for implementing the testing policies of central agencies with no power and authority to resist. This phenomenon is especially noticed in contexts in which national and state-wide tests are used.

In this chapter, I describe the preceding process and demonstrate its effects on second language teaching in the classroom. I argue that the top-down approaches to testing are undemocratic and unethical, as they treat teachers as agents for carrying out orders rather than as authoritative, professional decision makers. In this chapter, I conclude with a proposal for alternative assessment procedures that involve teachers and are driven by teachers based on pedagogical considerations. By using such procedures, tests and other assessment tools are used in interactive, democratic, and constructive ways. Thus, it is in the power of teachers to turn tests into effective pedagogical tools capable of empowering teachers and improving second language learning.

TESTING IN CONTEXT—"TRADITIONAL" VERSUS "USE-ORIENTED" TESTING

Traditional Testing

Traditional testing is a scientific field with precise boundaries and defined criteria. It consists of a well-defined body of knowledge that is systematic and accurate. High-quality tests need to follow the rules of psychometrics so they are reliable and valid, and their items and tasks are expected to possess certain required properties. Once a test is designed and developed, its items written, its format piloted, and items statistics, reliability, and evidence of validity obtained, the role of the tester is complete, and the test is ready to be delivered to those who contracted it and used with "real" people. Traditional testing is not interested in the use of tests.

Use-Oriented Testing

Use-oriented testing is concerned with how tests are used. Specifically, it focuses on what happens to the test takers who take tests, to the knowledge that is created by tests, and to the teachers who prepare students for tests. It asks questions about the effect of tests on the material and content that teachers teach, the methods used by teachers, and the intentions and motivations in introducing tests. It also examines the decisions made based on tests' results, the parents whose children take tests, the ethicality and fairness as a result of tests, and the long- and short-term consequences that tests have on education and society. It is clear that in use-oriented testing, tests are not viewed as isolated events but rather as connected to educational, pedagogical, psychological, social, and political variables that affect curriculum, ethicality, social classes, bureaucracy, politics, and knowledge. Messick (1981), for example, claims that these values that tests embody, that is, their connection to the variables previously listed, too often are unrecognized and unexamined.

THE POWER OF TESTS

In examining their uses, it is clear that tests are used for power and control. Tests possess features that allow them to be used in such ways because they are introduced and administered by powerful organizations, whereas the test takers are powerless and are dependent on these organizations for decisions with regards to the content of the tests, format, scoring procedures, and timing. In addition, tests make use of the language of numbers and science, and these are very powerful and influential, as numbers are often awarded blind trust from the public. Tests also employ written forms and documentation, devices that according to Foucault (1979) enable control as the data scores obtained from tests are preserved by central authorities and are there to stay. Furthermore, tests rely on objective formats, which avoid direct connection between the tester and the test takers while giving unquestionable trust to the test as an objective informer. This is all interesting, given the fact that tests were originally developed as democratic tools to allow equal opportunity to all, including women and minorities; yet over the years, tests have turned into devices of power and control in particular. This is especially noticed in centralized educational systems, which use tests to control the curriculum and learning and where test takers claim that tests have a detrimental effect on their lives.

In Shohamy (2001), test takers provide narratives that describe their experiences of second language test taking as well as the effect of these tests on their lives and future. These narratives clearly point to the low trust test takers have in tests and their beliefs that tests are not at all indicative of their true knowledge. In addition, they claim that tests are detached from real learning and from real-life performances. They often feel that success on tests is not dependent on their real knowledge but rather on "luck" and on supernatural forces. Test takers note that teachers in classrooms often use tests as tools for punishment, control, discipline, or to "kill time." Yet, test takers learn to "play the testing game" as they comply with the demands of the tests and change their behaviors and learn what is covered on tests. There are at least two explanations for this phenomenon, the first being the detrimental effects of tests and the second that tests are used as disciplinary tools.

The Detrimental Effects of Tests

Results obtained from tests often lead to high-stake decisions for individuals (and often for society as a whole); they create winners and losers, successes and failures, rejections and acceptances. Test scores are often the sole indicators that lead to decisions about placing people in class levels, granting certificates and prizes, and determining whether a person will be allowed to continue in future studies, decide on a profession, enter special education classes, participate in honor classes, get accepted to higher education, and/or obtain jobs.

Tests Used as Disciplinary Tools

Authoritative groups use tests to impose behaviors on those who are tested and/or on others (e.g., school systems) who are affected by their results. Test takers develop fear of tests, as they feel that tests have control over their behavior and that they are in the hands of the tests and the testers. Tests are capable of dictating what test takers will study and what will be taught and eventually what they will know. Tests takers comply with the demands of the tests by changing their behavior as they need to maximize their scores given the detrimental effects of the scores explained previously. It is often the realization by those in authority that test takers will change their behaviors to succeed on tests that leads them to introduce tests as disciplinary tools to make those who are affected by tests change their behavior in accordance with their own priorities. Thus, tests are used as arms of policy and for imposing control.

RESEARCH ON THE USE OF TESTS

Research on the use of tests confirms the preceding phenomena. It focuses on two dimensions—*intentions*, which refer to the rationale, purposes, and expectations of those in authority who introduce tests, and to *effects* or *consequences* of tests, that is, the impact that tests have on education and society (Shohamy, 1994, 1997, 2001).

In terms of intentions, research has shown how policymakers explicitly state that language tests are used as a means for controlling and affecting educational practices (see, e.g., Shohamy, 2001). That is, at times, tests are deliberately intended to lead to changes in curriculum or to a redefinition of language knowledge. They may also affect teacher behavior and lead teachers to focus on teaching test language and emphasize the material that is to be included on the test. As certain material is selected for tests, other material is not, and this has the potential to narrow the linguistic knowledge that teachers embed in their classes and students learn. Even when such intentions are not explicitly stated, they result in major effects on individuals and impact beyond any expectations. Yet, the pattern of effect varies as it depends on whether the test is of high or low stake (high-stake tests have more impact than low-stake tests), the status of language and skills (tests of high-status languages and skills have more effects than those of low-status languages and skills), and the purposes of the test and skills tested (classroom tests will have less effect than external tests that aim to place people).

In terms of the greater consequences of tests, it has been shown that the introduction of tests does not lead to meaningful changes but only to procedural changes. In fact, the introduction of tests has negative effects on the quality of knowledge as it creates "test language," which is very different from "real language." It also creates parallel forms of education (there is the testing language and the language as stated in the curriculum, yet the testing language becomes the de facto knowledge). In many situations, there is a contradiction between the tested language and the language as it is expressed in the official curricula.

Testing is a policy act that is carried out in covert and unethical ways by those in authority, as in most cases tests are introduced for disciplinary purposes, to carry out policy agendas of those in authority, and for manipulating educational systems. Such uses of tests for dictating what test takers will learn and know and what teachers will teach is possible with high-stake tests, as they cause those who are affected by them—students, teachers, and educational systems—to change their behavior along the agendas of the tests to maximize their scores given the consequences of successful or unsuccessful performance on tests.

The preceding phenomenon is especially noticed in multicultural societies in which it is through high-stake standardized tests that the unique knowledge of "different" groups receives no recognition. In such situations, tests are capable of affecting and redefining knowledge, as hegemonic groups who are interested in perpetuating their domination and excluding unwanted groups use tests to suppress and eliminate cultural differences by selecting test content that represents the knowledge of those in power. These are situations in which tests serve as gatekeepers and as tools for eliminating unique knowledge of different groups (Shohamy, 2004).

Bourdieu (1991) claims that the power of tests is derived from the trust that those who are affected by tests place in them, as there is an unwritten contract between those in power who want to dominate and those who want to be dominated and who grant them the power and authority so they can perpetuate and maintain their power. Tests, then, are instrumental in reaffirming societal powers and maintaining social order.

There are numerous examples of such situations and processes. For example, when a certain topic is being included on tests, the message that is being conveyed is that these very topics have certain priorities for those in authority and that the educational system should follow these priorities by having students learn and study the content of the tests. The tests then become the means through which these priorities are communicated. In the United States, 2001 marked the reauthorization of the Elementary and Secondary Education Act, called the "No Child Left Behind Act," which includes accountability measures that require mass testing of all learners in reading, writing, math, and science. It is a clear message that reading as explicitly characterized in the content and format of the tests is the definition of literacy and of what children should acquire in schools. It is through the test that these messages are being transferred to schools. Given that these are high-stake tests and can lead to major sanctions imposed on schools and districts, many are asking what impact might these tests have on schools and districts having high numbers of language minority learners? In Japan, the mandatory university entrance examinations for English require grammatical knowledge and literacy skills; the content of the test, then, is in direct contrast to a recent national reform effort requiring oral communication classes in the high school English curriculum (see Hiramatsu, chap. 7, this volume). In Israel, there are similar examples when tests are being introduced in situations when the Ministry of Education is unhappy with the type of leaning that is taking place in schools. The introduction of high-stake tests ensures that certain topics that the Ministry perceives as important will be learned in schools. When the Ministry decides on a new topic and would like it to be widely implemented, such as a new English curriculum, the introduction of tests perpetuate it. In short, regardless of the national context, tests serve as a guarantee tat teachers will teach the test content in their classrooms.

Yet, the dominance of tests remains unquestioned, unchallenged, unmonitored, and uncontrolled. Tests have enormous trust and support on the part of the public and institutions because results obtained from tests are used as rites of passage, create dependence, and grant economic value, especially when the power of tests is combined with the power of language. Further, those introducing tests create myths and propaganda about their usefulness and brainwash the public to believe in their infallibility, fairness, and meaningfulness (Spolsky, 1998).

THE ROLE OF TEACHERS WITHIN THE POWER PARADIGM

Teachers play a major role within the process described previously. There are currently two views with regards to teachers—there are those who view teachers as bureaucrats and others who view them as professionals. In most cases, teachers are viewed as bureaucrats; they are being used by those in authority to carry out testing policies and thus become servants of the system. In other situations, teachers are viewed as professionals who take an active role in creating testing policies and who initiate meaningful dialogue about tests and their uses and effects.

Teachers as Servants of the System

When teachers are viewed as bureaucrats, this implies that they become agents who carry out the testing policies of those in authority; they are the soldiers or servants of the system. It should be noted that those in authority have great temptations to use tests as disciplinary tools for policy-making, as tests are perceived by the public, especially parents, as authoritative. In addition, tests guarantee control, they are effective for "proving," are capable of redefining knowledge, allow flexible cutting scores, provide visible evidence of action, and are cost effective because they are tools that do not require investment in teacher development, material writing, or creation of new curricula. In most cases, teachers are not involved in decisions to introduce national and/or state-wide tests. Yet, at the same time, teachers are expected to carry out the order of "teaching to the tests" and to change their pedagogical strategies accordingly. Even in situations when it is not explicitly stated, teachers view tests not only as testing the language performance and proficiency levels of their own students but also as assessing or testing their own performances. Those who introduce the tests know very well that teachers and students will change their behavior to succeed on the high-stake tests, and this is often, as noted earlier, the rationale for introducing such tests. Thus, centralized tests are capable of dictating to teachers what to teach and what test takers will study, as teachers and test takers comply with the demands of the tests by changing their behavior so as to maximize the scores given the detrimental effects of the tests. Broadfoot (1996) demonstrates how teachers become the new servants of the central systems, which she refers to as "a new order of domination" (p. 87).

Teachers as Professionals

The other view perceives teachers as professionals—responsible and involved leaders in the field of second language testing. This means that teachers take an active part in making decisions about tests and do not only carry out orders. Viewing teachers as professionals implies a number of steps and procedures that are described in the following section.

Teacher Education. For teachers to be viewed as professionals, they need to take part in testing policies, and they need to demand to be included. Yet, a prerequisite for that is the importance for teachers to become professionals in their assessment practices by obtaining training and knowledge in assessment and by proposing alternative assessment procedures that are more in line with classroom learning as well as to become more understanding and knowledgeable about the consequences of tests and their different uses. Specifically, this includes the need to expand the role of teacher education programs in which teachers are exposed not only to procedures and methods of testing and assessment but also to aspects related to the consequences of tests.

Critical Testing. Part of the professionalization of teachers involves the need to develop critical strategies to examine the uses and consequences of tests, control their power, minimize their detrimental forces, reveal their misuses, and empower test takers. Teachers need to become more aware, more socially responsible and socially reflexive about the uses of tests by pointing out such misuses to the public at large and by resisting the "one size fits all" approach. They should also encourage test takers to question tests and their uses, the material that tests are based on, and to critique the values and beliefs inherent in them.

Interactive Models of Assessment. Teachers also need to become aware of and involved in interactive models of assessment (Moss, 1996; Shohamy, 1998, 2001). The words of Paolo Freire (1985) speak to such interaction in his characterization of evaluation:

> Evaluation, that is, and not inspection. Through inspection, educators just become objects of vigilance by a central organization. Through evaluation, everyone is a subject along with the central organization in the act of criticism and establishing distance from the word. In understanding the process in this way, evaluation is not an act by which educator A evaluates educator B. It's an act by which educators A and B together evaluate an experience, its development, and the obstacles one confronts along with any mistakes or error. Thus, evaluation has a dialectical character.... It's essential that members of the evaluating organization deeply believe that they have as much to learn from educators directly linked to popular bases as those who study at the bases. (pp. 23-25)

Interactive models of assessment involve shared power. They are based on a broader representation of different agents, central and local, who together go through a process of contextualization of the evidence obtained from the different sources. Through constructive, interpretive, and dialogical sessions, data are collected by different participants and are then used in interpretive and contextualized manners. It is a two-way relation based on assumptions that nobody knows everything, but both parties know something and that by dialoging, they will know more. It consists of a willingness on the part of both parties to acknowledge that each side has limitations, to understand that it is a continuous process, to ensure that information brought to the table is relevant, and that each party is responsible for consequences of tests. Lynch (1997) argues that such practices can ensure that individuals participate effectively in the political process. Such a view builds on the true power of tests, that of offering pedagogical benefits in the form of feedback leading to more effective learning and teaching. This means that tests as well as other assessment procedures can be used for beneficial and constructive purposes but at the same time can be used to guard against central bodies and authoritative agencies who seek ways to use tests in unethical and undemocratic ways for power and control.

ADOPTING A MORE DEMOCRATIC/INCLUSIVE APPROACH TO TESTING

Adoption of a more democratic or inclusive approach to testing implies mostly considerations of different groups of test takers from a variety of multicultural groups so that the different knowledge will be acknowledged and not be viewed as deficient. Even in societies that recognize multiculturalism as part of society trends, there is rarely recognition of the specific and unique knowledge of the different groups in schools. Thus, multiculturalism becomes lip service, as there is no de facto recognition, and educational or political leaders continue to strive for homogeneous knowledge to be owned by all.

Thus, there is a need to do the following:

1. Monitor and limit the uses of powerful tools, especially those that have the potential of excluding or discriminating groups. It is important, therefore, to apply critical testing approaches to monitor the powerful uses of tests, challenge their assumptions, and examine their consequences.
2. Have citizens in democratic societies play a participatory and active role and transfer and share power from elites with local bodies. They should follow inclusive models whereby test development and practice are conducted in collaboration and cooperation with those tested.
3. Hold those who develop powerful tools responsible for their consequences. Those involved in the testing act must assume and examine the consequences of tests and therefore assume responsibility.
4. Consider voices of diverse and different groups in multicultural societies. There is a need in multicultural societies to consider and include knowledge of different groups on tests and consider representatives of these groups as partners.
5. Protect the rights of citizens from powerful institutions. The rights of test takers must be protected and guarded.

6. Apply democratic practices in the classroom. Teachers need to involve students in decision making about tests, ensure that students are evaluated based on a variety of sources, apply process-oriented evaluation strategies, empower test takers, and try to understand and acknowledge the rights of test takers.

These are the challenges that teachers need to face—How can such testing practices be carried out; what are some of new methodologies that have to be developed to follow such practices; how can more democratic testing be pursued while ensuring the validity of the assessment procedures; and most of all, how can test users be convinced not to accept teachers as servants of the systems but rather to use their professional knowledge about assessment policies that are pedagogical in nature and can lead to better learning? This is the true power of teachers over tests, when tests become the means and not the agent.

Tests provide a reflection, a mirror, of the complexities and power struggles of society, and too often they serve as tools in these struggles. They fall in the midst of two forces—of those who try to see tests as tools for control and those who view tests as constructive pedagogical tools. Teachers as professionals should try to protect, guard, and use tests as pedagogical tools as part of the process of preserving and perpetuating democratic cultures, values, and ethics.

REFERENCES

Bourdieu, P. (1991). *Language and symbolic power.* Cambridge, MA: Harvard University Press.

Broadfoot, P. (1996). *Education, assessment and society: A sociological analysis.* Buckingham, England: Open University Press.

Elementary and Secondary Education Act of 2002, Pub. L. No. 107–110 (2002).

Foucault, M. (1979). *Discipline and punish: The birth of the prison.* New York: Vintage.

Freire, P. (1985). *The politics of education.* Hadley, MA: Bergin and Garvey.

Lynch, B. (1997). In search of the ethical test. *Language Testing, 14,* 315–327.

Messick, S. (1981). Evidence and ethics in the evaluation of tests. *Educational Researcher, 10*(9), 9–20.

Moss, P. (1996). Enlarging the dialogue in educational measurement: Voices from interpretive research traditions. *Educational Researcher, 25*(1), 20–28.

No Child Left Behind Act of 2001, 20 USC 6301. U.S. Dept. Of Education.

Shohamy, E. (1994). The use of language tests for power and control. In J. Alatis (Ed.), *Georgetown University round table on language and linguistics* (pp. 57–72). Washington, DC: Georgetown University Press.

Shohamy, E. (1997). Testing methods, testing consequences: Are they ethical? Are they fair? *Language Testing ,14,* 340–349.

Shohamy, E. (1998). Critical language testing and beyond. *Studies in Educational Evaluation, 24,* 331–345.

Shohamy, E. (2001). *The power of tests. A critical perspective on the uses of language tests.* Singapore: Longman.

Shohamy, E. (2004). Assessment in multicultural societies: Applying democratic principles and practices to language testing. In B. Norton & K. Toohey (Eds.), *Critical pedagogies and language learning.* New York: Cambridge University Press.

Spolsky, B. (1998). The ethics of gatekeeping tests: What have we learned in a hundred years. *Language Testing, 14,* 242–247.

Chapter **7**

Contexts and Policy Reform: A Case Study of EFL Teaching in a High School in Japan

Sachiko Hiramatsu
State University of New York at Buffalo

INTRODUCTION

In the last two decades, the movement toward a communication-oriented approach or communicative language teaching (CLT) has been a remarkable phenomenon in the contexts of both English as a second language (ESL) and English as a foreign language (EFL). However, it has been suggested that in some countries where EFL is taught, teachers find it difficult to implement communicative language teaching in their contexts (Li, 1998). Japan is not an exception. Over the last 15 years or so, it has not been easy for Japanese English language education to move from a traditional grammar-translation method to the communicative language teaching approach (Gorsuch, 2000). Nonetheless, change is taking place in Japan, helped by strong government initiatives that involve teachers, teaching methods, and curricular reform. In this study, I examine a context of change initiated by the implementation of two reform initiatives in English education as seen by a case of one high school in Japan.

TWO REFORM INITIATIVES IN JAPANESE EFL

EFL education in Japan started to change when the Japanese Ministry of Education and Science, Sports, and Culture (*Ministry of Education thereafter*) announced two reform initiatives in 1987. The first, the Japan Exchange and Teaching (JET) program, was introduced in 1987, and the second, the revision of the English curriculum, was first announced in 1987 and went into effect at the high school level in 1996.

JET Program

The JET program was created in 1987 by the Japanese government with the objectives of improving foreign language education in Japan and enhancing internationalization by helping to promote international exchange at the local level and mutual understanding between Japan and other countries (Ministry of Education, Science and Culture, 1994, p. 6). With this in mind, this program invites young college and university graduates, 22 to 35 years old, from overseas to participate in international exchange and foreign language education throughout Japan. In 2000 to 2001, there were 6,078 participants from 39 countries (Ministry of Foreign Affairs, n.d.). More than 90% of them hold the Assistant Language Teacher (ALT) position (Council of Local Authorities for International Relations [CLAIR], 1997). They are placed mainly in public schools or local boards of education. The ALTs engage in duties that include assisting the Japanese teachers of English (JTEs) with classes and team teaching with them. Thus, the concept of a team of two teachers, a JTE and an ALT, teaching together is the core of the JET system. It should be noted that ALTs are not required to have teaching qualifications, and most of them are not language teachers or education majors. In team teaching, JTEs have to take a leading role, and in principle, ALTs are not allowed to teach alone.

Revision of the English Curriculum

The second reform, the revised English curriculum, was implemented in 1996 in senior high schools. This was based on the Revised Course of Study, which was first announced in 1987 and finalized and published in 1989 by the Ministry of Education (1989).

Educational policies are created and implemented in a top-down fashion in Japan. First, the Ministry of Education lays down national standards for the curricula for all school levels, which is called the "Course of Study." Then, individual schools organize their own curricula within the framework of the Course of Study.

What is notable about the Revised Course of Study of 1989 is that new courses, called "Oral Communication" (OC), were created for senior high school English. These courses place an emphasis on the teaching of oral/aural skills; thus, they are quite different from the other more reading- and writing-oriented courses. With the inclusion of OC courses, the resulting English curricula at each school elevated the importance of communication in teaching English. Traditionally, JTEs have had a tendency to speak Japanese in English classes because the grammar-translation method does not require extensive oral/aural practice, and thus, high levels of oral proficiency were not an important criterion for the JTEs in the past. The two initiatives, the implementation of OC courses and team teaching in the JET program, however, have a good chance of changing this traditional practice. It is expected that there are communication-oriented activities and practices and in-class interactions between JTE and ALT in OC courses. In this sense, OC courses and team teaching fit together naturally and theoretically can promote communicative language learning in classroom.

POLICY IMPLEMENTATION AND PRACTICE

The intended changes in the English education policy reform are drastic, involving two levels: new practice—team teaching (JET Program), and new content—OC courses. The creation of the JET Program itself was somewhat political (McConnell, 1996), and it created great confusion to the JTEs whose voices were not heard in the decision-making process and who were not prepared to team teach with native speaking teachers (Moore & Lamie, 1996). The implementation of OC courses, on the other hand, allowed schools and the teachers more time, 7 years, to prepare for the new courses.

During these 7 years, the Japanese Ministry of Education provided a series of conferences and seminars designed to give JTEs the guidance and support necessary to carry out the directive to move toward CLT. Some of these conferences and seminars were voluntary and others mandatory. In the meantime, the number of the ALTs steadily increased, resulting in more schools hosting an ALT or more visits of ALTs to nonhosting schools. In this way, the circumstances surrounding the JTEs began to change gradually but substantially.

At this point, one may wonder how actual teaching will change as a result of the reform. Can the ideas of the new policy be achieved at the classroom level and at the teachers' level? Here, one needs to realize that policy change and its effect on practice may not be a simple linear relation. Then, what are the factors that come into play between the policy change and its implementation at the level of individual teachers? For this question, it is important to examine selected educational policy studies.

Teachers and Policy Changes

The State of California's reform initiative of mathematics teaching, called "Framework," provides a good case in point (Ball, 1990; Cohen, 1990; Wiemers, 1990). These Framework studies, which examine teachers' responses to and understandings of the reform, are helpful and applicable to this study despite the difference of the subject matter.

The studies on Framework report that each teacher takes Framework into his or her existing beliefs and knowledge of the subject differently, resulting in individually unique classrooms where each teacher exhibits different levels of understanding of this initiative (Ball, 1990; Cohen, 1990; Wiemers, 1990). This is because each teacher individually interprets the change and adapts his or her teaching depending on the students they have, their prior knowledge and experience, their views of the content of the subject matter, and textbooks and tests (Grant, Peterson, & Shojgreen-Downer, 1996). As McLaughlin (1987) states, "At each point in the policy process, a policy is transformed as individuals interpret and respond to it" (p. 174).

These findings of the Framework research suggest that the reform initiated by the Ministry of Education in Japan is one thing, and the understanding and teaching of the JTEs who team teach with ALTs in OC courses may be another. Despite the mandated curriculum changes and the prevalence of team teaching, there is no guarantee that individual JTEs who team teach with ALTs understand the changes or change their teaching accordingly to the direction of the reform.

There have been only a few studies conducted on the JET program or on individual English teachers in Japan. Among the findings reported, there is a gap between the ideals of CLT and the reality of the entrance exams, which focus on grammar, reading, and translation (Gorsuch, 2000; McConnell, 1996); the teachers' attitudes toward team teaching are an important issue (Sturman, 1992); and different teaching situations and teaching teams lead to diversity in curricular content and activities in team teaching (Smith, 1994).

These studies did not address the implementation of OC classes, the newest reform. Moreover, they failed to attend sufficiently to the individual teachers' voices, especially the voices of the ALTs with whom the JTEs team teach, nor did they provide thorough examinations of individual contexts. The ALTs generally have several team-teaching partners in a school; therefore, they may have the potential to influence several JTEs in their daily routine of team teaching. It is important that ALTs' perceptions be included in research studies. Furthermore, because teachers are part of a larger school system, the context where teachers are situated should be thoroughly examined to analyze possible factors underlying the teachers' interpretation of the reform (Grant, et al., 1996). An investigation of a specific context and the teachers' (JTEs' and ALTs') perceptions of the reform within that context may provide insight into the complexities and individual differences in the way teachers understand the reform. In this study, I examine how changes are talking place in the context of one particular high school, giving equal emphasis to both the JTEs and the ALT. Although small in scale, this study contributes to previous studies, thus adding to the larger knowledge base concerning communicative language teaching policies and practices in EFL contexts.

METHOD

Research Questions

In this study, three research questions were posed in the context of one Japanese high school: (a) How have JTEs adapted to the changes caused by the JET program and the new OC courses?; (b) How do the individual teachers, the JTEs and the ALT, perceive team teaching and the OC courses?; and (c) What are the factors influencing the JTEs' and ALTs' perceptions?

Data Collection

Site. To explore my research questions, I made a series of visits to Tobu Senior High School,[1] which is located in a small rural town in the southern part of Japan. The school has approximately 1,200 students and can be characterized as an academic, college preparatory school with more than 90% of its graduates going on to receive tertiary education. At Tobu, there are 12 English teachers, but only 4 of them were team teaching with the ALT during the data collection period. During the study, I participated in all school activities and observed activities, teachers, and physical aspects of the school as a participant observer (Spradley, 1980) while keeping field notes. I also collected documents, memos, and handouts.

---

[1]All the names of the people and places that appear in this chapter are pseudonyms.

Interviews With JTEs. Among the 12 English teachers at Tobu High School, I interviewed 8 teachers who had taught or were currently teaching OC classes. Of those eight, Mr. Oda, Mr. Kusaka, and Ms. Kawada taught OCA the previous year, a course that is offered only to 1st-year students (10th graders). Teachers teaching the OCA courses during this study were Mr. Muto, Mr. Toyoda, and Ms. Kono. Mr. Ohmi was teaching an elective course for 3rd-year students, OCB, the year of the study, and Mr. Obita taught it the previous year.

Mr. Oda and Mr. Kusaka were both experienced teachers in their 40s and had been working together for 3 years. Ms. Kawada was in her 2nd year in teaching. The previous year, she had 60 hr of in-school training (required for all new teachers in Japanese schools) with Mr. Oda.

Mr. Muto was an experienced teacher who had been the head English teacher for 2 years, and he was in charge of the ALT program. Mr. Toyoda, in his 50s, was the most experienced teacher but was new to Tobu that year. Ms. Kono was a young lecturer in her 2nd year in the teaching career and was also new to Tobu. Mr. Ohmi was in his 30s and had the unique experience of working in the United States for a year as a chef prior to becoming a teacher. Mr. Obita was a very experienced teacher who had been working on communicative English for many years. All of these teachers, except Ms. Kawada and Ms. Kono, had previous experiences in team teaching with ALTs, either at Tobu with former ALT(s) or at other schools.

I conducted individual interviews with the eight JTEs. Each interview lasted about 45 to 60 min, and all interviews were conducted in Japanese and tape-recorded. Due to time constraints, I had one interview with each JTE, although with Mr. Oda, who was the most involved in the implementation of OC courses, I had two interviews. Each semistructured interview started with a request that the JTEs recollect their past team-teaching experiences and then expand to their current teaching.

Interviews With the ALT. The ALT at Tobu High School was Dan Harrington from the United States. He had been teaching at Tobu for 3 years, the limit set by the JET program, and at the time of this study, he was about to finish his teaching duties. He did not have any teaching experience prior to this teaching duty.

Dan[2] was scheduled to team teach 11 classes per week. When he was not teaching, Dan would sit at his desk in the teachers' room and grade 2nd-year students' writing assignments for the writing class, or he would read the newspaper; he did not interact with other teachers much. I con-

---

[2]At Tobu, the ALTs were called by their first name.

ducted three interviews with Dan, each lasting 50 to 60 min. I followed the procedures suggested by Seidman (1991), which allows the informants to reconstruct their experiences in their own words.

Observations of OC Courses. At Tobu High School, OC courses had begun in April of the year prior to the study. OCA was offered to all 1st-year students, and approximately 20 third-year students were enrolled in the elective OCB.

There were two OCA classes per week according to the curriculum, but only one of them was team taught by the ALT and a JTE, and the other was taught by the JTE alone, which may have been due to the scheduling difficulties. In addition to this classroom contact, the ALT took part in the final exam's listening comprehension section.

During the period of my study, I observed six OCA classes taught by one of three JTEs (Mr. Muto, Mr. Toyoda, and Ms. Kono) and Dan and two OCB classes taught by Mr. Ohmi and Dan. Thus, all four teachers who were team teaching at Tobu during my visit were observed. When observing classes, I took notes on lesson procedures and the interaction between the teacher and the ALT and interactions between teachers and students, among other things.

Data Analysis

I followed Seidman's (1991) procedures for the analysis of interview data, which progresses from transcribing the tapes, marking and labeling the passages that seem relevant to the research questions, constructing categories, and searching for connections between categories that would lead to themes. I started with analyzing data from individual JTEs and then grouped together the themes that emerged from all the JTEs. I analyzed the data from the ALT separately and then examined how themes from this analysis converged or diverged with those of the JTEs. For triangulation purposes, observation data, which focused on actual team teaching, as well as my field notes and other school documents that I obtained during the study, were all utilized to help me make sense of the interview data. In particular, the data from team-teaching classes were useful in examining what gap, if any, existed between what the teachers reported in interviews and how they actually taught in the classroom.

FINDINGS

This is a study of teachers who experienced team teaching and OC courses within the context of an academic high school. The following themes emerged in data analysis: JTEs' communicative competence in English, team teaching—threat or stimulus, team teaching in practice, lack of opportunities for learning and for building collegiality, and dual reality.

JTEs' Communicative Competence in English

Some JTEs reported that they were not very confident in their spoken English. Some admitted that they had difficulty in communicating with Dan due to their weakness in listening and speaking English:

> Most of the JTEs, including me, can't speak English. I can't say what I want to say, because I can't think of the words, or I can't catch what Dan is saying. When Dan speaks at a natural speed, I don't understand him. It's a guessing world. (Mr. Ohmi)

> I am not confident in my knowledge and competence in English, so I sometimes become incoherent when I am speaking in English, not knowing what to say. I think this is my lack of competence.... In team teaching, there are times when we JTEs have to debate with the ALT over things, not just simple things, but more complicated things, such as grading. In these cases, I think we have to be able to speak and get our meaning across. I wish I had such an ability to debate with the ALT. (Mr. Oda)

Dan felt Mr. Oda's English was good, but with other JTEs, he pointed out that their lack of competence was an obstacle in communicating with them:

> I felt like [Mr. Oda's] English is good enough.... I felt confident that he understands what I'm saying when I speak to him.... With the other teachers, for a variety of reasons, I just don't feel that comfortable because either their English is not very strong or their whole sense of reasoning is just different than mine. Very often, I don't like to do this, but often I would have Mr. Oda talk to another teacher for me because I knew that Mr. Oda understood and I knew that he could explain it in Japanese so that the other teacher would understand. (Dan)

The preceding quote indicates that a JTE's adequacy or inadequacy in communicative skills is likely to influence how effectively the JTE and Dan can communicate. The insufficient English proficiency of the JTEs has already been identified as one of the hindrances to effective communicative language teaching (Gorsuch, 2000; McConnell, 1996; Moore & Lamie, 1996). Considering joint class preparations and discussions necessary to carry out a team teaching class, these daily communication difficulties appear to work against effective team teaching.

Team Teaching: Threat or Stimulus

This feeling of competence or incompetence in spoken English that JTEs expressed may lead to two perceptions of team teaching with the ALT: as a threat or stimulus. When the JTEs speak English while team teaching, they may have to face their lack of competence, which could result in embarrassing situations. Even in solo teaching, "there is the possibility of mistakes and vocabulary lapses at every moment of every class" (Horwitz, 1996, p. 367). To make matters more complicated, JTEs have the ALT to teach with and interact with in class in front of the students. As Mr. Oda simply stated, "For the JTEs, the presence of ALTs is a threat." Embarrassing moments in class with an ALT present can be felt as particularly threatening in a culture in which teachers are expected to know everything.

> Because JTEs have to talk with the ALT before the class, construct a lesson with him and have to communicate with the ALT in class, those who are not very good at doing these things will have problems such as facing embarrassment in front of the students. (Mr. Obita)

On the reverse side, it is possible for teachers to perceive team teaching as a positive challenge and to use this opportunity for their own benefit:

> I think without a threat, we JTEs won't improve our current competence.... I think a threat is an absolute necessity. I think it's good for us that we can't be idle and are forced to change by being threatened by the foreign teachers.
>
> I think we have been given a good "pressure from outside." I think it's like somebody telling us, "The situation has to change. You JTEs have to become able to speak English and to comprehend English." I think [with the ALTs] we were given a lot of that stimulus. (Mr. Oda)

It is along this line that Dan perceived that the true benefit of team teaching, that is, having an ALT at school, is for the JTEs to improve their competence in spoken English:

> I think the biggest benefit [of having ALTs] is for the teachers, the teachers who can use us as a resource or practice their English with us.... Because the teachers are coming from a much higher level [than are the students], they are having much more intelligent conversations with us, and if they really want to, they can improve their English by leaps and bounds if they are spending a lot of time talking to us. (Dan)

However, this realization does not appear to be shared by all the teachers. Dan thought that not all the JTEs actively took advantage of the opportunity to improve their English and teaching. He said, "The impact is the greatest on the teachers, but that impact is not at work in some cases [with some JTEs]."

Using the ALT as a resource could mean the roles are reversed for the JTEs who are supposed to be the leader officially and the ALT, the assistant. The JTEs may feel some reservation toward the JET program, which in a sense means that the ALT is here to coach them and teach English to them:

> I felt like there was a little bit of ... jealousy. I guess, in a way, that I am brought here to do a job, and [the Japanese government] feels like the teachers are not doing well enough.... I can understand the teachers' sort of reluctance in a way to accept me. But I have felt the least amount of acceptance, I guess. (Dan)

In this way, there seems to be various feelings among the JTEs toward team teaching and having an ALT at school, be they related to their perception of team teaching as a threat or stimulus or to feelings of jealousy. Team teaching has compelled at least some JTEs to improve their communicative English. Threat and stimulus, in fact, can be two ends of a spectrum, not necessarily two opposing perceptions. If a JTE feels she or he is not good at spoken English, the presence of an ALT and team teaching may be more of a threat. However, as they become more accustomed to interacting with the ALT and conducting team-teaching classes, they may come to perceive team teaching more as a stimulus than as a threat. How far one goes on the spectrum may depend on the individual JTE.

Team Teaching in Practice

Although some JTEs reported lack of competence in English, when the JTEs were teaching, they all appeared confident in speaking English in class, and their English use sounded natural. No communication breakdowns or miscommunications between JTEs and Dan in class were observed during this study.

There seemed to be several characteristics to describe team teaching at Tobu. First, all classes were alike and had a very similar procedure no matter who the JTE was. After greetings and a short introduction of the day's topic by the JTE, Dan read words and phrases from the textbook, and the JTE explained their meanings in Japanese. Then the students repeated the words after Dan for pronunciation practice. Then the JTE and Dan would read a model dialogue together followed by students' practice in pairs. Adherence to the textbook may have caused this similarity across teachers.

Second, it was clear from my observations that there were certain roles a JTE and the ALT took in team teaching despite who the JTE was. For instance, it was always Dan who read vocabulary and true or false questions. On the other hand, a JTE always introduced the topic of that day, checked students' comprehension of words or sentences in Japanese, and explained grammar.

One time Mr. Toyoda started the introduction by posing questions to the students: "Do you belong to any club?"; "We have many clubs. Would you tell me what clubs we have?"; "Do you sometimes practice on Sundays?" The question and answer session lasted about 5 min., during which Dan was standing silently in front of the room about 10 ft. away from Mr. Toyoda. When I asked Dan the next day during the interview why he didn't ask some of the questions himself, he simply said, "[Mr. Toyoda] came up to me ... and said, 'I'm going to do this part. And you will do this part.' So we kind of broke it down like that." This type of division of teaching duties was clearly visible in all of the team-taught classes that I observed.

The only difference, then, was whether the JTEs were willing to break with the routine when necessary. For instance, in Ms. Kono's class, when she spoke English, it was limited to dialogue reading, classroom greetings and commands (e.g., "Open your textbook."), and exchanges of a few words with Dan. On the other hand, in Mr. Muto's class, when Dan was explaining his house in the United States and mentioned "porch," Mr. Muto asked him, "What is the difference between porch and patio?" This was an impromptu question. He also asked Dan for confirmation (e.g., "How big is it, did you say?"; "Your family bought a house in 1985, right?"). It was a natural flow of questions and answers and indeed a spontaneous interaction.

The studies on language anxiety among nonnative foreign language teachers can clarify the similarities and difference of the JTEs' use of English in class. Even though language teachers are supposed to be high-level speakers of their target language, teachers themselves are learners and thus may have uncomfortable moments speaking the target language. Summarizing several studies on this issue, Horwitz (1996) states that teachers who suffer a higher level of foreign language anxiety will tend "toward linguistic interactions that are predictable and more easily controlled" (p. 366). Seen this way, adherence to the textbook, fixed procedures, and divisions of teaching roles could be interpreted as JTEs' strategies to reduce the possibilities of embarrassing moments. If the anxiety level of the JTE is high, she or he may not go beyond routine classroom greetings and expressions. This may be what some JTEs at Tobu were experiencing in class. Considering the fact that there were only routine, scripted interactions, many team-taught classes at Tobu unfortunately may not represent successful communicative language teaching.

Lack of Opportunities for Learning and for Building Collegiality

The need to improve their communicative skills was shared by all the JTEs. The opportunities available to the JTEs were off-site seminars and workshops and daily interactions with the ALT at school.

Seminars and Workshops. At the initial stage of team teaching, the JTEs were bewildered and unsure of how to team-teach with an ALT:

> When I team taught with the first ALT (of Tobu High School), I have to admit, I was not willing to do team teaching.... I thought, "Why are we doing this? Is it worth doing?" I felt the team teaching system started all of a sudden with no time for preparation. So I thought the ALT was just a substitute for a tape recorder. "Yes, I can use him instead of the tape recorder. Then I don't need to take the trouble of playing and rewinding the machine." So what I did was to have him read repeatedly. (Mr. Muto)

This comment shows that there was lack of basic information about what team teaching is and how to team teach, which led to ineffective use of ALTs at this stage. Then, the prefectural board of education held mandatory team teaching seminars in 1993 to 1995. This seems to have helped at least some JTEs to adjust to team teaching and develop positive attitudes toward team teaching. Mr. Toyoda summarizes the experience:

> We were put in a situation where we have to team teach, that is, we have to teach oral English, and so, we had to have training.

> Because of the training, we have made progress and overcome our hesitation. (Mr. Toyoda)

Mr. Toyoda's remark shows that inservice training may ease teachers' hesitation and bring forth more positive attitudes. As is shown in the studies by Lai (1993) and Saraswathi (1992), the benefit of inservice workshops is providing teachers with practical "how-to" tips and activities, thus making a difference in the way teachers perceive what is possible for them to do in their classroom.

Even after the implementation stage, the board of education continuously offered the seminars and workshops every year, although they were not mandatory. Some workshops included a demonstration class with an ALT. Those were the opportunities available for the JTEs to learn tips for successful team teaching and to become more competent in communicative English. However, availability of those opportunities is one thing and JTEs' utilization of them is another, because, in principle, participation in seminars and workshops was voluntary. Mr. Toyoda explains this when reflecting on his past experience of doing a team-teaching demonstration with an ALT:

> After [the demonstration assignment], I got good feedback and all ended well, but until reaching that point, there were hesitation and passiveness on my side. There is something more to this, in addition to being busy. I know it's going to be good for me but I don't know why, I sometimes don't feel like doing it.... So, I think when teachers don't want to go to the seminars, that's not only because they are busy. There may also be a feeling like "Again?" (Mr. Toyoda)

Mr. Toyoda's explanation of why some teachers are not willing to participate in seminars may indicate that they are not well designed, or they do not provide an opportunity to learn something useful. At the same time, however, it may suggest that once one has gotten accustomed to team teaching, she or he may reach a plateau, and it is difficult to continue improving and learning. It seems to me that the word "again?" suggests both possibilities.

On the other hand, Mr. Oda, who participated in many seminars and workshops, perceived those occasions as opportunities to learn and experience something beneficial for teaching:

> I went to the regional seminar last year and there were 600 ALTs there. I was grouped with 10 ALTs and we did debate and

> a mock class. Among the things we did, there was one assignment for which we had to create a drama after talking about how to develop a plot for 15 minutes; we had to present the drama in front of all the people there afterward. So we made a plot and acted and got big applause. I was very happy about it and thought, "Well, my students would be happy if they did this." So I did the same thing in my class. (Mr. Oda)

Mr. Oda's comment seems to support the findings of several studies that indicate that depending on the nature and content of off-site workshops, teachers' perceptions of them can be positively changed (Lai, 1993; Ney, 1989; Saraswathi, 1992). According to a survey by Ney (1989), it is shown that the more "active involvement" a workshop or training requires from teachers, the more beneficial the workshop is and the more teachers prefer that type of workshop. Saraswathi (1992) shows a benefit of assigning teachers the role of learners and making them aware of what learners would experience in an inservice workshop. However, workshops, no matter how useful, could influence only those who attend them. Because participation in most of the workshops is voluntary, individual JTEs' motivation and willingness to participate, or lack of them, becomes critical.

In-school seminars and workshops can also be a way to improve teaching skills and communicative English skills. In the case of Tobu High School, however, they were not offered. Difficulty in building consensus among the JTEs who individually differ in terms of age and competence in spoken English seems to be one reason why they did not have departmental workshops. Mr. Obita said, "There are always individual differences among us teachers. You can't say to other teachers something like, 'You have to do this.'"

> I think everybody wants to change individually, but if you really want to change the system, at the grade level, and at the school level, or at the department level, that would require a lot of work.... Also, there are differences in opinions about the use of ALTs and seminars and workshops. (Mr. Oda)

In classrooms and in decision-making, teachers have great autonomy, as Rohlen (1983) describes, but such independence may sometimes cause this type of difficulty in cooperating with others and creating something new.

Dan acknowledged the benefits of having in-school seminars and workshops and tried to initiate them but with no success. He saw this as a limitation to what an ALT can do and that pressing hard on this issue would cross the boundary between the ALT's job and JTE's job:

> ALTs can have seminars and workshops within the school to which he invites the JTEs and that can help improve their English.... I suggested a number of such occasions in my first and second years here. They didn't really receive a very good welcome.... You get the feeling that something like that is not necessarily within the bounds of what they expect me to do.... That kind of professional interaction has not been made an option. (Dan)

This boundary was apparent in the fact that Dan was never invited to the English faculty meeting, although they met every week regularly. Dan also said, "I have little input in JTEs' grading system." Perceiving the ALT as having only a limited responsibility, he felt that this job is not really for professional teachers, especially ESL teachers:

> I probably would not recommend it to a teacher, or at least I would recommend it with reservations to somebody who had a teaching certificate or somebody who had already taught class in America. Because I think those people probably would have the most frustrations when they come here. (Dan)

Limited responsibility or exclusion from the decision-making process would be a great discouragement for the ALTs who can make contributions not only to classroom teaching but also to the improvement of the JTEs' English. Being discouraged, ALTs may become hesitant to initiate something beneficial to the JTEs, and that is an opportunity lost in professional development. In the English department of Tobu High School, although opportunities were there, they were not made a reality.

Interactions With the ALT. One may not need a formal seminar or workshop with the ALT to improve one's own English. Daily interactions with the ALT at school may be sufficient in some cases. These are the occasions in which JTEs can exchange dialogues with the ALT and improve their communicative skills and understanding of English-speaking culture. Individually, JTEs at Tobu tried to take advantage of having a native speaker at school. I observed them having a small chat with Dan or asking him for explanation of some examination questions. There seemed to be a common perception that ALTs are a very valuable resource for them on the individual teacher level.

On a more professional side of the relationship, teachers have much to gain by exchanging ideas among themselves. Unfortunately, Dan felt that, except for Mr. Muto and Mr. Oda, there was lack of dialogue about and joint preparation for classes:

> Part of being prepared for class is knowing what the other person is expecting you to do and doing it, your knowing what they are going to do, and both being perfectly clear about that and being comfortable in discussing it, and their being comfortable in discussing with me, not being afraid to give me suggestions or willing to accept my suggestions. I never felt like [most JTEs] were comfortable for the most part in working through the dialogue like that.... That bothered me a little bit. (Dan)

In exchanging ideas, teachers can foster a personal and possibly a professional relationship among themselves. The more two-way interactions take place, the stronger the professional and personal relationship will be and the better the team teaching will be. There will be not only planned collaborations but also spontaneous interactions in class.

Cruz and Zaragoza (1997) state that effective communication is essential in any collaborative relationship, and it requires frequency and regularity. Successful communication helps to "initiate the expression of respect and trust needed for the development and continued growth of a positive endeavor" (Cruz & Zaragoza, 1997, p. 148). There is a need for the teachers to establish regular meeting times when they can discuss issues and air concerns. This type of effective communication, however, did not seem to exist between the JTEs and the ALT at Tobu. I did not observe any regular meetings or occasions for exchanging dialogues for an extended period of time between Dan and JTEs. That could be due to JTEs' busy schedules, the lack of JTEs' fluency in English, or it could be due to each teacher's (Dan's and JTEs') personalities or characteristics of Japanese teachers in general. As Rohlen (1983) states, the majority of teachers may be "rather private and disinclined to socializing with their colleagues" (p. 176). If this is an attribute of Japanese high school teachers, it is natural that they do not actively seek opportunities to talk to each other much less carry out discussions or exchange opinions on teaching, be it with a Japanese colleague or the ALT. With regard to this, it seemed that one of the official purposes of team teaching, "to enable Japanese foreign language teachers to learn new approaches and gain an understanding of Western ways of thinking" (CLAIR, 1995, p. 11), was not being fulfilled in this high school.

Dual Reality

Since the implementation of OC courses, the long-neglected communicative aspect of English has gained much attention and support in high school English. However, that does not seem to mean that conventional teaching that emphasizes grammar and reading comprehension was abandoned at Tobu High School. Although all JTEs reported that teaching oral communication is necessary and something they would welcome, teaching for universities' entrance exams, which still focus mostly on grammar and reading comprehension, remained important for the JTEs. Mr. Motot said, "We can't do only oral communication. There are reading and writing exams as part of universities' entrance exams, and so, we have to prepare our students for these exams. We can't ignore reality now." It appears that particularly older JTEs accept the notion that both English for exams and communicative English are essential, thus seemingly creating the existence of two Englishes. Nobody expressed his or her preference for one English over the other. As Mr. Muto said, oral communication and exam English "have come to coexist."

The pressure of the universities' entrance examinations is already well known and commonly cited as a detriment to communicative language teaching (CLT) implementation (Gorsuch, 2000; McConnell, 1996). What my interview data show is the comfort level the JTEs, especially the older teachers, had with the two orientations. They did not perceive them as contradictory, as McConnell (1996) and Gorsuch (2000) explain in their studies. On the other hand, the two young teachers, Ms. Kawada and Ms. Kono, talked more strongly and articulately about communicative English, and they were more aware of the dilemma over how to balance the two orientations.

> I think oral communications will be more and more necessary from now on. But because of the current education system in Japan, we have to teach exam English, that is, English geared to exams. Otherwise our students will be left behind. They can't graduate with the learning of oral English only.... I do want to emphasize oral English if the system of university entrance exams can change, but for now, I have no other way but to teach exam English. (Ms. Kawada)

> You can make yourself understood with a few words [not complete sentences]. But even if you can do that, there are exams in the end and you can't ignore them. I feel, "What's the meaning of doing this stuff? We can get by even if we can't answer this type of gram-

> mar question." But there is always a bigger question, "What about the exams? Students have to pass the exams." (Ms. Kono)

Despite the coexistence of two Englishes, the actual emphasis was much more on English for exams than on communicative English in this high school context. Only 1st-year students and a handful of 3rd-year students had OC classes, and even for the 1st-year students, team teaching took place only 1 out of 2 hr designated for OCA. Dan said, "I think to [teach] only the 1st-year students is leaving students with a lot of time not having a chance to learn from the ALT." Most of the students would have only 1 hr a week contact with the ALT during the 3 years.

Then what role was Dan playing in the picture in which there are two orientations of teaching English? The ALTs still could contribute to a change in the JTEs' orientation or increase the JTEs' motivation to integrate CLT into the traditional teaching. Unfortunately, at Tobu, Dan's contribution seems to be kept minimal in this aspect due to his perception of the limitations of the job and also due to Dan's personality, as he stated, "Generally speaking, I am a bit passive toward giving my ideas.... I don't want to sort of push the teachers to do something they aren't comfortable doing in class." There may be also Dan's preference to go along with the existing system:

> [I asked "If there was somebody who has to change, who would it be?"] I would volunteer to change before I ask them to change. Because it's not just worth getting into all the hassles.... I've just been here so long that I find it much easier to go along with the system rather than trying to change it. (Dan)

This expressed difficulty in changing the system could point to a cultural issue. It is often said that Japanese culture places a great emphasis on keeping harmony (Reischauer & Jansen, 1995). If Dan had pushed too hard to change the system, it may have jeopardized the peace maintained in the current system. Dan explained, "[I] toned down my expectations," and he came to feel complacent in the situation.

In summary, although the creation of OC courses has increased the share of communicative English taught in high school English classes, no strong initiatives to challenge the split between the two orientations were taken at Tobu High School.

IMPLICATIONS OF THE STUDY

To make communicative language teaching workable in the EFL context, each country should carefully examine their situations and consider how best this approach serves their needs and interests. Communicative language teaching has to be adapted, not adopted into the particular context (Li, 1998). Team teaching in its current form may be one way of how the Japanese government is attempting to adapt this approach to English teaching in high schools. The process of transforming the teaching of English is still ongoing. In this study, I illustrate how the teachers came to accommodate team teaching and OC courses in the preexisting context of teaching at an academic high school.

At Tobu, there was a general acceptance of and satisfaction with the current form of team teaching and OC courses among the JTEs and the ALT. This seeming success, however, must be taken with caution because it does not assure that communicative language teaching (CLT) is actually taking place in the classroom. As was described earlier, a typical team teaching class at Tobu with its adherence to the textbook and prescribed procedures and interactions does not appear to reflect effective communicative language teaching in practice. There seems to be much room for further improvement to give it the substance to be called successful CLT. Attention should be given to the following areas.

Inservice Professional Development

The JTEs' participation in seminars and workshops for team teaching and/or OC courses should be supported, and I argue that it has to be made mandatory to attend at least one seminar or workshop per year. There are several reasons for this. First, to compensate for the insufficient preservice training (Yonesaka, 1999), inservice professional development should be offered so more JTEs can benefit from it. The JTEs may know what CLT is, but they may not be familiar with the theory and research helpful in adapting this approach to fit their own teaching contexts. Second, after 15 years of the JET Program, there was a general acceptance of the need for CLT among JTEs. I believe that the JTEs are now ready to listen and learn from what seminars and workshops can offer without negative feelings. Last, as described earlier, the mandatory participation in seminars in the past did make a difference to at least some JTEs at Tobu who may have missed the chance had those opportunities been voluntary.

This study shows that utilizing the learning opportunities is a key to changing a JTE's perception and practice. What the seminars and workshops can offer is a chance to get JTEs who may lack motivation or interest to rethink their own teaching and hopefully to change their perception and practice. Even for those who think they are teaching communicatively, inservice professional development can help them reflect their teaching with regards to CLT and its research.

Moreover, the content of these seminars may need to be revised to support the JTEs in a more practical way (Lai, 1993; Ney, 1989; Saraswathi, 1992). They should include how to assist teachers with "revising, refining, or changing their educational theories and attitudes"(Li, 1998, p. 697). Furthermore, the issue of JTEs' language anxiety needs to be addressed. Needless to say, it is essential for JTEs to improve their spoken English. However, there may be inhibition even for a seemingly competent teacher due to fears of making errors and the traditional view of teaching as a transfer of knowledge. As Horwitz (1996) suggests, a unique nature of the process of foreign language learning has to be recognized, and seminars can be a good occasion to educate the JTEs in this regard. Another suggestion is to invite more ALTs to JTEs' seminars and workshops, which can bring forth more positive cross-cultural awareness and build professional relationships among them.

Improvement of the Teaching Environment

There should be continuous support for the JTEs from the Ministry of Education, which translates into support from the rest of the system, that is, the prefectural board of education and the school. Support for the improvements of the JTEs' spoken English and their surrounding environment should remain a priority. Here, the Ministry of Education is moving the system in a favorable direction. For example, teachers can now take a sabbatical for up to 3 years to pursue a graduate degree full-time in Japan or overseas, during which they can improve not only their communicative competence but also pedagogical knowledge. Also, the Ministry announced a strategic plan to improve the English language education throughout the school system in which improving the qualifications of English instructors, promoting a more effective use of ALTs, and improving university examinations are included as central strategies (Ministry of Education, Culture, Sports, Science and Technology, 2002). Also, hiring native speakers as regular faculty is a welcomed plan because this is encouraging to the ALTs who excel in teaching but whose contributions may be kept minimal currently due to their "assistant" status.

It remains to be seen how effectively this plan is implemented in the immediate future; nonetheless, this could have a tremendous potential to change the English teaching in Japanese schools and could be a substantial step toward the realization of CLT in the Japanese context.

CONCLUSION

This study illustrates the complex context in which the JTEs and the ALT in one particular high school have coped with the demand for change in the midst of English education reform in Japan. The picture that this study presents may be partial; however, this study still provides some valuable insights into the process of adapting to changes and the complexity of contextual factors within one high school's English department. It seems that even this single high school cannot be free from the larger contexts of educational reform, university examinations, and teacher training. Further investigation that encompasses both national and school-specific issues is called for to make the two reform initiatives truly substantial and powerful instruments of promoting CLT in English education in Japan.

Despite the small scale and scope of this study, its implications may apply to other EFL contexts. Teachers are central to long-lasting changes (Li, 1998). To advance communicative language teaching in any EFL context, practical and constructive suggestions should be generated to assist teachers along the spectrum of change despite various constraints and factors embedded in the context.

REFERENCES

Ball, D. L. (1990). Reflections and deflections of policy: The case of Carol Turner. *Educational Evaluation and Policy Analysis, 12,* 247–259.

Cohen, D. K. (1990). A revolution in one classroom: The case of Mrs. Oublier. *Educational Evaluation and Policy Analysis, 12,* 311–329.

Council of Local Authorities for International Relations (CLAIR). (1995). *The Japan Exchange and Teaching (JET) Programme 1995: General description.* Tokyo: Author.

Council of Local Authorities for International Relations (CLAIR). (1997). *The JET Programme: Ten years and beyond.* Tokyo: Author.

Cruz, B. C., & Zaragoza, N. (1997). The road to collaborative and integrated education: Success and struggle in a university classroom. *The Teacher Educator, 32*(3), 135–151.

Gorsuch, G. J. (2000). EFL educational policies and educational cultures: Influences on teachers' approval of communicative activities. *TESOL Quarterly, 34,* 675–710.

Grant, S. G., Peterson, P. L., & Shojgreen-Downer, A. (1996). Learning to teach mathematics in the context of systemic reform. *American Educational Research Journal, 33,* 509–541.

Horwitz, E. K. (1996). Even teachers get the blues: Recognizing and alleviating language teachers' feelings of foreign language anxiety. *Foreign Language Annals, 29,* 365–372.

Lai, E. F. K. (1993). *Report of a TEFL workshop in China.* (ERIC Document Reproduction Service No. ED 371 590)

Li, D. (1998). "It's always more difficult than you plan and imagine": Teachers' perceived difficulties in introducing the communicative approach in South Korea. *TESOL Quarterly, 32,* 677–703.

McConnell, D. L. (1996). Education for global integration in Japan: A case study of the JET program. *Human Organization, 55,* 446–457.

McLaughlin, M. W. (1987). Learning from experience: Lessons from policy implementation. *Educational Evaluation and Policy Analysis, 9,* 171–178.

Ministry of Education, Culture, Sports, Science and Technology. (2002, July). *Developing a strategic plan to cultivate "Japanese with English Abilities."* Retrieved August 20, 2002, from http://www.mext.go.jp/english/news/2002/07/020901.htm

Ministry of Education, Science and Culture. (1994). *Handbook for team-teaching.* Tokyo: Monbusho.

Ministry of Education, Science and Culture. (1989). *The course of study for high schools.* Tokyo: Monbusho.

Ministry of Education, Culture, Sports, Science and Technology. (2002, July). *Developing a strategic plan to cultivate "Japanese with English Abilities."* Retrieved August 20, 2002, from http://www.mext.go.jp/english/news/2002/07/020901.htm

Ministry of Foreign Affairs. (n.d.). *About the JET Programme.* Retreived May 3, 2001, from http://www.mofa.go.jp/j_info/visit/jet/outline.html

Moore, G., & Lamie, J. (1996). *Translate or communicate?: English as a foreign language in Japanese high schools.* Commack, NY: Nova Science Publishers.

Ney, J. W. (1989). *Teacher attitudes toward new strategies for educational policy and program development: Illustrations from Togo Training Project.* (ERIC Document Reproduction Service No. ED 307 800)

Reischauer, E. O., & Jansen, M. B. (1995). *The Japanese today: Change and continuity.* Cambridge, MA: Harvard University Press.

Rohlen, T. P. (1983). *Japan's high schools.* Berkeley: University of California Press.

Saraswathi, V. (1992). *Coping with teacher resistance: Insights from INSET.* (ERIC Document Reproduction Service No. ED 369 279)

Seidman, I. E. (1991). *Interviewing as qualitative research: A guide for researchers in education and the social sciences.* New York, NY: Teachers College Press.

Smith, R. C. (1994). Contents and activities in team teaching: Lessons from observation. In M. Wada & A. Cominos (Eds.), *Studies in team teaching* (pp. 72–89). Tokyo: Kenkyusha.

Spradley, J. P. (1980). *Participant observation.* Fort Worth, TX: Harcourt Brace.

Sturman, D. (1992). Team teaching: A case study from Japan. In D. Nunan (Ed.), *Collaborative language learning and teaching* (pp. 141–161). Cambridge, England: Cambridge University Press.

Yonesaka, S. (1999). The pre-service training of Japanese teachers of English. *The Language Teacher, 23*(11), 9–15.

Wiemers, N. J. (1990). Transformation and accommodation: A case study of Joe Scott. *Educational Evaluation and Policy Analysis, 12,* 281–292.

Chapter 8

Toward a Comprehensive Conceptualization of Teaching Assistant Education: Contents, Commitments, Structures

Heidi Byrnes
Georgetown University

INTRODUCTION

This chapter focuses on a small segment of language teacher education, but one that is of great importance for the future of the profession: the preparation of graduate students for teaching within graduate foreign language (FL) departments. In the wake of changing beliefs about language learning and teaching but also as a result of oftentimes dramatically changed conditions for language departments, the preparation of teaching assistants (TAs) has, in the last decade or so, received much attention in publications and conference presentations. Important changes have resulted from these deliberations, not the least of these being a desire to hire into the position of TA coordinator and language program supervisor colleagues whose educational background explicitly prepares them for the extraordinary demands that go with the position. At the same time, recognizing the multiple knowledge bases and competencies that characterize the ideal coordinator can also create a sense of having "solved the problem" of assuring quality teacher education and therefore quality teaching, with few adjustments being required of other faculty members or of the program as a whole.

By comparison, I suggest that the changes required in TA education are so pervasive as to be beyond one person's professional reach. This is so because they must address deep cultural shifts in society, in education as an academic field and as a practice, as well as in FL education. Therefore, it will not suffice to leave untouched the marginal position of TA education within the intellectual-academic work of graduate programs. It is unsatisfactory to retain the structures that have institutionalized that marginalization and even trivialization of language instruction. It is too little to provide occasional relief to those who bear responsibility for preparing the graduate students for productive and successful careers as teacher researchers. It is even too little to acknowledge the value of their work when the stakes in that work are being raised significantly, and the demands of that work are being noticeably reconfigured in the current environment (Guthrie, 2001a; 2001b).

Instead, an appropriate response requires programs to acknowledge that the changed social, cultural, and political contexts outside the walled gardens of the academy can only be adequately addressed with changes in the socialization patterns and cultural contexts that departments create internally as they prepare teachers for those contexts. The goal is to enable the profession to imagine how it might educate its future members, including those entering higher education, to teach in ways that respond to the increasingly diverse institutional and programmatic contexts for increasingly diverse learners and toward increasingly diverse learning goals that characterize the educational landscape. To begin to meet these, we must find ways of linking TA education to the core of the intellectual life of departments and reshaping our practices accordingly. At the same time, we are challenged to understand teaching as the core of the programmatic existence of departments because that is what in the end distinguishes all faculty members from their researching colleagues at, say, humanities research institutes or at research libraries.

Accordingly, I argue in this chapter that the FL profession in general and graduate programs in particular must aggressively pursue a mutually reinforcing twofold strategy: a comprehensive reconceptualization of the preparation of graduate students for teaching that comes to life in and is itself shaped by new practices in their preparation. Although institutional contexts differ, programs tend to share a number of broad characteristics that an unsparing analysis readily identifies as highly detrimental to an appropriate socialization of graduate students into a diverse field. The following are particularly limiting:

1. The preparation of graduate students for future teaching in higher education is usually restricted to language teaching considered as a skill, particularly at the beginning and intermediate levels. It does not explicitly include upper level content courses, much less issues that arise in conjunction with the teaching of literary and cultural studies content and texts to nonnative users of a second language (L2) so that they may simultaneously develop differentiated, perhaps even sophisticated forms of literacy in the L2.
2. It takes place within essentially bifurcated departments, split between a language component that is separated from the intellectual work of the undergraduate content courses and, even more egregiously, from the intellectual-academic pursuits of the graduate program as an educational activity that is dedicated to apprenticing students as researchers in literary-cultural studies.
3. Responsibility for the education of graduate students as teachers typically falls to only one generally overworked faculty member: the TA supervisor or language program director/coordinator, frequently a younger colleague. Due to the recent push toward professionalization, he or she now often possesses the requisite educational background in applied linguistics with an emphasis on L2 teaching and learning, augmented by expertise in supervisory and administrative tasks. Yet, the position itself often remains so conflicted in departmental practice as to limit the extent to which these colleagues can actually bring their knowledge and expertise to bear on the issues. They tend to be excluded from many aspects of departmental life and decision making, they lack security of employment, are thought of primarily as administrators rather than faculty colleagues, and have only limited access to research support and the reward structures of the ordinary faculty. Even when they do hold tenure-track positions, by no means a customary matter, they find it difficult to affect larger programmatic decisions, to help specify suitable broad educational goals and specific pedagogies for an entire undergraduate program in a FL department, and, most important, to put into place those faculty and programmatic practices that socializing graduate students as teacher researchers in these changing times calls for.

4. Finally, further illustrating the isolation of supervisors as well as TA preparation programs taken as a whole, graduate FL departments rarely build up well-considered relations to Schools of Education, the academic unit with natural affinity to the work they must accomplish in the preparation of their students as teachers. In fact, unproductive dichotomies between these two units are often of long standing, part of well-established lore that is all the more resistant to being debunked as it enshrines the dichotomies of teaching versus scholarship or the acquisition of skills, techniques, and methods versus intellectually meritorious work of inquiry and interpretation. The result is continued reductive treatment of TA education.

For these reasons, I pursue in this chapter a line of thinking begun elsewhere that explicitly locates TA education within a department's full range of intellectual work, as that is expressed both in teaching and in scholarship (Byrnes, 2000a, 2001, 2002a, 2002c; Byrnes, Crane, & Sprang, 2002). I explore that possibility in two interwoven strands that broadly organize the chapter. First, reiterating terms that already appeared in the title, issues pertaining to content, to commitment, and to structures serve as broad frames for the intended reconceptualization: "Contents" addresses the need to find an academic focus that is encompassing enough to accommodate teaching and research issues in an inclusive fashion as well as content issues for the resultant TA program itself; "commitments" refers to new roles and responsibilities for all faculty members as they share in the responsibility of educating a department's graduate students as teachers; and "structures" looks at consequences for programmatic and administrative conduct if such an approach were taken. The second strand is a case study that relates experiences with such a reorientation in my home department, the German Department at Georgetown University.

BRIDGING THE GAP IN TA EDUCATION—A CURRICULAR SOLUTION

Beyond specifying the chapter's organization, this twofold approach reflects a deeper concern, namely, the increasingly debilitating avoidance in the FL profession, but particularly in graduate FL programs, of a discussion about the relation between knowledge and first-language (L1) and evolving L2 abilities and, by extension, the nature of L2 learning and teaching. On one hand, both traditional literature and cultural studies departments assert an intimate, even symbiotic relation between knowledge or culture and language and consider that fact to be a key characteristic of the humanities. On the other hand, prevailing practice in program construction and in faculty research and teaching reveals little of that conviction: Knowledge acquisition and language acquisition are essentially kept apart except in the most trivial sense, as is well exemplified by the frequent use of English in undergraduate and graduate courses. The consequences of this conflictedness are particularly debilitating for TA education.

Therefore, to plan and implement changes that reassert and use to advantage the sophisticated relation between knowledge and the L1 and L2 in a FL programmatic context, at least three issues must be confronted. First, we must ask how we can link content or meaning and language form and how we can conceptualize that link so as to result in an extended instructional sequence for adult L2 learners. The second question is, how will the essential qualities of that link come to life in carefully considered pedagogical choices within individual courses and classes so as to facilitate the complex and long-term process of adult literate learners' acquiring a FL to professional levels of performance? Third, and most pertinent to this discussion, what would an integrated approach to helping learners acquire content knowledge as well as upper levels of L2 performance mean for the preparation of TAs as teachers in such a reconceptualized educational environment for the FL profession?

Answers to these questions might be found along the following lines. From the programmatic standpoint, we might begin to imagine graduate students' education for teaching as one component of a twofold responsibility that graduate programs have toward their students: They are to educate them to make valued, long-term contributions to the field in a range of scholarly areas; *and* they are to educate them to make knowledgeable and competent choices in diverse teaching contexts to the benefit of their students as FL and culture learners. From the intellectual standpoint, we could endeavor to expand our horizons regarding education toward teaching by conceptually linking research and teaching through the integrating potential of the FL itself. As stated, language is not an addendum to acquiring other cultural knowledge. It is not a mere instrument, nor is language learning merely the skillful use of that instrument applied to preexisting meanings. Instead, language is itself a construer of knowledge, and learning a language is learning how to mean differently. Finally, from the structural standpoint and in terms of delivery, we should explore the benefits of relocating the responsibility for educating graduate students as teachers from the individual person of the supervisor into the entirety of a graduate FL department and its faculty.

This proposed direction is motivated by the often voiced demand that departments provide both an intellectual and a social foundation for the preparation of graduate students and that they do so in both research and in teaching. Extended opportunities for observation, repeated occasions for mentored action, modeling, apprenticing, reflection in action, and reflection on action are the practices that we know to address both of these needs (for discussion of the last two terms in the decision-making processes of professionals, see Schön, 1983). Graduate programs have always offered such opportunities; but they have offered them almost exclusively on a one-on-one basis and with a focus on research. By contrast, an approach that claims that intellectual practices, whether they pertain to teaching or to research, are socially anchored suggests that the qualities that enable departments to successfully socialize graduate students as future members of the profession derive not so much from well regarded individual faculty scholarship or well regarded individual teaching as they derive from jointly created and jointly pursued programmatic goals, curricular frameworks, and publicly held pedagogical practices. This is so because, as microeducational contexts, departments are defined by the totality of behaviors of a discursive academic community that shares and realizes an educational vision. Indeed, departments taken as a whole constitute the primary functional-structural unit within which the full range of intellectual pursuits associated with FL study, in teaching and research, is located and manifested. As the fields of anthropology and linguistics use that term, one could say departments are an "-emic" unit, that is, a unit within which otherwise disparate "-etic" behaviors are made meaningful in light of the entire faculty's goal of realizing ways of being teacher-researcher educators. Consequently, if graduate students are to experience at some depth and with some awareness the complex work and decision-making processes of college-level FL professionals and to begin to understand some of the educational policy issues that confront the field, they must see how these matters are differentially negotiated and put into practice by each and every faculty member within a functional graduate FL department.

In summary, I advocate that we establish a two-way linkage between teaching and research through creating a comprehensive intellectual-academic center that touches on all practices in research and teaching by all of the department's members, faculty and graduate students. Such a foundation provides a context that hopefully will lead to new practices and new ways of being in a department, in short, a new departmental culture.

In the following, I relate how my home department, the German Department at Georgetown University, obtained such a linkage through a carefully conceptualized, integrated 4-year, content-oriented and task-based curriculum with a literacy focus. As it overcame the traditional split of language and content, an integrated curriculum set in motion a reconsideration of nearly all departmental practices. Most important for this discussion are those practices that pertain to teaching and the relation between teaching and research, all the more so as these, perhaps more than any other departmental work, engaged all members of the department, faculty and graduate students. In the remainder of the chapter, I pursue these issues by concentrating on two areas: (a) the consequences of the curricular reorientation with regard to assumptions about language, language learning, and language teaching and by implication with regard to educating graduate students as teachers in FL departments; and (b) the reconfigured roles of all parties—graduate students, supervisor, and faculty—in this environment and by extension the nature of the socialization of graduate students into academic life and the construction of their identities as scholars and teachers who can be effective in a range of institutional settings.

THE CURRICULUM PROJECT "DEVELOPING MULTIPLE LITERACIES"

The curricular reform project Developing Multiple Literacies[1] that provides the backdrop for my observations has the following characteristics (for a more detailed account, see the department's Web site listed under "Developing Multiple Literacies;" also Byrnes, 2001; Norris, 2004[2]): Spanning all aspects of the department's 4-year undergraduate program and taking a content-oriented and task-based approach in all

[1]The curriculum project, Developing Multiple Literacies, is extensively described on the department's Web site, http://data.georgetown.edu/departments/german/programs/curriculum/ That description includes, among other topics, information about the history and motivation behind the curriculum renewal: administrative and program considerations; goals; syllabi for courses in Levels I through IV; intellectual sources, including bibliographical information; practices for continued curriculum enhancement; considerations regarding pedagogy in a content-oriented environment; an overview of placement testing practices; the department's approach to developing writing ability across the curriculum, including the assessment of writing; agreements regarding assessment in the entire curriculum; various research initiatives undertaken in conjunction with the curriculum; manuscripts from presentations pertaining to the curriculum renewal project; and, most pertinent to this discussion, the document entitled "Developing Graduate Students as Teachers," adopted by the department in final form in October 2002.

[2] Norris' (2004) dissertation fieldwork was conducted, over several semesters, in the revised curricular context of the department. At the time holding the position of a visiting researcher, he provides an outsider's perspective and at the same time a particularly close look at the consequences of such a shift for assessment practices for all participants, including the FL assessment research community, and beyond that for practices of teaching and TA education in FL departments.

courses, it focuses on content from the beginning of the instructional sequence and commits to explicit attention to the acquisition of German until the time of students' graduation. It is divided into five levels, with courses in Levels I through III having to be taken in sequence and Levels IV and V encompassing a variety of courses which, nevertheless, share certain learning goals.

The curriculum is built on the centrality of narrativity and a presumed facilitative relation between diverse genres as reflected in texts and topics and real-world and pedagogical tasks that foster language acquisition by literate adult learners. It uses thematically clustered content areas that are exemplified by a range of textual genres and the actual texts chosen, including literary texts. The curriculum as a whole and each course in turn derives from these texts a variety of carefully sequenced pedagogical foci and forms of instructional intervention.

The close link between genre, theme, text, and task enables different pedagogical opportunities and also requires different pedagogical practices at different instructional levels (cf. Long & Crookes, 1993; Robinson, 2001; Skehan, 1998). These varied pedagogical interventions are chosen from within a developmental trajectory. That means they are intended to enhance learners' continually shifting forms of attentiveness to meaning–form relations, as these characterize different topics, different texts, and different tasks at different stages of language learning (Doughty & Williams, 1998a, 1998b; Long & Robinson, 1998; Mohan, 1986). In particular, pedagogical choices consider task complexity, task difficulty, and task performance conditions as psycholinguistically important notions that affect learner processing, learners' likely performance, and therefore their language development (Skehan, 1998; Yule & Powers, 1994). In this fashion, the curriculum and its pedagogies support efficient and effective interlanguage development toward advanced levels of competence, including the interpretive abilities at the heart of work with literary, other discipline-specific academic, or essayistic texts.

The project required considerable materials development because, with the exception of Level I, no commercially produced textbooks are used. This took place over successive summers as well as during the semester, followed by numerous revisions during the 3-year implementational phase, a process characterized by a strong sense of agency regarding materials and pedagogies that the curriculum renewal had engendered through a heightened awareness of the interrelations between curriculum, materials, and pedagogies. In effect, materials development became an intensive and continuous faculty development effort that incorporated results from teaching experiences, from collegial classroom visits, informal and formal observations, sharing of instructional suggestions and, of course, assessment outcomes, all washed back into the curricular goals themselves.

Naturally, the project also necessitated a thorough rethinking of all assessment practices. In particular, it called for explicitly stated assessment criteria based on the notion of task supplemented by performance indicators as derived from previously stated curricular goals and recommended pedagogical practices. This knowledge base was gained in a needs-derived series of faculty development workshops, in extensive discussion in diverse groupings (e.g., by instructional level, among level coordinators, or by language modality), and, of course, in hands-on work (Byrnes, 2002b; Norris, 2004).

The effort has been highly collaborative, both by necessity and by design, engaging in various ways all 10 tenured or tenure-track faculty and essentially all of the department's graduate students that held teaching assignments over that time. Surprisingly quickly, this intense collaboration brought about a notable change in departmental culture toward a confident and openly shared competence vis-à-vis our program as a whole and vis-à-vis our teaching as a public good. I attribute this change to the redistribution of participant structures and responsibilities both among the faculty and between the faculty and graduate students.

ACCEPTING NEW COMMITMENTS: THE CURRICULAR EMBEDDEDNESS OF FL TEACHING AND FL TEACHER EDUCATION

Although I have thus far emphasized major aspects and consequences of the curriculum renewal itself, I relate them because the integrated content-oriented and task-based nature of the curricular sequence has had a profound effect on graduate students' knowledge and practices as developing teacher researchers. In light of the reluctance in most departments to engage in substantive, cooperative curricular planning, this is both a most encouraging and a thought-provoking development. Specifically, reflecting and projecting the department's shared intellectual work, the curricular framework acquired both high validity and high buy-in, as it rendered irrelevant and dispersed the insidious hierarchizing distinctions that otherwise sustain bifurcated practices and structures. Over time, faculty members and graduate students developed the kind of pedagogical reasoning that Shulman (1987) locates in a cycle involving the activities of comprehension, transformation, instruction, evaluation, and reflection (p. 14). Three aspects stand out:

1. The priority of content instruction through an in-depth exploration of the language of texts in all modalities for the purpose of learning content and language together. That exploration pertained to the texts in a twofold way: first, as genre, understood as a staged, goal-oriented social process, and second, as individual text, understood as situated social action. Pedagogical tasks were created on that basis.

2. A deliberate relating of our pedagogies to best knowledge in the field. Published research and pedagogical recommendations had to be interpreted in light of our educational setting, our teaching situation, and our students' needs and abilities because many research contexts involved rather different presuppositions and goals for language learning, not to mention different learners. Because of these discussions, the department evolved from an initially largely experiential and private knowledge base regarding teaching and learning toward a principled knowledge base that is publicly held and shared within the group (Byrnes et al., 2002; Byrnes & Kord, 2001; Shulman, 1993).

3. A willingness to consider the curriculum project and its attendant pedagogical reorientation an open and social process. The dialogic nature of the process and the communal nature of much of our thinking are unmistakable. Indeed, dialogue shaped all aspects of the curriculum, from its inception, to materials, to pedagogies, to assessments and back into the curriculum.

In that sense, this project exemplifies how a postmethods condition is by no means an "anything goes" environment, even though the terminology of well-defined "skills" or "methods" no longer adequately describes the educational processes (Freeman, 1989, 1991, 1994; Kumaravadivelu, 1994; Larsen-Freeman, 1983, 1990; Pica, 1994, 1995). To some extent even "mentoring," often a paired activity, does not adequately describe the fact that learning now occurs within an academic discourse community whose members have become well accustomed to addressing its educational -intellectual interests and practices in a cooperative and mutually supportive way within a group. For example, faculty and graduate students deliberate the appropriateness of particular pedagogical choices on the basis of an expanding awareness of options and knowledge structures that the project has facilitated (Richards & Lockhart, 1996). In its totality, the impact of this experience might be described as the practitioners' version of what perceptive second language acquisition (SLA) researchers also attempt to capture, namely, context-sensitive information about the nature and processes of instructed FL learning.

In fact, our experience highlights a necessary symbiotic relationship between teachers and researchers: (a) a content-oriented and task-based approach to language teaching depends on well-researched insights into the nature of learner processing at different points of the extended interlanguage continuum to facilitate appropriate educational decisions; and (b) instructed SLA research requires a well considered curricular context to foster sound judgments with regard to the relation of teaching and learning and the relation of language use and language development (Byrnes, 2000b).

Most encouraging, within the enlarged context of the new curriculum graduate students and faculty began to see new relations between the role of literary-cultural content and the acquisition and use of an FL to upper levels of performance, including careful literary analysis as their own research demands it. This is a highly desirable development not only because research and teaching are now seen as being connected through the FL but because it affirms the intellectual merit of our work and, hopefully, enhances its long-term sustainability.

It goes without saying that such interests enable graduate students to consider important issues that pertain to their own identity as future members of the academy: (a) a sophisticated metalinguistic awareness of their L2 use and continued development, a central concern because the profession regularly demands of nonnative students elaborated discursive practices to support both teaching and research, a demand that becomes nearly nonnegotiable at the point of hiring (Byrnes, et al., 2002); (b) an expanding ability to make motivated choices as reflective practitioners in the classes they themselves teach; and (c) an integration of the demands of research and teaching and, by implication, their emerging identities as researchers and as teachers.

Curricular Commitments and Teacher Identity

The following points further highlight how the integrated curriculum facilitated the kind of socialization into a professional community of researchers and teachers that experts have advocated for a number of years (Richards, 1994; Richards & Lockhart, 1996; Tedick & Walker, 1994; Tedick, Walker, Lange, Page, & Jorstad, 1993):

First, the education of graduate students is not about TA training "as a set of behaviors (as if they were manners, and not central), but as a set of *activities, that influence every facet of a future professional's life*" (Arens, 1993, p. 45). Becoming a teacher should instead be regarded and practiced as a process of socialization that depends on a dual conceptual and affective linkage into an evolving identity as researchers and as teachers. Central to that education is the notion of pedagogy as a publicly negotiated and publicly held good.

Second, graduate students must experience as broad an interpretation of the intellectual foundation of FL departments as possible. A literacy approach or, more correctly, a multiple literacies approach, seems to address that need particularly well. By conceptualizing language learning as social semiosis and focusing on the practices that describe both primary and secondary discourses, a well-designed curriculum and its pedagogies offer one of the strongest counterarguments to a reductionist expertise orientation vis-à-vis the work of FL departments and particularly with regard to language teaching.

Third, what graduate students need to acquire then is not so much a way of applying particular skills at a given instructional level as it is a broad understanding of interlanguage development, an awareness that they can translate into attentive choices in their own instruction and that will also aid their understanding of other instructional contexts, including quite explicitly Kindergarten through 12th grade (K–12) instruction. For example, the National Standards in Foreign Language Education project (1996) that has become so influential in precollegiate instruction presumes that teachers have reflected on content-oriented and task-based language learning and teaching in terms of long-term development, curriculum construction, materials development, pedagogy, assessment, and, indeed, in terms of teacher education. Thus, the proposed reorientation into content-oriented programs and instructional approaches is not an abstract and remote issue for graduate programs only. It is, instead, at the heart of the paradigm shift in FL education both in the K–12 environment and at the college level, undergraduate and graduate.

Finally, a curricular context, supported by the engagement of faculty and graduate students, applies many of the tenets that recent scholarship emphasizes for all learning: knowledge construction and situated cognition; the relation of identity to the range of activities that social actors are encouraged to perform and feel able and willing to engage in; scaffolding and mentoring as being conducive to acquiring complex decision-making capacities and abilities, discursive or otherwise; and the development of structured insights. It also applies critical theory to FL departments as peculiar sites of power. By taking up such work, the profession would prepare its graduate students to learn to "read" departments, a prerequisite for substantive contributions to the field in administration, governance, and leadership roles. I suggest that graduate students would greatly benefit from such a departmental Zone of Proximal Development, as it were, an environment that Vygotsky (1978) describes as "*the distance between the actual developmental level as determined by independent problem solving and the level of potential development as determined through problem solving under adult guidance or in collaboration with more capable peers*" (p. 86).

In sum, a comprehensive curriculum that engages faculty at all levels seems a particularly felicitous way for introducing graduate students into the academic discourse community, as reflective teachers (Antonek, McCormick, & Donato, 1997; Freeman, 1992; Freeman & Richards, 1993; Richards & Lockhart, 1996) who find coherent systems for decision making (Kinginger, 1997) and perhaps even as teacher activists (Crookes, 1997b) or as teacher researchers (Crookes, 1997a). For mentoring to be most useful, mentoring activities should address as many aspects of the work of a department as possible at the conceptual and at the practical level and ideally should involve all colleagues. Graduate departments have traditionally and quite competently responded to this need in research. It is now time to expand the purview of mentoring from research to teaching and to expand the responsibility for doing so from one individual faculty member to an entire department.

Evolving Structures for Stability and Growth

Although much of the work in my department continues to evolve and retains a certain fluidity and flexibility, in no small part because of the manageable size of the program, we have also sought stability and the capability of building on successes that comes with putting into place certain structures. The practices and structures that respond to both of these needs are summarized in two document, the first titled "Curriculum Enhancement" and the second titled "Developing Graduate Students as Teachers," and are both available on the Web site. Together, these documents govern the practices, opportunities, and mutual responsibilities of all members of the department in an environment that has created relatively stable curricular, pedagogical, and increasingly, assessment practices but that continually faces the challenge of having to socialize new cohorts of graduate students into an arguably unusual way of conducting both an undergraduate and a graduate program. Anticipated changes notwithstanding, I can also say that these practices, along with their foundational assumptions, have by now been completely "naturalized": We would no longer know how to do the department's work in any other way. Their resulting major provisions as they currently stand conclude this case study (see the departmental web page).

In line with my earlier observations, two features stand out in this approach to the education of graduate students as teachers: the intimate connection between TA education and the comprehensive curriculum and assignment of responsibility for educating graduate students as teachers to the entire faculty. Faculty members serve as Level Coordinators at the instructional Levels I through III, a position that charges them with close supervision of and contact with graduate students teaching at that level and with assuring that curriculum and pedagogies are aligned with stated educational goals. Those responsibilities are carefully planned and coordinated with the Curriculum Coordinator who, together with the department chair, holds administrative responsibility for the program as a whole.

Supporting this change, the department has made the following provisions. From the knowledge standpoint, the graduate program requires a minimum of two courses that address programmatic and pedagogical issues. The first of these courses is currently taken during the 1st semester of graduate study prior to any teaching duties. However, the department is currently considering shifting that course to the spring semester to begin the socialization process for incoming graduate students with extensive observation time in the fall, a practice that would be accompanied by workshop-like periodic meetings and particular observational tasks. The course itself would continue to tie broad information about L2 learning and teaching to our curriculum and its classes and would augment its classroom observations with additional meetings with the respective instructors. In either configuration, the goal is that graduate students should experience, right from the start and extensively, the relation between knowledge and situated pedagogical action within a curriculum by becoming aware of different learner characteristics and needs and also different demands on and different responses by faculty throughout the undergraduate sequence. The course also familiarizes students with key curricular and pedagogical documents that underlie departmental practice and with the resource management of a shared computer drive that contains all relevant curricular and pedagogical materials available to the entire teaching staff.

Connecting knowledge from various fields (e.g., SLA research, education, social psychology) with practical experience continues throughout the program. Depending on resource needs and availability, one option is paired teaching in lower level classes, which pairs a junior and a more senior graduate student with the expectation that they will share teaching responsibilities. Another possibility is mentored teaching that involves extensive observation of an upper level class, particularly Level III courses and above taught primarily by faculty, for which students have few models in their own educational history. The faculty member remains the teacher of record for this class but includes the graduate student in teaching activities as appropriate. Students typically take sole responsibility for a beginning class either during the 2nd semester or no later than the beginning of their 2nd year of graduate study toward the PhD. At that point, they are also encouraged to take the second graduate class that deals with additional teaching and learning issues. Recent topics have been aspects of advanced instructed L2 learning and teaching and curriculum construction and supervision. A jointly taught course on the opportunities for enhancing L2 learning with literary texts and particularly in literature courses is in preparation.

These formal activities and stages are flanked by numerous informal opportunities for developing an identity as a teacher. As they begin teaching, all graduate students are incorporated into diverse procedures related to the multiple observations of their teaching and also the activities planned by the faculty Level Coordinator. In addition, the department sponsors formal all-departmental events that pertain to teaching at the beginning and end of the semester and usually once or twice during the semester. Recently these have pertained to in-depth exploration of the development of writing throughout the curricular sequence (Byrnes, 2002b, and "Developing Writing" on the Web site), beginning discussion of developing and assessing speaking across the curriculum, and the special place of genre in our program.

On the basis of classroom visits with written feedback and the close faculty–graduate student advising relationship, the entire faculty makes recommendations for enhancing graduate students' teaching expertise. Possibilities include (a) assuring that they have the required German language abilities, by no means a minor matter if they are to teach throughout the curriculum and use their language for careful literary-cultural research; (b) giving them the opportunity to repeat courses at the same level to refine both their own teaching as well as the existing materials. In a number of cases such refinement has involved the use of various technologies, including Web-based technology for course delivery. Also (c) advancing them through all the sequenced levels, which not only involves varied teaching but increasing familiarity with diverse approaches to teaching as different faculty members favor them; (d) inviting them to propose a Level V course in their area of interest or specialization, usually as the result of working over an extended time with a faculty member before presenting the proposal for departmental approval; (e) giving them supervisory roles that are tied to aspects of the curriculum and outcomes assessment; (f) engaging them as teacher researchers in well-defined areas; (g) advising them in the creation of a teaching portfolio that is formally presented just prior to their graduation and documents their growth as teachers, including their evolving teaching philosophy.

The department recently completed a 2-year grant from the Spencer Foundation under its "Practitioner Research Communication and Mentoring Grants Program" that enabled graduate students working with faculty mentors inside and outside the department to pursue their own development as teacher researchers in additional dimensions.[3] The three practitioner-research areas that they themselves chose to pursue in depth indicate well the lively interests to linking teaching and research that all graduate TA's share, even as their specific research interests as pursued in dissertation work differ, ranging from literary studies to cultural studies to applied linguistics. Their seriousness and depth of commitment is obvious by the extent to which many of them have repeatedly presented in national fora and even published on these matters (for details, see "Dissemination" on the department's curriculum Web site)

Not surprisingly, given the central role of texts in the curriculum, one group studied genre, particularly from the pedagogical, curricular, and language acquisitional perspective. The group's work has taken on central importance as the department increasingly came to interpret its curriculum and pedagogy in terms of genre (Crane, 2002; Crane, Galvanek, Liamkina, & Ryshina-Pankova, 2002; Crane, Liamkina, & Ryshina-Pankova, 2004). A second group clarified for itself the complex topic of materials development in a content-oriented and task-based curriculum, where innovative work is most in demand at the upper levels of the curriculum.[4] Here the question was, what kinds of course and materials development would best assure that students continue to enhance their language use toward academic and professional level discourse capabilities? That project resulted, among other products, in the development of a Level V course by one graduate student (Rinner, 2002) and extensive application of its insights to a Business German course (Weigert, 2004). Finally, indicating the TA's keen desire to un-

---

[3]For information about all aspects of the Spencer Foundation grant, including yearly reports as well as the final report and the graduate students' write-ups of the focus of their research, project summaries, and their own assessment of participant learning, see http://data.georgetown.edu/departments/german/faculty/byrnesh/grants/index.html (accessed on January 31, 2004).

[4]Broad guidelines for materials development in upper level courses are part of the above-cited Web site.

derstand more completely how they are being prepared for the profession, one group examined the topic of TA socialization and professional development in the Georgetown German Department curriculum (for an example of these reflections, see Sprang, 2002).

Although space does not permit detailed discussion of these projects, one issue has arisen in all three contexts: the graduate students' desire that the kind of attention the program has devoted to linking content and language acquisition in the undergraduate program, particularly to upper levels of language learning, should now be expanded to the graduate program. In other words, the department as a whole is now challenging itself to take another unfamiliar turn on the road toward an encompassing reconceptualization of TA education through assuring that nonnative graduate students' language ability, whether the nonnative language is German or English, is explicitly enhanced in graduate courses.

Having completed the actual curriculum renewal project, we have no doubt that as a departmental unit we have developed a completely different set of praxes than those we held even a few short years ago. As already indicated, there is also no doubt that the department now faces quite different challenges with regard to the education of graduate TAs for teaching. To some extent, these challenges will repeat themselves inasmuch as new cohorts of graduate students have to be socialized into our particular educational environment; on the other hand, they will also change because the learning-by-doing focus of the curriculum implementation phase cannot be replicated for subsequent groups of graduate students, which means that at least the content focus, perhaps also the nature, of that socialization process will also change.

However, not everything is a challenge. We have come to appreciate just how much this work has opened up for us a host of benefits and opportunities, not least because it has been collaborative intellectual work. For example, on that foundation, we can now build focused investigations of our students' evolving multiple literacies both in their native and in the foreign languages (see Byrnes, et al., 2002; Crane et al., 2004). On that foundation too, all of us, faculty and graduate students, hope to continue to grow, a prospect that is both welcome and gratifying as it goes to the heart of the educational work that colleges and universities do. It is our way of practicing what Shulman (2000) calls fidelity—"to the *integrity of the discipline* or field of study; to the *learning of students* one is committed to teach and serve; to the *society, polity, community, and institution* within which one works; and to the teachers' own *identity and sense of self* as scholar, teacher, valued colleague, or friend" (p. 96).

REFERENCES

Antonek, J. L., McCormick, D. E., & Donato, R. (1997). The student teacher portfolio as autobiography: Developing a professional identity. *The Modern Language Journal, 81*, 15–27.

Arens, K. (1993). Applied scholarship in foreign languages. A program of study in professional development. In D. P. Benseler (Ed.), *The dynamics of language program direction* (pp. 33–63). Boston: Heinle & Heinle.

Byrnes, H. (2000a). Languages across the curriculum—intradepartmental curriculum construction: Issues and options. In M. R. Kecht & K. von Hammerstein (Eds.), *Languages across the curriculum: Interdisciplinary structures and internationalized education* (pp. 151–175). Columbus: National East Asian Languages Resource Center, The Ohio State University.

Byrnes, H. (2000b). Meaning and form in classroom-based SLA research: Reflections from a college foreign language perspective. In J. F. Lee & A. Valdman (Eds.), *Meaning and form: Multiple perspectives* (pp. 125–179). Boston: Heinle & Heinle.

Byrnes, H. (2001). Reconceptualizing TA education: It takes a department! *The Modern Language Journal, 85*, 512–530.

Byrnes, H. (2002a). Language and culture: Shall ever the twain meet in foreign language departments? *ADFL Bulletin, 33*, 2, 25–32.

Byrnes, H. (2002b). The role of task and task-based assessment in a content-oriented collegiate foreign language curriculum. *Language Testing 19*, 4, 419–437.

Byrnes, H. (2002c). Toward academic-level foreign language abilities: Reconsidering foundational assumptions, expanding pedagogical options. In B. L. Leaver & B. Shekhtman (Eds.), *Developing professional-level language proficiency* (pp. 35–61). Cambridge: Cambridge University Press.

Byrnes, H., & Kord, S. (2002). Developing literacy and literary competence: Challenges for foreign language departments. In V. Scott & H. Tucker (Eds.), *SLA and the literature classroom: Fostering dialogues* (pp. 31–69). Boston: Heinle & Heinle.

Byrnes, H., Crane, C., & Sprang, K. A. (2002). Non-native teachers teaching at the advanced level: Challenges and opportunities. *ADFL Bulletin, 33*, 3, 25–34.

Crane, C. (2002, November). Genre analysis: A step toward understanding the different stages of advanced language instruction. Paper presented at the ACTFL/AATG conference, Salt Lake City, UT. Accessed at http://data.georgetown.edu/departments/german/programs/curriculum/manuscripts/cranegenre.html on January 31, 2004.

Crane, C., Galvanek, J., Liamkina, O., & Ryshina-Pankova, M. (2002, March). Genre, where art thou? Tracing the role of genre in the foreign language curriculum. Paper presented at the UC Consortium Conference on Language Learning and Teaching, Irvine, CA. Accessed at http://www.georgetown.edu/faculty/byrnesh/grants/genreirvinepaper2002.html on January 31, 2004.

Crane, C., Liamkina, O., & Ryshina-Pankova, M. (2004). Fostering advanced-level language abilities in foreign language graduate programs: Applications of genre theory. In H. Byrnes & H. H. Maxim (Eds.), *Advanced foreign language learning: A challenge to college programs* (pp. 151–177). Boston: Heinle & Heinle.

Crookes, G. (1997a). SLA and language pedagogy: A socioeducational perspective. *Studies in Second Language Acquisition, 19*, 93–116.

Crookes, G. (1997b). What influences what and how second and foreign language teachers teach? *The Modern Language Journal, 81*, 67–79.

Developing multiple literacies: A curriculum renewal project of the German Department at Georgetown University, 1997 - 2000. Accessed at http://data.georgetown.edu/departments/german/programs/curriculum/ on January 31, 2004.

Doughty, C., & Williams, J. (Eds.). (1998a). *Focus on form in classroom second language acquisition.* Cambridge, England: Cambridge University Press.

Doughty, C., & Williams, J. (1998b). Pedagogical choices in focus on form. In C. Doughty & J. Williams (Eds.), *Focus on form in classroom second language acquisition* (pp. 197–261). Cambridge, England: Cambridge University Press.

Freeman, D. (1989). Teacher training, development, and decision making: A model of teaching and related strategies for language teacher education. *TESOL Quarterly, 23*, 27–45.

Freeman, D. (1991). "Mistaken constructs": Re-examining the nature and assumptions of language teacher education. In J. E. Alatis (Ed.), *Linguistics and language pedagogy: The state of the art* (pp. 25–39). Washington, DC: Georgetown University Press.

Freeman, D. (1992). Three views of teachers' knowledge. *Teacher Development, 18*, 1–3.

Freeman, D. (1994). Educational linguistics and the knowledge base of language teaching. In J. E. Alatis (Ed.), *Educational linguistics, crosscultural communication, and global interdependence*, (pp. 180–198). Washington, DC: Georgetown University Press.

Freeman, D., & J. R. Richards (1993). Conceptions of teaching and the education of second language teachers. *TESOL Quarterly, 27*, 193–216.

Guthrie, E. (2001a). New paradigms, old structures: Disciplinary tensions in TA training. In B. Rifkin (Ed.), *Mentoring foreign language TAs, lecturers and adjunct faculty* (pp. 19–39). Boston: Heinle & Heinle.

Guthrie, E. (2001b). The language program director and the curriculum: Setting the stage for effective programs. *ADFL Bulletin 32*, 3, 41–47. (Special issue: Chairing the foreign language and literature department, part 2.)

Kinginger, C. (1997). A discourse approach to the study of language educators' coherence systems. *The Modern Language Journal, 81*, 6–14.

Kumaravadivelu, B. (1994). The postmethod condition: (E)merging strategies for second/foreign language teaching. *TESOL Quarterly, 28*, 27–48.

Larsen-Freeman, D. (1983). Training teachers of educating a teacher. In J. E. Alatis, H. H. Stern, & P. Strevens (Eds.), *Applied linguistics and the preparation of second language teachers: Toward a rationale* (pp. 264–273). Washington, DC: Georgetown University Press.

Larsen-Freeman, D. (1990). On the need for a theory of language teaching. In J. E. Alatis (Ed.), *Linguistics, language teaching and language acquisition. The interdependence of theory, practice and research*(pp. 261–270). Washington, DC: Georgetown University Press.

Long, M. H., & Crookes, G. (1993). Units of analysis in syllabus design: The case for task. In G. Crookes & S. M. Gass (Eds.), *Tasks in a pedagogical context: Integrating theory and practice* (pp. 9–4). Clevedon, England: Multilingual Matters.

Long, M. H., & Robinson, P. (1998). Focus on form: Theory, research, and practice. In C. Doughty & J. Williams (Eds.), *Focus on form in classroom second language acquisition* (pp. 15–41). Cambridge, England: Cambridge University Press.

Mohan, B. A. (1986). *Language and content*. Reading, MA: Addison-Wesley.

National Standards in Foreign Language Education Project (1996). *Standards for foreign language learning: Preparing for the 21st century*. Yonkers, NY: Author.

Norris, J. M. (2004). *Validity evaluation in curriculum-based foreign language assessment*. Unpublished Ph.D. dissertation, The University of Hawai'i at Manoa.

Pica, T. (1994). The language educator at work in the learner-centered classroom: communicate, decision-make, and remember to apply the (educational) linguistics. In J. E. Alatis (Ed.), *Educational linguistics, crosscultural communication, and global interdependence* (pp. 264–288). Washington, DC: Georgetown University Press.

Pica, T. (1995). Teaching language and teaching language learners: Expanding roles and expectations of language teachers in communicative, content-based classrooms. In J. E. Alatis, C. A. Straehle, B. Gallenberger, & M. Ronkin (Eds.), *Linguistics and the education of language teachers: Ethnolinguistic, psycholinguistic, and sociolinguistic aspects* (pp. 378–397). Washington, DC: Georgetown University Press.

Richards, J .C. (1994). The sources of language teachers' instructional decisions. In J. E. Alatis (Ed.), *Educational linguistics, crosscultural communication, and global interdependence* (pp. 384–402). Washington, DC: Georgetown University Press.

Richards, J. C., & Lockhart, C. (1996). *Reflective teaching in second language classrooms*. Cambridge, England: Cambridge University Press.

Rinner, S. (2002, November). Text choice in task development for the differing needs of advanced language learners. Paper presented at the ACTFL/AATG conference, Salt Lake City, UT. Accessed at http://data.georgetown.edu/departments/german/programs/curriculum/manuscripts/rinner_text.html on January 31, 2004.

Robinson, P. (2001). Task complexity, cognitive resources and second language syllabus design: A triadic framework for examining task influences on SLA. In P. Robinson (Ed.), *Cognition and second language instruction* (pp. 287–318). New York: Cambridge University Press.

Schön, D. A. (1983). *The reflective practitioner: How professionals think in action*. New York: Basic Books.

Shulman, L. S. (1987). Knowledge and teaching: Foundations of the new reform. *Harvard Educational Review, 57*, 1–21.

Shulman, L. S. (1993). Teaching as community property. *Change, 25* (6), 6–7.

Shulman, L. S. (2000). Conclusion: Inventing the future. In P. Hutchings (Ed.), *Opening lines. Approaches to the scholarship of teaching and learning* (pp. 95–105). Menlo Park, CA: The Carnegie Foundation for the Advancement of Teaching.

Skehan, P. (1998). *A cognitive approach to language learning*. Oxford, England: Oxford University Press.

Sprang, K. A. (2002, May). *"Awareness" as assessment tool in teacher professional development*. Language symposium, Northwestern University. Evanston, IL. Accessed at http://data.georgetown.edu/departments/german/programs/curriculum/manuscripts/sprang.html on January 31, 2004.

Tedick, D. J., & Walker, C. L. (1994). Second language teacher education: The problems that plague us. *The Modern Language Journal, 78*, 300–312.

Tedick, D. J., Walker, C. L., Lange, D. L., Paige, R. M., & Jorstad, H. L. (1993). Second language education in tomorrow's schools. In G. Guntermann (Ed.), *Developing language teachers for a changing world* (pp. 43–75). Lincolnwood, IL: National Textbook Company.

Vygotsky, L. S. (1978). *Mind in society: The development of higher psychological processes*. Cambridge, MA: Harvard University Press.

Weigert, A. (2004). What's business got to do with it?: The unexplored potential of Business language courses for advanced foreign language learning. In H. Byrnes & H. H. Maxim (Eds.), *Advanced foreign language learning: A challenge to college programs* (pp. 131–150). Boston: Heinle & Heinle.

Yule, G., & Powers, M. (1994). Investigating the communicative outcomes of task-based interaction. *System, 22*, 81–91.

Chapter 9

A Conscious and Deliberate Intervention: The Influence of Language Teacher Education

Leslie Poynor
University of New Mexico

INTRODUCTION

By February of 1992, I had been a kindergarten/first grade teacher for nearly 4 years in rural Alabama, and I had struggled along the way. One day, sitting in front of Earl Niles[1] and 19 other first graders, I realized that my social studies transaction methods class was most likely the turning point in my life, the epiphany that opened my eyes to my real journey, the journey that cannot ignore the social, cultural, linguistic, and economic contexts of teaching and learning in public schools.

February 1992

"Would anyone like to share something about the story?"

[1]All names of students, schools, and districts are pseudonyms. Also, when my descriptions could be interpreted in a less than positive light, I use pseudonyms. In all other cases, with permission, I use real names.

My first graders can't see the deep breath I take as I turn to put the book about Rosa Parks up on the chalk tray. My first graders can't know how risky it is for me to open up this conversation.

Last night, I stayed up late reading and rereading all the books I had on Rosa Parks. Around midnight, I finally narrowed it down to two that I thought my first graders would understand—this one that talks about Rosa Parks, the activist who took a stand by taking a seat, and another that talks about Rosa Parks, the tired, black woman who just wanted to rest her feet. By midnight, I was tired and just wanted to go to sleep, but the decision of what to read was hanging over me. I thought about abandoning both books, but this is National Black History Month, and I teach in rural Alabama where more than 60% of the population is African American. How could I NOT talk about Rosa Parks? The bus boycotts were started less than two hours south of here.

Not for the first time, I cursed my (now) good friend, Barbara Rountree, and her social studies methods class that I took as an undergraduate in the fall of 1987. At midnight, when I was trying to make this decision, it was her face I saw. It was her voice I heard saying

Why is it that history is always presented from the perspective of the White, middle-class male? Why is it that social studies are always about memorizing dates, plotting capitals, regurgitating facts? Can't kids look that stuff up in a book? When do we teach kids to think, to question, to reflect, to analyze, to dissect? When do we engage in conversations with kids about what they know instead of what they don't know?

I had taken Barbara's words to heart. Since I began teaching in the fall of 1988, all teaching, not just social studies, became for me an opportunity to engage in conversations with children. Every story became an invitation for children to share their thoughts. Over the past 4 years, my role became less the asker of questions and evaluator of answers and more the facilitator of discussions and encourager of risk taking. Teaching and learning became transactions between the kids, the stories, and me. It was a philosophy that started in Barbara's class, one that I built upon my 1st year of teaching and one that continues now in my 4th year. And it is not one that I can simply abandon when the conversation gets controversial. I'm not even sure I would know how to go back to the old days when I was in school, the days of teacher questions and student answers. I could read about Rosa Parks, the tired woman who just wanted a seat, or I could read one of the many benign stories about Martin Luther King, Jr., being a great speaker and leader. Or I could just skip it altogether. It's not likely that any of the mostly White teachers in my school would notice. And it's not likely that any of my stu-

dents' parents would question it, since the kids are only in first grade. But I would know. And what could I say to Barbara?

At 1:15, I finally decided on Rosa the activist, let the chips fall where the may. But now, at 9:15 in the classroom, I wonder if Barbara knows how risky it is to raise social and political issues in a classroom where I have established a pattern of discussion, reflection, questioning, and sometimes acting upon the outcomes. Just last week, I had to change the bathroom policy because the kids pointed out that it wasn't fair that I could go whenever I wanted, but they had to ask my permission. It's crazy to think that in a classroom that promotes reflecting, questioning, and acting, kids are suddenly just going to be quiet when the topic turns political. Out of the corner of my eye, I can see Earl Niles, an African American student looking at me with his eyebrows knitted together. I turn in my chair so that I am facing him.

"Miss Leslie, why did they make that Black lady get out her seat?"

Keeping my voice deliberately neutral, I answer, "Well, it used to be that everything for Black people and White people was separate." I say this as if all has changed by 1992. "There were schools for Black children and schools for White children." As if all schools are now equally integrated. As if there isn't gross inequity in funding for schools for mostly White kids and schools for mostly Black kids. "There were water fountains for Black people and water fountains for White people." As if those water fountains were exactly the same in location and quality. As if they weren't incredibly unequal. "And on buses, there was a place for Black people in the back and a place for White people in the front."

There it is: Black people in the back and White people in the front. No amount of neutrality can cover up the inequity here. I am on dangerous ground. I can just see some of my White parents storming up here demanding to know why I'm bringing up all that stuff that ain't got nothing to do with them or their kids. They weren't in Montgomery when all that stuff happened. They ain't got nothing against Black folks, long as they keep to themselves. They ain't prejudiced or nothing; they just think that God didn't intend for White folks and Black folks to mix. That's all.

Earl stares at me, his already wrinkled forehead wrinkles some more and his eyes flash, "Miss Leslie, that ain't fair!"

Good lord, what have I gotten myself into? How did I end up here? I wanted to be an early childhood teacher because I wanted to make a difference in the world. Before I took Barbara's class, I had it all figured out. I was going to be a kind, fun-loving teacher who taught kindergarten or maybe first grade. My kids were going to love school. And after me, no matter what, they would stay in school. They would graduate. Maybe they'd go on to college, but for sure they'd get a decent job. I had a notebook full of ideas of how to make learning fun. Kids could paint their spelling words instead of writing them five times each. How boring. We'd do all the science experiments in the book instead of just one or two. I'd let the kids take their tests over and over again until they passed it so everybody could get an A. Kids would leave my classroom with their self-esteem intact and with a love of school. But then, the semester before my student teaching, Barbara turned all that upside down.

And now I find myself sitting before a 7-year-old who can see through my forced neutrality in part because I have encouraged him to look beneath the surface, to question what is really there.

Is that what Barbara did for me? Did she encourage me to look beneath the surface of traditional teaching, to question what teaching is really about? Could it be that unlike most of my teacher education classes, Barbara's class made a difference in how I thought about teaching and learning? And am I the only one? Is there anybody else who has ended up here? Sitting in front of a 7-year-old who is raising issues of political and social inequity? I look at Earl. I could diffuse this situation by downplaying the inequity—well, people didn't know back then, but now it's different, now it's fair. But it's not fair. There is huge disparity between the life chances of African American children in Alabama and White children in Alabama. If Barbara opened my eyes in her course, then I have chosen to keep them open in my classroom. Without blinking, I look at Earl.

"No, Earl. No it isn't fair."

My experience with Earl Niles was the first time that I had a meta-awareness of the connection between the transaction teaching practices learned with Barbara Rountree and the application of those practices in the context of my own classroom. It was the first time that I began to think about what being a transaction teacher with real children, particularly culturally, linguistically, and economically marginalized children, really means.

Transactional teaching practices are tied to very specific beliefs about the purpose and nature of schooling, beliefs drawn from Rosenblatt's (1978) reader response theory that "asserts that meaning lies not only in the text, nor only in the reader's mind, but in the transactions between the reader's background knowledge and the information provided by the text" (El-Dinary & Schuder, 1993, pp. 1–2). Transactional teaching practices (a) accept all social, cultural, and linguistic background knowledge and experience as valuable; (b) include those experiences in the explicit curriculum; and (c) regard all children, including culturally, linguistically, and economically marginalized children, as capable and developing human beings (Poynor, 2001, pp. 156–157 paraphrased).

In contrast, traditional teaching practices are also tied to very specific beliefs about the purpose and nature of schooling, which Apple (1990) describes in the following manner:

> [Traditional] schools partly recreate the social and economic hierarchies of the larger society through what is seemingly a neutral process of selection and instruction. They take the cultural capital, the habitus, of the middle class, as natural and employ it as if all children have had equal access to it. However, "by taking all children as equal," while implicitly favoring those who have already acquired the linguistic and social competencies to handle middle-class culture, schools take as natural what is essentially a social gift, i.e., cultural capital. (p. 33)

Culturally, linguistically, and economically marginalized students do have rich and varied cultural backgrounds, but as Apple (1990) points out, they often do not possess the cultural capital that is typically valued by traditional teaching practices. Hence, these practices have been exceedingly damaging to language minority students because they presuppose a particular type of background knowledge and experience. On the other hand, transactional teaching practices can offer language minority students a level playing field simply because the background knowledge and experience of the child is an integral and explicit part of the curriculum without regard to what that knowledge and experience is.

My experiences in Barbara's transaction teacher education class had influenced me in becoming a transaction teacher but had done very little to prepare me for what that would mean in practice—especially my practice in the 1st year of teaching and especially my practice with language minority students. Thus, the meta-awareness that began in 1992 became a nagging question: How can an undergraduate methods course prepare preservice ESL and Bilingual[2] teachers to be transaction teachers in the real world? This was a question that eventually led me to Carmen and Paul and this study.

---

[2]I am capitalizing the word *Bilingual* when referring to Bilingual education and/or a Bilingual teacher who uses Bilingual methods and materials in the education of children who are learning two languages to distinguish it from the word *bilingual* that refers to proficiency in two languages.

PURPOSE OF THE STUDY

This study is part of a larger study in which I followed two ESL preservice teachers and one Bilingual preservice teacher through their language arts and reading methods course. I then continued to follow one of the ESL preservice teachers and the Bilingual preservice teacher through student teaching and the 1st year of teaching. In this chapter, I briefly address all three segments of data collection (i.e., the methods course, student teaching, and 1st year of teaching) but concentrate primarily on the data analysis of the 1st year of teaching. The purpose of this chapter is to examine (a) the influence, if any, that an ESL/Bilingual transaction reading and language arts methods course has on preservice teachers when they become 1st year teachers, and (b) how such influence withstands the pressure inherent in the context of traditional schooling.

REVIEW OF THE LITERATURE

Trying to understand how an undergraduate methods course prepares preservice teachers from a primarily traditional transmission educational background to be progressive transaction teachers is a huge undertaking. Many people have done it before me. Darling-Hammond, Wise, and Klein (1995) wrote that preservice teachers who have traditional kinds of teacher training are consistently better prepared than those who enter education via alternative routes. Preservice teachers who participate in more progressive teacher education programs are better prepared than both. Mary Kennedy (1998) supported these assumptions in her study of teacher education and the process of becoming writing teachers. Kennedy (1998) found that teachers who were involved in reform-oriented teacher education programs on writing tended to move away from traditional prescriptive writing concerns and toward concerns about student strategies and purposes, whereas teachers enrolled in more traditional management-oriented programs remained concerned about the traditional prescriptions of writing. These researchers and others (Darling-Hammond et al., 1995; Kennedy, 1998; Richardson & Kile, 1992; Tatto, 1998) have argued that teacher education programs with a jointly defined philosophy, reform-oriented curriculum, and an emphasis on nontraditional pedagogy are likely to have an impact on how preservice teachers teach. Still others (Hollingsworth, 1989; Johnson, 1994) have argued that teachers' traditional understandings and beliefs can change when they confront their own past experiences and current beliefs and when they become cognizant of the contradictions between what they themselves experienced and what they want their students to experience. Johnson (1994) in particular concluded that preservice teachers' beliefs can shift as long as they have an alternative to switch to. Cochran-Smith (1991) concurred, writing that a progressive teacher education program can educate teachers to be both educators and activists, to teach against the traditional grain.

Lortie (1975), however, argued that the lifetime apprenticeship of students to teachers is more powerful than any teacher education program. In other words, teachers will teach the way they were taught. Lortie is not the only one who has argued this. Several researchers (Cortazzi, 1993; Hanson & Herrington, 1976; Kagan, 1992; Kennedy, 1991; Lortie, 1975; McDiarmid, 1990; Petty & Hogben, 1980; Zeichner, Melnick, & Gomez, 1996) have offered empirical evidence that teacher education programs do little to change the lessons learned during a childhood apprenticeship. Some (Britzman, 1991) have taken it a step further and argued that it is the context of schools both prior and present that are more likely to influence teachers rather than teacher education courses. Still others (Berliner, 1990; Freeman & Johnson, 1998; Genburg, 1992) have argued that teacher understandings of how to teach do not develop in teacher education programs but rather as a part of the long-term process of becoming teachers throughout their careers. The ones who have described teacher education programs as having some minimal influence (Maxson & Sindelar, 1998; Zeichner, 1996) have argued that there is still a great need for research on the long-term impact of that intervention on how preservice teachers develop and change.

THE RESEARCH QUESTION

However, if teachers teach the way they were taught, then how could we ever have any teachers who teach "against the traditional grain?" Barone (1987) argued that progressive teacher education can make a difference if the students entering the profession are already predisposed to the ideas espoused in the teacher education program. In other words, the preservice teachers have to be aware of the failings of traditional transmission education and be seeking an alternative model. For Barone, the problem is in recruitment. Recruiting preservice teachers with a predisposition for an alternative to traditional teaching is an ideal long-term goal, but it does nothing for the short-term problem of reaching the pool of preservice teachers we currently have.

Having read the applications of students seeking admission into the ESL/Bilingual Initial Teacher Certification program at Arizona State University for several semesters and having taught these same students for several semesters, it has been my experience that these students are here because they want to make a difference. Many have had bad experiences with public education and want to keep other youngsters from going through what they went through. A few had such great experiences that they want to duplicate them for others. However, if they enter with an awareness of the failings of traditional transmission education, are they seeking a true alternative or simply a kinder, gentler method of transmitting knowledge (Edelsky, Altwerger, & Flores, 1991)? If they are seeking a true alternative, how is it that they move from their traditional educational backgrounds toward a more progressive perspective? My nagging question from 1992 turned into research questions: How is it that ESL and Bilingual preservice teachers from traditional transmission educational experiences move toward becoming transaction teachers of language minority students? Or do they? And how could I find out?

BACKGROUND OF THE STUDY

The ESL/Bilingual reading and language arts methods courses in which this study is grounded had for years been nontraditional in that the methods were theoretically grounded in sociopsycholinguistic research and transaction pedagogy. Further, there was a strong emphasis on multicultural children's literature that raised issues about and offered challenges to the status quo—challenging stereotypes (Paulsen, 1993), offering alternative understandings of history (Yolen, 1992), and utilizing dialects or languages other than English (Flor Ada, 1997). The courses were taught in conjunction with one another and included (a) literature study groups, writing workshops, theme cycles, and small-group discussions; and (b) readings and discussions in which the status quo of traditional transmission education was called into question.

The Participants

I met Carmen and Paul in the Fall of 1998 when they were in exactly the same place as I was when I entered Barbara's class in 1987. That is, I met them as preservice teachers in the ESL/Bilingual reading and language arts methods class the semester prior to their student teaching.

I chose Carmen from my cohort group because she is a Mexican American who does not speak Spanish and is therefore seeking an ESL endorsement. I thought that her particular ethnic and cultural background might have a strong impact on how she approached literacy/biliteracy, and I was curious as to whether our class would have any impact on that.

I chose Paul from the Bilingual cohort group because he is a bilingual Mexican American. I was also interested in Paul because he seemed willing to question what was going on in class. In addition, Paul was male and a bit older (40 as opposed to early or mid-20s) than most of the students in the class.

Data Collection

During the methods course, I took field notes of class interactions with Carmen and Paul. I kept copies of their written weekly reflections and assignments and I audiotaped and transcribed an hour and a half interview with each of them. During their student teaching semester and their 1st year of teaching, I observed and recorded notes on class events and interactions between Carmen and Paul and their students. Following each observation, I met briefly (between 10 and 25 min, depending on the demands of the classroom) with Carmen and Paul to conduct a follow-up interview in which I asked them to describe what had happened in the classroom, why they thought it had happened, how they felt about it, how it related to what we had discussed in the methods course, and whether or not it was a practice that they would continue in their own classrooms. I expanded the field notes immediately following the observations and transcribed the interview tapes during and after the data collection period.

Data Analysis

By the end of data collection in the methods course, the student teaching, and the 1st year of teaching, I transcribed more than 40 hr of taped interviews. As I transcribed, I wrote memos to myself about patterns, trends, incidents, and stories that captured my attention and imagination. I used all of the evidence to reconstruct a narrative account of Carmen and Paul as complex individuals involved in the multilayered process of becoming a transaction teacher.

The Written Report

I wrote the narrative so that the emerging plot remained consistent with Carmen and Paul's stories as I understood them. In looking for consistency, I was not looking for a literal account of history, but rather, I was looking for the fiction that would be a faithful representation of the two participants' lives as they saw them (Polkinghorne, 1995). After I had written what I considered to be a faithful representation of this slice of their life, I offered the story to both to read. I asked each of them to read the story with the concept of fidelity in mind. Had I represented them in a faithful way? It is important to note that I was not seeking verification of the facts or incidents but rather a verification of the essence of their experiences. I was not trying to represent what O'Brien calls the "happening-truth" but rather the "story-truth." The distinction between happening-truth and story-truth that O'Brien, Vietnam veteran and author of *The Things They Carried* (1990), made is, I believe, a useful one in understanding narrative constructions:

> I want you to know why story-truth is truer sometimes than happening-truth.
>
> Here is the happening-truth. I was once a soldier. There were many bodies, real bodies with real faces, but I was young then and I was afraid to look. And now, twenty years later, I'm left with faceless responsibility and faceless grief.
>
> Here is the story-truth. He was a slim, dead, almost dainty young man of about twenty. He lay in the center of a red clay trail near the village of My Khe. His jaw was in his throat. His one eye was shut, the other eye was a star shaped hole. I killed him.
>
> What stories can do, I guess, is make things present. (pp. 179–180)

In asking Carmen and Paul to read, edit, and approve their stories, I was seeking to make their lives present. I was attempting to ensure that the story-truth of my construction represented the essence of their lives as ESL/Bilingual preservice teachers as they understood them. They returned their stories to me with requests for changes, deletions, and additions. I revised the stories according to their comments and once again returned the story to each of them for their approval. Once we were assured that the story met our requirements for fidelity, revision on the story stopped. This to-and-fro movement that I used to make sense of the data and construct the story-truth is best described by Polkinghorne (1995):

> [Narrative analysis] requires testing the beginning attempts at emplotment with the database. If major events or actions described in the data conflict with or contradict the emerging plot idea, the idea needs to be adapted to better fit or make sense of

> the elements and their relationships.... The creation of a text involves the to-and-fro movement from parts to whole that is involved in comprehending a finished text. (p. 16)

It is important to note that although I was the primary writer, Carmen and Paul had complete control over the editing and revising of their story, and in this way, I attempted to avoid the silencing of their voices. Further, I must note that it is beyond the scope of this chapter to present the entire text of the narratives. Rather, what follows are the themes from the narratives constructed for each segment of data collection (the methods course, student teaching, and 1st year of teaching) with illustrative excerpts from the original narratives.

THE FINDINGS

In constructing the narratives, I discovered what Linda Christensen (2000) calls the collective text.[3] In Christensen's high-school writing classes, she and the students (and sometimes her U.S. History co-teacher, Bill Bigelow) participate in what she calls a "read-around"; "The students, Bill and I [sit] in a circle and read our papers. As we read our stories we [take] notes on the common themes that emerged from our pieces" (Christensen, 2000, p. 60). The read-around produces the collective text, which is comprised of stories from one or two adults and 30 or so students.

This study contains not only the stories of Carmen and Paul and their first year of teaching but my own 1st year teaching story as well. The text offered here joins the voices of three 1st-year teachers separated by time, space, age, gender, ethnicity, dialect/language, and culture. Yet, despite such separateness, we still have common themes—a strong collective text. The telling of our stories offered us and I hope the reader the opportunity to step back "and figure out what our individual stories [say] about ourselves and our society" (Christensen, 2000, p. 16) and about the process of becoming (or not) a transaction teacher of language minority students. Christensen (2000) adds, "In the read-around kids understand they aren't alone, but they also learn to ask why they had these similar experiences" (p.

[3]I am using the term *text* in the same manner that Lidchi (1997) uses it to refer "not only to the written word, but fabrics of knowledge that can be used as reference, including oral texts, social texts, and academic texts. These perform the same function—they facilitate interpretation" (p. 166).

60). In the sharing of our stories, Carmen, Paul, and I have learned that we are not alone, but, more important, we began to ask why we had these similar experiences. This study as well as the larger study offers a challenge to the traditional systems of power that govern schools and determine our experiences.

The First Collective Text

When I first met Carmen and Paul and the 39 other ESL/Bilingual reading and language arts methods students, I had hoped that our methods course would influence them to become transaction teachers with an understanding of pedagogical strategies that support language minority students. Throughout our methods course, I had reason to believe that my hopes would be realized. I watched Carmen and Paul's ideas, intentions, and awareness come to reflect those theoretical, pedagogical, and political understandings that formed the foundation of our course. They had a commitment to transaction teaching and a burgeoning political awareness of ESL/Bilingual education that had not been evident when they entered the course. However, Carmen and Paul were worried about, confused about, their ability to put that theory and pedagogy into practice. Their changing ideas and worries resonated with me. I remembered those same feelings in Barbara Rountree's class. "Yes, Yes, this makes sense. But what does it look like? How do I do it?"

The Second Collective Text

The second collective text was that of student teaching. As I reflected with Carmen and Paul about their student teaching, I also reflected on my own student teaching experience. My student teaching was divided in half—half in kindergarten, half in third grade, which mirrored Carmen's experience in a dual language kindergarten and Paul's in a bilingual third-grade classroom. Carmen and I both learned how to set up and manage centers and multiple activities that had the appearance of transactional practices, but the underlying theory in both of our kindergarten student teaching experiences was still that of transmission. Paul and I did not learn how to manage multiple activities, organize centers, or provide choice to the children in our third grade student teaching experience, but we were (as Carmen had also been) invited into the community of teaching. Our cooperating teachers treated us as equals and encouraged us to try out our new understandings. Although we had come to endorse transaction pedagogy in our methods courses, we had little understanding of that pedagogy in practice. Furthermore, in our student teaching, over which we had no control, we did not see a commitment to that theory or pedagogy in practice (Edelsky, 1993). Thus, our ability to enact our theory remained virtually unchanged and our commitment to transaction teaching was left in a very tenuous position.

The Third Collective Text

The third collective text is that of our 1st year of teaching. The overarching theme of our collective text was the difficulty of being transaction teachers of language minority students in a traditional (White, middle-class) transmission world, supported by three subthemes: (a) the tyranny of efficiency and the pressure to conform, (b) the need for agency and experience to be transaction teachers, and (c) the pain and isolation of transaction teaching. For each theme, I offer excerpts from our narratives and a brief summary. The first narrative relates to the theme of the tyranny of efficiency and the pressure to conform. It is an excerpt from my own narrative about my 1st year of teaching.

> *The tyranny of efficiency and the pressure to conform.*
>
> *"I'm supposed to do it!" Vanessa shouts.*
>
> *I turn to look. Janey is holding her hand with tears running down her face. I go over and snap off the tape.*
>
> *"What happened?" I demand.*
>
> *"She was trying to turn the page, and you told me to do it!" answers Vanessa.*
>
> *I look at Janey, "What happened?"*
>
> *"She wasn't turning the page even though the bell rang, and so I was trying to turn it and she slapped my hand."*
>
> *"Vanessa! That's it!" I raise my voice for the second time in less than an hour. I grab her by the arm and say right in her face, "You may not slap people. If you do that one more time, I am going to have to paddle you. Now go sit in the circle by yourself!"*
>
> *I lead her to the circle and then I sit back down with my group. Good lord! What have I done? A paddling? I don't believe in paddling. My own parents didn't even spank me. But all the other teachers here paddle. If I've heard it once, I've heard it a thousand times. "You better get control of them early. If you paddle one, then they'll know you aren't going to put up with their foolishness."*
>
> *And when I have been talking to the kindergarten and 1st grade teachers about Vanessa, they've all said the same thing. "Leslie, you are just going to have to give in and paddle her. You might as well do it now, because when*

she gets in first grade we aren't going to put up with her acting like that. You've got more patience than I do, because I'd tear that tail up if she acted like that in my classroom. The longer you let it go, the worse it is going to get. Just go on and do it."

I sigh. I hope I don't have to find out if they're right.

Like me, Carmen and Paul felt the pressure to be successful and get things done. It is much more efficient to paddle a child or send a child out of the room than to spend the necessary time in facilitating transactions to create a class community in which the children's background knowledge and experience is central. The pressure we felt to keep moving, keep covering material, keep being efficient worked against our beliefs that all children have cultural and linguistic strengths, that all children are developing and capable human beings, and that the cultural context of the classroom should represent and support children and their strengths. In short, the tyranny of efficiency and the pressure to conform left us with few opportunities to be transaction teachers. To capitalize on those opportunities that we did have, we needed experience with explicit transaction practices, but we also needed a safe space (Weis & Fine, 2000) to exercise agency in being transaction teachers: And we needed courage. In Paul's case, that meant freedom from his mentor teacher's watchful eyes. When his mentor teacher was present, Paul felt compelled to follow the curriculum as she dictated it. This next excerpt from Paul's 1st year of teaching illustrates how her absence gave him the space to exercise agency, the power to act on his intentions.

The agency and experience to be transaction teachers.

> *Paul shuts the door and sinks into his chair. The past 2 weeks have been hell. Mrs. White has been absent for 10 days. And in all the days she's been absent they have only been able to get a sub twice. It has been pandemonium. They just consistently rotate aides.*

"And it disrupts this class too," thinks Paul.

> *We can't switch. My kids are consistently missing out on math and her kids are missing out on science and social studies. But the hardest thing is that the aides are constanly coming to me and saying Mr. Mendoza you need to go in there because they have nothing to do.*

Paul sighs. It's been hectic. Paul picks up a stack of reports on African American leaders and smiles.

> *But the one thing I'm really happy about is that I got them writing. I got them writing on African American leaders! And they all did a really good job, thinks Paul as he flips through the finished reports. So it wasn't a*

waste to spend the whole day on this. But it's hard to break away from just doing what's in the textbook. I just had to say to myself NO! NO! I'm going to spend as much time as I want to, as much time as I can. Besides if Mrs. White can waste 10 days being absent, then I can waste a day or two!

To be transaction teachers, we needed experience with explicit transaction practices such as those of facilitating independent writing projects on African Americans, but we also needed space such as the space that Mrs. White's absence opened up for Paul. It was space that we often did not have. Thus, we were left with the tension and contradiction between what we knew to be good teaching for language minority children—the theory learned in our methods courses—and what we were actually doing (practice). Yet, despite our positions of powerlessness, like Paul, we each found some small space, perhaps by the very absence of an overbearing colleague or through the superficial, albeit positive administrative support through which we could exercise agency to be transaction teachers. Although small, these openings did give us the courage, if not the experience, to implement transaction practices—practices that made the cultural and linguistics strengths of the students an integral part of the curriculum, practices that challenged traditional literacy instruction. However, our sense of agency did not prepare us for the pain and isolation that occurs for those who make any small attempt to change the status quo. The next story is from Carmen's 1st year of teaching during which she made great strides as a transaction teacher—strides that carried her away from the traditional practices of her dual language partner teacher and third-grade teammates.

The pain and isolation of transaction teaching.

"Come in Carmen, Alma and I want to talk to you," Sharon says as she pulls up an extra chair for Carmen. "You know that Alma and I have a very good relationship," she continues, "We've just developed a very strong friendship. And we're really interested in working together."

Carmen nods, working hard to keep her face blank but interested. What does this mean? Where is this going?

"So, we went to talk to Dr. Turner and told her that we wanted to team together next year."

"Oh, OK." Carmen opens her eyes wide to stop the tears from coming. She forces herself to ignore the knot in her stomach and the lump in her throat. She woodenly moves her head up and down like she understands, but she's shocked. Alma is her partner, her teammate.

Alma jumps in, "It probably will not even work out. Dr. Turner said that it was nice to know but that she can't guarantee anything."

Carmen blinks and nods, "Well thank you for being so honest and up front with me. I really appreciate that. I can tell why you guys want to team; you have a really great friendship."

Sharon leans forward and touches Carmen's knee, "You know, it's not anything personal. And it certainly doesn't mean that you aren't welcome to plan with us any time."

Alma nods, "No, no of course not. We still want to plan with you."

Carmen swallows the lump in her throat again and says, "Well thank you. That's good to know. And I really want to thank you both for the past couple of weeks. I have been really stressed out and I know I haven't been staying the long hours and planning with you like I used to. Thank you for helping me so much."

Carmen takes a quick breath and continues. She just can't seem to stop herself from rambling on. When she finishes, Alma begins to talk about next week. Carmen nods and tries to concentrate on what Alma is saying, but mostly she just keeps telling herself not to cry. "Don't cry. Don't cry." Finally, Alma finishes. Carmen chit chats with the two of them for a few more minutes before she can finally leave. "Just keep it together until you get to the car. Just keep it together until you get to the car."

When I struggled painfully with the paddling issue (I did end up paddling, to my dismay and humiliation then as now), there was no one to whom I could turn because paddling was the culture of the school. When Paul felt the frustration of an overbearing mentor and partner teacher, there was no one to whom he could turn because of the importance of seniority and hierarchy in the culture of his school. Nor was there anyone to whom Carmen could turn when she felt the pain of rejection by her partner teacher in their dual language team. In all cases, the traditional systems of power worked first to conform us and second to isolate us.

IMPLICATIONS

The choices that we as 1st-year teachers of language minority students made were influenced by our cultural and historical contexts, which included our preservice transaction methods courses. As both student teachers and first-year teachers, the questions we asked ourselves and the awareness we had of transaction teaching practices were a result of our methods experience. However, because we were not the sole owners of our choices but rather co-owners (Shannon, 1995) with our cultural and historical contexts, we found our choices in competition with, in contradiction to, and, more times than we liked, in reluctant compliance with the traditional systems of power that govern the culture of schools and education.

For Carmen and Paul, the ESL/Bilingual transaction methods experience significantly altered their understandings of teaching and learning with language minority students and ultimately did have an influence on their teaching practices; however, I suggest that the influence could have been more profound had they participated in building a collective text about teaching and learning with language minority students.

If, as methods students, Carmen and Paul had the opportunity to create with me their own collective text about their educational experiences, together we could have exposed the tyranny of efficiency and other traditional systems of power that govern schools, particularly inner-city schools for culturally, linguistically, and economically marginalized children. Language teacher education grounded in transaction theory and pedagogy can influence preservice teachers, but it is through the collective text that preservice teachers will come to understand the knowledge, experience, agency, and courage necessary to be transaction teachers of language minority students. It is through the collective text that they will have the opportunity to understand the traditional systems of power that perpetuate the tyranny of efficiency that is so damaging to language minority students. If more 1st-year transaction teachers of language minority students had the opportunity to share their honest and critical stories before us, perhaps through the reading of their collective text we would have been better prepared for the potential pain and isolation of transaction teaching with language minority students, and we would have learned more of the tools necessary to be transaction teachers ourselves.

As methods students preparing to teach language minority students, we needed a place to share our stories and to figure out what our collective text said about teaching and education. We needed a place where we could read the collective text of those methods students and 1st year teachers before us. We needed a place where we understood that we were not alone and we could question why we had these similar experiences. We still need that place in language teacher education. We need it for our preservice teachers of language minority students. We need it for our 1st-year teachers of language minority students. And we need it for ourselves, teacher educators committed to the education of language minority students, because it is through the collective text that we all become better equipped to challenge these seemingly unchanging hierarchical and marginalizing systems.

REFERENCES

Apple, M. W. (1990). *Ideology and curriculum.* New York: Routledge.

Barone, T. (1987). Educational platforms, teacher selection, and school reform: Issues emanating from a biographical case study. *Journal of Teacher Education, 38*(2), 13–18.

Berliner, D. (1990). If the metaphor fits, why not wear it? *Theory into Practice, 29*(2), 85–93.

Britzman, D. (1991). *Practice makes practice: A critical study of learning to teach.* Albany: State University of New York Press.

Christensen, L. (2000). *Reading, writing, and rising up: Teaching about social justice and the power of the written word.* Milwaukee, WI: Rethinking Schools.

Cochran-Smith, M. (1991). Learning to teach against the grain. *Harvard Educational Review, 61,* 279–309.

Cortazzi, M. (1993). *Narrative analysis.* London: Falmer.

Darling-Hammond, L., Wise, A. E., & Klein, S. P. (1995). *A license to teach: Building a profession for 21st-century schools.* Boulder, CO: Westview.

Edelsky, C. (1993, November). *Democracy and the teaching of English.* Keynote address presented at the conference of the National Council of Teachers of English, Indianapolis, IN.

Edelsky, C., Altwerger, B., & Flores, B. (1991). *Whole language: What's the difference?* Portsmouth, NH: Heinemann.

El-Dinary, P. B., & Schuder, T. (1993). *Teacher's first year of transactional strategies instruction* (Reading Research Rep. No. 5). College Park, MD: National Reading Research Center.

Flor Ada, A. (1997). *Gathering the sun: An ABC in Spanish and English.* New York: Lothrop.

Freeman, D., & Johnson, K. (1998). Reconceptualizing the knowledge-base of language teacher education. *TESOL Quarterly, 32,* 397–417.

Genburg, V. (1992). Patterns and organizing perspectives: A view of expertise. *Teaching and Teacher Education, 8,* 485–496.

Hanson, D., & Herrington, M. (1976). *From college to classroom: The probationary year.* London: Routledge & Kegan Paul.

Hollingsworth, S. (1989). Prior beliefs and cognitive change in learning to teach. *American Educational Research Journal, 26,* 160–189.

Johnson, K. (1994). The emerging beliefs and instructional practices of preservice English as a second language teachers. *Teaching and Teacher Education, 10,* 439–452.

Kagan, D. M. (1992). Professional growth among preservice beginning teachers. *Review of Educational Research, 62,* 129–169.

Kennedy, M. (1991). Some surprising findings on how teachers learn to teach. *Educational Leadership, 49*(3), 14–17.

Kennedy, M. (1998). *Learning to teach writing: Does teacher education make a difference?* New York: Teachers College Press.

Lidchi, H. (1997). The poetics and the politics of exhibiting other cultures. In S. Hall (Ed.), *Representation: Cultural representations and signifying practices* (pp. 151–222). London: Sage.

Lortie, D. C. (1975). *Schoolteacher: A sociological study.* Chicago: University of Chicago Press.

Maxson, M., & Sindelar, R. (1998). Images revisited: Examining preservice teacher' ideas about teaching. *Teacher Education Quarterly, 25*(2), 5–26.

McDiarmid, G. W. (1990). Challenging prospective teachers' beliefs during early field experience: A quixotic undertaking? *Journal of Teacher Education, 41*(3), 12–20.

O'Brien, T. (1990). *The things they carried.* New York: Broadway Books.

Paulsen, G. (1993). *Hermanas/sisters.* San Diego: Harcourt Brace.

Petty, M., & Hogben, D. (1980). Explorations of semantic space with beginning teachers: A study of socialization into teaching. *British Journal of Humanistic Education, 7,* 6–8.

Polkinghorne, D. E. (1995). Narrative configuration in qualitative analysis. In J. A. Hatch & R. Wisniewski (Eds.), *Life history and narrative* (pp. 5–24).

London: Falmer.

Poynor, L. (2001). A drop of color: What's the point of ESL/bilingual language arts teacher education? In B. Johnston & S. Irujo (Eds.), *Research and practice in language teacher education: Voices from the field. Selected papers from the First International Conference on Language Teacher Education* (pp. 151–169). Minneapolis: University of Minnesota, Center for Advanced Research on Language Acquisition.

Richardson, V., & Kile, S. (1992, April). *The use of videocases in teacher education.* Paper presented at the annual meeting of the American Educational Research Association, San Francisco.

Rosenblatt, L. (1978). *The reader, the text, the poem: The transactional theory of literary work.* Carbondale: Southern Illinois University Press.

Shannon, P. (1995). *Text, lies & video tape: Stories about life, literacy & learning.* Portsmouth, NH: Heinemann.

Tatto, M. T. (1998). The influence of teacher education on teachers' beliefs about purposes of education, roles and practice. *Journal of Teacher Education, 49,* 66–77.

Weis, L., & Fine, M. (2000). *Construction sites: Excavating race, class, and gender among urban youth.* New York: Teachers College Press.

Yolen, J. (1992). *Encounter.* San Diego: Harcourt Brace Jovanovich.

Zeichner, K. (1996). Educating teachers for cultural diversity. In K. Zeichner, S. Melnick, & M. L. Gomez (Eds.), *Currents of reform in preservice teacher education* (pp. 133–175). New York: Teachers College Press.

Zeichner, K., Melnick, S., & Gomez, M. L. (Eds.). (1996). *Currents of reform in preservice teacher education.* New York: Teachers College Press.

Theme **III**

COLLABORATIONS IN SECOND LANGUAGE TEACHER EDUCATION

A key element in language teacher development is effective collaboration—be it between those individuals and institutions preparing teachers and their professional counterparts currently engaged in language teaching and learning or among teachers or teacher educators themselves in an institutional context. The four chapters in this section serve as illustrations of the power that second language teachers and teacher educators have to collaborate in their own professional development.

The lead chapter in this section (Edge, chap. 10) begins with the author's personal, philosophical framework of the values that underlie his work in TESOL teacher education. In chapter 10, Julian Edge reminds us that English is often associated with the political, economic, military, and cultural values espoused by the dominant cultures whose first language is English, perhaps even more so in this post-9/11 world in which we live. Edge explores these values and ponders whether TESOL teacher education may serve as a way of expressing the values that he holds as different from those often associated with English language. This analysis is followed by a description of his own personal values related to liberty, equality, and community, in which Edge thoughtfully draws connections to the other three chapters in this section of the book. Edge then shares some of the work in which he and his colleagues are engaged that reflect the values they hold, namely, collaborative group development in which one colleague takes on the role of "speaker" and others participate in reflection and interaction as "understanders."

Edge closes with a charge to language teacher educators that we have to believe that passing on values that foster a global society in which "care and mutual respect are cultivated in the interests of a cooperative future" (p. 196) is possible in teacher education. In short, through an analysis of collaborative work and the values that underlie it, Edge's chapter reminds us of the vital importance of the work that we do.

The second chapter in this section (Smith, chap. 11) is another example of the value of collaboration, this time among ESL adjunct instructors in an English Language Institute housed in a 4-year college in the United States. Lorraine Smith reports in chapter 11 on a study with three coteachers in which over the course of a year, they engage in collaborative work that impacts their professional growth. Data sources in the study included field notes and transcriptions of weekly meetings, journals written by the teachers, five joint interviews focused on "reflection-on-collaboration," as well as biographical interviews with each teacher. Throughout the chapter, Smith describes the relationship that Claire, Faith, and Pat build together as they work over the course of the year with the same learners and learn to use the study's design and resources to further their individual growth. Their collaboration—and the opportunity to reflect on it through their participation in the study—were powerful experiences for these teachers, so powerful that they continued the collaboration they started even after the study was complete.

The power of collaboration again emerges in chapter 12 (Cormany, Maynor, & Kalnin) which focuses on a "Researchers in Residence" program at a high school in a large urban district in the upper Midwest of the United States. Two of the teachers involved in this program, Sharon Cormany and Christina Maynor, are coauthors of this chapter along with a university teacher educator, Julie Kalnin, who works closely with this Professional Practice School (PPS) to support beginning teachers in a variety of ways. Cormany, Maynor, and Kalnin describe the origins of and need for the PPS and the Teacher Residency Program, which involves engagement in action research through the Researchers in Residence group. Then Cormany and Maynor each describe their respective action research projects, Maynor focusing on how curricular activities and teacher approach affect student engagement and retention in high school French and Cormany on the interaction of instructional techniques and the acquisition of English grammar in the context of an advanced English as a second language class. Through the voices of these teachers, we learn the value of teacher collaboration in action research. Cormany, Maynor, and Kalnin complete the chapter with reflections on how their practice was changed through collaboration and engagement in inquiry.

Also situated in a Professional Development, or Practice, School—this time an urban elementary school in the East that houses a bilingual program—chapter 13 (Dubetz) explores the work of a teacher study group whose goal was to improve English acquisition and content learning in the context of the bilingual program. The study conducted by Nancy Dubetz focused on how the teacher study group evolved over 8 months and whether the participation in this collaborative, inquiry-based group influenced teachers' theories of practice. Participants in the teacher study group included a range of bilingual teachers and other support staff as well as the college's liaison to the Professional Development School, Dubetz herself. Dubetz uses the voices of teacher participants in the study group to illustrate the various lines of inquiry that emerged over time. Dubetz further explores their transformed theories of practice, presenting a composite model to illustrate the five sources of knowledge that together comprise these theories.

Ultimately, the work of teacher educators through the work of teachers is intended to have a positive impact on student learning. Edge's chapter (chap. 10) reminds us of this, and in the Smith (chap. 11), Dubetz (chap. 13), and Cormany, Maynor, and Kalnin (chap. 12) chapters we are given a glimpse of that impact. These four chapters together and separately speak to the power of collaboration in the work that second language teachers and teacher educators do.

Chapter **10**

Build It and They Will Come: Realising Values in ESOL Teacher Education

Julian Edge
Aston University, Birmingham, England

INTRODUCTION

When I set out to plan a chapter such as this or to prepare myself to write one (a distinction to which I return later), I always begin with a feeling of being overwhelmed by the scale of what needs to be said. The theme, "Collaborations in Second Language Teacher Education," is broad, and many aspects of it range beyond my knowledge and experience. I remember (and probably still partly identify with) the very strongly held view that I had as a young man that any statement that claimed to be relevant to language teaching but did not contain some ideas on how to do something was just so much hot air—what one might these days call an unnecessary and unwelcome contribution to global warming. At the same time, I now feel a need—encouraged by the appearance of Clarke (2003) and Johnston (2003)—to take account of the significance of action beyond its immediate context of impact. I want to consider a wider horizon and in that larger context, to be as sure as I can that the actions of which I speak truly realise the values that I value.

With these thoughts in mind, I intend in this chapter to sketch one version of a wide horizon and hope that it might serve (whether accepted, amended, or disputed) as a kind of general backdrop to the theme of this section of the book. Having done that, I move on to a brief, data-based presentation of some work of my own that I value for its collaborative underpinning. If this particular fire burns well, then I hope that a spark from it may be carried on the hot air and ignite a response from among my readers.

These then, are the two communicative acts that I have in mind: a statement of broad principle and a report on work that is meant to be in tune with those principles. The chapter is personal. It is not meant as a review of relevant issues but as an engagement with them. I neither insist that the principles meaningful to me should necessarily be meaningful to others nor that the approach on which I report should necessarily be as successful for everyone as it is proving to be for some. I see this as one of the changes of our times: As educators theorise their practice in writing, they do not (have to) set out to prove what is right or wrong or even what would be better or worse for others. They (may) set out to report their experience and to articulate their understandings. They offer their own evaluation and they invite their readers to ask, as they themselves ask when reading, "What can I learn from this?," and when a reader's response to that question is "*Not much!*," it might yet be useful to reflect on why the articulation was important to the writer. One enriching outcome of reading is to have one's ideas confirmed; another enriching outcome is to learn something new, even to the point of changing one's mind; a third enriching outcome is to accept and respect difference. I believe that we need all these outcomes.

A WIDER HORIZON

When I first began to be involved in teacher education in the late 1970s, I was struck by Lynch and Plunkett's (1973) observation that teacher education is one of the most important ways in which a society organises the passing on of the values that it deems to be important. I want to hold on to that thought, and I take its power to relate not only (or even perhaps most significantly) to the content of what we as teacher educators say in and about teacher education but to the ways in which we act.

This position is complicated by the fact that those of us who teach English as a second language (ESL) or foreign language (EFL) work, by definition, cross culturally. We are not, therefore, talking here about passing in-culture values on to the next generation of "our own," so to speak. The English language, furthermore, is necessarily associated with the political, economic, military, and cultural values transmitted by the globally dominant societies whose first language English is. As a British TESOL teacher educator, I risk appearing, at least, to be aligned with the transmission and perhaps the imposition of those same values. I believe that it is worth pausing for a moment to consider what some of these messages are with which I may be associated.

Political

Politically, western electorates are becoming increasingly convinced that their individual votes and voices are unimportant. This is a long-term trend well documented in the United States and Britain where we are now becoming accustomed to the fact that even with regard to national elections for central government, only around half of those eligible to vote actually turn out to do so. Hertz (2001b) adds the following data: "During the European elections in 1999, less than half the electorate voted, and less than a quarter came out in the UK. In the Leeds Central by-election last year only 19% of those eligible to vote did so" (p. 22).

The working assumption across the western democracies is that it is not really important who is in government because the interests of big business have already taken over the reins of policy (Hertz, 2001a). Following the U.S. American presidential election in 2000, Borger (2001) quotes the former White House advisor Robert Reich as saying, "There is no longer any countervailing power in Washington. Business is in complete control of the machinery of government. It's payback time, and every industry and trade association is busily cashing in" (p. 2).

Economic

Commercially, globalisation and free trade is understood to mean the freedom of capital to move in predatory fashion around the world using up local resources of all kinds, whether material or human, and moving on when conditions for profit elsewhere are more favourable, leaving behind environmental and social degradation. In Bauman's (1998) terms, "Some can now move out of the locality—any locality—at will. Others watch helplessly the sole locality they inhabit moving away from under their feet" (p. 18).

Military

The first draft of this chapter was written in the spring before the 11 September 2001 attack on the World Trade Centre; the United States and Britain have since waged war on Afghanistan and, as I make these final amendments, stand on the brink of war with Iraq. I realise that I take a risk with the perspectives that I choose to report here. I could have chosen different, more comforting ones. My purpose, however, is to remind us, in the words of cultural insiders, how we can be seen and, in Vidal's (2002) terms, "How we got to be so hated." Vidal (2002) writes

> Although we regularly stigmatize other societies as rogue states, we ourselves have become the largest rogue state of all. We honour no treaties. We spurn international courts. We strike unilaterally wherever we choose. We give orders to the United Nations but do not pay our dues. We complain of terrorism, yet our empire is now the greatest terrorist of all. We bomb, invade, subvert other states. Although We the People of the United States are the sole source of legitimate authority in this land, we are no longer represented in Congress Assembled. Our Congress has been hijacked by corporate America and its enforcer, the imperial military machine. (p. 158)

Cultural

Our Culture (with a capital "C") has perhaps gone the way of our governments, at least in the assessment of John Malkovich, in a *New York Times* article reprinted in *The Guardian* (Malkovich, 2001): "Because in the America of today, the sole arbiter of nearly every kind of art (or even entertainment) is not what it provides but only what it makes" (p. 7).

In terms of social relationships, our society expresses the power of men over women by choosing a subset of the latter, undressing them to various degrees, photographing them and using the resulting images to sell everything and anything, including, in the final analysis, the bodies themselves. This is called freedom, and we attack other cultural expressions of the power of men over women as though we ourselves were free from this most fundamental form of human domination and debasement.

When I think of the power of this essentially coordinated message that is sent out uninterrupted around the world—a message of bottom-line-led, rapacious competitiveness and consequent disillusion—I find it hard to be optimistic about the effectiveness of TESOL teacher education as a medium for the passing on of the values that I do, in fact, value. And when I see in the field of education itself the extent to which the whole discourse of "best practice" is malleable to this same overall message of centralised, commercially driven, manipulative, dispiriting hegemony, I can come quite close to despair.

When I then think about the values that I do want to send out with my teacher education, I recognise that they can be expressed in various ways, and it is enriching and useful that they should. One articulation that I put forward in this chapter has the advantage of being easy to remember: It is a message of liberty, equality, and community. I allow myself a few words on each before concentrating on the last:

Liberty, in the sense of the onerous freedom of each teacher to take on the continuing responsibility of becoming the best that he or she can be for his or her students, independent where necessary of the changing fashions of language teaching methods and free of the demeaning role of technician in the delivery system of someone else's best practice. This is a liberty that has to be earned, seized, and defended, a tradition frequently celebrated in our culture: "Freedom is not something that anybody can be given; freedom is something people take" (Baldwin, 1961, p. 17).

My own preferred vehicle is an action research approach, one that has learned from general education and is building its own tradition in TESOL (Burns, 1999; Edge, 2001; Edge & Richards, 1993; Freeman, 1998; Nunan, 1989; Wallace, 1998). I believe that I hear a resonance of this demanding liberty in Cormany's statement (see Cormany, Maynor, & Kalnin, chap. 12, this volume):

> Ultimately, action research has a significant, although somewhat unexpected, impact on my [Cormany's] practice. It simultaneously bolsters my confidence and causes me to question everything I believe about teaching. It has led me to believe that I am the primary constructor of knowledge about how my students learn, which is both incredibly empowering and somewhat daunting. I cannot blame Selinker, Chomsky, Krashen, or Larsen-Freeman for not understanding my students; they have never met them. I have. (pp. 227–228)

Equality, first in the sense of a mutual respect for the various traditions that feed into different educational cultures. There is no sense in earnestly asserting that students can only learn by starting from where they are while expecting teachers to apply pedagogic principles that are not rooted in their own value systems. In TESOL, for example, we teacher educators could spend less time ridiculing rote learning and more time interesting ourselves in the (to me) astonishing ability of Arab and Chinese students to memorise data. This ability becomes even more relevant, perhaps, in the current language and second language acquisition research scenario of extended lexical chunks and prefabricated sentence stems (Haastrup & Viberg, 1998; Ketko, 2000). A sense of respect for difference operates equally importantly, of course, at the level of individual interaction and begins with a sensitivity to the equalizing of discourse opportunity. We can hear this sensitivity in Smith's report (see Smith, chap. 11, this volume) of action research with part-time ESL teachers at the college level. "Pat reported that she had read the transcripts and noticed that in initial meetings, she tended to dominate the conversations. Consequently, she made an effort to speak less at subsequent meetings for her coteachers to have a greater part in the conversations" (p. 208).

Community, with its attendant demand for cooperation because I follow Reason's (1994) claim that this is what being fully human is about. "Cooperation is not merely an actual or potential attribute of human nature, but constitutes human nature; we are not human without the extended socialization of the young and the mother–child relationship" (p. 38).

In institutional terms, there are frequently divisions built into our working practices that require our attention. Dubetz (chap. 13, this volume) emphasizes this in her chapter on work in a Professional Development School (PDS). Of the support groups operating there, Dubetz writes, "They are structured for community building among the participants. In a PDS setting, participants include preservice teacher candidates and college faculty in addition to practicing teachers and administrators" (p. 233).

Our broader TESOL community is, of course, a far-flung one in geographical terms. Its diffuseness, however, might also be protective in the sense that we can build a community that avoids or at least gives us succour in the face of some of the more heavy-handed directives of any state apparatus. To the extent that this is true, it is a reminder that a protocommunity of TESOL educators can be local in its own ways. I know Japanese, Pakistani, Polish, and Mexican teachers of English who would claim to have more in common with each other in their teaching than with many of their compatriots without at the same time feeling that they have lost the national or cultural roots that nourish their lives as a whole. In complementary fashion, I know long-resident British, U.S. American, and other foreign nationals deeply encultured in their adopted countries who have learned the validity of the local perspective without losing their sense of a broader belonging, one that celebrates our common humanity as well as our differences. Indeed, one of the main opportunities offered by modern communications is the chance to build this type of global community (while avoiding the dangers of globalisation as it is more usually understood).

My task as a teacher educator working with experienced teachers on a distance-learning program is to use my global reach to facilitate local development—this in the consciousness of my own localness, my own parochiality, and in the recognition of my extra responsibility to keep all localities up to speed with developments elsewhere while not implying that any successful development has global applicability (a term we could well practice doing without). I agree here with Warschauer (2000) that a key term in our global endeavours is *agency*—most particularly here the structuring of space for the agency of others in a way that sets out at least to counterbalance the degrading effects of bottom-line-led competitiveness. (A company selling educationally relevant magazines to students at my university leads its advertising with the slogan, "Keep ahead of your classmates!" Is this really what we want?)

There is a legitimate demand on all of us who work as teacher educators that we should practice what we preach. In response to this, I now want to turn to a brief presentation of the cooperative strand of my own work that most helps me realise in my practice the values, sketched previously, that I hold to be important.

A SMALL FIRE

For over 10 years now (Edge, 1992; Edge, 2002), I have been working with a style of nonjudgmental discourse in which one person takes on the role of Speaker, and one or more colleagues take on the role of Understander. When I am Speaker, it is my development that is the specific focus of the group's work. It is my responsibility to take further my awareness of a self-selected issue and to use this awareness as the basis for devising appropriate action. I must, therefore, be prepared to risk speaking in an exploratory fashion, opening up areas that I do not yet fully understand. The role of my colleagues is to Understand me as empathetically as they can and to reflect that Understanding back to me while withholding their own opinions and experience out of respect for my desire to formulate my own way forward. This is a scheme based on agreed rules of nonjudgmental interaction and a repertoire of learned moves. I shall not go through the details of the whole underlying scheme here but deal with issues as they arise from the interaction. I have maintained the use of the upper case to distinguish the use of the terms, *Speaking* and *Understanding*, from their everyday meanings, but otherwise no specialist knowledge is required and the transcriptions are kept deliberately reader friendly. Edge (2002) presents the cooperative framework in detail, based on a number of authentic sets of pair and group data such as the one used here.

The participants in the data below are teacher educators in a university department. In fact, they are my colleagues and myself who take one hour a fortnight to meet together in this fashion. In this Group Development format, colleagues take turns to act as Speaker. On this occasion, Bill is the Speaker.

Particularly on Bill's mind is the need to give a talk at an upcoming conference, but the issue he is working on is one that is common to other situations in a teacher or teacher educator's professional life: how to get oneself ready for formal, public performance. In Extract 1, we see how Bill initially expresses the issue he wants to work on (lines 01–07) and how this is reflected back to him (lines 08–14). We then see how the reflection itself leads to a further articulation of the focus (lines 15–18), making explicit Bill's feeling that he fails to communicate when he engages in planned discourse:

Extract 1

Bill: For whatever reason, I've got a strong sense that I'm much better at improvising and off-the-cuff talking than I am at planning. As soonas I enter into a planning world in terms of talking, it seems to put on some kind of stress, which I feel imposing on me, and this imposition, this structure that I've pre-planned, is, is a saddle, a chain, something that inhibits me.

Joe: So, if I can just check that with you, this area of focus that you Want to work on is a preference for off-the-cuff talk, as opposed to planned talk. (Bill: Mmm). You feel that when you plan something, that when you start to talk, you feel that plan as an imposition on you and it constrains you and ties you down, and you feel that you're not being as productive as you could be in your talk (Bill: Yes) Is that right?

Bill: That's right. It has a ... in the experiences of public talk that I've had, where I've planned to a higher degree, I've had a very strong feeling that I haven't ended up communicating very much at all, because of that structure.

In Extract 2, we see how Harry asks for further clarification of the stress/pressure/imposition that Bill has spoken of, at the same time offering a possible way of narrowing the focus of the work still further (lines 01–05). As he is asked to dig deeper into this area, Bill accepts this refocusing option (line 06) and also develops further the communication element of what he has said (lines 06–23), drawing on his earlier background in acting (lines 08–12) and making an analogy also with music (lines 12–15). The length and enthusiasm of this turn indicates how helpful Harry's previous move has been, and the closing lines (lines 20–23) suggest that Bill is now accessing long-standing and deeply held personal preferences. Bill is, perhaps, making space for his own strengths to operate more effectively in an area of his work in which he has previously been guided more by his ideas on what a person is supposed to do. Sara's (lines 24–27, 30) and Lucy's (lines 34–36) reflections pick out the audience/communication focus that is clearly important to Bill and allow him to express the strength of the constraints that he feels (lines 28–29, 31–33, 37):

Extract 2

Harry: Can you just clarify something for me about this pressure? When you say it's like an imposition, is that an imposition in the sense that consciousness of the plan places a psychological pressure on you, or is it that having the plan constrains what you can say? Or is it both?

Bill: I think it's both, and the interesting thing about the second one, the constraint element, is that a lot of the thoughts, or this vague thought that I've got, relates to drama, where you have a choice between scripted performance and improvisation. Back in the eighties, I was part of a theatre group, Improv, it was called, where you had very loose structures, and you'd walk onto stage as a group, and you improvise.—I suppose this is very much like jazz, where you play together and the more you get to know each other, the more you know what you might do.—But the actual line that you're going to take is often supplied by the audience. And I think there's a parallel there with the kind of public talking that we do, where the more constrained you are, the more planned it is, the less able you are to respond to your audience, the people you are trying to communicate with. And I think for a long time I've believed that really I would be better having a very loose structure and walking in to do whatever I do, a lecture, a presentation, a talk ...

Sara: Just picking up on what you said about the audience, do you feel that you've had experiences where you've received some kind of signal from the audience and you've been unable to change in response to it?

Bill: I think it's partly that and partly the fact that I don't feel open to any signals.

Sara: So, you don't feel that you see them?

Bill: I see the two things, you know, in opposition: This driving force to get through the plan does meant that I don't even see the signals let alone invite them or deal with them.

Lucy: As though you're looking back into your head all the time, rather than looking out to your audience and communicating with them?
Bill: Yes!!

In Extract 3, we see how Paul returns to Bill's drama analogy, reflecting his Understanding of what is involved (lines 01–03) and checking how this transfers to Bill's present situation (lines 05–08). Again, this elicits quite a lengthy response (lines 09–22), and one that turns out to be significant to the session as a whole. Bill develops a clear distinction between being prepared (line 11–12) and having a plan (lines 16–19). Once again, we see a contrast in Bill's mind between what is best for him (lines 12–15), and what people expect from him as a good professional (lines 16–22):

Extract 3

Paul: You mentioned audience involvement, audience participation, or the audience actually changing the story line—Have I got that right?
Bill: Yeah, yeah.
Paul: Is that right? How important is that element in this? In other words, I can understand that you don't know where to go, ... *Is* it the case that you don't know where to go until somebody has made a contribution?
Bill: I think there are plenty of places I *could* go with a talk opportunity. I'm not talking about knowing nothing about the area you've allotted to talk about. I'm not talking about no *preparation*, no *reading* no *thinking* around the area, but the more experience I have of this kind of teacher education, the more comfortable I am with the idea of taking my thoughts and my current understanding in, without a clear structure. (Joe: Mmm) And at the same time, I know that audiences sometimes like to see a clear structure, because they take that as the sign of a good, of a professional, somebody who has planned, and I think there will always be those who, if you don't say , "Look, there are five stages to the presentation today and I'm going to cover this, that and the other," then they will assume that you haven't *prepared*, even.

In Extract 4, Joe picks out the two terms, *prepared* and *planned*, that Bill has used and offers them back to him as a possibly significant contrast (lines 01–07). As Bill recognises what he has been saying, the impact of it on him enables a further, supporting insight, signalled here by the words, "And another thought hits me from that" (line 08). It is perhaps at moments such as this that we come as close as we are ever likely to get to seeing the evidence of development in the data of linguistic exchange:

Extract 4

Joe: Mmmm. And that's the big distinction I hear now in what you're saying: between being prepared, to enter the arena, and to deal with the topic in the context of the people, on the one hand, which is what you do want to do. And the idea of having a plan (Bill: Mmm), which you think will ride roughshod over the discourse possibilities that could have occurred in that arena.

Bill: Yes, yes! And another thought hits me from that, from this preparation/planning distinction, is that an athlete doesn't necessarily prepare for a hundred metres by doing a hundred metres. They prepare in lots of different ways. That to *plan* for a speech event, if you take that metaphor to its conclusion, is not a good way to *prepare* for a speech event.

Bill then returns for a while to the issue of an audience's expectation that there will be a plan. He introduces a distinction important to him between a debilitating tenseness that he sometimes feels and a creative tension that he believes is necessary to high-quality performance. From this, in Extract 5, he then takes up again the sporting metaphor that we saw in Extract 4 and develops it in terms of a warming-up metaphor (line 01–02). We see here, explicitly signalled (lines 03–04) and expressed (lines 04–06), how Bill's developmental goal is taking shape for him. Joe's checking of his Understanding of connections between the different points that Bill has made (lines 07–08) again draws an enthusiastic response (line 09), and Bill's goal setting is now articulated in terms of possible action strategies (lines 09–16):

Extract 5

Bill: That's where the warming up comes in, the preparation, you need to reach that pitch where you're excited enough to talk and I think that, what, one realisation that is becoming even clearer to me now is that I need, I need to *try* to not wrap myself up with a highly planned product, and to take a few risks with a couple of presentations.

Joe: Because the highly planned product brings you tenseness, whereas a well-prepared improvisation gives you tension?

Bill: Yes! Yes, I've got to, I started to say this earlier and I somehow got side-tracked, but, in terms of preparation, I have never been able to say, "Right, this presentation is an hour, I'm going to rehearse this. I'm going to put a clock down and give this presentation to nobody." I just can't do that. And there are, there are other things: I can do snippets, I can read, I can voice things. There are other forms of warming up that I think, that I feel more comfortable with.

Through these data, we have looked at the way in which Bill used his personal experience and analogical thinking to bring individual preferences to bear on professional difficulties and goals. He articulated important personal preferences in terms of his own style of communicative action and also identified other people's expectations—and his need to live up to them—as getting in his way. He discovered a way of expressing this contrast that allowed him to evaluate his preferred style highly enough to validate goals and actions based on them. In the necessarily brief extracts above, I have tried to present the essential data of this process.

As well as the developmental progress achieved here by the Speaker, there were other outcomes. The planning/preparation distinction captures two important dimensions of how we work and has since become a part of the technical terminology of our group. Lucy commented later,

"This has definitely sharpened my thinking about preparing talks, and has had a real developmental effect for me."

I also found myself affected. After working with Bill, I thought again about my preferred working strategy if I am faced with the prospect of giving a talk at a conference: (a) write a full written text of an appropriate length; (b) read the text onto a tape, checking the timing; (c) listen to the tape a couple of times and make headline notes from it; (d) on the way to the conference, listen to the tape while reading the text; and (e) before the talk, listen to the tape while looking through the notes.

When I get up to speak, I am not only *prepared*, I am *planned*! I do not find this constraining. I believe that the planning frees me up to be relaxed, aware, and present in the moment of my presentation. I find the procedure lengthy and arduous, sometimes even tedious, but eventually liberating. I find that *my* best chance of communication (and of improvisation) lies in the clarity that I believe I produce from this kind of planning. This is how I am best prepared.

But I cannot always manage this kind of planned preparation, and I have found that reflection on the distinction between the two—on a distinction that had not been explicitly available to me before this session—has proved enormously helpful. I see more clearly now that a planned message without personal preparation may not communicate well at all, whereas if I am prepared, in myself, to communicate, then I am likely to have things to say that will be meaningful to my audience. To give a specific instance, shortly after Bill's session as Speaker, I ran a weekend workshop for participants on our distance-learning "Master of Science in TESOL" program, all of whom are experienced EFL/ESL teachers working around the world. In the time available to me, I reduced the period I might have spent planning content for the session, and I prepared myself by rereading the participants' background files. The workshop went well, in part because I was able to give individually appropriate responses to sometimes isolated distance-learning course participants who were in need of exactly that kind of interpersonal support.

The general point to note here, arising from Lucy's and my response to Bill as Speaker, is that when one makes oneself available as an Understander, one makes oneself vulnerable to change. As you make the effort to withdraw your own evaluation and to empathize with the Speaker, you let in the logic and power of perspectives other than your own.

This brief sketch has attempted to show one of the ways in which my colleagues and I work to implement the values that we espouse: how we try to take responsibility for our liberty, to affirm our equality, and to deepen our sense of community.

SPARKS ON A BREEZE

This, then, is one of the fires that my colleagues and I are tending out of a commitment to the power and importance of cooperation both in terms of our own continuing professional development and that of our course participants. When I lift my head from the little local glow and compare the resources put at the disposal of the communication of this message to the resources devoted to the other cultural messages that our society sends out into the world, I sometimes do not know whether to laugh or to cry. Referring back, however, to the idea of a community that is both far-flung and local, I take heart from a message received from a course participant in Switzerland who is using the approach to professional development exemplified previously (S. Hegglin, personal communication, January 28, 2003):

> Looking at the Iraq crisis, looking at Palestine, looking at what happens at my school, in my family, my parish, it very often boils

> down to taking the time to understand what others want to express, to give them your attention, to leave them a chance to develop an idea on their own, their own approach, and contribution to a solution. This letting others contribute to their own solutions probably has to do with enhancing human dignity.

Which brings me, finally, to my title. It is taken from a Hollywood movie called *Field of Dreams*. Taken at one level, this is the story of a farmer in Iowa who believes that he hears a voice urging him to dig up his cornfield and build a baseball field there instead. The voice simply says, "Build it and he will come." In the face of strong economic arguments against the idea, he builds it, and there are interesting, life-enhancing outcomes. See the movie—it's funny, too.

The relevance for me runs as follows. To fall in line with the dominant values of economic exploitation, global expansion at the cost of local depredation, political despair, and professional de-skilling via "best practice" is unthinkable. For so long as I can manoeuvre sufficiently to escape the various constraints that face me, I believe that I have a responsibility to offer frameworks, models, and structures of collaboration that offer teachers and prospective teachers the opportunity to experience the satisfaction of making a professional contribution to their society based on something like the principles of liberty, equality, and community that I have tried to outline and exemplify in this chapter. Anyone reading the other chapters in this volume will be reassured that there are many other examples of similar ideas at work and at play among us. Recent publications such as Gebhard and Oprandy (1999); Bailey, Curtis, and Nunan (2001); Johnson and Golombek (2002); Johnston (2003); and Clarke (2003) broaden the base of this message. I also believe that there will continue to be enough people who will respond to these values to make all our efforts worthwhile. To indulge my taste for popular culture one more time, I join with Kristofferson (1999) in saying, "I don't believe that no one wants to know."

This is, for the most part, a matter of belief, an act of faith, a statement that I have no choice but to make and would make were the situation even bleaker than it appears to be. As a male, middle-aged, humanist, Anglo-Saxon, heterosexual, married, father of a daughter, and well-educated child of manual labourers implicated in institutional, national, and other group actions and attitudes that I can neither support nor control, I, too, to borrow Clarke's (2003) phrase, need a place to stand and from which to lean over, reach out, or jump. When faced with the challenge that, "various concepts in critical multicultural education, such as democracy, pluralism, and equality, which challenge racial, cultural and other kinds of inequalities, are in fact built on White Eurocentric epistemologies" (Kubota, 2002, p. 90), I can only acknowledge the limitations of what I have to offer along with my readiness to learn. I am not well situated to offer "a total rejection of any epistemology associated with Whiteness ... [or] an entirely new epistemology arising from a world view of the marginalized," (Kubota, 2002, p. 90), and so I offer what I can and will defend what I must (Edge, 1996). If I seem to some to overemphasise the importance of the individual, it is because I believe that that is where responsibility ultimately falls. There are certainly ironies and paradoxes involved in "using the master's tools to rebuild the master's house" (B. Kumaravadivelu, personal communication, March 6, 2003) and the whole venture may, of course, fail.

To those from whatever background who share similar commitments, I can only repeat that we may fail in the attempt to erect a structure inside which care and mutual respect are cultivated in the interests of a cooperative future. We may fail in the attempt to fashion a home for multicultural acceptance and intercultural communication. Yet if the attempt is not to be made in teacher education, then where should we look for it? Where should the millions of people anyway obliged to learn English look for such values to be given substance? We have to proceed as though it is possible, as though it is feasible, as though it is appropriate, and we proceed in the knowledge that sometimes it is what actually happens. For this and future generations of English language teachers, we have to build it and believe that they will come.

ACKNOWLEDGMENTS

My sincere thanks to Dee Tedick for her enthusiasm and perseverance with this project and for her comments on the original manuscript. As ever, warm acknowledgment is due to my colleagues in the Writing for Academic Publication (WRAP) group at Aston University whose critique and care regularly combine to make things better and certainly did so here. Responsibility for views expressed and examples chosen remains, of course, with me.

REFERENCES

Bailey, K., Curtis, A., & Nunan, D. (2001). *Pursuing professional development: The self as source*. Boston: Heinle & Heinle.

Baldwin, J. (1961). *Nobody knows my name: Notes for a hypothetical novel*. London: Penguin.

Bauman, Z. (1998). *Globalization: The human consequences*. Cambridge, England: Polity Press.

Borger, J. (2001, April 27). All the president's businessmen. *The Guardian G2,* pp. 2–3.

Burns, A. (1999). *Collaborative action research for English language teachers*. Cambridge, England: Cambridge University Press.

Clarke, M. (2003). *A place to stand: Essays for educators in troubled times*. Ann Arbor: University of Michigan Press.

Edge, J. (1992). *Cooperative development: Professional self-development through cooperation with colleagues*. Harlow, England: Longman. (see www.les.aston.ac.uk/lsu/staff/je/CD)

Edge, J. (1996). Cross-cultural paradoxes in a profession of values. *TESOL Quarterly30*(1), 9–30.

Edge, J. (2001). Attitude and access: Building a new teaching/learning community in TESOL. In J. Edge (Ed.), *Action research* (pp. 1–12). Alexandria, VA: TESOL.

Edge, J. (2002) *Continuing cooperative development: A discourse framework for individuals as colleagues*. Ann Arbor: University of Michigan Press.

Edge, J., & Richards, K. (Eds.). (1993). *Teachers develop teachers research*. Oxford, England: Heinemann.

Freeman, D. (1998). *Doing teacher research: From inquiry to understanding*. Boston: Heinle & Heinle.

Gebhard, J., & Oprandy, R. (1999). *Language teaching awareness: A guide to exploring beliefs and practices*. Cambridge, England: Cambridge University Press.

Haastrup, K., & Viberg, A. (Eds.). (1998). *Perspectives on lexical acquisition in a second language.* Lund, Sweden: Lund University Press.

Hertz, N. (2001a). *The silent takeover: Global capitalism and the death of democracy.* Oxford, England: Heinemann.

Hertz, N. (2001b, April 8). Why we must stay silent no longer. *The Observer,* pp. 22–23.

Johnson, K., & Golombek, P. (Eds.). (2002). *Teachers' narrative inquiry as professional development*. Cambridge, England: Cambridge University Press.

Johnston, B. (2003). *Values in English language teaching*. Mahwah, NJ: Lawrence Erlbaum Associates, Inc.

Ketko, H. (2000). Importance of multi-word chunks in facilitating communicative competence. *The Language Teacher, 24*(12), 5–11.

Kristofferson, K. (1999). To beat the devil. On *The Austin Sessions* [CD]. New York: Atlantic Records/WEA International.

Kubota, R. (2002). (Un)Raveling racism in a nice field like TESOL. *TESOL Quarterly, 36*(1), 84–92.

Lynch, J., & Plunkett, H. (1973). *Teacher education and cultural change*. London: Unwin.

Malkovich, J. (2001, April 27). Captured by the terrorist. *The Guardian Review,* pp. 7–8.

Nunan, D. (1989). *Understanding language classrooms: A guide for teacher-initiated action*. London: Prentice Hall International.

Reason, P. (1994). *Participation in human inquiry*. London: Sage.
Vidal, G. (2002). *Perpetual war for perpetual peace: How we got to be so hated*. New York: Thunder's Mouth Press/Nation Books.
Wallace, M. (1998). *Action research for language teachers*. Cambridge, England: Cambridge University Press.
Warschauer, M. (2000). The changing global economy and the future of English teaching. *TESOL Quarterly, 34*(3), 511–535.

Chapter 11

The Impact of Action Research on Teacher Collaboration and Professional Growth

Lorraine C. Smith
Adelphi University

This chapter is based on a 1-year study of teacher collaboration among part-time college-level teachers. Although higher education depends increasingly on part-time teachers—their numbers are in the hundreds of thousands—they have rarely been a topic of research. Part-time college teachers' work often involves teaching at two or more campuses and typically requires multiple course preparations and considerable travel time. Clearly, such work conditions are not conducive to teacher collaboration; they also limit professional development opportunities. Because college teachers are not usually discussed in the research and because of the time constraints inherent in their work, I believed it was especially important to learn how part-time teachers might develop a collaborative relationship, what form it would take, and how their work might impact on their students.

The original purpose of my research (Smith, 1998) was to set up a study in which a small group of willing college-level English as a second language (ESL) teachers would collaborate. I would then observe, document, and describe their experiences for two consecutive semesters and report the extent to which the teachers' collaborative experience enhanced their professional growth from their perspective. I did achieve these goals, but I did not foresee that the teachers would develop a sense of ownership in the research and use its design, and the researcher herself, in unexpected and effective ways.

PROFESSIONAL DEVELOPMENT

Professional development is a term with a wide range of meanings, but for the purposes of this study, Fullan's (1995) definition is appropriate. According to Fullan (1995), professional development involves "learning how to bring about ongoing improvements" (p. 255), and thus, it needs to be an integral part of teachers' daily lives.

An essential aspect of professional development involves its individual nature. Clark (1992) states that "it is impossible to create a single, centrally administered and planned program of professional development that will meet everyone's needs and desires" (p. 77). Clark asserts that teachers need to design their own self-directed program of professional development. Clark further argues that this process must be voluntary for teachers to feel in control. When teachers develop their own goals, they perceive themselves to be more effective, and their efforts are more likely to meet with success (Hargreaves & Dawe, 1990; Husband & Short, 1994; O'Connor, Jenkins, & Leicester, 1992). For growth to take place, teachers need to overcome resistance to change, to engage in professional development activities tailored to their individual needs, within the context of their working environment. However, although these factors are essential, they are insufficient to ensure that professional growth will take place.

Important Components of Professional Growth

A teacher's professional growth does not take place in isolation. Woods (1993), in his case study of a teacher's career through that teacher's life history, found that the self develops throughout a person's life. Furthermore, this process is a "social process, as the self continues to form in interaction with others" (p. 451). Collaboration can thus be an effective means for the improvement of teaching as indicated in Ellis' (1993) findings. The teachers in Ellis' study reported that collegial interactions were instrumental in facilitating the changes they had made in their instruction.

Other research on professional development has revealed additional factors that may enhance or hinder teacher change. In their 3-year study on teacher development, Bell and Gilbert (1994) identified three main features of teacher development: professional, personal, and social development. Bell and Gilbert's study highlights several aspects of professional growth: (a) it is multidimensional, involving social and personal as well as professional elements; (b) teachers experience a sense of risk when learning new knowledge and developing new expertise; (c) teachers need support, feedback, and opportunities for reflection as they engage in professional growth; and (d) professional development takes time. Bell and Gilbert's findings have useful implications in the context of this study because they illustrate the complex nature of professional growth and identify areas of concern for teachers as they work toward improvement of their practice.

TEACHER COLLABORATION

Teacher collaboration has potential as a vehicle for professional growth (Bell & Gilbert, 1994; Briscoe, 1994; Christiansen, Goulet, Krentz, & Maeers, 1997; Ellis, 1993; Woods, 1993). Like professional development, *teacher collaboration* is a term with many meanings. According to Austin and Baldwin (1991), "people who collaborate work closely together and share mutual responsibility for their joint endeavor.... It emerges from shared goals and leads to outcomes that benefit all partners" (p. 21). Teacher collaboration involves viewing teaching as a professional practice that needs to be reflected on, evaluated, and refined. Teachers cooperate when they agree on textbooks or class schedules. They collaborate when they examine their practice together and make changes as a result of their collaborative efforts.

Collaboration has been shown to benefit teachers both personally and professionally. In fact, collaboration is a key component in teacher growth (Bell & Gilbert, 1994; Briscoe, 1994; Ellis, 1993; Harnish & Wild, 1992). Collaboration facilitates teacher reflection on practice, promotes collegial interaction, and involves teachers in school change. As Hargreaves (1992) points out, "the relationships between teachers and their colleagues are among the most educationally significant aspects of teachers' lives and work. They provide a vital context for teacher development" (pp. 217–218).

Although this chapter ultimately focuses on the teachers' use of the study design, collaboration and professional growth are at the heart of the research presented here.

METHODOLOGY

In this study, I documented the collaborative relationship of three ESL coteachers over 1 year and recorded the teachers' report on the relation between their collaborative work and their professional growth. The research questions guiding this inquiry are the following:

1. How does the facilitated collaborative relationship of a triad of teachers responsible for the same classes of students develop over 1 year?
2. How do these teachers view the relation between their efforts to collaborate and their professional development?

The purpose of this study was to (a) create the opportunity for teacher collaboration; (b) observe, document, and describe the collaborative experiences of these three teachers for 1 year; and (c) report the extent to which this collaborative experience enhanced the teachers' professional development, from their perspective.

Action research is particularly relevant in educational contexts because it has as its goals "the improvement of practice, the improvement of the understanding of practice by its practitioners, and the improvement of the situation in which the practice takes place" (Carr & Kemmis, 1983, p. 155). The goals of action research are compatible with the aim of this study. As a study design, action research allowed me to create conditions that would support professional development. The supportive conditions involved in this study included (a) identifying three teachers willing to engage in a collaborative relationship with each other for 1 year, (b) arranging for these three teachers to be scheduled to coteach the same classes, (c) scheduling a 1 hour per week meeting time for myself and the participating teachers in which they could discuss their practice and I could observe and record their meetings, and (d) scheduling periodic interviews in which I could facilitate the teachers' reflection on their work together. Once conditions thought to be supportive of professional development were in place, I could then study what occurred by documenting the teachers' collaboration and reporting whether the teachers felt their collaboration led to professional development.

The Setting

The study took place at the English Language Institute (ELI), an intensive ESL program located on the campus of a 4-year college. The ELI is geared primarily for international students who plan to attend colleges or universities in the United States and return to their native countries on graduation. The ELI serves approximately 400 students per semester. At the time of the study, the faculty consisted of 45 teachers, all of whom were part-time. ELI classes meet for 18 hours per week. Each class has three teachers: one for reading, one for writing, and one for listening/speaking. Each teacher sees each class for 6 hours per week. The teachers typically teach two classes per semester. The three teachers who instruct each class of students do not teach them at the same time. Because of scheduling constraints, the teachers of a given class rarely meet and generally do not coordinate their instruction. In subsequent semesters, each teacher may be assigned to classes with two different coteachers. Consequently, interaction among coteachers is sporadic, and collaboration rarely occurs.

Participant Selection

As noted earlier, I decided to work with part-time college faculty because they are rarely represented in research on collaboration or on professional growth. I had access to the ELI because at the time I was also a member of the faculty. I chose the ELI as the setting for my study for two reasons: It is in a college environment, and the ELI program has a scheduling arrangement that holds potential for facilitating teacher collaboration. Specifically, each intact group of students has three teachers. My being a member of the faculty put me in a unique situation as a researcher; I was not a stranger to the other teachers, having been at the ELI for several years. I was initially concerned about issues of researcher bias. As I explored the literature on this subject, however, I discovered that the relationship between researcher and participant need not always be one of distance and formality but may range along a continuum from distanced observer to full participant (Bickel & Hattrup, 1995; Merriam, 1998; Miller, 1990; Ulichny & Schoener, 1996; Wagner, 1997). Still, I determined to carefully document my role and involvement as researcher.

Because research clearly indicates that collaboration, by its nature, is voluntary (Bell & Gilbert, 1994; Christiansen et al., 1997; Cole, 1992; Hargreaves & Dawe, 1990), it was imperative that the teachers be willing participants. I identified 10 potential research participants based on the following criteria: each teacher had at least 3 years of teaching experience, had taught in the ELI for at least 1 year, had never collaborated, and had never cotaught with me. I outlined the study to them and described what was involved if they agreed to participate: For 1 year, each participating teacher would collaborate with two other teachers, hold weekly 1-hr meetings, participate in periodic off-campus interviews, keep a personal journal, and give me an autobiography. Three teachers, Faith, Pat, and Claire, immediately agreed to participate in the study. The ELI's Assistant Director assigned Faith,

Pat, and Claire[1] to teach the same two classes for two consecutive semesters. The Assistant Director also scheduled both me and them to have a common 1-hr break on Friday mornings, which gave them the opportunity to hold a weekly teacher meeting, and which I could observe. In fact, these two accommodations were the only differences between their schedules and those of the other teachers in the ELI.

RESEARCH METHODS

For two consecutive semesters, as the three teachers met weekly to discuss their work, my researcher role was primarily participant observer. I took field notes and audiotaped and transcribed the teachers' 1-hr weekly meetings. The teachers also kept individual journals in which they reflected on their work together (daCosta, 1993; vanManen, 1990). Five times during the study, I held off-campus, reflection-on-collaboration interviews with all three teachers together, during which they reflected both individually and as a group on their work. These interviews were also audiotaped and transcribed. I obtained the teachers' life histories through individual interviews with the teachers. These various data sources provided a means of triangulating data, because the meetings represented the teachers' actual week-to-week interactions; the journal entries represented the teachers' individual, private reflections; and the group reflection-on-collaboration interviews represented the teachers' thoughts about their work together as they interacted in reflective conversation.

THE TEACHERS' COLLABORATIVE EXPERIENCE

When the teachers began their first semester together, they were assigned two advanced level ESL classes. The teachers were excited about the idea of collaborating but had no set plan for doing so. Pat, Faith, and Claire decided that during their weekly teacher meetings, they would keep each other informed as to what each of them was teaching in class and discuss the students' progress and difficulties.

Semester One

Claire, Faith, and Pat agreed that Faith would teach listening/speaking, Pat would teach reading, and Claire would teach writing. They also decided to coordinate reading and writing. For example, Pat would work with the students on narrative reading when Claire was teaching narra-

[1]Faith, Pat, and Claire are pseudonyms for the research participants.

tive writing. Finally, they decided to focus their independently taught classes around common themes such as family. During the first weeks of the semester, they continued to coordinate their work in their individually taught classes.

At the teacher meeting half way through the semester, the teachers made their first move toward interdependent work when they decided to have their two classes hold debates with each other. The debate project became the ongoing focus of Faith, Claire, and Pat's work together and strongly influenced the nature of their collaboration. The teachers recorded some of these effects in their journal entries. Pat wrote, "It is very comforting to know what 'the right hand' is doing. I think the students are responding well because there is a coordinated rationale behind what we do." Faith wrote, "We're a team. We work together for the good of the students. We share ideas and failures without feeling vulnerable."

The teachers developed their debate project over several weeks. They divided each class into groups of four students; each group worked on a different debate topic. As the writing teacher, Claire had the students keep personal journals in which they reflected on how their debate group was progressing. Claire read and responded to the students' entries every week. Pat and Faith depended on Claire to inform them of any problems within the debate groups that the students may have written about in their journals.

During subsequent weekly meetings, as the teachers continued finalizing their plans for the debates, they wrote their impressions in their journals. Faith described her excitement and her own growth in her journal:

> When we started working together I felt like an experienced teacher taking on a new job. I knew what I was supposed to do because of my prior experience but at the same time there was an air of anxiety and excitement about this project. The anxiety has gone but the excitement hasn't. I feel that personally I've become more focused, more aware of long range goals for the students.

Pat, Claire, and Faith scheduled the last day of classes for the debates. During the meeting they held immediately afterward, they evaluated the debate process and planned revisions for the next term. For example, they decided to set up student groups earlier in the term and to make writing an integral component of the debate process.

Semester Two

Claire, Pat, and Faith's initial meeting of the second semester was focused and purposeful. The teachers planned out the debate project for the entire semester. Pat noted in her journal, "The collaborative process makes it easier to develop good ideas. I know that I can develop my own ideas but they can be even better with more input from another teacher."

At the first reflection-on-collaboration interview of the semester, Pat and Claire discussed their work together. Pat said, "Say I have a particular lesson that I want to do. I know I have two people that I can call, and say to them, 'What do you think?' I feel I have this wealth of knowledge and experience that I can turn to as a teacher." Claire reflected, "It keeps me focused, it makes me think long and hard about what I'm doing with the students: how it affects me, how it affects Pat's class, how it affects Faith's class."

As their second semester drew to a close, Pat, Faith, and Claire decided to continue teaching together after the study officially ended. Claire would continue teaching writing to improve her skills. Pat and Faith switched skills so that Pat would teach listening and speaking, and Faith would teach reading. In her journal entry a week later, Claire reflected on her increasing self-confidence and on the students' responses to the debate process: "I feel more comfortable speaking to the students about the debate process. Also, they have been sharing their ideas and fears in their journals. It's interesting to do this (the debate) a second semester."

At the second reflection-on-collaboration interview of the semester, Pat suggested having the students complete a questionnaire in which they would be asked to evaluate the debate process, and Claire and Faith agreed. As they typically did after a reflection-on-collaboration interview, the teachers wrote about their work together in their journal entries. Claire wrote of her feelings about continuing to teach writing for a third semester: "I'm excited about doing the same skill. I really feel I've learned a lot this semester about how I want to pursue this 'wonderful' process of writing (hopefully not at the students' expense!)" Pat wrote, "I think that collaborating forces me to be more creative and not to slack off when I get tired. I don't want to let my 'comrades' down. These last two weeks I've been tired, but meeting with Faith and Claire has refreshed and stimulated me. I'm getting back my enthusiasm."

Claire, Faith, and Pat held their final teacher meeting of the semester immediately after the last two debates. This meeting served as a debriefing on the debate process. The following Monday, the students completed the questionnaire, and Claire had the students write a reaction to the debate process.

RESEARCH FINDINGS

A number of findings emerged from this study, but three are particularly relevant to this chapter: (a) the teachers' collaborative relationship evolved over time and was characterized by increasingly interdependent work; (b) the teachers established a long-term commitment to working together, which continued after the study formally ended; and (c) the research design and the data collection methods used by the researcher enabled the teachers to benefit from the research itself as well as other opportunities provided by the study. In the remainder of this chapter, I will focus on the teachers' use of the study design and the study's resources.

THE TEACHERS' USE OF THE STUDY'S DESIGN AND RESOURCES

When the study began, the teachers were not sure what collaboration would involve or how their work would develop, because none of them had collaborated before. In the same way, because they had never participated in any research, they did not have a vision of how the study itself would progress or what my role would be. Faith, Claire, and Pat's use of the researcher and the research design developed throughout the two semesters of the study.

The Researcher

Pat, Claire, and Faith had always viewed me as a fellow teacher at the ELI. Although none of us had ever cotaught, we were often together in the teacher's room before and after class and during our lunch breaks, and we had all known each other for several years. When I approached them as potential study participants, I added the role of researcher to my role of experienced teacher and colleague. We were all aware of the fact that their work together was theirs and that I was only to document it unless they invited me to do otherwise. I had made it clear that I was always available as a resource for them in whatever capacity they might wish to use me. During the study, the teachers used me in a variety of ways, depending in part on the role they envisioned for me at the moment. When I described the research to Pat, Claire, and Faith before the study began, I also explained what my data collection methods would be. At the outset of the study, Claire asked me if they could have copies of the transcripts to read ("I like to see what I said."). I gave the teachers the transcripts of their weekly meetings and periodic reflection-on-collaboration interviews every week for the duration of the study.

On occasion, the teachers relied on me to keep track of important dates both in the college schedule and regarding the study. When I attended TESOL conferences, they reviewed the conference program and asked me to bring back materials on specific topics of interest to them.

Occasionally, one of the teachers would bring in an article or a handout she had and show it to the other two. If the other two thought it worthwhile, they asked me to photocopy the materials for them. They sometimes asked me for books, articles, and teacher-made materials, and occasionally involved me in brainstorming sessions to develop materials for their classes. At one point in the second semester when the teachers decided to have the students evaluate their debate project and their teachers' work together, Claire, Faith, and Pat asked me to design the questionnaire for them. When they agreed to present at TESOL conferences with me, they asked me to write the proposals.

These examples demonstrate how my roles in the study ranged from complete observer, observer as participant, to complete participant, depending in large measure on Pat, Claire, and Faith's needs and requests. I served as teacher, resource person, secretary, writer, and presentation facilitator.

Transcripts of Teacher Meetings and Reflection-on-Collaboration Interviews

Because the teachers had asked for copies of the transcripts from their weekly meetings and reflection interviews, I transcribed the audiotapes every weekend and gave each of the teachers a copy the following Monday. I followed this practice for the entire two semesters of the study. The transcripts served two purposes: (a) they documented the teachers' collaborative interaction, and (b) they contributed to the teachers' reflection on their collaborative interactions. The importance of providing the transcripts of the meetings to the participants cannot be underestimated. At meetings throughout the study, Faith, Pat, and Claire frequently referred to the transcripts of prior meetings. If a teacher missed a meeting, she read the transcript of that meeting to update herself on what had been discussed so she would be informed before the next teacher meeting. In some instances, the transcripts served as reminders of decisions the triad had made with regard to planning, instruction, or evaluation. At other times, one or more of the teachers referred to their own or another's behavior and pointed out changes. This was a use of the weekly meeting transcripts for reflection, a purpose I had not expected. For example, Pat reported that she had read the transcripts and noticed that in initial meetings, she tended to dominate the conversations. Consequently, she made an effort to speak less at subsequent meetings for her coteachers to have a greater part in the conversations. The teachers often noted the nature of their conversation, for instance, how often they all finished each other's sentences, and used this observation as an indication of how well they were collaborating and how similarly they thought.

The Teachers' Journals

The teachers wrote regularly in their journals throughout the two semesters of the study. The journals were used in part to document the teachers' reflections in a way that their conversations during their meetings did not. DaCosta (1993) discussed the difficulty he had documenting teacher reflection. In fact, on many occasions, the teachers reflected on their work together, and on their own development, in their journals.

During the study, the teachers often referred to comments they had made in their journals and talked about how helpful the journal writing was for them. For instance, during the first semester, at the second reflection-on-collaboration meeting, Pat stated the following:

> I was concerned about the journal. I used to write in a personal journal quite often. And now I find I write on New Year's Day, and then I only write maybe once or twice a year, usually when something bad happens. And so I was thinking, am I going to be able to keep up with this journal? But I have, and I think it's been very helpful. Because it gives me a chance—after we talk; we talk on Friday, and then I teach the next week, and I've gotten ideas.... And then I'm taking those ideas and then do it, and then trying to sit down and write about it—it's really good. I wish I did it all the time.

At the same meeting, Claire told the group, "If I write in the journal, then I have to take time to think about myself and my job.... That's what I find for me: that it really focuses me. It's like I'm putting pressure on myself, writing in the journal. Forcing myself to really think about what I'm doing."

The teachers also used their journals as notebooks in which they wrote ideas, suggestions, and questions they had for each other, and which they wanted to remember to bring up at their meetings. On occasion, they wrote questions directly to me, asking about an idea or voicing a concern. For example, Pat wrote, "Yesterday, my class had a terrible time with direction prepositions. I am looking for some more material for them to work on. Any suggestions?" They found it helpful to reread their journals periodically; this practice gave them additional insights, which they discussed at the reflection-on-collaboration interviews.

The Study Design

The study called for three teachers to coteach the same classes for two consecutive semesters. As noted earlier, continuous coteaching was not the rule at the ELI, nor was scheduling all three teachers to be on campus on the same day and to have the same 1-hr break. However, once Claire, Faith, and Pat had been coteaching for two semesters, they saw this precedent as an opportunity to continue doing so and felt a strong enough commitment to their work together to approach the Assistant Director and request they be scheduled to coteach even though the study had officially ended. The study design had shown them what was possible.

The final reflection-on-collaboration interview took place during the teachers' third semester of coteaching, which was also when I interviewed each teacher to obtain her autobiography. This final reflective interview served us all as a debriefing and gave me the opportunity to ask questions I had not posed before because I did not want to ask any leading questions or because I simply had not thought of them. For example, I asked each teacher why she had agreed to participate in the study. Each teacher said that she had seen it as an opportunity to do something she believed in—collaborate with other teachers—and which she had not had the chance to do before. They also expressed the conviction that their collaboration had enabled them to develop a complex curriculum, the debate project, which was impossible for a single teacher to implement effectively. The study met the individual and collective needs of these teachers.

Pat, Claire, and Faith's experience seems somewhat unusual. They developed a sense of trust, openness, camaraderie, and commitment to each other that was virtually nonexistent in the ESL program where they worked. They also created a semester-long project that they initiated during their first semester together—class debates—whose benefits to the students they felt strongly enough about to continue for the entire five semesters they cotaught.

Some of their success may be attributable to the support structure provided by the study design. Some of it can be explained by the fact that Claire, Pat, and Faith enjoyed working together. A third factor, which is outside the scope of this chapter, may be seen through the lens of each teacher's autobiography, which provided insight into why each teacher wanted to collaborate as well as what each teacher brought to and drew from their work together (Smith, 2001).

IMPLICATIONS FOR RESEARCH AND PRACTICE

Further case studies of collaboration among part-time college-level teachers will add to the knowledge base of part-time college faculty, a group that has largely been ignored in the research on teachers. Additionally, case studies of administrative attempts to overcome institutional constraints to encourage and facilitate part-time teachers' professional growth through collaborative work as well as through other means will broaden the current limited knowledge base on administrative efforts to support part-time faculty. By building up a body of research on teachers in this context, it may become possible to draw up guidelines for supporting these teachers as they work under their unique, and often difficult, conditions and thus to facilitate their professional growth, which should affect the kinds of experiences they provide for their students and, ultimately, student learning.

Further research might more directly involve the participants in the study design, leading to true collaborative action research. Teachers would have a sense of ownership, as their concerns and questions are taken into consideration at the outset. The teachers' collaborative relationship would serve as a springboard for reflection on teaching, improved practice, and enhanced student learning.

This study focused on the collaboration of three part-time ESL teachers at the college level. It provides a detailed record of these teachers' work together. The teachers' collaborative experience provided them with a social climate far removed from the isolating conditions under which part-time college faculty so often work. From an administrative perspective, the effort involved in accommodating teachers who wish to collaborate—scheduling willing teachers to teach the same classes and ensuring a common meeting time once a week, for instance—is minimal, costs little, and may facilitate their professional growth. However, administrators' responsibility to their part-time faculty goes beyond merely accommodating those teachers who have a vision of collaboration that they are sufficiently motivated and self-directed to engage in. As this and other studies have shown, outside support is a critical factor in facilitating teachers' professional growth. Given the hundreds of thousands of part-time faculty currently employed in colleges and universities throughout the United States, administrative cooperation and support for these teachers is compelling. Institutional constraints such as scheduling problems and budget limitations must be dealt with in creative ways to support this legion of part-time faculty on which colleges and universities depend so heavily.

REFERENCES

Austin, A. E., & Baldwin, R. G. (1991). *Faculty collaboration: Enhancing the quality of scholarship and teaching* (ASHE–ERIC Higher Education Report No. 7). Washington, DC: George Washington University, Washington, DC. School of Education and Human Development. (ERIC Clearinghouse on Higher Education No. ED 347 948)

Bell, B., & Gilbert, J. (1994). Teacher development as professional, personal, and social development. *Teaching and Teacher Education, 10,* 483–497.

Bickel, W. E., & Hattrup, R. A. (1995). Teachers and researchers in collaboration: Reflections on the process. *American Educational Research Journal, 32,* 35–62.

Briscoe, C. (1994). Cognitive frameworks and teaching practices: A case study of teacher learning and change. *Journal of Educational Thought, 28,* 286–309.

Carr, W., & Kemmis, S. (1983). *Becoming critical: Knowing through action research.* Geelong, Victoria, Australia: Deakin University Press.

Christiansen, H., Goulet, L., Krentz, C., & Maeers, M. (1997). Making the connections. In H. Christiansen, L. Goulet, C. Krentz, & M. Maeers (Eds.), *Recreating relationships: Collaboration and educational reform* (pp. 283–290). Albany: State University of New York Press.

Clark, C. M. (1992). Teachers as designers in self-directed professional development. In A. Hargreaves & M. G. Fullan (Eds.), *Understanding teacher development* (pp. 75–84). New York: Teachers College Press.

Cole, C. M. (1992). *Collaboration: Research and practice.* (CASE Information Dissemination Packet). Bloomington: Council of Administrators of Special Education, Indiana University, Department of Special Education.

daCosta, J. (1993, April). *A study of teacher collaboration in terms of teaching-learning performance.* Paper presented at the annual meeting of the American Educational Research Association, Atlanta, GA.

Ellis, N. E. (1993). Collegiality from the teacher's perspective: Social contexts for professional development. *Action in Teacher Education, 15*(1), 42–48.

Fullan, M. G. (1995). The limits and the potential of professional development. In T. R. Guskey & M. Huberman (Eds.), *Professional development in education: New paradigms and practices* (pp. 253–267). New York: Teachers College Press.

Hargreaves, A. (1992). Cultures of teaching: A focus for change. In A. Hargreaves & M. G. Fullan (Eds.), *Understanding teacher development* (pp. 216–240). New York: Teachers College Press.

Hargreaves, A., & Dawe, W. (1990). Paths of professional development: Contrived collegiality, collaborative culture, and the case of peer coaching. *Teaching and Teacher Education, 6,* 227–241.

Harnish, D., & Wild, L. A. (1992). In the words of the faculty: What difference does professional development make? *Community College Review, 20*(2), 20–29.

Husband, R. E., & Short, P. A. (1994). *Middle school interdisciplinary teams: An avenue to greater teacher empowerment.* College Park: The Pennsylvania State University.

Merriam, S. B. (1998). *Qualitative research and case study applications in education.* San Francisco: Jossey-Bass.

Miller, J. L. (1990). *Creating spaces and finding voices: Teachers collaborating for empowerment.* Albany: State University of New York Press.

O'Connor, R., Jenkins, J. R., & Leicester, N. (1992, April). *Collaboration among general and special educators: The influence teachers exert on the process.* Paper presented at the annual meeting of the American Educational Research Association, San Francisco.

Smith, L. C. (1998). *Professional development through teacher collaboration: The experiences of a co-teaching triad in an intensive ESL program.* Unpublished doctoral dissertation, Teachers College, Columbia University, New York.

Smith, L. C. (2001). Life history as a key factor in understanding teacher collaboration and classroom practice. *Teacher Education Quarterly, 28,* 111–125.

Ulichny, P., & Schoener, W. (1996). Teacher-researcher collaboration from two perspectives. *Harvard Educational Review, 66,* 496–524.

vanManen, M. (1990). *Researching lived experience: Human science for an action sensitive pedagogy.* Albany: State University of New York Press.

Wagner, J. (1997). The unavoidable intervention of educational research: A framework for reconsidering researcher-practitioner cooperation. *Educational Researcher, 26*(7), 13–22.

Woods, P. (1993). Managing marginality: Teacher development through grounded life history. Britis*h Educational Research Journal, 19*(5), 447–465.

role play

French teacher

ESL teacher

p. 19

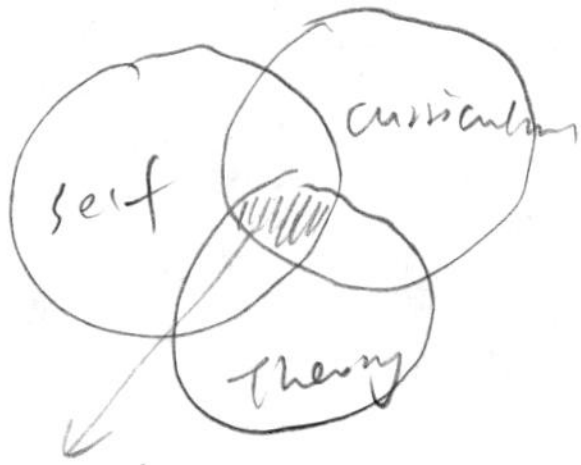

self

curriculum

theory

practice

for example using past tense!

theory → transformation → knowledge

practice

Chapter 12

Developing Self, Developing Curriculum, and Developing Theory: Researchers in Residence at Patrick Henry Professional Practice School

Sharon Cormany
Patrick Henry High School

Christina Maynor
Patrick Henry High School

Julie Kalnin
University of Minnesota

THE DEVELOPMENT OF THE PROFESSIONAL PRACTICE SCHOOL AT PATRICK HENRY

In the late 1980s, Patrick Henry High School was identified as a school at risk. With enrollment at barely 800 in a school designed for 1,200, spotty student attendance, low morale, and high teacher turnover, the school was in danger of being shut down. Yet, by March 2000, district data rated Patrick Henry more highly than five of the seven other Minneapolis public high schools (Minneapolis Public Schools, 2000). That year, *Newsweek* ranked Patrick Henry number 218 on its list of top high schools in the United States (Mathews, 2000).

Patrick Henry High School, situated in the northernmost section of Minneapolis, now serves 1,382 students. Forty-one percent are African American, 33% are Asian/Pacific Islander, 23% are Euro-American, 2 % are Native American, and 2% are Chicano/Hispanic American. Seventy-two percent of Patrick Henry students qualify for federally subsidized free or reduced-price lunches, one indicator of lower socioeconomic status. On any given day, 98% of the students are in attendance. Two generations of coordinators and a cadre of trained teachers have brought the school's International Baccalaureate program from a fledgling magnet with its first diploma candidates in 1993 to a highly competitive program that annually admits nearly 120 students to its ninth grade preparatory program and administered 332 tests to the school's 115 certificate and 25 diploma candidates this year. Sixty-five percent of the students who test at Patrick Henry are low income as demonstrated by their status as free and reduced-lunch recipients.

Although many factors influenced the dramatic changes at the school, the creation of a Professional Practice School (PPS) was a significant one. When they were faced with possible reconstitution, the faculty of Patrick Henry High School made a commitment to turn the school around. A group of teacher leaders drafted an application for the school to become part of a national restructuring project, The Professional Practice School. In 1990, Henry was selected as one of three sites to win grant support from the Exxon Foundation and the American Federation of Teachers. This funding allowed the faculty to establish significant structural changes.

The original vision of the Professional Practice School at Patrick Henry was that teachers are lifelong learners engaged in a continuum of reflection and practice to improve teaching and learning. The goals in the original planning discussions were to (a) foster student success, (b) provide clinical experiences and induction for new teachers, and (c) support and sustain inquiry into practice.

The Professional Practice School aimed, through its collaboration with the Minneapolis Federation of Teachers and the University of Minnesota (U of M), to transform the school by transforming how teachers viewed the profession of teaching. New roles for teachers were formally established in the school. Initially, redefined positions were established for teacher coordinators of the PPS and teacher mentors. These individuals developed the Teacher Residency Program—a sane and humane introduction to teaching in an urban setting. Resident Teachers teach a reduced load (three classes) and participate in focused professional development within the school and at the university. Resident Teacher positions simultaneously create opportunities for release time for experienced staff. The program has been extremely successful—past Residents now serve as coordinators of the Professional Practice School; 88% of the Residents still teach in the district. In 2001, the school established additional instructional leadership roles to move responsibility for curriculum, accountability, and professional development from assistant principals to teachers. All individuals who hold these leadership positions continue to teach about half time.

In addition to developing differentiated roles for novice teachers and teacher leaders, the Professional Practice School has fostered visible and vital intellectual exchange among the faculty as a whole through the establishment of monthly staff forums, a yearly retreat, ongoing professional development cohorts, and a preparatory group for National Board Certification. In these professional contexts, teachers assess, revise, and refine their individual teaching and school procedures in conversation and collaboration with their colleagues.

Researchers in Residence

In accord with the Professional Practice School's emphasis on teacher reflection and ongoing development that begins in the Residency Program, an action research group was established in 1999. Funded by the Spencer Foundation,[1] the Minneapolis Researchers in Residence research group serves as a support network for teachers interested in deeply studying their own practice. Members of the group rely primarily on a recursive action research structure (Bassey, 1998; Carr & Kemmis, 1986; Whitehead, 1989), but phases of the research are supported by drawing on qualitative research methods suited for classroom contexts (Freedman, 1999; Hubbard & Power, 1993; MacLean & Mohr, 1999) as well as analysis of published teacher research (e.g., Fecho, 1996; Juarez, 1999).

Over the course of the 2-year project, teacher researchers have developed research questions, designed a data collection plan, and analyzed data. The goal of the project was to develop new understandings about teaching academic content in an urban setting. The teacher researchers have each structured a research plan that incorporates multiple forms of data (e.g., student work, instructional artifacts, field notes, interviews, surveys, existing records, observational charts, etc.). Within the group, university and teacher researchers have worked together to cre-

[1]This work was generously supported by a Spencer Foundation Practitioner Research Communication and Mentoring Grant.

ate instruments for data collection (where necessary) and to formalize a suitable approach for data analysis. Teacher researchers participated in ongoing informal analysis—reflective writing and discussion—and received feedback on more structured qualitative data analysis. Action research methodology provided teacher researchers with a framework that can wed substantive, systematic data collection and analysis drawn from established qualitative research methodologies with a flexible approach that incorporates evolving understandings and practices. Some members of the group followed a more traditional research approach, formalizing their research question and design before collecting data, whereas others, drawing more deliberately on an action research cycle, incorporated design/reflection and analysis throughout, progressing through the spiral of developing new plans and questions as they learned from their earlier data collection.

In the Researchers in Residence group, six teachers and two U of M facilitators met monthly. Teachers in the group represent multiple subject areas. To support each individual teacher researcher, the team developed a routine for their research meetings in which individual reflection, paired discussion, and whole-group meetings were balanced. After an opening discussion of some aspect of research method (e.g., developing coding categories, writing research memos, etc.) and a round-robin in which each teacher researcher identified a focus for the day, team members would work independently, meet in pairs with colleagues, or discuss with a university-based facilitator for an hour. These options supported authentic collaboration by allowing each individual researcher to determine when interaction would be productive. Some teacher researchers in the group would collaborate at nearly every meeting; others would work independently until the need for feedback became apparent.

The final hour of the meetings was set aside for whole-group collaboration through research presentations. Drawing on protocols used within the Coalition for Essential Schools (Allen & McDonald, 2002), the group used research presentations to offer focused response to an individual's evolving research. This technique provided structure for group discussion and reinforced issues of research methodology through concrete dilemmas. Most important, in these discussions, the diversity of teaching experience, research knowledge, institutional roles, and subject-matter expertise served as significant resources that could be brought to bear as a teacher researcher examined the intersection of research and teaching decisions.

In addition to these meetings, the Henry teacher researchers met informally—usually once a month. Group members drew on their knowledge of each other's teaching goals and research purposes, as well as their shared understanding of students and the educational context, to talk through roadblocks, articulate new ideas, develop data analysis frameworks, brainstorm new teaching approaches, and plan future research steps.

In this chapter, we explore the role that participating in action research played for members of the group through the voices of two language teachers: Christina Maynor (French) and Sharon Cormany (English as a Second Language [ESL]). In our reflections, we see that conducting research in the classroom brings multiple dimensions of teaching into interaction. For each individual, the nature of those interactions will differ depending on the research question and the issues that individual is drawn to and perplexed by. We captured the interactive dimension of action research as a series of overlapping circles (see Fig.12.1).

In the following sections, Maynor and Cormany describe in detail how their action research has led to new understandings of self, curriculum, and theory and through these understandings to changes in teaching practice.

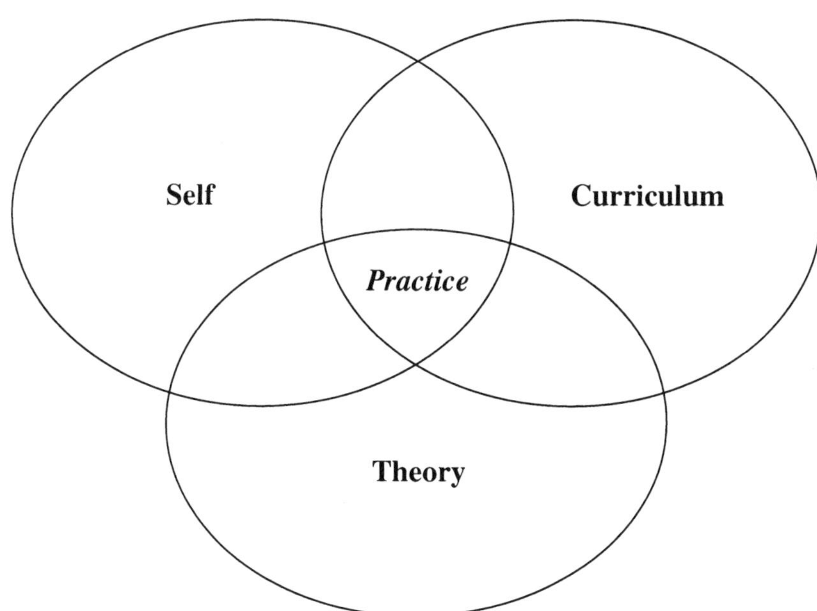

FIG. 12.1 The interactions of action research.

THROUGH SELF AND CURRICULUM TO PRACTICE: CHRISTINA MAYNOR

I ran into the classroom with warm copies in hand just as the bell rang. I explained that we would be using what we've learned so far by applying it to something real. Real French TV.... I watched the whole time as everyone followed along, as they diligently answered the questions and enjoyed the videos and ads. I admitted to them that I didn't catch every word either when they complained of having difficulty picking a word out.... We had fun together. I think partly it was magical because the students "owned" the videos.... Partly ... because it was real. (Journal entry, January 24, 2001)

There was an intense energy that day. I felt like I was at the top of my game—giving them the best in me. Ironically, I wasn't in front of the class that period. My role was that of engineer.

The students were spellbound watching the videos and working furiously in the packets I had assembled to go with them. Looking around the room, I saw that they were crowded up to the TV; no one's head was down. After finals, I counted the packets. Every single person who was present had completed it entirely. The magic number: 100%. It was exactly what I was looking for—total student engagement.

I analyzed the results when all the classes had completed the activity, looking especially at their answers to the question, "What did you learn from this activity?" In their own words, they said, "I learned that ... [the French] have good taste in music and that I like to listen to it even if I don't understand it"; "I learned that [Americans] have a big impact on French culture and music"; "I also learned that French people like, maybe love, American artists"; "I learned that the French like to hear music from all around the world ... that the French music is very interesting, their songs are different and in some ways better."

While I read their comments, I noticed a few corners ripped from the packets. They were the corners on which some students had scribbled the Web address of the French music television station to continue their French explorations at home. Some of these students later told me of the MP3s[2] of French music they now had in their music collections.

This approach was miles away from how I taught French the previous year. At the time, I didn't think I was a poor teacher; on the contrary, I took pride in my method. I used direct instruction, clear explanations of key grammar points, patterned practice as a class, regular worksheet homework, and individual quizzes. I offered the students some impor-

---

[2]MP3 (MPeg3) is an encoding format for audio files that allows them to be easily compressed and downloaded.

tant things: structure, organization, and practice building study skills. It wasn't until the summer when I was out of the fray that I realized what could possibly be missing. It occurred to me one day while I was thinking of our accomplishments that we hadn't ever produced anything real. We had never interacted with anything other than a textbook. I remembered the less successful students of the year, and they were generally ones whose parents had never been to college, who didn't imagine themselves traveling the world. I hadn't done much to change their minds, and maybe I could.

The music video activity I described previously was a direct result of my long-term engagement in action research. The foundational principals of authentic learning and communicative language use at work here are simple enough—so simple, I could've read it in a book. I have. I could've heard it in a class. I have. However, it was my guiding question, discussions with colleagues, input from my students, and my reflections—ultimately the processes of action research—that made planning the aforementioned activity so easy. Action research is about figuring it out for yourself from the ground up.

The Initial Question

My goal at the outset of the year, my first time teaching French I, was to reduce the numbers of students who drop out of French all too soon and to increase numbers who continue in Levels II through V. Although Patrick Henry enjoys a healthy enrollment in World Languages, with nearly 50% of students taking one of three languages, by the time students reach Levels IV and V, one can see at a glance that the classes are lacking in diversity. I believed that as a classroom teacher, I could affect student retention in all student groups (race, socioeconomic class, future academic plans, background, etc.) through my approach to students in the class and through my choice of curricular activities. I began a 2-year project surrounding the following question: "How do curricular activities and teacher approach affect student engagement and retention in the French classroom?"

At the beginning of the year, I was new to action research. I was drawn to try it because I was looking for a way to answer questions about curriculum and as a means of honing my teaching approach:

> It doesn't make sense for me to take on yet another project ... yet I was compelled by something within me to come here.... I got a sense that this experience would deepen my personal and professional relationship with teaching.... The daily grind of teach-

> ing has its ups and downs, but without a community of inquiring peers, it lacks an intellectualness that I crave. (Journal entry, September 27, 2000)

The Researchers in Residence offered me an opportunity to try formal inquiry with the support of group peers.

A Dynamic Approach

"The Researchers in Residence met again today, and it reminded me just how precious this [process] is to my sense of professionalism and how rejuvenating it is to talk with our group" (Journal entry, March 7, 2001).

In my 2nd year of teaching, my vision of myself as a teacher was in a state of continuous flux. This made looking at curricular activities and my approach toward students a bit like trying to fix on a moving target.

The Researchers in Residence helped me define my approach. The group was made up of teachers at the high school and university levels with a range of teaching and research experience. As one of the newer teachers and the newest to action research, I was able to benefit immensely from others' insights into my observations, suggestions for research approach, and curricular ideas.

Through free-writing activities and discussions in our September and October meetings, I articulated the beginnings of a simple theory related to my research question. Looking first at curricular activities, I theorized that activities that are purposeful (communicative), collaborative, and tied to the target culture will effectively engage a broad range of students and thereby increase student retention in Henry's French program. I set out to look at this at six through nine specific points in the year. I created unit projects designed to synthesize about 4 weeks of learning language "building blocks," which were pulled from our class text (Valette & Valette, 1990).

Over the year, a patterned research approach emerged for me. At our monthly meetings, we would discuss questions and recent observations from our classrooms. I would go back to the classroom with new ideas centered on my initial research question and enriched by collegial discussion. I used these ideas to create the synthesis projects like the one described previously. After each project, I looked at student engagement levels and considered student reactions to the projects though journaling. Fortified with new observations and reflections, I returned to the group to continue the process. Included in the synthesis projects were a range of activities from writing lengthy pen pal letters to making family photo albums and introducing their families and telling about them in French to the class. Through cycles of discussion, action, observation, and reflection, action research helped me live fully and intentionally in the class.

An Episode From the Classroom— The Effects of Action Research on Curriculum

In more than one way, the activity I described at the beginning of this article went on to form a cornerstone of our classroom culture and curriculum. Students continued to make reference to the artists and music from those videos for the rest of the school year, thereby displaying a personal ownership of French.

I chose to use the artists from the videos as the basis for our next synthesis activity. In groups, students dressed up as the musicians and singers and TV interviewers and presented an original mock interview before the class. Participation was uniformly energetic.

The general results of the year were that an overwhelming number of students chose to continue to take French: 77 of 79. Although this number is hard to correlate to any one part of a classroom approach, it seems to be an indicator of the positive response I observed in my classes.

Epilogue, Year 2

The beauty of action research is that it not only answers questions about what happens in the classroom, but it also necessarily brings up new ones. Sure enough, as I looked at the class we had become at the end of the 1st year, I noticed something strange.

It was a day near the end of the year, and I tried something new. As I asked students to find a partner to work with for the day's activity, I heard more than one person say, "I don't know *him,*" or "I don't know *her.*" It occurred to me that although we had worked in groups during the year, it had only been for unit projects and that I had never asked them to get French information from their peers before. I sat back and watched as they worked with their newly discovered partners, and we all realized that this was a goldmine of untapped energy and knowledge.

I added a new part to my original question for Year 2 of the cycle: "How do daily elements of purpose, collaboration, and ties to French culture affect student engagement and retention in the French classroom?" Over time, as I study this question, it has brought a fresher and more organic feel to the class, and we continue to pursue understanding French language and culture together. In fact, my class mirrors more and more the experiences that I had with the Researchers in Residence.

Through my own experience, I realize in an authentic way what my students need to question, collaborate, and do to know.

FROM PRACTICE TO THEORY: SHARON CORMANY

> As researchers of their own practice, teachers can discover for themselves how deeply theoretical their work is and has always been. This discovery can position them in a new relation to university theory. For some teacher researchers, theory is no longer what "they" do at the university, but becomes what "we" do in our classrooms every day. (Kalnin, 2000, p. 296)

Nearly 20% of the students at Patrick Henry High School are English language learners. About 60% of these students are Hmong, whereas the remaining 40% is composed mainly of Liberian students. With both of these groups, their speaking and listening skills far outpace their reading and writing skills. As their ESL teacher, my task is to prepare them to succeed in mainstream classes as well as to pass the Minnesota Basic Skills Tests in reading and writing. Thus, a great deal of my curriculum and instruction is focused on helping my students become more effective at communicating their ideas in writing.

As a 1st-year teacher in the Residency Program at Patrick Henry, I had conducted an action research project that looked at student editing and revision processes, which I found to be among the most useful and enjoyable projects of my graduate program. In that study, I found that students were able to generate a list of things to look for when editing that included content, organization, and mechanics, but that when actually revising and editing their own work, they focused almost entirely on mechanics. I became interested in the gap between students' declarative knowledge and procedural knowledge: If students know what to do, why don't they do it? I realized that this applied to many other areas as well, especially grammar. My advanced English language learners are more than able to complete a past-tense worksheet, but when they write, the past-tense morpheme rarely makes an appearance. At the same time, I was frustrated that not many of my students were passing the Minnesota Basic Skills Writing Test;[3] grammatical errors seemed to be one of the main factors holding them back.

From this quandary, my next action research questions developed: "How does grammar production differ in controlled versus communica-

---

[3]The Minnesota Basic Writing Skills Test, along with other tests in mathematics and reading, are required for high school graduation in the state. The writing test is administered for the first time to students in the 10th grade.

tive contexts? How can a teacher facilitate transfer of students declarative knowledge of grammar to novel production tasks such as writing?" More specifically, I wanted to look at the impact of direct instruction and ongoing form-focused error correction on student production of the past-tense morpheme. First, I looked at correct usage of the past tense in a decontextualized task using my entire Academic Language (advanced ESL) class as participants. I gave students a list of 10 verbs and asked them to put them in past tense, first before and then after a 3-week period of form-focused instruction in past tense. Of course, I expected that correct usage of past tense would improve in this simple task. However, much to my dismay, when I looked at the results, it appeared that correct usage of the past-tense morpheme actually declined after we studied it in class. "Well, so much for teaching!" (Journal entry, January 10, 2001).

This initial data set called into question the very foundations of my teaching philosophy: I teach something, and students learn it. Of course, the whole point of my project was to find out more about why students have trouble transferring what they learn to new tasks, but it had never occurred to me that they might not actually be learning it at all. I thought back to the theories I had studied in graduate school for some explanation of this troubling discovery. Could this be a manifestation of interlanguage (Selinker, 1972), or was it an example of the gap between competence and performance (Chomsky, 1957)? Was Krashen (1981) right about input being more important than instruction? Were my instructional methods too focused on form without enough attention to meaning and use (Larsen-Freeman, 1986)? Perhaps my entire approach to teaching grammar and writing was misguided. I decided it was time to seek some guidance from the experts in the form of professional reading about second language acquisition and second language (L2) writing instruction.

As soon as I began reading about and revisiting these theories, I began to compare them to my own theories based on my experience in the classroom and my action research. Ironically, the more I looked at others' theories and research, the more confident I became in my own theory of L2 writing instruction. It seemed as if most of the major theories of L2 writing instruction focused on one aspect of writing at the expense of all others. From my own experience as a writing teacher, I know that English language learners have many needs; needs that cannot be met by any of these approaches used in isolation:

> I should not discount my role as the theorist who drives my own research and practice.... I have a working theory that L2 writing instruction needs to include attention to linguistic correctness, discourse structure, the writing process, fluency,

> enjoyment, pragmatism, and the strategies to make all of the above possible. I am nothing if not ambitious. However, what my theory currently lacks is credible research, both in the traditional academic sense and in its effectiveness in my classroom. I might be able to synthesize the first, given the time and resources. The second is my own personal cross to bear. (Journal entry, February 17, 2001)

The task of articulating my own theory of writing instruction was incredibly empowering. It set in motion an avalanche of ideas about how teachers construct their own knowledge and the role theory plays in that knowledge. It struck me that all teachers have a theory of instruction, which is constantly honed and redefined through daily practice. In fact, teachers' theories both begin and end in practice. What teachers, myself included, want to know is, "How do my students learn? How does what I do as a teacher impact that learning?" Like learning, the development of teacher theory is nonlinear. There is a constant interplay between theory, research, and practice:

> Obviously, teachers are not sheep—we do not just blindly embrace a theory generated at the university level and apply it hook, line, and sinker in our classrooms. We may take bits and pieces of academic theory to varying degrees, then modify, adjust, and re-theorize based on the realities of our practice. In this way, teachers' theories are truly working theories, not static entities to be recorded and subsequently discredited and disproven. Because our theories work backwards, they may be less well articulated, but infinitely more useful. (Journal entry, February 19, 2001)

I realized that, regardless of what other theorists said about the importance of focusing on form or linguistic correctness, I knew it was important for my students. They need to use grammar correctly to pass the Minnesota Basic Skills Writing Test and to succeed in future academic pursuits. They need an awareness of linguistic forms and structures to effectively communicate their ideas in a second language. As their ESL teacher, I cannot simply sit back and hope that they get enough input to acquire these structures on their own. I have to do everything in my power to help them master the conventions of English so that they can be successful in whatever endeavors they pursue.

> I view writing as a somewhat political act—it is important to teach students to operate within the dominant paradigm, in or-

> der that they may be empowered to change that paradigm or create new ones. What I haven't decided yet, however, it to what extent this belief applies to teacher theory. (Journal entry, February 19, 2001)

In fact, I have come to view action research as a political act as well. Not only can action research help teachers better understand our students' needs, it can help us take more ownership of our profession as well. It is a tool by which we can assume more control over our practice and the theory that guides it. It moves us from a role of passive recipients into active constructors of professional knowledge.

I have continued constructing knowledge about my students' use of grammatical forms in writing by looking at their use of the past-tense morpheme in communicative writing contexts. I conducted a detailed error analysis of past-tense verbs in five students' journals at four points over the course of the year. On first examination, the data showed no significant patterns, with some students increasing their correct usage of past tense and others decreasing. To better understand the data, I decided to separate regular and irregular verbs and see if any patterns emerged. In fact, they did. I discovered that all five of my students increased their correct usage of the regular past-tense morpheme (-ed) over the course of the year, whereas irregular verbs remained erratic. When I reanalyzed the initial decontextualized past-tense task for my five students using the same criteria, the same pattern emerged. So, in fact, form-focused instruction and error correction did appear to make a difference for my five students, but only with the verbs that followed the pattern we focused on. So, apparently, there is a reason to teach grammar after all.

As we prepared for this conference, my colleagues and I looked for quotes from our own journals and other writings on action research to illustrate the significance of this tool in our professional lives. When I read Julie Kalnin's quote, which begins this section, I nearly gasped—it perfectly describes my own experience with action research and mirrors many of the quotes I selected from my professional journal. In fact, it turned out that I had seen this quote at the beginning of the year at the first meeting of our action research group. Yet it took a year of struggling to make sense of data, reading, and reflecting for me to reach the same conclusions on my own. Simply reading someone else's insights was not enough to make them meaningful to me; just as with my action research findings, my own discoveries are far more significant to me than the same assertions made by someone else.

Ultimately, action research has a significant, although somewhat unexpected, impact on my practice. It simultaneously bolsters my confidence and causes me to question everything I believe about teaching. It has led me to believe that I am the primary constructor of knowledge about how my students learn, which is both incredibly empowering and somewhat daunting. I cannot blame Selinker, Chomsky, Krashen, or Larsen-Freeman for not understanding my students; they have never met them. I have. If my students forget to use "-ed" in their writing, it is my responsibility to find a better way to teach them, and now it is my responsibility to discover the secret of teaching irregular verbs as well.

FINAL REFLECTIONS

The chronicles of our experiences with the Researchers in Residence group describe side-by-side transformations. Each one of us experienced independent and yet interconnected changes in our practice through collaboration in the group. Tina's understanding of her role as a teacher/learning engineer and Sharon's understanding of herself as theorist in the classroom are the result of a true openness and honest mutual inquiry that illuminate the connections between the self, theory, and curriculum.

All teachers have theories about how their students learn best, but through action research, these theories become knowledge. For the Researchers in Residence at Patrick Henry High School, conducting action research has allowed us to know our students in a deeper, more meaningful way that goes beyond the vague sense of intuition we relied on previously. Often, this knowledge can be surprising, as the results of action research lead to new insights and deeper understandings that transcend our inevitable biases. Although this process can be humbling initially, it leads ultimately to an increased sense of efficacy and empowerment as we translate our knowledge into improved student learning.

The formalized knowledge developed through action research not only helps teachers solidify their own theories about how students learn language but also become more informed practitioners of others' theories as well. The more teachers know their students, the more they can use second language acquisition theory to help students learn because they have a strong awareness of students' learning needs and characteristics through which teachers can filter the latest trends and approaches. By conducting action research, teachers can truly claim that no one knows their students better than they do.

This kind of learning requires at least extended and focused time and may even require a reconceptualization of teachers' work. Although the goals of the PPS are well aligned with the Researchers in Residence project, and the structure of the Professional Practice School provided a few hours of release time, participating in ongoing classroom inquiry was an intensive process that challenged existing support structures. The stipends provided by the Spencer Foundation offered an additional incentive for teachers to participate in such a long-term project, yet becoming teacher researchers meant extending beyond current professional expectations and assigned job duties in ways that could be exhausting as often as they were exhilarating.

If we were to break down our process into bite-sized pieces and prescribe them to other teachers in search of transformation, we would necessarily fail. Transformation cannot be taught; it must be learned. Our experiences challenge superficial inservice activities and one-shot workshops and speak to the need to move teacher research from the margins of a teacher's work to a core component of practice. Participating in and witnessing the interplay of theory, curriculum, and self leads us to reject reductionistic research and professional development that isolate instructional behaviors. Only by seeing teaching in an integrated way can we begin to transform ourselves, our theories, and our daily lives with students.

REFERENCES

Allen, D., & McDonald, J. (2002). *The tuning protocol: A process for reflection on teacher and student work.* Retrieved January, 2003, from the Coalition for Essential Schools Website: http://www.essentialschools.org/cs/resources/view/ces_res/54

Bassey, M. (1998). Action research for improving educational practice. In R. Halsall (Ed.), *Teacher research and school improvement: Opening doors from the inside* (pp. 93–108). Buckingham, UK: Open University Press.

Carr, W., & Kemmis, S. (1986). *Becoming critical: Education knowledge and action research*. London: Falmer.

Chomsky, N. (1957). *Syntactic structures.* The Hague, Netherlands: Mouton.

Fecho, B. (1996). Learning from Laura. In *Cityscapes* (pp. 57–72). Berkeley, CA: National Writing Project.

Freedman, S. (1999). The M-CLASS approach to teacher research. In S. W. Freedman, E. R. Simons, & J. S. Kalni (Eds.), *Inside city schools: Investigating literacy in multicultural classrooms* (pp. 22–52). New York: Teachers College Press.

Hubbard, R., & Power, B. (1993). *The art of classroom inquiry: A handbook for teacher researchers.* Portsmouth, NH: Heinemann.

Juarez, D. A. (1999). A question of fairness: Using writing and literature to expand ethnic identity and understand marginality. In S. W. Freedman, E. R. Simons, & J. S. Kalni (Eds.), *Inside city schools: Investigating literacy in multicultural classrooms* (pp. 111–125). New York: Teachers College Press.

Kalnin, J. (2000). *Teachers learning: A teacher research group in action.* Unpublished doctoral dissertation, University of California, Berkeley.

Krashen, S. (1981). *Second language acquisition and second language learning.* New York: Pergamon.

Larsen-Freeman, D. (1986). *Techniques and principles in language teaching*. New York: Oxford University Press.

MacLean, M., & Mohr, M. (1999). *Teacher-researchers at work*. Berkeley, CA: National Writing Project.

Mathews, J. (2000). Education: The 100 best high schools. *Newsweek, 135,* 50–53.

Minneapolis Public Schools. (2000). *Measuring up: A summarized report on the Minneapolis*

Public Schools 2000. Retrieved June 23, 2001, from http://mpls.k12.mn.us

Selinker, L. (1972). Interlanguage. *International Review of Applied Linguistics, 10,* 209–30.

Valette, J., & Vallete, R. (1990). *Discovering French, bleu*. Lexington, MA: DC Heath.

Whitehead, J. (1989). Creating a living educational theory from questions of the kind, "How do I improve my practice?" *Cambridge Journal of Education, 19*(1), 41–52.

Chapter 13

Improving ESL Instruction in a Bilingual Program Through Collaborative, Inquiry-Based Professional Development

Nancy E. Dubetz
Lehman College

INTRODUCTION

In its statement on bilingual education, TESOL advocates for programs that promote bilingualism and have a strong, carefully integrated English as a second language (ESL) component (TESOL, 1993). In this chapter, I describe the study of a collaborative teacher development project that focuses on improving instruction in bilingual classrooms by engaging bilingual teachers in (a) using assessment information in the first and second languages to plan for ESL instruction, and (b) providing effective content-based ESL instruction that builds on what is taught in the native language. The project is one of several collaborative teacher development activities that take place in a Professional Development School (PDS) partnership between an urban public elementary school and an urban public university.

Professional Development Schools

A PDS is a wide-ranging and long-term partnership designed to improve the quality of teaching in ways that ultimately improve student learning (Abdal-Haqq, 1998; Chance, 2000; Houston, Hollis, Clay, Ligons, & Roff, 1999; Reynolds, 1999; Teitel, 2001). This is achieved in several ways. First, PDSs promote more ambitious conceptions of teaching and learning than do traditional school/university partnerships by focusing on simultaneous renewal at both participating institutions (Abdal-Haqq, 1998; Grisham, Laguardia, & Brink, 2000; Holmes Group, 1995; Walling & Lewis, 2000). Second, these partnerships promote opportunities for university-based and school-based faculty to identify and study problems of practice together (Holmes Group, 1995; Lyons, Stroble, & Fischetti, 1997; Simmons, Konecki, Crowell, & Gates-Duffield, 1999). Research in PDSs is characterized as enterprising, responsible and immediately relevant to teacher practice (Abdal-Haqq, 1998; Berry, Boles, Edens, Nissenholtz, & Trachtman, 1998; Boudah & Knight, 1999; Holmes Group, 1995). This type of inquiry adds to and reorganizes the knowledge base on teaching and learning (Abdal-Haqq, 1998; Holmes Group, 1995; Houston et al., 1999; Thompson, Maxwell, Kelley, & Carnate, 2000; Whitford & Metcalf-Turner, 1999). Finally, PDSs link experienced teachers' efforts to renew their knowledge and advance their status with efforts to improve their schools and to prepare new teachers (Holmes Group, 1995; Levine, 1997; Nihlen, Williams, & Sweet, 1999).

To foster an environment that promotes both adult and children's learning, PDS partners must create opportunities for professional development that fit within the organizational structures of the institutions involved and meet the needs of all participants including teacher education candidates, school-based faculty, and university-based faculty (National Council of Accreditation of Teacher Education, 2001). In the study reported here, I describe PDS work that involves representatives of all three of these constituencies working together to improve instruction for English language learners (ELLs) who constitute roughly one third of the student body at the PDS and have been the least successful in meeting state learning standards.

The PDS work described in this study is grounded in an inquiry-based professional development model that promotes an environment of learning for adults and children. Effective professional development offers participants opportunities to collaborate while experimenting with new practices (Joyce & Showers, 1995; Miller, 1988; National Partnership for Excellence and Accountability for Teaching [NPEAT], 1998; Sparks & Loucks-Horsley, 1990). Support during this process of experimentation must be ongoing, interactive, and cumulative (Gusky, 1995), and all of those participating in the professional development should have a say in determining the content and nature of the activities offered (National Foundation for the Improvement of Education [NFIE]; 1996; NPEAT, 1998). Finally, effective professional development opportunities are designed to accommodate participants who will be at different places in their professional knowledge, interests, and beliefs (Huberman, 1995; NFIE, 1996; Sprinthall, Reiman, & Thies-Sprinthall, 1996). Thoughtful consideration must be given to the integration of individual professional development needs with the institutional needs (Sparks & Loucks-Horsley, 1990; NFIE, 1996; NPEAT, 1998).

PDSs are ideal settings for effective professional development to take place because they value and allocate resources to professional development that is characterized by the qualities described previously. One model of inquiry-based professional development that encompasses these qualities are what have been called teacher study groups or support groups (Clair, 1998; Clark, 2001; Trueba, 1989), work groups (Biagetti, 2001), or more broadly, professional development and inquiry groups (Clark, 2001). These groups share four characteristics. First, they are learning oriented. The purposes of the discussions that take place are driven by the concerns of the participants. Typically, teacher study groups focus on issues around teaching practice and student learning. As such, they serve as a mechanism for building knowledge, providing emotional support, and problem solving. Second, they are structured for community building among the participants. In a PDS setting, participants include preservice teacher candidates and college faculty in addition to practicing teachers and administrators. Third, participation is voluntary and participants set the agenda. Fourth, study groups are ongoing and meet regularly. These four qualities make study groups fertile places for undertaking inquiry into the relationship between teaching practice and student learning. In this chapter, I present research into the evolution of a study group in a PDS and the potential impact of the model on one group of PDS participants: bilingual classroom teachers.

SETTING OF THE STUDY AND PARTICIPANTS

The PDS in which the study took place is a Kindergarten through fourth grade urban elementary school with a population of 630 students in a school designed for 573. In this working class community, 94% of the children are eligible for free lunch. Ninety-eight percent of the school population are children of color. A little over 30% of the children are

ELLs, and most of these are enrolled in a transitional bilingual program. The transitional bilingual program is designed to move children into English as quickly as possible. In kindergarten and first grade, all areas of the curriculum are taught in the native language except for social studies, which is the focus of ESL instruction. In second grade, children receive 3 days of language arts and science in Spanish and 2 days of language arts and science in English, 4 days of math in English and 1 in Spanish, and social studies in English. By third grade, all areas of the curriculum are taught in English except for two periods of native language arts and two of science. In fourth grade, ELLs who still need support are placed in a monolingual classroom with a bilingual teacher and a "push-in" ESL teacher.[1]

Although the ELLs have shown significant gains over the last 3 years in developing English language proficiency as measured by the Language Assessment Battery (New York City Public Schools Office of Testing, 1982), they are not meeting state standards in math and language arts as measured on the state standardized assessments in English or Spanish. Because these children represent a significant portion of the school population and because the university preservice programs have as a goal preparing all teachers to work with ELLs, the following priority goal was established for the PDS partnership: to support English language acquisition and content learning for ELLs. A study group was created as one form of PDS work that would help the partners move toward achieving this goal.

During the first 8 months of the study, the participants in the study group included six bilingual classroom teachers, one bilingual staff developer, one Title VII coordinator, one monolingual literacy staff developer; two bilingual paraprofessionals, a student teacher, and me, the college's PDS liaison and the researcher. The student teacher attended the meetings while she was completing a 7 week student teaching placement in a third grade bilingual classroom. In addition, two school administrators and an ESL teacher each attended one or two sessions. Of the bilingual teachers participating in the study group, one teacher was in her first year, two had two to four years of experience and three had more than 5 years. Four were certified to teach grades prekindergarten through sixth grade with a bilingual extension, and two were working toward the bilingual extension. There were five bilingual general edu-

[1]"Push in" refers to programs in which the ESL teacher works with ESL students in a grade level classroom that contains both ESL and English-speaking children. Two examples of push-in models area (a) the ESL teacher team teaches with the classroom teacher, and (b) the ESL teacher observes the classroom teacher's presentation of a content-based activity and then works with the ESL students to help them complete assignments related to the activity.

cation teachers teaching kindergarten to third grade, and there was one special education bilingual teacher who taught a class with children from Grades 2 to 4. All of the teacher participants in the study group were Latina women of Puerto Rican or Dominican heritage except for the college PDS liaison and the monolingual literacy staff developer, who were both Anglo.

The teacher study group met twice monthly and focused on issues raised by the teachers in the bilingual program. Meetings occurred during the common preparation period for bilingual teachers and on a city-wide staff development day. Each teacher also met regularly with me, the college PDS liaison and researcher, as a follow-up to the study group meetings. The study group was designed to pursue the teachers' questions as lines of inquiry within the PDS structure to effectively connect theory and practice. The findings reported in this chapter focus on the contributions made by the bilingual teachers to the study group.

RESEARCH DESIGN AND METHODOLOGY

Theoretical Framework/Research Questions

The study I report here explores how the PDS study group evolved over an 8-month period and whether participation in a study group influenced teachers' theories of practice. The term *theory of practice* is used in this study to describe the relation between the theory a teacher holds about teaching and learning and her or his enacted practice (Dubetz, 2002). This construct is supported by a body of research that characterizes teachers' thinking as context specific, activist, adaptive, nonlinear, and holistic (Clandinin, 1985; Elbaz, 1991; Genishi, Dubetz, & Focarino, 1995; Golombek, 1998; Paris, 1993; Rios, 1996). A theory of practice reflects a teacher's negotiation of multiple sources of knowledge including personal beliefs and values, pedagogical and content knowledge, knowledge of children, and the expectations of the school culture where she or he works when making instructional decisions. It is continually tested and modified as the teacher attempts to maintain coherence between what she or he thinks and what she or he practices.

Study groups are designed to engage teachers in making explicit their thinking through collaborative conversations about issues around teaching and learning, and therefore, they offer a fertile context for the study of what constitutes a theory of practice and whether it changes in the collegial context of a study group setting. The study of changes in teachers' theories of practice is important because it addresses a key function of PDSs, which is improving teaching practice, and because there is evidence that simply understanding the reasons behind the instructional decisions that they make may not lead language teachers to long term personal and professional development (Golombek, 1998).

The specific research questions guiding the study are the following:

> Research Question Set 1: How does the study group model evolve over time to accommodate the changing needs of participants? What lines of inquiry emerge and how are these discussed across time?
>
> Research Question Set 2: How do teachers' theories of practice emerge during participation in a PDS study group ? Does a theory of practice change as a result of participation in the PDS study group?

Data Collection and Analysis

The study was conducted using a qualitative research design characterized by naturalistic inquiry (Lincoln & Guba, 1985). Data sources included (a) transcriptions of audiotaped study group meetings and one meeting with the third grade bilingual teacher and her student teacher, (b) surveys, (c) anecdotal recollections of meetings between the study group facilitator and individual teachers, (d) artifacts from classrooms such as samples of children's work, and (e) the researcher's log. These data were collected over an 8-month period between September 2000 and May 2001.

Data were analyzed using the constant comparative method (Glaser & Strauss, 1967). As the researcher, I first engaged in repeated, holistic review of data to identify (a) significant events in social interaction (Zellermayer, 2001) and (b) the nature of the conversations associated with these events. *Significant events* were defined as those that involved risk on the part of a participant, for example, a teacher requesting feedback from colleagues on a sample of a child's work or sharing an opinion about a particular practice. To capture teachers' theories of practice, data were coded for sources of knowledge, and properties associated with these sources were identified. I then reviewed the results of this analysis to identify patterns in teacher learning, both gradual and accumulative as well as sudden and definitive. To establish credibility and dependability (Lincoln & Guba, 1985), the research design included triangulation of data sources and long-term, repeated data collection.

FINDINGS FOR RESEARCH QUESTION 1: EVOLUTION OF THE STUDY GROUP

In response to the first set of research questions for the study regarding the evolution of the study group, two general lines of inquiry emerged over the first 8-month period (a) planning for effective biliteracy instruction (September 2000 through March 2001) and (b) planning for sheltered content-based ESL instruction (March through May 2001). Each of these lines of inquiry was framed by concerns that teachers raised over time in study group meetings. Concerns that were discussed within the first line of inquiry were (a) how to assess children's oral and written language development and what to do with assessment information when planning for literacy instruction, (b) how to help children transfer their literacy knowledge from the native language to the second language, and (c) how to meet the needs of children whose literacy skills are not at grade level in either Spanish or English. Concerns that were discussed within the second line of inquiry were (a) how to teach social studies through ESL, (b) how to support comprehension of grade level social studies texts in English, and (c) how to structure ESL instruction for children who need basic English and children who are ready for more challenging academic content in English.

Discussions around a line of inquiry took four forms (a) descriptions of current teaching practices, (b) analyses of specific children's learning, (c) explanations of learning using academic theories, and (d) analyses of curriculum materials.

Descriptions of Current Teaching Practices

There is a strong emphasis on teaching reading and writing at the PDS, and much of the conversation that took place in the study group during the first months focused on how to teach literacy and how to assess children's literacy development. When discussing specific concerns about literacy instruction, for example, when to introduce a child to guided reading in his or her second language, teachers often shared stories of their current practices. In the first sample following, a first-grade teacher describes for me, the PDS liaison, how the bilingual teachers gather information about children's reading comprehension. In the second sample, a third-grade teacher describes her choices when grouping for guided reading.

Sample 1

First-grade teacher: [Regarding formal reading assessments] We have to do both. Everything is double for us, in Spanish and English[2] ... and also besides the testing, when you test them, it's the beginning of showing you and it gives you a star.... Besides the testing, like say you're doing modeling or the read aloud, then when you prepare the mini-lesson that they [the children] jump in, then you look at that, not only those books [part of the formal assessment instruments] because, see, when you do those books, it's not the same thing as when you use other books. I don't care what they say, but it's different.

College PDS liaison: So you also use your own observations.

First-grade teacher: Exactly, daily work, every day work. (Study group, 12/4/2000)

Sample 2

Third-grade teacher: What we do is, especially me, what I do is that I group them by needs, and then I group them by level according to what I'm going to teach them, according to whatever I'm focusing on that day. Then, I rearrange my group.... And so I disclose the grouping in that period of time. And I consider it's working with my children because they can express themselves more and they are acquiring the written language more than before. I know it's a step. We're going to go little by little because they can't jump one day to the next. I can't expect that. (Study group, 12/4/2000)

Descriptions of practice such as these offered insights into what teachers believed to be the strengths and limitations of various assessment and instructional approaches. When describing assessment practices, they valued informal assessment practices as much as formal assessment practices in deciding how to group

[2]The *Developmental Reading Assessment* (Beaver, 1997) and its Spanish counterpart, *Evaluación del Desarrollo de la Lectura* (Ruiz & Cuesta, 2000) are given to children three times a year and consist of a running record of the child's reading to assess the use of cueing systems followed by an interview with the child to assess comprehension. Results are reported to the District Office.

children for instruction and what practices to implement to support their learning. Over time, several formal assessment practices were discussed, such as the *Developmental Reading Assessment* (Beaver, 1997) and the *Evaluación del Desarrollo de la Lectura* (Ruiz & Cuesta, 2000) (endnote 2) and student portfolios, as were informal assessment practices, for example, teacher observations of level of student participation during small- and large-group instruction and language preferences. Linked to discussions of assessment were discussions of sheltered instructional strategies, as illustrated in the following excerpt:

Third-grade teacher: For bilingual it's great to act things out—
First-grade teacher: Talk about that TPR [Total Physical Response], that stuff, and it's really good.
Third-grade teacher: Cause I was reading book that says twisting, and they were like "what? twisted?" And I'm like, no, it's a twisting road [moving body] and you see me going through the same thing, and they finally "oh, it goes like a snake." I said, "yea that's exactly how it goes," so you have to act it out. (Study group, 2/2/2001)

Other strategies that were discussed included the language experience approach and the use of graphic organizers such as semantic webs.

Analysis of Children's Learning

When the study group first began meeting, teachers expressed frustration at not being able to effectively group children with such diverse language proficiency levels and reading abilities for literacy instruction. As the PDS liaison, I suggested that teachers share with the study group the work of a student whom they believed to be struggling to ground discussions about grouping in the needs of real children. Over a 2-month period, the teachers discussed work samples and formal assessment records of a kindergartner and a third grader. The following excerpts are two samples of conversations about a third grader named Rogelio[3] who was posing a particular challenge to one of the third-grade teachers because he had been in the transitional bilingual program since kindergarten and was a struggling reader in both Spanish and English.

[3]Rogelio is a pseudonym.

Sample 1

Kindergarten teacher:	[Referring to earlier comments that the child does not seem to have much oral language in either language] I'm really concerned with something they said. Because they said the child [Rogelio] in oral language has very limited vocabulary, but then they say he's very articulated [*sic*] but [do] you mean when he speaks, is he always repeating the little vocabulary he has?
Bilingual developer:	Like, "I am, he has."
Third-grade teacher:	Whatever little he has, it's the same thing over and over—
Kindergarten teacher:	Because he's very articulated [*sic*], but he's very lacking, major lacking in vocabulary. How can you be so articulated [*sic*]? [meaning how can a child be so articulate with such limited vocabulary]
Third-grade teacher:	If you could see his writing—
Bilingual developer:	No, he's not (inaudible). He can answer you in English—
Third-grade teacher:	He can answer, but it's not that he had the vocabulary.
Kindergarten teacher:	Because I didn't understand.
Third-grade teacher:	He can articulate. He can answer you, but it's very limited. You know, your usual little child kind of answers—
Kindergarten teacher:	So, he's not articulated [*sic*] much?

* * *

First-grade teacher:	Well I was just thinking, he can talk to you, bla, bla, bla, but he needs to realize that what he's saying that he can write it down, like we learned at the other [study group] meeting, too. Right?
Third-grade teacher:	Right.
First-grade teacher:	So he should be getting—
Third-grade teacher:	Making a connection with language to print.
First-grade teacher:	You know how to do that, right?

Third-grade teacher:	Right.
First-grade teacher:	So then he's going to be able to realize, "oh, what I'm saying I can write down and then I can read that." I think that would be—
Title VII coordinator:	The point is that the oral language might not even be—
Third-grade teacher:	It's not that advanced—
Title VII coordinator:	(inaudible) oral but how oral a level?
Third-grade teacher:	Limited, limited.
Title VII coordinator:	You might start building up his oral language; it's limited.
Principal:	So I think one thing he may need is a lot of listening skills, uh, listening to stories whether it be in his native language or in second language, a lot of read to strategies, and for the read to strategies, you can see the literacy staff developer and you can see the assistant principal, alright? And connecting, doing a follow up to that story. It could be to anything that he would picture that he can write something, whether it be a read aloud that you had done that morning or the day before or whatever, and you could only do that in read to. When you do language experience, then whatever follow-up you give can be around what you just talked about—
Kindergarten teacher:	I can bring in a sheet [description of the Language Experience Approach] (Study group, 1/4/2001)

Sample 2

First-grade teacher:	The thing also is that sometimes people have a little bit, I don't know if they don't know or a misunderstanding or wrong concept that not every body learns the second language as fast as the other one [be]cause I don't know if you remember, you remember that I had Carlos from the Dominican Republic. And by the end of the year he was speaking, writing, everything in English because his first language was very good.
Third-grade teacher:	That's why. He had something to transfer.

First-grade teacher: But, but, but if that's not the case [with Rogelio], but it depends on the individual, you know.

Bilingual developer: But with Rogelio they [his family] use Spanish a lot too. So he's not only being exposed to the English, he is also using a lot of the Spanish too, so when does he get to transfer? It will probably be only in school.

First-grade teacher: Yes, because when you get this group of first graders or second graders or whatever the grade, and [you ask yourself] how come they're not doing it? Some are, some aren't. It's not going to happen—

Third-grade teacher: Not everyone's at the same level—

First-grade teacher: You know how they put a level, like a time frame, like in 3 years[4]—

Third-grade teacher: They should [learn] English, [but] that's not possible—

First-grade teacher: Hello, that's not what ESL or bilingual education is and if you don't understand that, you're going to make those kids miserable.

Third-grade teacher: And frustrated. (Study group, 1/19/2001)

The analysis of Rogelio's difficulties illustrates the concerns related to literacy instruction that teachers chose to explore in their discussions, for example, the complex relation between oral and written language development and the role of knowledge transfer from one language to another in becoming biliterate. In the first sample, a teacher's challenge to explain what is meant by describing the child as having a limited oral vocabulary leads to suggested practices to overcome the limitation, for example, helping him to write down what he is saying or what he is hearing using the language experience approach. In the second sample, a discussion of the child's inability to yet transfer his knowledge from one language to the other leads to the acknowledgment of a discrepancy between the model of bilingual education mandated in state policy and that supported by sound pedagogical practice. What began as a concern about grouping evolved into an exploration of the relation between individual learning needs and best practices.

[4]This refers to the state policy that after 3 years, ELLs must take standardized tests in English unless a specific waiver is requested. The policy recommends transitional bilingual programs in which children transition to all English instruction after 3 years.

Explanations of Learning Using Academic Theories

Study group participants sometimes applied academic theories of language development and literacy development to their explorations of what was happening in their classrooms during literacy instruction. The following excerpt is from a conversation in which teachers are discussing a chapter from *Literacy Assessment of Second Language Learners* (Hurley & Tinajero, 2000). The chapter offers a description and examples of a Mexican fifth grader's writing in Spanish and English:

College PDS liaison:	One of the things that they talk about in the chapter is that Spanish speaking children organize their writing differently in Spanish than in English, but I'm curious about whether you've seen that to be the case when the children write. Do they organize their writing actually differently? Is that right?
Third-grade teacher:	Uhuh, because they're thinking in their language, so then they're going to write it down. It's like totally different because in English, I don't know if you've noted, to them it's like thinking backwards.
College PDS liaison:	That's because adjectives and the verbs and the nouns are backwards.
Third-grade teacher:	Right because when they are trying to write, they can not organize their thoughts because they are so much concentrating on what they're writing, not how they're organizing their paragraph. Because when they write it in Spanish—we're talking about [Spanish] dominant [children]—because when they're doing it in Spanish, they don't have to be thinking in any language but their own, so all they're thinking about is how they're organizing it. The other way they're thinking about the language more than organizing it, you know.
College PDS liaison:	No, I'm curious. I really don't know.
Kindergarten teacher:	We're talking about dominant, we're talking about the child has the CALPs [cognitive academic language proficiencies]—
Third-grade teacher:	No. Right. Dominant. They have the language.
Kindergarten teacher:	And that it means they have schooling in the native language and they have proficiency in the

language. And actually Spanish dominant, that we've read Spanish, it has a different logical pattern than in English. In Spanish you don't write the same way you write in English. I mean your ideas are not developed. You're not fixed to introduction, to supporting ideas, to a body. You are more (inaudible) like you'll develop the same idea in a different pattern. You will not be so tied to first idea, second idea, and a conclusion and wrapping up the second idea. So it's like it will flow, it's flow; that's how you write in Spanish. And that's what happens when dominant Spanish speakers learn English, they're so used to writing in that logical pattern that it will show.

College PDS liaison: So you see differences then, when you[r] kids write a story in Spanish, they actually use—

Kindergarten teacher: When they are dominant. They're not. That's what I said, [that] we have to really specify that they have the CALP, that they have the competencies, the cognitive language developed in the native language because when we're talking nondominant, you will not see that flow. When they don't have the proficiency in the native language, you will not see that flow.

College PDS liaison: In either one.

Kindergarten teacher: Right.

College PDS liaison: So you don't see it. So our two language kids that are sort of between both—

Kindergarten teacher: Their Spanish isn't going to have the fluency for writing.

College PDS liaison: Right. So they're writing may not be organized logically.

Kindergarten teacher: Exactly. It should be. That sample showed [in the chapter] that she [the fifth grader] has proficiency in her native language. (Study group, 2/16/2001)

This discussion suggests that teachers apply aspects of academic theories that have explanatory or predictive value to them. In the preceding discussion, there are references to Cummins' (1989) theory about cognitive academic language proficiency (CALP), for example, "... we have to really specify that they have the CALP ..." and his critical threshold hypothesis, for example, "... when we're talking nondominant, you will not see that flow. When they don't have the proficiency in the native language, you will not see that flow." In addition, a reference is implicitly made to a theory of cross-cultural variations in written discourse, for example, "[Spanish] ... has a different logical pattern than in English."

Analyses of Curriculum Materials

In the 6th month of meetings, the line of inquiry shifted from literacy instruction to a focus on sheltered ESL instruction in social studies. Two events prompted this new emphasis. First, a district social studies curriculum aligned with a new state social studies assessment had been introduced in the schools, and the principal requested that teachers prepare to engage in curriculum mapping at each grade level. Second, the district was changing the allocation of English and Spanish instruction in the transitional programs to require more ESL instruction and less native language instruction. As a result, all social studies instruction would take place in English from Kindergarten through third grade.

The bilingual teachers believed that grade level content materials in English posed a tremendous challenge to bilingual learners because they lacked background knowledge, vocabulary, and learning strategies they needed to make the facts and concepts comprehensible. To implement the new social studies curriculum in the bilingual programs, the teachers had to review grade level materials and identify potential challenges for their students. Thus, the focus of the study group turned to analyzing English texts that would be used to meet the social studies goals in English and to identify Spanish materials that addressed social studies topics and could be used during native language arts. A selection from an anecdotal recollection of a study group meeting illustrates the focus of conversations around the analysis of content materials. The teachers are reviewing an excerpt from the third grade social studies text about Kenya, which is one of the world communities that the children will study.

> The monolingual literacy staff developer said that there were key words at the beginning of the chapter that would obviously be important words to learn. Third Grade Teacher 1 said that a Swahili word "Harambee" was an unknown word.

> The college PDS liaison said that although this was a new word, it might not be a word that a teacher would feel that children should learn to apply in future contexts. Third Grade Teacher 2 pointed out that even words in embedded definitions would not help children understand them. She said that the embedded definition of wilderness as "unsettled" or "wild land" would not help her children understand the meaning of wilderness. Another teacher added that describing Nairobi as a "young" city would be difficult. The college PDS liaison added that "young" may being used in a different way than the children are used to seeing it. Third Grade Teacher 1 and the literacy staff developer disagreed about the definition of the word *tourist,* although they both thought that it would be a new vocabulary word for the third graders. Third Grade Teacher 2 suggested that she would explain to her students that when they went to Puerto Rico or the Dominican Republic, they would be tourists. The staff developer said that they would not be tourists because they would generally go there to visit family. Third Grade Teacher 2 argued that they did not live there so they would be considered tourists. The college PDS liaison said that another challenge the teachers might encounter is words that have different meanings to different people. (Study group, 4/27/2001)

The discussion reveals problems teachers encountered with both specialized vocabulary and common vocabulary. These concerns led to two decisions regarding future study group meetings, which would be documented in the 2nd year of the study. First, teachers decided to identify Spanish texts with social studies themes that they could use during native language arts to introduce as many social studies concepts as possible in children's dominant language. Second, teacher resources on sheltered instruction were ordered and teachers agreed to set specific goals for themselves in the fall of the coming year to meet both language and content goals during ESL instruction.

The samples of conversations presented in this section offer images of how the study group evolved as teachers explored their concerns through conversation. The process of exploring specific questions around their two lines of inquiry—literacy instruction and content-based ESL instruction—did not follow a linear path such as might be evident in teacher research projects in which problems and interventions are identified up front and documented through to their resolution. Because study groups are designed to respond to teachers' immediate problems, a line of inquiry can change suddenly, as it did when it shifted from literacy instruction to attending to the challenge of teaching social studies in English. Despite this, the discussions did reveal teachers' struggles in two areas of their practice across time and the sources of their decision making. The second set of research questions focuses on how the study group process illuminates teachers' theories of practice.

FINDINGS FOR RESEARCH QUESTION 2: TEACHERS' THEORIES OF PRACTICE

The Nature of Teachers' Theories of Practice

The theories of practice that were made explicit through collaborative conversation shared common characteristics with descriptions of teacher thinking derived from narrative studies of teacher practice (Clandinin, 1985; Elbaz, 1991). First, these teachers' theories of practice were context specific. The issues that mattered to them were grounded in their day-to-day work with children. Second, their theories were activist in nature; in study group discussions, practice was problematized and solutions were sought. Finally, these teachers' theories of practice were grounded in a complex network of sources of knowledge, which is illustrated in the model found in Fig. 13.1.

Teachers' theories of practice are represented in the model as a set of intertwining shapes because the teachers' thinking, as it became explicit through study group discussions, was synthetic and nonhierarchical, unlike early models of teacher decision making that tended to cast thinking as analytical and two-dimensional (Clark & Peterson, 1986). The bilingual teachers drew on five sources of knowledge during study group discussions (a) knowledge of individual learners (b) knowledge of assessment and teaching practices that they believe help children become literate in two languages, (c) an understanding of the political context of bilingual education and the policies that contradict best practice, (d) academic theories of learning and language development, and (e) cultural and linguistic knowledge grounded in their own experience as bilingual adults.

The excerpts of discussions presented earlier in this chapter illustrate the interplay of these multiple sources of knowledge during study group discussions. In the discussions about Rogelio, teachers drew on both their knowledge of children and of teaching practices to make sense of his challenges and to identify ways to help him overcome them. In talking about assessment practices, a first-grade teacher drew on her political knowledge when expressing her frustration with a policy that pushes children as quickly as possible into English at the expense of de-

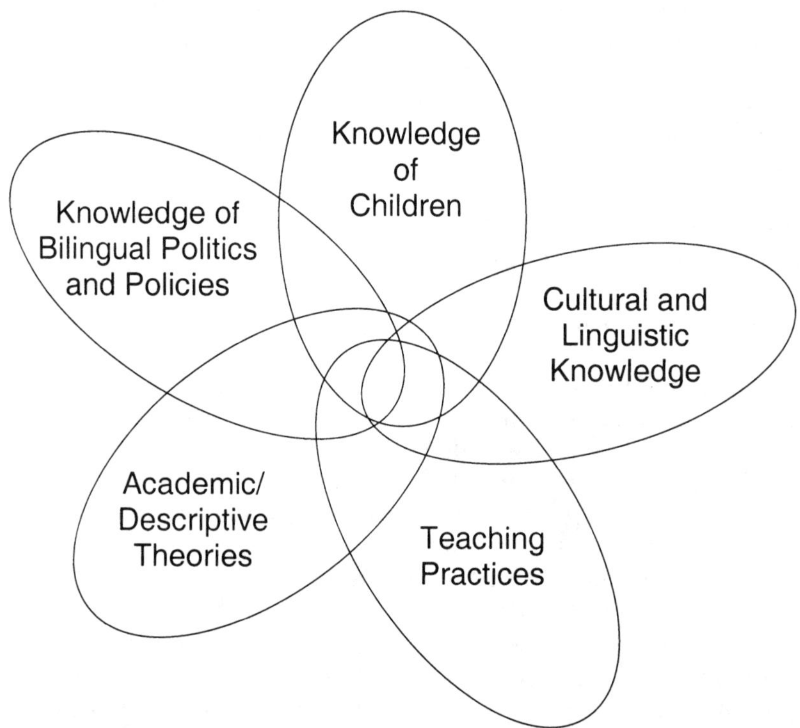

FIG. 13.1 Composite model of a teacher's theory of practice.

veloping the strong foundation in the native language required for transfer. Teachers applied Cummins' (1989) theory of a common underlying proficiency on multiple occasions to explain problems that students like Rogelio faced in transferring knowledge between two languages. When the kindergarten teacher talked about the different discourse structures of Spanish and English writing, she drew on her cultural and linguistic knowledge as a bilingual individual as well as her knowledge of children. The composite model in Fig. 13.1 serves as a framework for understanding how teachers think about their work and can offer insights into whether opportunities to explore questions and concerns collaboratively influence theories of practice over time.

Changes in a Teacher's Theory of Practice

I use a case of one of the third grade bilingual teachers who participated in the study group to illustrate how the collaborative, inquiry-based model of professional development described in this chapter has the potential for changing a teacher's theory of practice. It is important to present the case, however, with the caveat that adult learning is a gradual process and that changes occurring over 8 months may or may not suggest long-term changes in a theory of practice. Only evidence gathered over time and from multiple data sources can support the credibility and dependability of the interpretations. Therefore, the evidence presented here is only preliminary in suggesting that a theory of practice was changing as a result of participation in the study group.

When the third-grade teacher first volunteered to share information about a student in her classroom, she began by emphasizing what the child was unable to do, how he was not being successful, how he was unmotivated, and how little support he had from home. The following excerpt is representative of the way she described the child:

> [Referring to his vocabulary development] It's very limited. Very, very limited. Seems to be I, I, I, I, I. Everything is I. He's still at that stage of a first grader. Well, as a matter of fact, she [bilingual staff developer] also has him. He's still at the first-grade-level stage mentally and in his academics. (Study group, 1/4/2001)

At the following study group meeting, she explained why she tended to focus on a child's problems:

> I don't know but I tend [to think] that if I don't know what the problem is, how can I target the solution? So I have to know what the problem is instead of looking, "Okay, he knows what a period is. He knows how to start a sentence." That's not going to help me because he already knows how to do that. I'm looking to target [the problems], but that's me. What should we look at first is my first question. (Study group, 1/19/2001)

Other study group participants offered reasons why information about what the child already knows might be important in terms of planning for instruction and analyzing students' work for strengths and problems. This type of discussion continued to be a focus of subsequent study group meetings over the next 2 months. The teacher's reactions to these discussions were recorded in an individual meeting with the PDS liaison 4 months later in May:

> The teachers in the 1st grade level had helped me by giving me ideas about what I can use with his [Rogelio's] writing. I

> automatically thought that a third grader would be able to write using other pronouns and that by telling him, "don't use I," he would be able to use other names or pronouns. The other teachers suggested, OK, use a name. In other words to give Rogelio suggested ways to get a first sentence down using a noun or pronoun. By doing this I got him to write. He still has spelling errors, but he doesn't always use I. I also found that instead of focusing on quantity—I assumed all third graders should be able to write at least a paragraph—I focus now on quality in his writing. Let me get two or three sentences. I was not thinking like a lower grade teacher, OK I'm a third grader teacher, but I am now able to say OK, let's work up, he's writing there.... The language preference discussions helped me too. I started asking people about Rogelio's language preferences. [Based on these conversations I found that] he preferred English. It was confusing. I realized that I have to observe him better and not automatically assume the instructional language is Spanish. (Anecdotal transcript of individual meeting, 5/14/2001)

2 weeks later, the teacher approached the college PDS liaison explaining that she had been asked to create portfolios of children's writing to serve as the basis for an end-of-the-year conference with each child. She had begun a portfolio for the child who had been discussed extensively in the study group and wanted to discuss her concerns about the child's progress. The teacher, PDS liaison, and the student teacher met, and the conversation began with the following exchange. The three have samples of Rogelio's writing in front of them as they are talking:

Third-grade teacher:	Remember that we had been speaking about the I, I, I, I. We can clearly see that he's getting some difference sentence structure "My" it's starting to be a difference. He started here with I but I had, he's doing it with a "J" Spanish sound.
College PDS liaison:	Interesting, J which is the H.
Third-grade teacher:	So we're getting some sense of phonemics, so he started with that. He knows there's a period and [he knows] you begin with a capital letter once you have that, but here, yet here we go back to it, but that's again back to the period and has to begin with a capital letter. But yet, we've moved a little; we know he can begin with the pronouns and what not. And he has the period. So we were looking at what he had, what he had accomp-

lished from the last time. See, here he had an idea of that it has to be capital letters. "Let me go back and change that."

College PDS liaison: I just want to check the date. So this was done earlier.

Third-grade teacher: [Pointing to writing samples] This was the last one. This one was done earlier, which by this one he should have gotten it. This one was done earlier, but (inaudible) which had strongly [reading child's writing] "be on my first I had a birthday" kind of thing. So it's [his writing] moving up. Starts with an I. [pointing and writing sample] Period. [reading] "My gramma." So, we have "my" again. So see we're getting, you know, we're moving.

College PDS liaison: And they're personal stories so there has to be some I's and my's in it—

Third-grade teacher: My and I, Exactly, but he's not beginning every sentence with I. The sentences are longer.

College PDS liaison: Yea. The sample that we had way back attached to this [looking at writing sample from case study done in the study group] it was very short.

Third-grade teacher: Very sentence oriented, it wasn't even paragraph oriented. (Individual meeting, 5/30/2001)

In this exchange, the teacher chooses to initiate a conversation about the child's work by focusing on what he can do, which suggests a shift from what she emphasized when planning for instruction in the first months of the study group meetings, that is, the preference to focus on problems that the child was experiencing rather than his existing abilities. These preliminary findings will either be confirmed or refuted with data collected over time.

CONCLUSION

The conversations that took place over the first 8 months of the study group responded to both individual and organizational needs. Individually, teachers were able to find answers to questions and concerns they brought with them directly from their classrooms. At the same time, the focus on improving instruction for ELLs addressed an important organizational need because these students, who represent almost one third of the school's population, were failing to meet learning standards. Because it is a priority goal for the PDS partnership to improve student learning among ELLs, the study group received support from the college and the school to continue another year. Because it has fulfilled individual needs, the 1st-year's participants volunteered to participate in the study group for another year. To determine whether this opportunity for teacher development ultimately has an impact on student learning, baseline data on the ELLs in the bilingual classrooms were collected during the 1st year of the study group. Data will continue to be collected for another year to see what, if any, evidence can be found to link the content of the collaborative PDS work to student learning.

The work that takes place in a PDS must meet the needs of both college and school partners. This chapter focuses on the work of the bilingual teachers involved in a study group. However, the work described here is part of a larger, integrated professional development plan for the PDS to promote renewal in both institutions. Therefore, it is important to document change in all participants, including student teachers and college faculty. Studying the experiences of student teachers and college faculty who work with ELLs in the bilingual program is also being documented. This work is exciting, albeit labor intensive. However, given the growing evidence that PDSs do make a difference in the lives of the adults and the children that inhabit them, it will be extremely beneficial to identify PDS practices that help teachers effectively address the needs of their ELLs and help teacher educators effectively prepare teachers for the challenges they will face as teachers in urban schools.

REFERENCES

Abdal-Haqq, I. (1998). *Professional development schools: Weighing the evidence.* Thousand Oaks, CA: Corwin Press.

Beaver, J. (1997). *Developmental reading assessment.* Parsippany, NJ: Celebration Press.

Berry, B., Boles, K., Edens, K., Nissenholtz, A., & Trachtman, R. (1998). Inquiry and professional development schools. In N. J. Lauter (Ed.), *Professional development schools: Confronting realities* (pp. 121–148). New York: National Center for Restructuring Education, Schools and Teaching.

Biagetti, S. C. (2001). Teachers creating frameworks to understand their students' algebraic thinking. In U. D. Ranier & E. M. Guyton (Eds.), *Research on the effects of teacher education on teacher performance: Teacher education yearbook IX* (pp. 209–223). Reston, VA: Association of Teacher Educators.

Boudah, D. J., & Knight, S. L. (1999). Creating learning communities of research and practice. In D. M. Byrd & D. J. McIntyre (Eds.), *Research on professional development schools: Teacher education yearbook VII* (pp. 97–114). Thousand Oaks, CA: Corwin Press.

Chance, L. (Ed.). (2000). *Professional development schools: Combining school improvement with teacher preparation.* Washington, DC: National Education Association.

Clair, N. (1998). Teacher study groups: Persistent questions in a promising approach. *TESOL Quarterly, 32,* 465–492.

Clandinin, D. J. (1985). Personal practical knowledge: A study of teachers' classroom images. *Curriculum Inquiry, 15,* 361–385.

Clark, C. M. (Ed.). (2001). *Talking shop: Authentic conversation and teacher learning.* New York: Teachers College Press.

Clark, C. M., & Peterson, P. L. (1986). Teachers thought processes. In M. C. Wittrock (Ed.), *Handbook of research on teaching* (3rd ed., pp. 255–296). Washington, DC: American Educational Research Association.

Cummins, J. (1989). *Empowering minority students.* Sacramento: California Association of Bilingual Education.

Dubetz, N. E. (2002). Teacher as negotiator: A teacher's theory of practice in an urban, multilingual setting. In L. Catelli & A. C. Divers (Eds.), *Commitment to excellence: Transforming teaching and teacher education in inner city and urban settings* (pp. 229–243). Cresskill, NJ: Hampton.

Elbaz, F. (1991). Research on teachers' knowledge: The evolution of a discourse. *Journal of Curriculum Studies, 23,,* 1–19.

Genishi, C., Dubetz, N. E., & Focarino, C. (1995). Reconceptualizing theory through practice:

Insights from a first-grade teacher and second language theorists. In S. Reifel (Ed.), *Advances in early education and day care* (Vol. 7, pp. 121–150). Greenwich, CT: JAI.

Glaser, B. G., & Stauss, A. L. (1967). *The discovery of grounded theory: Strategies for qualitative research.* New York: Aldine de Gruyter.

Golombek, P. R. (1998). A study of language teachers' personal practical knowledge. *TESOL Quarterly, 32,* 447–464.

Grisham, D. L., Laguardia, A., & Brink, B. (2000). Partners in professionalism: Creating a quality field experience for preservice teachers. *Action in Teacher Education, 21*(4), 28–42.

Gusky, T. R. (1995). Professional development in education: In search of the optimal mix. In T. R. Guskey & M. Huberman (Eds.), *Professional development in education: New paradigms and practices* (pp. 114–132). New York: Teachers College Press.

Holmes Group. (1995). *Tomorrow's schools of education.* East Lansing, MI: Author.

Houston, W. R., Hollis, L. Y., Clay, D., Ligons, C. M., & Roff, L. (1999). Effects of collaboration on urban teacher education programs and professional development schools. In D. M. Byrd & D. J. McIntyre (Eds.), *Research on professional development schools: Teacher education yearbook VII* (pp. 6–28). Thousand Oaks, CA: Corwin Press.

Huberman, M. (1995). Professional careers and professional development: Some interactions. In T. R. Guskey & M. Huberman (Eds.), *Professional development in education: New paradigms and practices* (pp. 193–224). New York: Teachers College Press.

Hurley, S. R., & Tinajero, J. V. (Eds.). (2000). *Literacy assessment of second language learners.* Boston: Allyn & Bacon.

Joyce, B., & Showers, S. (1995). *Student achievement through staff development: Fundamentals of school renewal.* White Plains, NY: Longman.

Levine, M. (1997). Can professional development schools help us achieve what matters most? *Action in Teacher Education, 19*(2), 63–73.

Lincoln, Y. S., & Guba, E. G. (1985). *Naturalistic inquiry.* Newbury Park, CA: Sage.

Lyons, N., Stroble, B., & Fischetti, J. (1997). The idea of the university in an age of school reform: The shaping forces of professional development schools. In M. Levine & R. Trachtman (Eds.), *Making professional development schools work: Politics, practices, and policy* (pp. 88–111). New York: Teachers College Press.

Miller, L. (1988). Unlikely beginnings: The district office as a starting point for developing a professional culture of teaching. In A. Lieberman (Ed.), *Building a professional culture in schools* (pp. 167–184). New York: Teachers College Press.

National Council of Accreditation of Teacher Education. (2001). *Standards for the professional development schools*. Washington, DC: Author.

National Foundation for the Improvement of Education. (1996). *Teachers take charge of their learning: Transforming professional development for student success.* Washington, DC: Author.

National Partnership for Excellence and Accountability for Teaching. (1998). *Improving professional development: Eight research-based principals.* Washington, DC: Author.

New York City Public Schools Office of Testing. (1982). *Language assessment battery.* New York: Author.

Nihlen, A. S., Williams, M., & Sweet, A. (1999). Teachers' stories of professional development school restructuring. In D. M. Byrd & D. J. McIntyre (Eds.), *Research on professional development schools: Teacher education yearbook VII* (pp. 142–156). Thousand Oaks, CA: Corwin Press.

Paris, C. L .(1993). *Teacher agency and curriculum making in the classroom*. New York: Teachers College Press.

Reynolds, A. (1999). *NEA Teacher Education Initiative: Seven-site replication study of teacher preparation, cross-site report.* Unpublished manuscript, National Education Association, Washington, DC.

Rios, F. A. (Ed.). (1996). *Teacher thinking in cultural contexts*. Albany: State University of New York Press.

Ruiz, O., & Cuesta, V. (2000). *Evaluación del desarrollo de la lectura*. Parsippany, NJ: Celebration Press.

Simmons, J. M., Konecki, L. R., Crowell, R. A., & Gates-Duffield, P. (1999). Dream keepers, weavers, and shape-shifters: Emerging roles of PDS university coordinators in educational reform. In D. M. Byrd & D. J. McIntyre (Eds.), *Research on professional development schools: Teacher education yearbook VII* (pp. 29–44). Thousand Oaks, CA: Corwin Press.

Sparks, D., & Loucks-Horsley, S. (1990). Models of professional development. In W. R. Houston (Ed.), *Handbook of research on teacher education* (pp. 234–250). New York: Macmillan.

Sprinthall, N. A., Reiman, A. J., & Thies-Sprinthall, L. (1996). Teacher professional development. In J. Sikula, T. J. Buttery, & E. Guyton (Eds.), *Handbook of research on teacher education* (2nd ed., pp. 666–703). New York: Macmillan.

Teachers of English to Speakers of Other Languages. (1993, Winter/Spring). TESOL statement on the role of bilingual education in the education of children in the United States. *Bilingual Basics: The Official Publication of the Bilingual Interest Section Teachers of Speakers of Other Languages*, pp. 1, 3, & 5.

Teitel, L. (2001). *How professional development schools make a difference: A review of the research.* Washington, DC: National Council of Accreditation of Teacher Education.

Thompson, B., Maxwell, E., Kelley, L., & Carnate, B. (2000). Project learn: Closing the gap. In M. Johnston, P. Brosnan, D. Cramer, & T. Dove (Eds.), *Collaborative re-*

form and other improbable dreams: The challenges of professional development schools (pp. 189–208). Albany: State University of New York Press.

Trueba, H. T. (1989). *Raising silent voices: Educating the linguistic minorities for the 21st century.* New York: Newbury House.

Walling, B., & Lewis, M. (2000). Development of professional identity among professional develop school preservice teachers: Longitudinal and comparative analysis. *Action in Teacher Education, 2*(2A), 63–72.

Whitford, B., & Metcalf-Turner, P. (1999). Of promises and unresolved puzzles: reforming teacher education with professional development schools. In G. Griffin (Ed.), *The education of teachers: Ninety-eighth yearbook of the National Society for the Study of Education, Part I* (pp. 257–279). University of Chicago Press.

Zellermayer, M. (2001). Resistance as a catalyst in teachers' professional development. In C. M. Clark (Ed.), *Talking shop: Authentic conversation and teacher learning* (pp. 40–63). New York: Teachers College Press.

Theme **IV**

Second Language Teacher Education in Practice

The fourth and final section of the book is devoted to showcasing examples of second language teacher education in practice. In these five chapters, readers will see how the other three themes of the book— knowledge base, contexts, and collaboration—are conceptualized and put into practice in teacher education programs.

In chapter 14 (Snow), the first chapter of this section, Marguerite Ann Snow identifies six key themes that guide a vision of what constitutes a high quality teacher education program. The program showcased is the Master's of Arts (MA) TESOL program offered at California State University in Los Angeles, where they prepare teachers for Kindergarten through 12th grade (K–12) English as a second language (ESL) programs, for adult ESL, and for English as a foreign language (EFL) teaching in international contexts. Snow explores (a) how teachers are initiated into the professional discourse community, (b) how the roles of native and nonnative speaking teachers are considered, (c) ways in which technology is infused in their teacher education curriculum, (d) how they tackle issues related to standards and accreditation in the program, (e) how performance-based assessment is practiced and taught in their program, and (f) how they help new teachers understand and take on new partnership and roles in the profession. Most interesting about Snow's contribution is that although the themes are presented within the context of ESL teacher education, they are themes that cross second language teacher education contexts and serve to inform best practices for all.

Dual language education in the United States is the teacher education context highlighted in chapter 15 (Cloud). Nancy Cloud explores innovations in teacher education for dual language education with particular attention to school-based study groups, program visits, networking among dual language teachers, curriculum development, and intensive institutes. Cloud then explains how the effectiveness of such innovations is being documented in the field. Finally, Cloud offers an analysis of some of the challenges faced in implementing dual language programs.

The three questions that frame Cloud's chapter (chap. 15)— innovations, documentation of effectiveness, and challenges—also provide the organizational framework for the next chapter by Tony Erben (chap. 16). In chapter 16, Erben describes a program in Australia that prepares teachers through immersion for teaching in immersion programs. The Language and Culture Initial Teacher Education Program (LACITEP) is a 4-year, undergraduate degree program in which some courses are taught in Japanese to native English speakers seeking certification to teach in Japanese immersion programs. Erben highlights the innovations, describes how the program has been documented in terms of its effectiveness, and raises the challenges faced by LACITEP, many of them parallel to challenges faced by immersion programs in K–12 schools such as curriculum and materials development.

In chapter 17 Martha Bigelow and Diane J. Tedick describe preservice and inservice programs at the University of Minnesota that combine second and foreign language teacher education. Their preservice program allows students to seek licensure in a foreign language and/or ESL. The inservice program includes an array of program options for ESL/EFL, foreign language, bilingual, and immersion teachers. Bigelow and Tedick identify the rewards that come with the integration of second language teaching contexts in their programs, noting how teachers find common ground and benefit from understanding how second language (L2) teaching works in a variety of L2 contexts. They also identify a number of major challenges that accompany such integration.

The final chapter of the book (Walker, Ranney, & Fortune, chap. 18) speaks to the expanding role of second language teacher educators, namely, needing to provide teacher education for grade level (elementary) and content area (secondary) classroom teachers who are faced with ever increasing numbers of learners for whom English is not a native language. This issue has become very important in countries around the world where large numbers of immigrants populate schools. In chapter 18, Constance L. Walker, Susan Ranney, and Tara W. Fortune describe how teacher educators in one context—the University of Minnesota—have dealt with this issue by developing a course that has multiple sections designed to correspond to the unique needs of preservice teachers in different content areas. They begin with an analysis of the reasons for the course, explain how it evolved, and illustrate how the course plays out in cohorts for elementary education, math, English literature/language arts, and social studies. These illustrations are followed by an analysis of the benefits and limitations of such an approach as well as the institutional barriers that make this innovative approach difficult. Finally, Walker, Ranney, and Fortune highlight a number of key insights that have emerged as they have worked with beginning teachers across subject matter areas on issues related to language minority learners.

It is hoped that these descriptions of second language teacher education in practice will spark further ideas and innovations on the part of the teacher educators who read this volume. How are the themes in the MA program in TESOL at California State University embedded and addressed in second language teacher education programs around the world? What can second language teacher educators learn from innovations in dual language teacher education? How might the Australian approach to language immersion teacher education inform programs for immersion teachers in other countries? How might an integrated approach to preservice and inservice teacher education serve to bring together second language teachers in other institutional contexts? How might the content-based approach for preservice teachers who will serve large numbers of language minority learners inform other teacher educators that are faced with this issue? How do these program models help us to envision how the knowledge base, contexts, and collaborations in second language teacher education may be implemented in practice?

Chapter **14**

Key Themes in TESOL MA Teacher Education

Marguerite Ann Snow
California State University, Los Angeles

INTRODUCTION

The processes of language teacher education are necessarily a broad and complex topic. In this chapter, I will confine my discussion to preparing teachers for English as a second language (ESL) and English as a foreign language (EFL) teaching settings and filter my comments through the vision statement following. This statement guides the teacher education program we offer in our TESOL Master's of Arts (MA) program at California Sate University, Los Angeles (Cal State LA), a mid-size urban, state university where I have been a faculty member for the past 15 years and currently serve as program coordinator. In our TESOL MA program, we prepare teachers to work in Kindergarten through 12th grade (K–12) public school settings and to teach adults in community colleges, intensive English programs, community-based settings such as libraries, workplace or corporate settings, and, of course, those who plan to go abroad to teach EFL.

Vision Statement for the TESOL MA Program at Cal State LA:

> The TESOL MA program endeavors to prepare teachers to be both informed practitioners and effective researchers by providing a pedagogically and theoretically sound knowledge base and by encouraging respect for differences in language, culture, belief systems, and values.

In this chapter, I identify six themes, which, I believe, reflect important processes in language teacher education and underlie our vision of what constitutes a high quality teacher education program. The six themes are as follows (a) initiation into the professional discourse community, (b) the role of native and nonnative speakers in the profession, (c) infusion of technology, (d) knowledge of standards and accreditation processes, (e) performance-based assessment, and (f) new partnerships and roles.

INITIATION INTO THE PROFESSIONAL DISCOURSE COMMUNITY

I was first influenced to think about the challenge of initiating students into the professional discourse community when using Frank Smith's (1988) book *Joining the Literacy Club: Further Essays Into Education.* I had selected this venerable book to introduce the notion of discourse community membership for ESL students when I came to the realization that this perspective should inform processes in language teacher education as well. Our teacher education students are indeed joining a new type of literacy club, and curricula that reflect this initiation process need to be designed.

An important component of English for academic purposes (EAP) instruction is consideration of ways in which ESL teachers can assist second language students to acculturate into the U.S. academic discourse community, whether K–12 or postsecondary. Wong-Fillmore and Snow (2002) refer to this role of teachers as "agents of socialization." Interestingly, however, teacher educators often overlook the need to explicitly initiate our own language education students into the professional language teaching discourse community. How can we make this initiation a part of the teacher education curriculum?

One initiation strategy is through explicit modeling of the conventions of the TESOL and applied linguistics community. For example, Ann Johns' (1995) article on the use of classroom and authentic genres in an adjunct course for incoming freshman ESL students influenced me to develop my course assignments around authentic genres. Johns defines *authentic genres* as the activities that reflect the kinds of discourse actually used by members of the discourse community in the course of their work. Although I continue to use classroom genres such as reaction papers in my teaching, I am trying to move toward greater use of authentic genres. One example is the textbook review. In my materials and curriculum development class, we conduct a discourse analysis of selected textbook reviews from the *CATESOL Journal* and *TESOL Quarterly*, noting the common formulas and formats used including a discussion of academic style conventions. As an assignment, students then write their own reviews, incorporating appropriate discourse patterns and content from class readings, with the goal of producing a review of publishable quality like the ones they have analyzed in class. This kind of assignment requires students to integrate course content (i.e., criteria for effective textbooks) with the conventions of an authentic genre. In recent years, several of our students have published their reviews in professional journals. Other examples of authentic genres I have incorporated into my syllabi are oral presentations, collaborative materials development projects, and poster presentations by students at the research colloquium our College of Education organizes each spring. Still other examples include giving students credit for volunteering at local ESL conferences or copresenting with other students at regional or state conferences—all are fruitful avenues for reinforcing authentic genres by teacher educators.

The initiation process should also focus on what Donald Freeman (1996) has called the "unstudied problem" of teacher learning in language teaching. Our teacher education courses must give students opportunities to explore their belief systems and develop reflective reasoning systems in the ways presented, for example, in Karen Johnson's 1999 book *Understanding Language Teaching: Reasoning in Action*. The initiation process should expose our students to the range of challenges they will face on the job. In this regard, case studies are an excellent teaching tool, as they offer descriptions of commonly recurring dilemmas that teachers encounter in their work and illustrate the complex thinking and decision making teachers must employ as they teach. TESOL's case study series is very useful in this regard. For example, using the short case studies in *Teaching in Action: Case Studies From Second Language Classrooms* (Richards, 1998), prospective teachers can be exposed to such important issues as "A Balance or a Battle: L1 Use in the Classroom," "One class, Two Levels," "Responding to Plagiarism," and "Intercultural Faculty Meetings." All introduce real-life teaching challenges for students to discuss and reflect on an appropriate course of action.

I have also found Kathleen Graves' (1996) book *Teachers as Course Developers* to be very valuable, not only for teaching principles of curriculum and materials design but also for providing actual examples of real teachers talking through their successes (e.g., developing a writing component that motivates teenagers at an after-school private English institute in Brazil) and failures (e.g., neglecting to include the targeted learners in the needs assessment on which a curriculum for Chinese health care workers in the United States was based).

Other techniques include providing explicit statements of the evaluation criteria by which assignments will be graded and rubrics for all assignments, modeling of expectations by making sample papers available for students to examine, and assigning multistep writing assignments in which students complete assignments such as research papers in phases and get feedback throughout the term, not only at the end. A focus on initiating students into the discourse community will allow our students to excel within the graduate program but also prepare them to be active participants within their professional communities on graduation. What all these examples have in common is that we, teacher educators, must develop creative ways to initiate new teachers into the community of TESOL and applied linguistics professionals.

THE ROLE OF NATIVE AND NONNATIVE SPEAKERS IN THE PROFESSION

There is a fledgling movement and growing literature (cf. Braine, 1999) on the role of nonnative speakers in the TESOL profession.[1] It is often a startling revelation for ESL teachers in training to realize that many (in some cases, most) of the students they teach will primarily use English to interact with other nonnative speakers of English; this is obviously the case in EFL settings, but is increasingly true in urban centers of the United States. As such, TESOL MA curricula must treat the topic of world Englishes (cf. Kachru, 1992) and consider the implications for language teacher training. Furthermore, for TESOL MA programs that enroll large numbers of nonnative speakers of English, the issue of the role of nonnative speakers in the profession is increasingly relevant in terms of designing TESOL MA programs that meet the needs of both native and nonnative teachers. What does this imply for the processes of language teacher education?

Lia Kamhi-Stein (2000a) notes four perceived needs and concerns of nonnative teachers from the extant literature (a) low confidence and

[1]A caucus has been established for nonnative speakers in TESOL. See the Web site at http://nnest.moussu.net/

self-perceived challenges to professional competence, (b) self-perceived language needs, (c) lack of voice and visibility in the TESOL profession, and (d) self-perceived prejudice about ethnicity or nonnative status. Kamhi-Stein suggests a variety of ways to address these concerns and to enhance the preparation of prospective native and nonnative teachers in teacher education programs. Among these are to (a) explore beliefs as teachers and learners, (b) engage in collaborative projects, (c) assign experienced nonnative teachers to serve as mentors and role models, and (d) develop informal support networks.

Encouraging nonnative speakers to pursue their thesis research on the topic of nonnative speakers in the profession validates it as a worthwhile area of inquiry. A recent graduate of our TESOL MA program, Kristy Liang (2002), for example, investigated ESL students' attitudes toward the degree of accentedness of nonnative teachers' speech. Liang's quantitative analysis revealed that the students rated pronunciation as very important; however, her qualitative analysis indicated that teachers' personal and professional characteristics or "perceived professionalism" was a more important factor contributing to teacher preference.

Meeting the needs of nonnative English teachers within the TESOL MA program might require adding a prerequisite course to help nonnative students with their academic language proficiency or a course such as Introduction to Applied Linguistics so that the conventions of the discourse community such as writing literature reviews and citations/referencing can be modeled and practiced. *Academic Writing for Graduate Students: Essential Tasks and Skills* by Swales and Feak (2004) provides an excellent genre-based resource for such a component. Adding readings on the topic of nonnative speakers in the profession to course syllabi is another way to stimulate both native and nonnative teachers to explore their roles and challenges. Lynne Diaz-Rico (2000) describes many other strategies for making nonnative speakers part of the community of learners in TESOL MA programs. One such strategy is the creation of weekly "CommuniConfidence" sessions that focus on oral language and cross-cultural socialization. The point is that language teacher education programs must address the needs of both their native and nonnative English-speaking students to better educate the entire student population and also to maintain currency in course offerings.

INFUSION OF TECHNOLOGY

Many teacher educators are seeking innovative ways to increase the use of technology in the curriculum. How can technology be infused into the curriculum to benefit all students?

In our TESOL MA program, we have added training in online and electronic databases in the first term of the program. The sessions are incorporated into our introductory theory course, and follow-up assignments in the class are built around the library and database research training. We also offer a course Using Computers in the Language Classroom in which students are introduced to the computer assisted language learning (CALL) literature, develop lesson plans using Web-based, video-based, and PowerPoint resources, and design a web page as a course project. Reports from our recent graduates reveal that in addition to adding to their instructional repertoire in the ESL classroom, their technology "know how" has helped them in the extremely competitive search for full-time ESL teaching positions.

In addition to developing information competence, there are other benefits to infusing technology into the teacher education curriculum such as promoting greater participation of students of diverse learning styles and personality types. It may also be an excellent medium for enhancing the participation of students from nonnative English speaking backgrounds. For example, Kamhi-Stein (2000b) compared whole class, face-to-face discussions with Web-based bulletin board discussions in a TESOL methods class. Kamhi-Stein (2000b) found that in the whole-class discussions, students directed most of their discussion to the instructor who was responsible for keeping the conversations going and for evaluating what the students had to say. In contrast, the Web-based bulletin board option promoted collaboration and interaction that were driven by the needs and interests of the students. It was also interesting to note that although the native English speakers exhibited more initiations and responses in both formats, these differences were not significant; however, both the novice native speakers and the nonnative speakers reported that the Web-based discussions allowed them to develop knowledge at their own time and pace, and the nonnatives felt that the computer-mediated communication reduced cultural and linguistic barriers. Results of the Kamhi-Stein (2000b) study provide a glimpse of the varied benefits of infusing technology into TESOL MA programs.

KNOWLEDGE OF STANDARDS AND ACCREDITATION PROCESSES

Accountability is the buzzword of current efforts at educational reform. ESL teachers may be required to teach to specific standards; teacher educators may have to respond to the standards of their professional associations and other accreditation demands. As a faculty member in an

NCATE-accredited[2] College of Education, all my course syllabi, for example, must contain content and performance standards. How can teacher educators respond to this increasing focus on standards in the teacher education curriculum? What are the challenges for this process of teacher education?

One challenge is to ensure that teachers are aware of the various sets of ESL-related standards developed by different entities such as professional associations, state departments of education, and local districts or institutions. We introduce, for example, the *ESL Standards for Pre-K–12 Students* (TESOL, 1997), but realize that our K–12 teachers have to incorporate California's English Language Development Standards[3] into their instructional planning. We also make our K–12 teachers aware of the *Standards for English as a New Language* so that teachers can chart their long-term career development.[4] For our adult and intensive English program-bound students, we introduce the *Standards for Adult Education ESL Programs* (TESOL, 2003) and the draft standards for Teachers of Adult Learners. From time to time, we also have foreign language or heritage language teachers in our program who seek an MA focusing on methodology instead of literature, so we introduce the American Council on the Teaching of Foreign Languages (ACTFL) standards[5] (ACTFL, 1996). Finally, we discuss the fledgling movement toward standards for the EFL context (cf. Fujimoto, 2000), and I offer a case study of a project in which I am involved to develop standards for English teachers and inservice teacher trainers in Egypt (Katz & Snow, 2003).

Another challenge for the teacher educator is how to implement TESOL's Standards for P-12 Teacher Preparation Programs, recently approved by NCATE,[6] given that responsibility for TESOL training is often divided up between different departments or colleges. For example, in California, K–12 ESL training is typically conducted in Colleges of Education; all other levels are typically under the purview of departments of English, Linguistics, or Foreign Languages. Still others are trained in Learning Centers. We tend to be a fragmented profession op-

---

[2]NCATE stands for the National Council for Accreditation of Teacher Education.

[3]California's English Language Development Standards can be found at the California Department of Education Web site: www.cde.ca.gov

[4]The *Standards for English as a New Language* can be found at the Web site of the National Board for Professional Teaching Standards: www.nbpts.org/candidates/guide/whichcert/09EarlyMiddleChildEnglish.html

[5]An executive summary of ACTFL's Standards for Foreign Language Learning can be found at http://www.actfl.org/public/articles/Winter1997.paf

[6]Information about TESOL's Standards for P–12 Teacher Preparation Programs may be found at http://www.tesol.org/assoc/p12standards/index.html

erating out of many different settings (Tedick & Walker, 1994). How can we ensure that our students have sufficient exposure to the standards relevant to their current or future instructional settings?

Implementing the ESL Standards for Pre-K–12 Students in Teacher Education (Snow, 2000) is a step in the right direction toward meeting the challenges of the standards movement in K–12 education. To really ensure this process of teacher education, teachers in training must have experience preparing lesson plans that incorporate standards in instruction and assessment. A practical suggestion for providing this exposure is to demonstrate model lessons developed by practicing ESL teachers such as those contained in *Integrating the ESL Standards into Classroom Practice Series*[7] and then have students develop their own lesson plans. Similarly, this same kind of activity can be carried out in a Language Testing class using a resource such as *Scenarios for Classroom-Based Assessment* (TESOL, 2001), with students designing assessment activities based on selected standards. The proliferation of standards has created a bewildering array of materials to which teacher educators and practicing teachers will be held accountable, and teachers in training need practice applying these standards to their classroom practice. (See also Bigelow & Tedick, chap. 17, this volume.)

PERFORMANCE-BASED ASSESSMENT

There are increasing calls in the testing literature for authentic, performance-based assessment and for the implementation of multiple measures to achieve fairness in testing (cf. Bailey, 1998; Katz, 2000). Furthermore, as student and program standards are implemented, standards-based assessment must be conducted. How can we practice what we preach in terms of assessment practices in teacher education?

In our TESOL MA program, we have endeavored to provide authentic fieldwork experiences as one route to performance-based assessment. We developed initiatives across campus that provide practice teaching opportunities for TESOL MA students. For example, my colleague, Lia Kamhi-Stein, and I developed a workshop series for ESL students in the MBA program, which is team taught by TESOL MA students. We then expanded the model to the Nursing School where TESOL MA students observed nursing classes to conduct a needs assessment and then designed and taught a workshop series for ESL Nursing students. We have also

[7]There are four volumes in this series: 1) Integrating the ESL Standards into Classroom Practice: Grades K–2; 2) Integrating the ESL Standards into Classroom Practice: Grades 3–5; 3) Integrating the ESL Standards into Classroom Practice: Grades 6–8; 4) Integrating the ESL Standards into Classroom Pracitce: Grades 9–12.

sought to develop more authentic assessments while taking into consideration the variety of ESL and EFL settings in which our students will work. By developing take-home comprehensive examinations, we have eliminated memory and time-constraint factors and given students time to actually develop appropriate lesson plans and sample test items. Furthermore, they can apply the questions to settings with which they are familiar or in which they plan to teach, such as a primary school classroom or a community college course, depending on their interests and experiences. We have also developed a grading rubric that we share with students in advance. The rubric communicates clear evaluation criteria to students and improves reliability among exam readers.

Another strategy used by many TESOL MA programs is requiring portfolios for each class and a final portfolio as an evaluation component for program completion. All of these examples attempt to accommodate the diversity existing in many teacher education programs and to create assessments that are valid, reliable, and fair.

NEW PARTNERSHIPS AND ROLES

Crandall (1999), Cloud, Genesee, and Hamayan (2000), and Hones (2000), among others, have called for new partnerships in the educational community. Approaches such as content-based instruction, thematic teaching, and dual language education (see Cloud, chap. 15, this volume) are placing new responsibilities on teachers at all levels to become content experts as well as language experts. Language and content teachers are being asked to collaborate to make difficult content accessible to language minority students and to teach learning strategies and study skills. In fact, I have made the case that for ESL students to develop academic literacy, the curriculum must offer some form of focused instruction for integrated language and content teaching (Snow, in press). Partnerships such as the university–school collaboration described by Bunch, Abram, Lotan, and Valdés (2001) in which middle school ESL students enrolled in a social studies course specifically designed to identify, model, and offer guided practice of academic language skills and to meet Goal 2, "Students will use English to obtain, process, construct, and provide subject matter information in spoken and written form" of the *ESL Standards for Pre-K–12 Students* provide vivid examples of these new roles. Project LEAP (Learning English for Academic Purposes) at Cal State LA is another example of successful collaboration. In this case, language specialists worked with content faculty to rework their course delivery and assignments in an effort to teach academic literacy skills to language minority university students (Snow,

1997; Snow & Kamhi-Stein, 2001). In all cases, professional development support for collaboration must be offered to participants.

How can we prepare students to enter into new partnership and roles? What are the implications for teacher training? One avenue is to introduce our students to critical pedagogy (cf. Wink, 1997) and what Jim Cummins (2000) calls "tranformative pedagogy," which challenge teachers to rethink their roles. ESL teachers are often their students' best advocates and in the K–12 context, may be parents' only link to the school. Political events with immediate instructional implications like the passage of Proposition 227 in 1998 in California, which banned bilingual education, have added even more pressure on ESL teachers to move students into mainstream classes.

Teacher educators must be willing to raise awareness of the concept of partnerships and diversified roles in our courses and model exemplary programs through case studies. We must also be ready to respond to new educational and political developments in the interest of our students and their students.

CONCLUSION

To achieve the goals we set out in our vision statement at Cal State LA, we are committed to ongoing conceptualization and operationalization of the knowledge base in TESOL teacher education. The issues raised in this chapter are just six of the many critical processes of language teacher education that guide our instruction and assessment practices.

REFERENCES

American Council on the Teaching of Foreign Languages. (1996). *Standards for foreign language learning*. Yonkers, NY: Author.

Bailey, K. M. (1998). *Learning about language assessment*. Cambridge, MA: Heinle & Heinle.

Braine, G. (Ed.). (1999). *Non-native educators in English language teaching*. Mahwah, NJ: Lawrence Erlbaum Associates, Inc.

Bunch, G. C., Abram, P. L., Lotan, R. A., & Valdés, G. (2001). Beyond sheltered instruction: Rethinking conditions for academic language development. *TESOL Journal, 10*(2/3), 28–33.

Cloud, N., Genesee, F., & Hamayan, E. (2000). *Dual language instruction: A handbook for enriched education*. Boston: Heinle & Heinle.

Crandall, J. (1999). Preparing teachers for real classrooms: Aligning teacher education with teaching. *TESOL Matters, 9*(3), 1, 21.

Cummins, J. (2000). Academic language learning, transformative pedagogy, and information technology: Towards a critical balance. *TESOL Quarterly, 34,* 537–548.

Diaz-Rico, L. (2000). TESOL education in the context of diversity. In K. Johnson (Ed.), *Teacher education: Case studies in TESOL practice series* (pp. 71–84). Alexandria, VA: TESOL.

Freeman, D. (1996). The "unstudied problem": Research on teacher learning in language teaching. In D. Freeman & J. C. Richards (Eds.), *Teacher learning in language teaching* (pp. 351–378). Cambridge, England: Cambridge University Press.

Fujimoto, D. (2000). Looking ahead to international standards. *TESOL Matters, 10*(1), 9.

Graves, K. (Ed.). (1996). *Teachers as course developers*. Cambridge, England: Cambridge University Press.

Hones, D. E. (2000). Building bridges among university, school, and community. In K. Johnson (Ed.), *Teacher education: Case studies in TESOL practice series* (pp. 11–27). Alexandria, VA: TESOL.

Johns, A. M. (1995). Teaching classroom and authentic genres: Initiating students into academic cultures and discourses. In D. Belcher & G. Braine (Eds.), *Academic writing in a second language: Essays on research & pedagogy* (pp. 277–291). Norwood, NJ: Ablex.

Johnson, K. (1999). *Understanding language teaching: Reasoning in action*. Boston: Heinle & Heinle.

Kachru, B. K. (Ed.). (1992). *The other tongue: English across cultures* (2nd ed.). Chicago: University of Illinois Press.

Kamhi-Stein, L. D. (2000a). Adapting U.S.-based TESOL education to meeting the needs of nonnative English speakers. *TESOL Journal, 9*(3), 10–14.

Kamhi-Stein, L. D. (2000b). Looking to the future of TESOL teacher education: Web-based bulletin board discussions in a methods class. *TESOL Quarterly, 34*, 423–455.

Katz, A. (2000). New paradigms in assessment. In M. A. Snow (Ed.), *Implementing the ESL Standards for Pre-K–12 students in teacher education* (pp. 137–166). Alexandria, VA: TESOL.

Katz, A. M., & Snow, M. A. (2003). Process and product in educational innovation: Implementing standards in Egypt. *Prospect, 18*(1), 53–67.

Liang, K. Y. (2002). *English as a second language (ESL) students' attitudes toward non-native English-speaking teachers' (NNESTs') accentedness*. Unpublished master's thesis, California State University, Los Angeles.

Richards, J. C. (Ed.). (1998). *Teaching in action: Case studies from second language classrooms*. Alexandria, VA: TESOL.

Smith, F. (1988). *Joining the literacy club: Further essays into education*. Portsmouth, NH: Heinemann.

Snow, M. A. (1997). Teaching academic literacy skills: Discipline faculty take responsibility. In M. A. Snow & D. M. Brinton (Eds.), *The content-based classroom: Perspectives on integrating language and content* (pp. 290–304). White Plains, NY: Longman.

Snow, M. A. (Ed.). (2000). *Implementing the ESL standards for pre-K–12 students in teacher education*. Alexandria, VA: TESOL.

Snow, M. A. (in press). A model of academic literacy for integrated language and content instruction. In E. Hinkel (Ed.), *Handbook on research in second language teaching and learning*. Mahwah, NJ: Lawrence Erlbaum Associates, Inc.

Snow, M. A., & Kamhi-Stein, L. (2001). Teaching and learning academic literacy through Project LEAP. In J. Crandall & D. Kaufman (Eds.), *Content-based instruction in higher education settings* (pp. 169–181). Alexandria, VA: TESOL.

Swales, J. M., & Feak, C. B. (2004). *Academic writing for graduate students: Essential tasks and skills* (2nd ed.). Ann Arbor: University of Michigan Press.

Tedick, D. J., & Walker, C. L. (1994). Second language teacher education: The problems that plague us. *Modern Language Journal, 78,* 300–312.

Teachers of English to Speakers of Other Languages. (1997). *ESL standards for pre-K–12 students*. Alexandria, VA: Author.

Teachers of English to Speakers of Other Languages. (2001). *Scenarios for classroom-based assessment*. Alexandria, VA: Author.

Teachers of English to Speakers of Other Languages. (2003). *Standards for adult education ESL programs*. Alexandria, VA: Author.

Wink, J. (1997). *Critical pedagogy: Notes from the real world*. New York: Longman.

Wong Fillmore, L., & Snow, C. E. (2002). What teachers need to know about language. In C. Temple Adger, C. E. Snow, & D. Christian (Eds.), *What teachers need to know about language* (pp. 7–53). Center for Applied Linguistics and Delta Systems Co. Inc: Washington D.C. and McHenry, IL.

Chapter **15**

The Dialogic Process of Capturing and Building Teacher Practical Knowledge in Dual Language Programs

Nancy Cloud
Rhode Island College

INTRODUCTION

Until very recently, the available literature on dual language immersion (DLI) had tended to focus on advocating for such programs or describing the features of particular models being implemented (Lindholm-Leary, 2000). Relatively little attention had been paid to the "practical knowledge of teachers" (Clandinin, 1986) working in such programs. This is despite the fact that the heart of language teaching is action—performance in the classroom (Wein, 1995)—and despite the fact that the accreditation of teacher education programs will rest on graduates meeting specific performance indicators (National Council for Accreditation of Teacher Education [NCATE], 2002).[1]

We know that teaching practice is built on language teachers' beliefs about language and language teaching, attitudes or dispositions toward

[1]See www.ncate.org to learn about NCATE's emphasis on performance-based assessment.

learners and programs, knowledge about language and literacy development, knowledge of specific curriculum and instructional approaches, and the development of other practical skills needed in classrooms such as advocacy and collaboration (see Teachers of English as a Second Language, 2003, e.g.). However, the specific knowledge base needed to inform the teacher preparation and/or professional development of dual language teachers had not been documented or operationalized.

To address this unmet need, in 1998, Fred Genesee, Else Hamayan, and I began a project that resulted in the handbook: *Dual Language Instruction: A Handbook for Enriched Education* (Cloud, Genesee, & Hamayan, 2000). The purpose of this collaborative effort was to frame and develop the practical knowledge needed by teachers working in immersion, developmental bilingual, and DLI programs; programs we refer to as enriched education (EE) programs because they seek to develop bilingualism and biculturalism along with all of the other objectives of a basic public education. The handbook was a response to the concerns raised by language teachers working in EE programs who expressed a need for guidance with the many complex teaching decisions they face on a day-to-day basis or who simply desired confirmation that the approaches they were using were sound and defensible. Starting with the premise that teacher practical knowledge should both inform and be informed by the existing research, theory, and practice, we set out to develop a handbook drawing from a variety of sources (the professional literature, our own experience as teacher educators and researchers, the experience of teachers and administrators working in such programs) that would provide dual language educators with guiding frameworks, models of teaching, and practical guidance to guide their daily work in classrooms. In the process of this work, we discovered quite a lot about the professional development needs of teachers working in these programs and current efforts designed to address those needs.

The discussion that follows concerning dual language teachers' professional development needs related to classroom practice is organized according to the following three questions:

1. What characterizes innovative teacher education programs in the field of DLI?
2. How are innovations in teacher preparation in the field of dual language education being documented in terms of their effectiveness?
3. What specific challenges must be faced in implementing DLI programs?

WHAT CHARACTERIZES INNOVATIVE TEACHER EDUCATION PROGRAMS IN THE FIELD OF DLI?

In 1995, the National Staff Development Council (NSDC) developed standards for staff development that have recently been revised to reflect current understandings about what contributes to effective professional development (NSDC, 2001). Twelve standards have been articulated that fall into three categories: context standards, process standards, and content standards. The kinds of things that they recommend such as forming adult learning communities; delivering locally relevant, data-driven professional development; using existing research to support decision making in classrooms; the need to provide educators with the knowledge and skills to collaborate; and the need for ongoing support and resources to support adult learning and collaboration are reflected in innovative teacher education efforts in the field of dual language education. Five innovations that are commonplace in current preservice and inservice teacher education efforts are described in the sections that follow.

On-site/School-Based Study Groups

Collaboration and collegiality among professionals is known to support the delivery of effective programs to students with diverse learning characteristics and needs (Johnson, Pugach, & Devlin, 1990). Such interaction also facilitates teacher growth (Idol, Paolucci-Whitcomb, & Nevin, 1987). Often this aspect is missing from professional development efforts in which professionals in different roles are trained in isolation with little access to each other's knowledge, skills, and experience. By so doing, little opportunity is available to forge partnerships and relationships that will support teachers' joint work in schools. Bilingual, second language, and mainstream teachers participating in dual language programs need to forge a common understanding and discourse that will permit them to work effectively together. The use of school-based study groups is one commonly used structure that permits these kinds of conversations and collaboration to develop in meaningful ways at a school or program level. (See Dubetz, chap. 13, this volume for an example of such a study group in a bilingual program.) Study groups are one of the structures recommended by the NSDC. Other groups also endorse such ongoing, locally focused professional development efforts over sporadic, short-term staff development activities conducted at a district-wide or regional level with little chance of having any measurable impact on individual schools (Holmes Group, 1990).

Visits to Other Programs

Peer support and modeling are also being conducted through visits to other programs. Especially in cases of new programs seeking the guidance of experts, visits to other programs provide invaluable insights about program formulation as well as offer the modeling of key techniques and approaches used by effective dual language teachers. Because sharing among programs is critical to the advancement of this program model, the Center for Applied Linguistics has compiled a directory of DLI programs in the United States[2] In our *Dual Language Handbook,* (Cloud et al., 2000), we created links to other programs through a boxed-text feature called "Voices from the Field" in which professionals from coast to coast, working at all levels in the implementation of dual language programs, share specific information with colleagues about their efforts. Such networking extends the sense of community to a much broader level. Virtual visits are also accomplished through the development and use of videotapes that chronicle specific features of existing programs.[3]

Networking Among Dual Language Teachers

To encourage collaboration and peer support, opportunities to learn from peers must be cultivated (NSDC, 2001). In addition to visits to other programs, be they virtual (online, on the phone, through writing) or in person, networking among dual language teachers is critical because they have a shared need to apply their knowledge and skills as second language/bilingual educators to the unique program context in which they teach. In Illinois, for example, through the Illinois Resource Center, the Enriching Language and Culture Education (ENLACE) network was established to facilitate such communication among dual language teachers working in programs in Illinois.[4] This spawned a whole host of resources from special resource collections, to training institutes based on local teachers' needs, to curriculum development projects. This kind of networking facilitates the development of the DLI program model in a particular geographic region and supports the development of individual programs through mentoring and networking by those working under similar political and social conditions.

---

[2]See http://www.cal.org for the directory of DLI Programs.

[3]For a list of informational videotapes, see Appendix D in Cloud et al., (2000) and page 38 in Lindholm-Leary (2000).

[4]For a description of the ENLACE network, see pages 186 to 187 in Cloud et al. (2000).

Curriculum Development Projects

It has long been known that the active involvement of participants best facilitates professional growth and development. Active decision-making calls on all of the existing knowledge, skills, and dispositions of professionals. For this reason, the application of professional development sequences to one's own life experience and professional role is urged by staff development specialists (NSDC, 2001; Sparks & Hirsh, 1997). Through curriculum development projects, participants are provided with the opportunity to make key instructional decisions and prepare needed classroom resources under the guidance and feedback of "experts" and with the support of peers. The reflection that takes place as groups of professionals work together to construct curriculum is very beneficial to program and teacher development. In addition, such efforts insure common understandings among teachers of each grade's curriculum. Such understandings are essential if the DLI program is to function effectively and support the continuous language, literacy, and academic development of the learners served (Cloud et al., 2000).

Intensive Institutes

Intensive institutes, designed to address the ongoing concerns of participants, are ideal mechanisms for promoting growth in teachers. This is true because they offer sustained professional development opportunities and take place outside of the daily routine of teaching (Saturday series, summer institutes). In addition, they allow staff developers to use a "layered" approach—presentations that are amplified by films, readings, activities, reflection, and discussion. Such intensity and duration are needed to make real progress in advancing teachers' teaching practices. At the same time, changes in practices initiated through intensive institutes must be complimented by ongoing support on site to insure sustained use of newly acquired techniques. Examples of such intensive teacher institutes are the Illinois Resource Center Summer Institute in Oaxaca, Mexico where dual language teachers from around the country explore methods and materials for teaching bilingual students in dual language programs while furthering their linguistic and cross-cultural skills.[5]

---

[5]For more information about the Illinois Resource Center summer institute, see http://www.thecenterweb.org/irc/irc_home.htm

HOW ARE INNOVATIONS IN TEACHER PREPARATION IN THE FIELD OF DUAL LANGUAGE EDUCATION BEING DOCUMENTED IN TERMS OF THEIR EFFECTIVENESS?

Currently, most dual language teacher preparation programs are documenting their effectiveness in a variety of ways. These include, for example, participant feedback (e.g., student attitudes; parental involvement, attitudes and satisfaction), ethnographic research conducted in classrooms (e.g., on teacher talk, nature of peer interactions), and student outcome measures (state-wide assessments and program specific evaluation results in language, literacy, and academic achievement; Lindholm-Leary, 2001).[6]

As is clear from the preceding listing, and because this is a relatively new program model, the emphasis thus far has been on program outcomes rather than on the professional development of dual language teachers. Indeed, relatively little information documenting the effectiveness of teacher preparation specific to this model is available. Thus, this is an area in which major contributions could be made by those seeking to conduct research on this program model.

WHAT SPECIFIC CHALLENGES MUST BE FACED IN IMPLEMENTING DLI PROGRAMS?

There are many challenges facing teachers working in DLI programs and those that prepare them for their work in classrooms. Among these are teachers' and administrators' fundamental lack of understanding of the program models they are attempting to implement. In some districts, DLI programs exist in name only, for the fundamental characteristics that define those programs do not exist in reality. For example, some programs do not begin early enough or last long enough to reap the benefits DLI programs are designed to produce. Others do not use both languages of instruction according to the recommended guidelines or group students effectively to insure frequent, well-planned interaction among speakers of both languages; rather, they place emphasis on the learning of English and only secondarily on the learning of the other language and separate children by language group unnecessarily for instruction.

---

[6]Readers are referred to the major clearinghouses and resource centers, such as the National Clearinghouse for English Language Acquisition (http://www.ncela.gwu.edu/), the Center for Research on Education, Diversity and Excellence (www.crede.ucsc.edu), and the Center for Applied Linguistics (www.cal.org) for up-to-the-minute research information on the DLI program model.

Dual language programs depend on well-prepared teachers who are trained to be strong collaborators. They must have administrative support (necessary time and resources) for frequent and extended joint instructional planning both within and across the grades of the program. They need to understand how to promote second language acquisition for language minority and language majority students. They need to understand how to promote high levels of literacy in both languages and have strong preparations in the teaching of academic subjects. They need to work well with parents and have strong roots in their local communities. They need to be fully proficient in the languages in which they teach. In short, well-prepared, experienced, and committed professionals are needed for these programs.

A huge challenge to teachers currently working in these programs is to support the full development of the language other than English and also to avoid the "drift" to English that is common in an English dominant environment. This includes establishing testing policies that do not create an overemphasis on English to the detriment of the development of full proficiency in both languages for both groups of students (language minority and language majority). This caution also pertains to insuring an equivalent quantity and quality of instructional materials in both languages.

The knowledge base for teachers working in dual language programs must be developed starting in initial teacher preparation programs and continuing through their ongoing professional development offerings in schools, as their needs change radically as they move from preparing for the programs versus working in the programs on an ongoing basis. These efforts need to be field based to capture the reality of the teaching/learning process. The actual day-to-day needs for support that teachers working in dual language programs require and deserve are challenging yet cannot be fully anticipated in preservice offerings. This continued support must be leveled according to the stage of development of individual teachers. Therefore, a seamless, individualized system must exist to build basic knowledge, skills, and dispositions by preservice programs and follow teachers into the field with continued inservice offerings.

CONCLUSION

Teacher practical knowledge is best developed when it is (a) grounded in theory and guided by defensible principles, (b) informed by the knowledge base on effective language and content teaching, and (c) developmentally appropriate to the stage of a program's and individual teacher's development (Cloud et al., 2000). The articulation of frameworks and models, provision of virtual and real-time demonstrations, the offering of collegial collaboration, and sharing of reality-based solutions all further the work of teachers in classrooms.

As we have seen in this brief review, there are many notable and innovative teacher education efforts emerging to support those working in dual language programs focused on classroom practice. These initiatives are beginning to be documented, but additional research is sorely needed pertaining to effective initial preparation and continued professional development for dual language teachers. There are also specific challenges faced by those implementing such programs that teacher educators can systematically address. With everyone's attention focused on these enriching programs, they will begin to realize their promise in our diverse and increasingly global society.

REFERENCES

Clandinin, J. (1986). *Classroom practice: Teacher images in action.* London: Falmer.

Cloud, N., Genesee, F., & Hamayan, E. (2000). *Dual language instruction: A handbook for enriched education.* Boston: Heinle & Heinle.

Holmes Group. (1990). *Tomorrow's schools: Principles for the design of professional development schools.* East Lansing, MI: Author.

Idol, L., Paolucci-Whitcomb, P., & Nevin, A. (1987). *Collaborative consultation.* Austin, TX: PRO-ED.

Johnson, L. J., Pugach, M. C., & Devlin, S. (1990). Challenges of the next decade: Professional collaboration. *TEACHING Exceptional Children, 22*(2), 9–11.

Lindholm-Leary, K. (2000). *Biliteracy for a global society: An idea book on dual language education.* Washington, DC: Center for the Study of Language and Education, National Clearinghouse for Bilingual Education.

Lindholm-Leary, K. J. (2001). *Dual language education.* Clevedon, England: Multilingual Matters.

National Council for Accreditation of Teacher Education (NCATE). (2002). *Professional standards for the accreditation of schools, colleges and departments of education.* Washington, DC: Author.

National Staff Development Council. (2001). *National Staff Development Council's standards for staff development, Revised: Advancing student learning through staff development.* Oxford, OH: Author.

Sparks, D., & Hirsh, S. (1997). *A new vision for staff development.* Alexandria, VA: Association for Supervision and Curriculum Development and the National Staff Development Council in Oxford, Ohio.

Teachers of English to Speakers of Other Languages. (2003). *Standards for the accreditation of initial programs in P–12 ESL teacher education.* Alexandria, VA: Author.

Wein, C. A. (1995). *Developmentally appropriate practice in "real life": Stories of teacher practical knowledge.* New York: Teachers College Press.

Chapter **16**

Teacher Education Through Immersion and Immersion Teacher Education: An Australian Case

Tony Erben
University of South Florida

In this chapter, I address three focus questions in relation to the development of a university immersion teacher education program called Language and Culture Initial Teacher Education Program (LACITEP). LACITEP is a 4-year Bachelor of Education degree program in which, depending on the semester, between 50% and 100% of the courses are delivered through the medium of Japanese to native speakers of English. The three questions that I deal with are (a) What characterises this innovative immersion teacher education program in Australia?; (b) How have those innovations been documented in terms of effectiveness?; and (c) What challenges are faced in implementing such a program as LACITEP?

INTRODUCTION

It may be claimed that the genesis of immersion education was the result of the intersection of two historical developments. One centered around an amalgam of sociocultural, political, and economic transformations that occurred during the 1960s in Québec, Canada. The other involved an ever-increasing body of linguistic research that highlighted the positive effects of bilingualism. Together, these developments signaled the educational potential as well as both a societal and individual imperative for immersion education. Each development has provided in turn an impetus for the sustained growth of the language immersion phenomenon to the present time.

In the nearly 40 years that have passed since the St. Lambert experiment (Lambert, 1974), immersion education has been exported throughout the rest of Canada and the world. Although the pedagogical outcomes of immersion education remain comparatively constant across education systems and national boundaries, the sociopolitical and educational agendas to which they contribute may vary quite substantially from one another. One needs to accept that immersion pedagogy as described following is located in a range of sociopolitical, cultural, and economic debates (Johnson & Swain, 1997).

The Languages Other Than English (LOTE) Agenda in Australia

Since the mid-1980s, an important ingredient in the federal government's agenda for national microeconomic reform has been the need to multiskill the Australian workforce. In schools, such microeconomic reform has translated into improving learning outcomes, which in turn have obliged schools into reshaping curricula so that students are taught skills in conjunction with content knowledge, including foreign languages, and the capacity to transfer these to new tasks and situations (Finn Report, 1991; Mayer Committee, 1992). Current policies set a framework within which the proliferation of improved modes of LOTE education now serves a national interest catering to all sections of the community. By promoting second language proficiency, teachers are encouraged to acquire specialist skills as well as to achieve higher levels of L2 proficiency themselves in order to operate successfully in alternative LOTE teaching environments (Council of Australian Governments [COAG], 1994).

TEACHER EDUCATION THROUGH IMMERSION

LACITEP was established in answer to the mainstreaming of LOTE education in Australia. It is the result of educational restructuring at both macro and micro levels. LACITEP is an endeavour to operationalise the concepts of immersion education at university to graduate highly proficient speakers of Japanese. It aims to equip LOTE teachers to be able to meet the growing demands in the profession by graduating teachers educated as generalist primary school teachers with a specialisation in

LOTE (Japanese) pedagogy capable not only of teaching the whole primary school curriculum as well as teaching Japanese but also of teaching the whole curriculum through the medium of Japanese. By creating such a pool of multiskilled LOTE teachers who have a solid grounding in immersion teaching practices and who are highly proficient in Japanese, the LACITEP program is aiming to meet the needs of employing authorities, particularly in Queensland. It is here envisaged that LOTE will become a compulsory part of the curriculum from Year 4 through to Year 10 within the next few years (COAG, 1994).

When it was established in 1993, LACITEP became in effect the first immersion initial teacher education degree program in the world to employ language immersion (Japanese) as a means to graduate multiskilled primary teachers specialised and proficient in the areas of Japanese language, primary education, Asian literacy,[1] and immersion pedagogy. The aim of LACITEP is to deliver a minimum of 50% of curriculum subjects through the medium of Japanese. In effect, a subject is either (a) totally delivered through Japanese language immersion, (b) delivered in such a way that the lecture is given in English and the tutorials or seminars are given in Japanese, or (c) totally delivered through the medium of English.

Fieldwork Experiences

To keep in line with the types of changes advocated by recent reports dealing with foreign languages and employment issues in Australia (COAG, 1994; Finn Report, 1991; Leal, 1991; Mayer Committee, 1992), learning opportunities are enhanced through a variety of practicum experiences organized within the degree. Of all the components in LACITEP, it is the practicum that allows the students to engage fully with the knowledge they have acquired in the content classes through immersion. To gain expertise in all specialisations in LACITEP (primary, Japanese, immersion, Asian Studies) there are several kinds of practical experiences other than the traditional block practicum. These consist of 1-day school visits, microteaching, Saturday Morning School, in-country practicum, and an internship.

Recent studies into the practicum component of preservice immersion teacher education indicate that it is preferable for student teachers to attempt immersion teaching after having experienced success in regular monolingual and foreign language classes (Majhanovich & Gray, 1992).

[1]This term was coined in Australia in the early 1990s to describe the study of anything Asian. A person who is Asian literate is seen to have communicative proficiency in at least one language of Asia and is able to function culturally appropriately as well as having an in depth knowledge of the sociocultural, political, historical, and economic landscape of one or more Asian countries.

The Central Queensland University teacher education immersion degree programs have such sequenced built-in practicums. These offer students ample opportunity for observation and time to build confidence in mainstream monolingual and foreign language teaching before having to deal with actual immersion teaching itself. By having such a variety of experiences and methods made available to them, future teachers can adopt the teaching techniques that most suit the circumstances and best cater to the individual needs of the school language learner.

In the Bachelor of Education for LOTE, students are required to complete a number of block practicum experiences in schools over the course of the degree program. The teacher development focus of each practicum differs from semester to semester. To gain expertise in all areas of specialisations (primary, secondary, Japanese, immersion, Asian Studies, plus one other discipline area), students are advised to conform to the school types as outlined in the recommended practicum schedule listed in Table 16.1.

As part of the practicum experience, the idea of a Saturday Morning Japanese School (SMJS) has been devised for Year 1 and Year 2 immersion student teachers. This School operates at Central Queensland University's Rockhampton Campus on a Saturday morning and is open to the wider Capricornia community. The composition of these classes consists of beginner learners of any age group as well as family groups.

The subjects Professional Practice 1 and Second Language Teaching Methodologies are integrated into and articulate with the experiences of the SMJS practicum and provide the theoretical focus of what Eltis (1991) describes as a practicum-driven curriculum. In preparing lessons for the SMJS, the immersion student teacher is expected to internalise new ideas, develop lesson plans, deliver lessons, and videotape lessons that are subsequently deconstructed the following week in Second Language Teaching Methodologies tutorials. SMJS also provides the immersion student teachers with the opportunity of team teaching with registered LOTE teachers.

To educate teachers who are capable of teaching in a number of different environments as well as achieving fluency in work-related competencies, the SMJS is structured in such a way that the student teachers themselves have an opportunity to run the school. Student teachers take on administrative roles on a 5-week rotational basis. A school executive (principal, deputy principal, curriculum advisers, and resource aide) establishes SMJS policies and guidelines to which all immersion student teachers conform. The SMJS is implemented for two 10-week blocks. After each 5-week module, a new executive is elected. In other words, for every 5-week unit of teaching, one immersion student teacher takes on the role of the SMJS principal, another

TABLE 16.1

Overview of the LACITEP Practicum Schedule

Year	*School Type*	*Semester*	*Focus*	*Days*
1		I and II		
	1-day Primary School		Generalist Primary	10
	Professional Practice 1		Generalist Primary	10
2		III and IV		
	Saturday Morning School		LOTE/Japanese	20 ½
	Professional Practice 2		Primary & Immersion	20
	Subject Specific Microteaching		Immersion & LOTE	
3		V and VI		
	Professional Practice 3		Generalist Primary	20
	Subject Specific Microteaching		Immersion & LOTE	
4		VII and VIII		
	Professional Practice 4		LOTE & Immersion	20
	Miscellaneous Tutoring		Generalist, LOTE, Immersion	10
TOTAL				100

Note. LOTE = Languages other than English.

takes on the role of the deputy principal (as well as being the de facto school accountant), three immersion student teachers become curriculum advisors, one becomes a resource person, and the remaining students take on the role of classroom teacher. These roles are rotated at the end of each 5-week period of work.

HOW HAVE THESE INNOVATIONS BEEN DOCUMENTED IN TERMS OF EFFECTIVENESS?

An understanding of effectiveness may be derived from the literature on schools effectiveness. One finding of this literature is that some schools are more successful than others. So too, it may be argued, approaches to language learning in schools including immersion (there are few immersion programs in teacher education) may be more effective and show a greater variety of successes than others. This situation when applied to teacher education emphasizes the fact that there are probably no simple generalisations that can be made about immersion programs across institutions or contexts. However, the study and reporting (Bartlett & Erben, 1995; Erben, 1993, 1999, 2001a, 2001b; Erben & Bartlett, 1997) of a more demonstrably successful immersion program such as LACITEP can be instructive for the education of future course design and development in preservice immersion teacher education.

Selected assumptions made about the effectiveness of immersion during the implementation of LACITEP may be defined as follows.

The Immersion Method Appropriately Conceived Does Have a Real Influence on Student Teachers. Before entry to the LACITEP program, most students did not realize what immersion entailed even though all potential applicants were provided with a range of documentation explaining the nature of the degree program. In a 1995 study, Bartlett and Erben uncover beginning students' inability to discern the interrelatedness of immersion, content, and language.

Meanings of immersion were more often than not relegated by respondents to a level of language proficiency in a language classroom, "something which is done with Japanese." Most students interviewed had a limited understanding of immersion and felt that immersion was intrinsically related to something that indeed only accommodated the study and acquisition of language. Students were forced to reorientate and reevaluate their expectations once the program had commenced. As a result, the 1st semester for most students was a period of adjustment and acclimatisation to the whole idea of immersion in LACITEP. In effect, students felt that they had to understand at least partially the idea of immersion to be able to learn through immersion.

The Student's Background and Social Context Will Influence Achievement and Outcomes/Effects of Immersion. In the same study (Bartlett & Erben, 1995), students frequently made the point that they needed to be more involved in their studies than regular Bachelor of Education students: that they couldn't afford to daydream because of the danger of missing out on something of importance. As a result, students were guided to take greater responsibilities when learning in immersion. In LACITEP, this manifested itself in a number of instances, reflective in the following student comments:

> Saturday Morning School is unreal. We've learnt how to deal with people; how to use resources; how to teach; just to make things interesting, it gives everything a practical side of things. You get to use Japanese and explain in Japanese.... It's different from fieldwork ... all you do is observe—you have to do what the teachers says—here we do/we can truly experiment. This is ours. We write, we teach, we create a syllabus, we decide directions, it's run by us. It is ours. We've learnt about administration, and organization, people management.

Being more involved in the process of language learning and learning per se allowed "each to work at [his or her] own level of understanding, no one should be bored, there's always things to do."

The Effects of Immersion Learning Should Be Measured Quantitatively and Qualitatively. In the 1995 study, Bartlett and Erben conclude that it is exceedingly important to use a variety of theoretical and methodological perspectives. Apart from statistical approaches to measure growth, the contextual factors within an immersion program are very rich and often further elucidate quantitative findings. While investigating language proficiency levels in LACITEP, Bartlett and Erben uncover relevant contextual data; they write the following:

> *Confidence*, *motivation*, and *fluency* reacted together to promote or hinder good learning practices. In each immersion class, the level of involvement was strongly influenced by [second language] L2 communicative competence. Some students expressed the idea that they felt "dumb" because their language ability or lack of it, did not allow them to follow the lesson. Rightly or wrongly, this led a few students to associate incorrectly low levels of proficiency with low IQ. This phenomena was evident with a number of students in Year One and was evident at the time of the study. The equation looked like the following; low proficiency = catch 22 leading to > low comprehension > greater confusion > more time needed to stay "on top" > internalization of the problem > frustration > burn out. (p. 86)

Effectiveness Can Be Measured at Least in Part by Changes in Levels of Achievement Over Time, For Example, in the Four Macroskills, but Particularly in Speaking Skills. Immersion within LACITEP encouraged students to learn a variety of Japanese registers and although students initially became more comfortable with using basic interpersonal communicative skills (BICS) type language, their initial hesitancy to use cognitive-academic language proficiency (CALP) style language (Cummins, 1980) gradually decreased. In LACITEP, CALP type language incorporated language registers that were used primarily by teachers. These included language that was the specific speech domain of the educational environment of the classroom.

Effectiveness is not the product of an accurate formulation of a recipe for success. Immersion learning is framed by broader contextual realities such as national policy, societal attitudes—that is, those influences that frame or govern and constrain what is possible for immersion teaching and learning. In any discussion about effectiveness, one must also acknowledge the location in which the learning takes place. Rockhampton is a rural Australian city whose population has been bolstered by the student population of Central Queensland University. There is a low ethnic population in the community, and there are very few native-speaking Japanese living in the area. However, the University has an active English Language Centre that sees numerous native Japanese arrive in Rockhampton for short intensive study tours. Although the city of Rockhampton doesn't provide much outside interaction with Japanese, the University does. It seems that what is not readily available or accessible is sought even more actively when it does become available.

Effectiveness in LACITEP Is not Seen as "Value Added" (as Are Curriculum Elements Reflected in Recent School Effectiveness Research). LACITEP is assessed for its success by the fact that it does achieve more than what is expected. Bartlett and Erben (1995) report

> Students were very much supportive of the idea that learning through Japanese provided new ways of looking at content; that it provided different perspectives on content and that most importantly one could relate knowledge to an increasing number of situations: "We are doing an English B.Ed. and a Japanese B.Ed.; we reconcile both by compromising and using what comes out of it." Thus for LACITEP students, learning through immersion meant learning language and culture; it meant learning at one's own pace through comprehensible input:

"The more perspectives one has of a subject the easier it is to learn it and you thus learn more" Some students expressed their learning of knowledge as: "I think you'd have to learn more because when you learn a language you'd have to see things from a different perspective and so I think we get a perspective through English and Japanese.... The Australian point of view is how this can benefit me and the Japanese point of view is how it can benefit others.... It's a gradual thing." For LACITEP students, immersion allowed for a better base knowledge in the area of teacher knowledges. (p. 98)

No One Characteristic Identified in the Immersion Literature or Empirically Observed During the Conduct of Research Within LACITEP Is Seen to Be Transferable Across All Immersion Settings, Although Immersion Characteristics Singularly and in Combination Are Assumed to Have an Influence on Student Learning. The overarching principal goal of LACITEP was to produce teachers of Japanese language for immersion programs. The pedagogical formation of students therefore was a critical purpose for the program's raison d'être, which would not necessarily become evident in other immersion programs with different goals. Within LACITEP, the word *pedagogy* should be understood as teaching or instruction, but within a broader discursive, sociocultural, economic, and political framework within which teachers work. In some sense, the LACITEP students, at least initially at the time of the 1995 Bartlett and Erben study (the situation may have changed since), acknowledged the possibility of developing multiple identities as teachers and proficient speakers of Japanese with all the cultural attributes that implies or requires.

Above all, it is the student successes that are a measure of the success of the LACITEP immersion degree programs. Since the first cohort of students graduated, 100% of graduates have gained employment, up to 90% of graduates have received an S1 or S2 rating by Education Queensland, all graduates have passed Education Queensland's LOTE proficiency interview[2] (a minimum of Australian second language-pro-

[2]S1 and S2 are a part of a system of performance indicators (S1–S4) used by Education Queensland to rank graduating teachers in terms of their suitability to teach in Queensland schools. The ASLPR is a communicative assessment scale used by governments in Australia. Trained raters engage L2 speakers in a range of tasks and by interview. L2 speakers are subsequently rated on a scale from 0 to 6 (0 being *no proficiency* and 6 being *native speaker*) by matching L2 speakers' communicative performance against benchmark descriptors in Listening, Speaking, Reading, and Writing. The scale was developed by Ingram and Wylie (1985); a version for L2 teachers was developed by Wylie and Ingram (1995), and a version for Japanese as a foreign language was developed by Wylie, Ingram, and Grainger (1995).

ficiency ratings [ASLPR] 3 is a passing grade), and the overall attrition rate within LACITEP has been a very low average of 5% to 10%.

WHAT CHALLENGES ARE FACED IN IMPLEMENTING SUCH A PROGRAM AS LACITEP?

The philosophical impetus around which the LACITEP degree program has been created in the desire to promote student learning has been (a) the idea of the linguistic bath called immersion, and (b) the constructivist notion that "through doing comes learning." In an effort to provide students with an ever-increasing multitude of innovative linguistic and professional experiences, challenges remain.

Classroom Teaching in Immersion

The very nature of immersion teaching, as explained, means that subjects that are normally delivered in English have to be converted to Japanese. This process is a complicated one and does not simply involve translation. Content in the form of concepts are used in a Japanese language and cultural context that is located in Australia and forms part of a program at an Australian university. This process, for those delivering the subjects, involves virtually complete redesign and rewriting of each subject. It also involves Japanese resources being used and altered to suit the pedagogical practice of an immersion program. The workload then becomes greater in volume than what it would be if the program were delivered in English. Knowledge of the area, the specialist language and contemporary context in Japan as well as Australia are necessary for effective execution.

Program-Based Teaching

To frame notions of teaching solely around what happens in a classroom is a narrow view of teaching. The LACITEP degree program operates on a team basis; a lot of teaching also occurs outside the classroom directly and indirectly through other activities. These outside classroom teaching activities may be seen as teaching work that has traditionally been hidden and unofficial yet is fundamental in making the immersion model work. It is the communication and organizational aspect of teaching within immersion units and as a program as a whole that merits closer consideration.

Resource Preparation

Resource preparation impinges on both language acquisition subjects and curriculum subjects. The radical nature of immersion methodology and the paucity of university markets for courses of this nature result in the absence of any commercially produced texts that might successfully be used by LACITEP staff. All materials, including those that would be regarded as "readings" in distance education material, must be prepared by staff. This is an ongoing process.

Difficulties in preparing such material are exacerbated by the absence of Japanese academics with whom to consult. Responsibility for all research related to resource preparation must be taken by the individual professor involved. This can be an extremely isolating as well as an onerous process. Consideration also needs to be given to the sheer volume of ongoing time involved in the constant search for appropriate materials.

Faculty staff who teach through the medium of English, for instance, have ongoing access to publisher advertising material that provides fairly detailed descriptions of texts and their content. LACITEP staff are unable to access similar material in Japanese.

Resource preparation in an immersion degree program is not merely a brief teleological process of preparing for a subject to an endpoint after which the material can repeatedly be reused. Because staff are simultaneously teaching Japanese and teaching in Japanese, the different characteristics of each cohort of students demands that materials must annually undergo significant and time-consuming adaptation.

Command of Subject Matter Including the Incorporation of Recent Development in the Field of Study

Of all points to consider when selecting appropriate staff, the need to have teachers who are proficient in the second language and have a resounding depth of content/curriculum knowledge is paramount to the success of any immersion degree program. If the teachers are comfortable with what and how they teach, then it doesn't take much more effort to embed within the program additional stimulating learning opportunities, initiatives, and activities.

Participation in the Effective and Sympathetic Guidance and Advising of Students

For an immersion program teacher education to work, it is of extreme importance to supervise the individual progress of all students. Students enter LACITEP having completed Japanese up to Year 12. It is a great step for the students to simultaneously become acquainted with university life but also to learn their university subjects through the medium of a second language. The LACITEP staff see each individual student enrolled in the LACITEP degree program and discuss their academic and professional teacher development at least once each term. Also, the teaching staff meet regularly every week for 1 to 2 hr meetings to discuss student progress. In this way, staff can gauge what is happening within LACITEP, help students with problems, provide advice, or share individual time with them for intellectual discussions. Such supervision has involved a lot of time for staff, although it is these types of support structures that have ultimately contributed to the overall success of LACITEP.

Provision of Appropriate Assessment With Feedback to Students on Their Learning

The LACITEP staff operates its assessment procedures according to the Faculty of Education and Creative Arts assessment guidelines; however, in addition to these procedures, a further means of evaluation and assessment of students' language development is implemented. This is called *profiling*.

Profiling is carried out twice every semester on every student in every year level enrolled in the LACITEP immersion degree programs. It involves a systematic and semistructured proficiency interview that includes a set of interactive tasks that students have to complete. Each profile takes approximately 30 to 45 min. It is recorded, and the results are written down on a profile proforma. Once completed, one proforma is given to the student and one is stored in each student's portfolio kept in the Faculty's library. Profiling means that each student's performance and learning development is assessed against the student himself or herself, not against the group or other members of the class. The administration of the profiling becomes a challenge in that it consumes a great deal of time. In addition, maintaining high levels of reliability is always a matter of concern especially in a context in which the raters may change from semester to semester.

Because students are learning Japanese through content area subjects, students develop communicative proficiencies in a range of vocational and professional discourse registers. Profiling allows staff to adequately describe, map, write down, and report each student's language development in a way that is transparent and easy for students to understand.

CONCLUSION: FLEXIBLE DIVERSITY

The strategy of flexible diversity offers language teacher education programs a better opportunity to reduce risk factors while improving returns. Of course, there are no guarantees. It is recognised that the success of this strategy has as much to do with the nature of a program's course offerings and the location and reputation of the institution as it does with the changing policy and economic context.

REFERENCES

Bartlett, L., & Erben, T. (1995). *An investigation into the effectiveness of an exemplar model of LOTE teacher-training through partial immersion* (A Report for the Innovative Languages Other Than English Project). Canberra: Department of Employment, Education and Training, Australian Government Printing Service.

Council of Australian Governments: (K. Rudd, Chair). (1994). *Asian languages and Australia's economic future: A report prepared for the Council of Australian Governments on a proposed Asian languages/studies strategy for Australian schools.* Brisbane: Queensland Government Press.

Cummins, J. (1980). The entry and exit fallacy in bilingual education. *NABE Journal, 4,* 25–60.

Eltis, K. (1991). Reshaping pre-service teacher education: Establishing a practicum-driven curriculum. *The Journal of Teaching Practice, 11*(2), 1–17.

Erben, A. (1993). The importance of the practicum in teacher development. What happens in an immersion teacher training program? *Australian Association of Language Immersion Teachers, 1*(1), 16–30.

Erben, T. (1999). Constructing learning in a virtual immersion bath: LOTE teacher education through audiographics. In R. Debski & M. Levy (Eds.), *WorldCALL* (pp. 229–248). Amsterdam: Kluwer.

Erben, T. (2001a). *Student-teachers' use of microteaching activity to construct sociolinguistic knowledge within a Japanese immersion initial teacher education program in Australia.* Unpublished doctoral dissertation, Lancaster University, Lancaster, England.

Erben, T. (2001b). The student-teacher school: Constructing second language competences. In G. Braeuer (Ed.), *Pedagogy of language learning* (pp. 195–220). Westport, CT: Ablex.

Erben, T., & Bartlett, L. (1997). Mediated interaction and the management of learning in an initial teacher education language immersion classroom. In T. Gale, A. Erben, & P. Danaher (Eds.), *Diversity, difference & discontinuity: (Re)mapping teacher education for the next decade*. Refereed Proceedings of the 27th Annual Conference of the Australian Teacher Education Association (ATEA). Yeppoon, Queensland, Australia: ATEA. Retrieved July 13, 2002 http://atea.cqu.edu.au/content/soc_base/erbart.html

Finn Report. (1991). *Young people's participation in post-compulsory education & training* (Report of the Australian Education Council Review Committee). Canberra: Australian Government Printing Service.

Ingram, D. E., and Wylie, E. (1985). *Australian second language proficiency ratings (ASLPR).* Brisbane, Queensland: National Languages and Literacy Institute of Australia, Language Testing Centre, Griffith University.

Johnson, R. K., & Swain, M. (1997). *Immersion education: International perspectives*. Cambridge, England: Cambridge University Press.

Lambert, W. E. (1974). A Canadian experiment in the development of bilingual competence. *The Canadian Modern Language Review, 31,* 108–116.

Leal, B. (1991). *Widening our horizons* (Report of the review of the teaching of modern languages in higher education). Canberra: Australian Government Printing Service.

Majhanovich, S., & Gray, J. (1992). The practicum: An essential component in French immersion teacher education. *The Canadian Modern Language Review, 48*, 682–696.

Mayer Committee. (1992). *Employment-related key competencies for postcompulsory education and training*. A discussion chapter (Australian Education Council & Ministers for Vocational Education, Employment and Training). Melbourne: Australian Government Printing Service.

Wylie, E., & Ingram, D. E. (1995). *Australian second language proficiency ratings (ASLPR) version for second language teachers.* Brisbane, Queensland: National Languages and Literacy Institute of Australia, Language Testing Centre, Griffith University.

Wylie, E., Ingram, D. E., & Grainger, P. (1995). *Australian second language proficiency ratings (ASLPR) version for Japanese.* Brisbane, Queensland: National Languages and Literacy Institute of Australia, Language Testing Centre, Griffith University.

Chapter **17**

Combining Foreign and Second Language Teacher Education: Rewards and Challenges

Martha Bigelow
Diane J. Tedick
University of Minnesota

INTRODUCTION

Second and foreign language (FL) teacher education have more commonalities than differences. Nevertheless, in the United States, English as a second language (ESL) teachers and FL teachers often complete their initial or continuing education in different departments or even different colleges. The reasons for this may be philosophical or historical or both. In the Second Languages and Cultures (SLC) Education program in the Department of Curriculum and Instruction at the University of Minnesota, we have long argued that second language (L2) contexts are fragmented and isolated from one another—in schools, in programs that prepare teachers for L2 settings, and in the profession at large (Tedick & Walker, 1994; Tedick, Walker, Lange, Paige, & Jorstad, 1993). In both preservice and inservice teacher education, FL teachers are primarily prepared in language departments, ESL teachers often receive their professional development in linguistics or English departments, and bilingual teachers are enrolled in isolated programs that are often linked to education departments administratively. Immersion teachers in the United States have little opportunity to have professional development that is designed to address their unique needs and issues (Met & Lorenz, 1997), although Canada and Australia are two countries where immersion-specific preparation programs exist (see, e.g., Day & Shapson, 1996; Erben, chap. 16, this volume). We maintain that language teachers, regardless of context, should engage in professional development together, and we have become aware of the rewards and challenges of combining FL and L2 teacher education.

In this chapter, we briefly describe our integrated preservice and inservice programs for L2 teachers. We then discuss some of the rewards that emerge when FL, ESL, bilingual, and immersion teachers come together. Finally, we identify a number of pedagogical and professional challenges that arise with such integration.

TEACHER DEVELOPMENT IN SECOND LANGUAGES AND CULTURES

The SLC program offers a variety of degree, licensure, and nondegree options for those interested in L2 teaching.[1] All of our courses and programs are offered at the graduate (postbaccalaureate) level. In addition to the preservice and inservice programs we describe in this chapter, we offer advanced Master of Arts and Doctor of Philosophy programs for individuals seeking to do research in the field. We begin with a brief description of our preservice program and then describe the options available for inservice professional development.

Preservice Teacher Education

The SLC preservice program typically accepts a cohort of 25 to 35 students who will obtain their first state licenses (certifications) to teach ESL and/or an FL in Kindergarten through 12th grade (K–12) settings in a 15-month, full-time program. The cohort includes students who are, for the most part, seeking an ESL license. There is a subset of those students who are seeking the dual licensure option by adding an FL. To obtain a license in a language in which the student is not native, a score of at least *Advanced-Low* is required (*Superior* if the L2 is English) on the Oral Proficiency Interview (Breiner-Sanders, Lowe, Miles, & Swender, 2000). A unique feature of this program is that students take classes and

---

[1]For more information about the variety of programs offered, visit the University of Minnesota Web site at http://education.umn.edu/ci/Areas/SLC.html

engage in student teaching throughout most of their program, spending their mornings in schools and their afternoons on campus.

Due to a large and highly qualified applicant pool, we have been able to admit many outstanding candidates. Students come to the program from a wide range of backgrounds both in terms of experience and undergraduate degrees. Because of this, the average age tends to be between 27 and 30. Students typically have spent time abroad—hence, their high levels of L2 proficiency—and have demonstrated commitment to immigrant communities through volunteer work and community activism. They are required to have spent at least 100 hr in K–12 language classrooms before applying to the program. This helps us ensure that the applicants are confident of their desire to obtain a K–12 license.

The curriculum of this program is integrated. After students spend their first summer in the program taking courses in foundations in education, linguistics, and L2 acquisition, they participate in a 12 semester-credit pedagogy course spanning the academic year. This course, although officially four 3-credit classes, follows one syllabus that integrates approaches to instruction and assessment, curriculum development, and issues in culture. This integration is possible because the two instructors who lead the program coteach the pedagogy course. Additional courses include a course on integrating English grammar in language instruction and a course in using technology for instructional purposes. These are the only courses in the program that are also open to practicing teachers. The fact that there are separate courses dedicated to English grammar and technology does not mean that students' development of their knowledge in these areas is limited to this course or stops after the course is over. There is much effort to integrate what students learn in these courses with the content of other courses they take, especially in terms of how they apply this knowledge in age- and level-appropriate ways.

Students in our program engage in two or four student teaching placements during the academic year depending on whether they are seeking a single or a dual license. This is required because in Minnesota, language licenses are K–12, and becoming licensed in elementary or secondary alone is not an option. Course work is complemented by a weekly 3-hr meeting held with small groups of students and facilitated by the student teaching supervisors. This is the time in which students are able to debrief at length the particular issues that arise in their student teaching placements. By integrating student teaching and course work, we have been able to keep the curriculum from fragmenting into components that do not connect to one another or fail to recycle content across contexts, according to the students' current student teaching placement.

Inservice Teacher Education

In addition to our program for preservice teachers, we have a range of options available for practicing teachers including a Master of Education degree program, endorsement programs (for those who wish to add another area to their existing license, e.g., an elementary teacher who wants to add ESL or a French teacher who wants to add Spanish), a certificate program in language immersion education,[2] special summer institutes,[3] and grant-funded professional development opportunities. One grant-funded program is Content-Based Language Teaching through Technology (CoBaLTT), which includes both a professional development program for K–16 FL teachers and a Web-based resource center.[4] Another current grant targets professional development for grade-level teachers who work with increasing numbers of language minority learners (Walker & Stone, 2003).

All of the degree, endorsement, and certificate programs have a distinct set of requirements, and some of those requirements are unique to a particular context. For example, ESL teachers take linguistics courses that other L2 teachers do not take; immersion teachers enrolled in the certificate program take two courses that are designed specifically for the immersion context. More often than not, however, the courses we offer cross programs. Therefore, it is common for us to find in our inservice classes teachers who represent a vast array of L2 contexts—ESL and EFL, FL, immersion, and bilingual[5]—and settings: K–12, university, and adult. In classes where we have this range of contexts, we assign "base groups" according to L2 setting and context. Thus, when the material in the course calls for context-specific discussion, group formation according to

---

[2]Certificate programs at the University of Minnesota are short, concentrated courses of study. They do not lead to state teaching licensure or a degree but rather are designed to provide teachers with courses designed around a specific area such as language immersion education. More information about this certificate program can be found at the University of Minnesota Web site at http://education.umn.edu/SPS/programs/certificates/LanguageImmersion.html

[3]Summer institutes for language teachers are organized and offered through the Center for Advanced Research on Language Acquisition (CARLA), one of 14 national language resource centers in the United States. Teachers may opt to take the week-long institutes for graduate credit. Institutes are offered in areas such as learning strategy instruction, culture, assessment, less commonly taught languages, and immersion. More information is available at the CARLA Web site at http://www.carla.umn.edu

[4]Information about the CoBaLTT program and the Web Resource Center can be found at the CARLA Web site at http://www.carla.umn.edu/cobaltt/ The CoBaLTT program is limited to FL teachers and language immersion teachers because of the parameters of the funding source.

[5]The state of Minnesota has not been proactive in supporting bilingual education over the years. Consequently, we have very few students in our programs from bilingual settings or pursuing a bilingual license.

the teachers' respective focus is facilitated. We are also careful to devise syllabi that offer a range of readings, some required for all contexts and others that are context specific. We design assignments that have a variety of options so that teachers will be able to select alternatives that are most valuable to their continued professional growth. Table 17.1 summarizes the features of the preservice and inservice programs in SLC.

Many of the teachers that have participated in our programs have shared with us how much they enjoy learning from and with L2 teachers across such a wide array of contexts, and our experience as teacher educators is that we wouldn't have it any other way. As our programs evolve and grow, it has been essential that all of our decisions be informed by the basic principles of integration and instruction that crosses contexts. In the following sections, we outline some of the specific rewards and challenges to our approach to language teacher education.

TABLE 17.1

Summary of Preservice and Inservice Program Features

Variable	*Preservice*	*Inservice*
Program/degree options	Master of Education (MEd) with licensure	MEd, endorsement(s), certificate, grant-funded programs, summer institutes
Teaching contexts represented	K–12 ESL and FL	K through adult ESL and FL, immersion, EFL, bilingual
Program model	Cohort model—full-time option only	A la carte course options in the evening; intensive summer offerings; weekend workshops
Time	15-month program duration	Programs take 2 to 7 years
Program parameters	Program designed around state licensure requirements	Programs include licensure requirements but are more flexible and tailored to teacher interests and needs

Note. K–12 = Kindergarten through 12th grade; ESL = English as a second language; FL = foreign language; EFL = English as a foreign language.

REWARDS BROUGHT BY THE REPRESENTATION OF MULTIPLE CONTEXTS

There are many rewards to having teachers who are focused on a number of different language learning contexts in our classes. We begin by describing these benefits and explain how they contribute to richer learning experiences for all.

Broadening Teachers' Understanding of Language Learning Contexts

One of the most significant ways teachers in our programs benefit is that by having classmates with primary interests in areas different from their own, they learn about the issues and dilemmas other language teachers face, which in turn rounds out their own professional development. This exchange often happens incidentally as they engage in small-group discussions or projects. At the same time, sharing is frequently deliberate and required because students often read studies conducted in contexts other than their own. Engagement across contexts inevitably promotes the realization in teachers that although there are certain fundamentals that seem to cross all classroom language-learning contexts, many core issues play out quite differently depending on the setting. For example, when we explore content-based instruction, each context tends to define content in different ways. ESL and immersion teachers will likely choose academic content that aligns with grade level/content curriculum and FL teachers often choose the L2 culture as content. Likewise, whereas ESL (TESOL, 1997) and FL (American Council on the Teaching of Foreign Languages [ACTFL], 1996) both have their own national standards, these sets of standards are framed quite differently. It has been our experience that comparing and contrasting the different sets of standards is very useful for language teachers in that it broadens their view of what is possible in a curriculum for language development.

In our classes, we feel that we serve teachers interested in EFL contexts very well because of the inclusion of the FL teachers in our programs. Their teacher development needs tend to parallel those of the FL teachers rather than ESL teachers. In this case, we have found that the shared language (English) is not as powerful a connection as a shared context in which that language is taught.[6] The EFL teachers

---

[6]Clearly, teaching English in, for example, Korea is far different than teaching Spanish in the United States. A key difference would be the importance given to FL instruction in the K–12 curriculum. Nevertheless, many core issues remain the same. One issue that consistently arises in our courses is the fact that FL teachers are often nonnative speakers. This seems to influence a myriad of other choices teachers make as they plan and carry out instruction.

bring additional perspectives to our classes that contribute to everyone's learning. For instance, they help us explore issues related to high-stakes testing, large classes, and coping with a standardized, government regulated curriculum—issues that teachers in the United States are facing more and more.

Gaining Greater Understanding of First Language (L1) and L2 Use in Classrooms

When language teachers of all types are together, they have the opportunity to examine and reflect on the norms that are often taken for granted in their respective programs or departments. Some of the most passionate discussions among ESL, immersion, and FL teachers, including EFL teachers, are with regard to the place of the L1 in the L2 classroom. For example, FL teachers lead ESL teachers to question the still common "English only" rules or beliefs they encounter or hold themselves and recognize that there are very good reasons for allowing learners to use their L1 or other bilingual resources in the classroom. In such discussions, FL teachers are often challenged by ESL teachers who teach beginners and use English very little because there are so many L1s present in the class. Similar challenges are voiced by immersion teachers. In this case, FL teachers learn from the techniques ESL and immersion teachers use to remain in the target language.

Finding Common Ground and Forging Alliances

Another advantage of having teachers representing multiple contexts in the same classes is that they begin to know more about each other's work and can see each other more as allies in both K–12 and university settings. They can see what unites them philosophically and institutionally. Unfortunately, institutional constraints often pull them in different directions. For instance, in the K–12 context in the United States, ESL teachers are far more likely to seek collaborations with grade level (elementary) or content (secondary) teachers than with FL teachers. This is due to pressures to help English language learners succeed in grade level/content classes as soon as possible. FL teachers are less likely to collaborate with colleagues from other departments because their curriculum is more self-contained. In university settings, their courses are offered in different departments. By being together, teachers from the various contexts can begin to see how their work is more similar than different and thereby are more likely to seek collegiality and institutional alliances.

Different Paths Toward Knowledge About Language

The teachers in our programs vary widely in how they learned the language(s) they teach, which results in a wide range of language awareness. This means, for example, that some teachers have a great deal of metalinguistic knowledge about the language, others are very proficient but have not experimented with a range of genres in the language, and others are educated monolingual native speakers who have had limited exposure to L2 study. These differences are challenges in our programs but are at the same time another example of why an integrated program with a diverse student body is beneficial.

Specifically, the majority of the ESL teachers in our programs are native English speakers, whereas most FL teachers and many immersion teachers tend to be nonnative speakers of the language they teach. The FL teachers tend to have learned their L2 through classroom learning in addition to time abroad. Many years of classroom language learning result in FL teachers having a great deal more explicit knowledge about language than the ESL teachers who may not have thought very much about the English language as a system since their middle school years despite required course work in linguistics and English grammar for the ESL license. Therefore, our FL teachers tend to be more conversant and confident in the grammar of their language. Immersion teachers, on the other hand, vary in their preparation and background (e.g., Walker & Tedick, 2000); some were originally prepared as traditional FL teachers and worked in that setting before joining an immersion school. Like FL teachers, they have stronger grammatical knowledge. Other immersion teachers, however, were prepared as elementary teachers and sought positions in immersion schools due to strong proficiency in the immersion language. They tend to be more like ESL teachers in that their formal knowledge of the immersion language may be lacking.

All of the teachers' strengths and weaknesses in their own language knowledge and fluency are only relevant in how they ultimately make pedagogical decisions in the classroom with regard to integrating a language focus. We find, for example, that FL teachers tend to be much more aware of their own language production and are better able to monitor their language use in the classroom (e.g., giving simple instructions). They also relate to their students' language learning challenges very easily, having learned the language to some degree in similar situations and with similar background experiences. ESL and immersion teachers benefit from learning how the FL teachers field grammar questions, modify their own language, and communicate expectations about linguistic accuracy.

We have observed that the FL teachers are often very clear about how their curriculum promotes developmental, sequential language learning. Our ESL, bilingual, and immersion teachers tend to bring a broad notion of social versus academic language (Cummins, 1980) and the real-world language demands on students. They do, however, struggle with keeping a language focus in their instruction as do most language teachers when they have a strong content focus (e.g., Bigelow & Ranney, 2001; Short, 2002; Snow, 2001; Tedick, Fortune, & Walker, 2003). The opposite seems to be true with our FL teachers. They tend to make language the center of their curriculum. For example, the ESL teachers are able to identify and teach strategies for coping with text that is beyond the learners' proficiency level, but they may not approach any portion of the text at a syntactic level. The FL teachers may choose a text to contextualize a new grammatical structure or may unnecessarily withhold difficult or authentic texts until they believe students know all of the vocabulary and grammatical structures presented in the text. In short, as all the teachers in our program strive to integrate content and language thoughtfully in their curriculum and instructional practices, they benefit from the diverse knowledge their peers bring to this very challenging enterprise.

Understanding Ironies and Valuing Multilingualism for All

In the United States, there are many contradictions in the world of language education depending on whether learners are part of the language minority or the language majority (Tedick & Walker, 1994; Tedick et al., 1993). On one hand, ESL programs may be seen as remedial, often (and inappropriately) linked to special education programs in public schools. ESL teachers are often marginalized because their work may be seen as remedial (Edstam, 2001). Their role may be seen as that of an aide rather than a fully licensed teacher. This is now magnified by the current trend toward inclusion in which ESL teachers are often relegated to a low-status position in the grade level/content teachers' classrooms. Additionally, ESL programs are often politically vulnerable when they are serving mostly immigrant children whose parents are often not in the position to become strong advocates for services. Bilingual programs are under constant scrutiny, reflecting the belief that programs that often result in subtractive bilingualism are acceptable for English language learners (Nieto, 2000). On the other hand, additive bilingualism for language majority children in immersion and FL programs in the United States is the goal. The power status of English is clear. As long as learners know English, adding another language is encouraged and praised. However, having a language other than English to begin with is seen as a deficit, and the emphasis is on teaching such learners English, often and sadly at the expense of their native language. By sharing classes with ESL and bilingual teachers who work with diverse learners, the FL and immersion teachers who work with native English speakers begin to question these school and societal ironies and perceptions and develop a deeper understanding about the contradictions involving language learning in the United States. This leads to a greater appreciation for the common goal of multilingualism for all learners.

Conversely, FL and immersion programs are too often perceived as elitist and reserved for high academic achievers. Such perceptions may even be perpetuated by FL teachers themselves and by scholars in the field. For example, we were dismayed to read Lindholm-Leary's (2001) statement that "many immersion programs are elite" (p. 30) when immersion programs in the United States go to great lengths to dispel this myth.[7] Yet many scholars are also careful to point to problems with FL instruction in the United States that in effect keep some learners from participating or succeeding in formal language instruction (Schulz, 1991); others have shown how diverse learners succeed in some FL contexts such as immersion (e.g., Genesee, 1992). Consequently, it is not a surprise that in K–12 contexts in the United States, ESL and FL teachers do not necessarily view each other as closely allied as they might due to the different student populations they teach.

The rewards that come with combining FL and L2 teacher education are many, but the synergy we describe previously does not happen incidentally. It takes thoughtful planning and coordination to achieve a balance among contexts to allow teachers in our programs the opportunity to learn from and with each other.

REWARDS DO NOT COME WITHOUT CHALLENGES

As described in detail previously, many rewards result from teacher education programs that bring teachers together from a variety of L2 contexts. It is, however, important to note the various challenges that come with this integrated program model.

Maintaining Currency in and Commitment to Multiple Professions

One of the greatest challenges to integrated L2 teacher education programs is ensuring that we maintain currency in the literature in the

---

[7]Immersion schools in the United States are normally public, not private schools as in many countries.

many fields represented in our programs. Each year there is a barrage of books, journals, newsletters, and online journals and resources published by the various L2 fields—applied linguistics, ESL, FLs, bilingual education, and immersion education—representing multiple settings, from early language learning to K–12, to adult and university level programs. Likewise, it is important that we keep abreast of developments in the L1 arena. For example, L2 reading research needs to be informed in part by advances in L1 reading research. For our work with teachers of language minority learners, we must be informed about developments in a number of other fields, particularly in the areas of literacy, standards, and assessment. This suggests that issues related to language minority learners no longer "belong" to the L2 professional community alone—every year there are more and more articles, book chapters, and books from the L1 professions on L2 learners, not to mention grant opportunities. The broader community has begun to attend to the issues of English language learners because the numbers are too large to ignore and because L2 issues sell—grant funding in many areas require at least a nod toward addressing the needs of English language learners in the proposal.

In addition to the vast array of published literature across multiple fields, there are several professional organizations for each of the fields (both L1 and L2), meaning ever-increasing professional dues and the potential for multiple conferences per year. In the United States alone, there are many L2 professional organizations, some highly specific (e.g., the American Council on Immersion Education) and others appealing to a range of L2 contexts (e.g., the American Association of Applied Linguistics). There are also L1 organizations that address L2 issues (e.g., the American Educational Research Association, which has several groups devoted to L2 issues). Of course there are also the state[8] and international organizations as well.

Another issue making it difficult to maintain currency is the proliferation of standards that have emerged in all educational fields. TESOL has developed ESL Standards for Pre-K–12 students (TESOL, 1997), and ACTFL introduced national standards for FL learning in 1996 (ACTFL, 1996); bilingual and immersion teachers need to be familiar with standards that have been developed for core subject matter areas (from science and math to social studies and reading/language arts). Teachers in our programs also need to be familiar with Minnesota's state standards; ESL teachers will need to follow newly revised standards that comply with federal guidelines requiring states to have standards specifically de-

[8]In Minnesota, we have Minnesota TESOL, Minnesota Council on the Teaching of Languages and Cultures, and Minnesota Advocates for Immersion Network.

signed for English language learners. These standards define progressive levels of competence in listening, speaking, reading, and writing and are linked to the content area standards in English language arts, math, and (eventually) science (*Minnesota English Language Proficiency Standards for English Language Learners*, 2003). To date, there are no state-level standards in Minnesota for FLs; instead, such standards are to be developed at the local level and will not be assessed by the state.

Although standards are an important part of any teacher's preparation, standards for teacher education programs have become a very powerful force as well. In Minnesota, the Board of Teaching reviews our programs to ensure that they meet state licensing standards, which allows us to be able to recommend candidates for teacher licensure in our state. We also undergo a voluntary review by the National Council for Accreditation of Teacher Education (NCATE) to achieve national accreditation for our programs. Additionally, our initial licensure program uses the standards created by the Interstate New Teacher Assessment and Support Consortium (INTASC), albeit not an accrediting body, to inform our curriculum. Although standards such as these are not without critique (e.g., Ladson-Billings & Darling- Hammond, 2000),[9] we are held to them, and they remain high stakes for us. Recently created FL programs now have two subject-specific standards we will use: a) INTASC Foreign Language Standards (INTASC, 2002) and b) ACTFL (2002) standards for FL teacher preparation.[10] FL programs that require accreditation through NCATE will use the new ACTFL standards starting in 2004. Standards require FL teacher candidates to have the necessary knowledge, skills, and dispositions to help their students in grades preschool through Grade 12 learn. In terms of the language proficiency of the candidate, the standards require a demonstrated *Advanced-Low* level in the language of license. In addition, TESOL (2003) recently developed standards for initial teacher preparation programs, although INTASC does not have plans to develop standards that are specifically designed for ESL teachers.[11]

---

[9]In this report, Ladson-Billings and Darling Hammond (2000) examine the research base related to effective urban teachers and find that these qualities are not well represented in the National Board of Professional Teaching Standards (NBPTS) Early Adolescent/English Language Arts assessment. In fact, NBPTS assessments have been found to have an adverse impact with respect to race. INTASC was found to have been used by too few urban teachers to draw any conclusion.

[10]ACTFL supported the INTASC Foreign Language Standards development, and these different sets of FL standards do not compete.

[11]INTASC is not currently planning to develop ESL standards. M. Jean Miller, the director of INTASC, when asked about this, stated, "If you look at our special ed standards, the ESL student is referenced and these standards generally apply to that population" (M. J. Miller, personal communication, December 3, 2001). According to their Web site, INTASC is still consistent with this position (INTASC, 2003). We view an ESL alliance with special education as problematic, and after examining the subject-specific special education standards, we are quite certain that no program that prepares ESL teachers would see them as suitable or functional.

Standards such as these are important for maintaining quality programs, promoting opportunities for teachers' professional growth, and discouraging rogue programs; however, they do put additional burdens on colleges of education as they prepare for the review. Snow (chap. 14, this volume) makes the important point that both teachers and teacher educators are challenged by this dizzying collection of standards in this era of accountability, and we agree—the sheer volume of standards is overwhelming. At the same time, we believe that this work is warranted because it adds status to our programs and is beneficial to the profession.

Dealing With Demanding Logistics That Accompany Integrated Programs

As described previously, our integrated preservice program prepares teachers for FL and/or ESL licensure, both of which are K–12 in Minnesota and require student teaching at both elementary and secondary levels. We have just one academic year to incorporate student teaching in four separate placements (for those seeking dual licensure) all while the beginning teachers are enrolled in full-time graduate course work. Scheduling the placements is one issue; finding enough placements with outstanding teachers is another. On average, with 30 students in the program and approximately two thirds of them working toward licensure in both ESL and an FL, we have 100 placements to secure each year (4 placements for each of 20 dual licensure candidates and 2 placements for each single licensure candidate). Each year it seems more and more difficult to find the outstanding teachers willing to take on the role of mentor, and we often have to compromise in the process. Our students, then, at times become torn between what we emphasize in the program (e.g., content-based instruction, use of the target language, performance assessment, etc.) and what they see happening in real classrooms.

Logistical concerns are also present for the endorsement programs we offer for inservice teachers. Although the initial licensure program is well supported institutionally with graduate assistant supervisors hired to support students through long-term mentoring, the inservice program does not have this type of support. In this program, supervisors meet with the teacher who is seeking the endorsement only two or three times, and the meetings tend to be more evaluative rather than opportunities to engage in reflective dialogue or mentoring. When a program serves as many contexts as ours, it is necessary to make difficult choices in allocating resources.

Keeping Pace With Politics and Choosing Where to Put Our Energy

Perhaps never before has it been more important to develop deep understandings about the impact of political decisions on language education and to become a strong advocate for the field. When a program serves many L2 contexts, the expectation is that we will be involved in key decision-making efforts and advocacy, but which political issues? For whom and how do we best advocate? Where do we put our energy? How do we choose?

In Minnesota, let alone at the national level, there are numerous issues that vie for the support of the L2 professional community. High stakes basic skills tests required for graduation make it difficult for many ESL learners to earn a high school diploma. ESL learners are at best an afterthought in the state's many attempts to develop standards for public schools and to meet the national call for accountability measures. As mentioned previously, FL has been left out of state standards in Minnesota (despite FL being recognized as a core academic subject in the federal No Child Left Behind Act). Immersion schools are under pressure to introduce English instruction earlier on because of state and federally mandated testing in third grade in English. Despite what we know about the importance of native language instruction for minority language learners, bilingual education has never received widespread support in the state, perhaps even less so now in the current national political climate (in spite of ever-increasing numbers of minority language learners). Severe state and local budget crises are leading schools to drop Foreign Language in the Elementary School (FLES) programs left and right. It seems that the past few years have brought too many invitations to serve and critical calls for support to count.

To advocate strongly for all L2 education contexts and to address the many issues that emerge in the political arena would be a full time job. Again, we have to choose our battles and determine how best to maximize our efforts.

Creating a Balance Between Respecting Individual Contexts and Finding Common Ground

A final challenge that arises from combining FL and L2 contexts in teacher education is one of creating and maintaining balance between acknowledging and respecting the unique needs and characteristics of the various teaching contexts while at the same time helping teachers to find common ground across their respective teaching contexts. Contextual difference is a reality. We know, for example, that elementary ESL teaching in a broad sense is different from adult ESL and different from high school FL teaching or FLES. Further, we know that vast contextual differences exist within each L2 context. For example, immersion programs vary enormously depending on a wide range of factors. Swain and Johnson (1997) developed a valuable framework for understanding commonalities and differences among immersion programs with their identification of core features that define immersion programs and variable features that differentiate them from one another. Walker and Tedick (2000) further identified what they called the "microcontexts" of immersion education related to schools (e.g., communities in which they are situated, the make-up of the staff, resources available), teachers (e.g., backgrounds, philosophies, language proficiency), and students (e.g., ethnic and socioeconomic diversity, proficiencies in L1 and L2, etc.).

Therefore, contextual differences are very real and as teacher educators, we must be ever mindful and respectful of those differences as we help teachers to understand them as well, particularly as they apply to research.[12] It is important to help teachers understand, for example, why language majority learners in immersion programs can successfully learn how to read through an L2, whereas L1 (native) instruction for initial literacy is recommended whenever possible for language minority learners.

At the same time, we have developed our programs with the epistemological assumption that the different L2 teaching contexts share important commonalities, one of the most powerful being our love for languages and cultures and belief in the benefits of bilingualism or multilingualism. The rewards of highlighting the commonalities we share and learning from each other's respective contexts have been discussed at length here. What is key is that we maintain a healthy balance between the common ground that unites us and the differences that make us distinct.

CONCLUSION

In this chapter, we have identified a number of rewards and challenges that accompany teacher education that combines FL and L2 contexts. We believe the rewards of an integrated language teacher education program such as ours greatly outweigh the challenges. The advantage of carrying out teacher education with teachers from such a wide range of

---

[12]Bernhardt and Tedick (1991) provide a discussion on the importance of context in interpreting L2 research results. Bernhardt and Tedick (1991) argued that "when research findings generated within one paradigm are applied to a setting that does not fit that first paradigm, serious misuse of the research findings is the result" (p. 58).

backgrounds enriches their experience in our programs. We have found that it provides all teachers with a broader view of the many circumstances in which classroom language learning occurs. It allows them to see that they are not alone in the desire to promote in their students bilingualism, cross-cultural understanding, broadened world views, and access to education. They are able to seek alliances and find collegiality among their peers. Professionally, this is very positive as it helps teachers understand their various roles in schools and in society. Through this understanding, L2 teachers are better able to advocate for their programs and their learners.

REFERENCES

American Council on the Teaching of Foreign Languages. (1996). *Standards for foreign language learning*. Yonkers, NY: Author.

American Council on the Teaching of Foreign Languages. (2002). *Program standards for the preparation of foreign language teachers.* Yonkers, NY: Author.

Bernhardt, E. B., & Tedick, D. J. (1991). On paradoxes and paradigms in language education research. In E. S. Silber (Ed.), *Critical issues in foreign language instruction* (pp. 43–62). New York: Garland.

Bigelow, M., & Ranney, S. (2001, May). *Learning how to keep the language focus in content-based instruction.* Paper presented at the International Conference on Language Teacher Education, Minneapolis, MN.

Breiner-Sanders, K. E., Lowe, P., Miles, J., & Swender, E. (2000). ACTFL proficiency guidelines—Speaking. Revised 1999. *Foreign Language Annals, 33*(1), 13–18.

Cummins, J. (1980). The entry and exit fallacy in bilingual education. *NABE Journal, 4,* 25–60.

Day, E. M., & Shapson, S. M. (1996). *Studies in immersion education.* Clevedon, England: Multilingual Matters.

Edstam, T. (2001). Perceptions of professionalism among elementary school ESL teachers. In B. Johnston & S. Irujo (Eds.), *Research and practice in language teacher education: Voices from the field* (pp. 233–249). Minneapolis: University of Minnesota, Center for Advanced Research on Language Acquisition.

Genesee, F. (1992). Second/foreign language immersion and at-risk English-speaking children. *Foreign Language Annals, 25*(3), 199–213.

Interstate New Teacher Assessment and Support Consortium. (2002). *Model standards for licensing beginning foreign language teachers: A resource for state dialogue.* Washington, DC: Council of Chief State School Officers.

Interstate New Teacher Assessment and Support Consortium. Retrieved July 9, 2003, from http://www.ccsso.org/projects/interstate_new_teacher_ assessment_and support_consortium/

Ladson-Billings, G., & Darling-Hammond, L. (2000). *The validity of National Board for Professional Teaching Standards (NBPTS)/Interstate New Teacher Assessment and Support Consortium (INTASC) assessments for effective urban teachers: Findings and implications for assessments.* Washington, DC: National Partnership for Excellence and Accountability in Teaching.

Lindholm-Leary, K. J. (2001). *Dual language education*. Clevedon, England: Multilingual Matters.

Met, M., & Lorenz, E. B.(1997). Lessons from U.S. immersion programs: Two decades of experience. In R. K. Johnson & M. Swain (Eds.) *Immersion education: International perspectives* (pp. 243–264). New York: Cambridge University Press.

Minnesota English Language Proficiency Standards for English Language Learners. (2003). Retrieved August 16, 2003, from http://education.state.mn.us/stellent/groups/public/documents/translatedcontent/pub_028657.pdf.

Nieto, S. (2000). *Affirming diversity: The sociopolitical context of multicultural education* (3rd ed.). New York: Longman.

Schulz, R. (1991). Second language acquisition theories and teaching practice: How do they fit? *Modern Language Journal, 75*(1), 17–26.

Short, D. J. (2002). Language learning in sheltered social studies classes. *TESOL Journal, 11*, 18–24.

Snow, M. A. (2001). Content-based and immersion models for second and foreign language teaching. In M. Celce-Murcia (Ed.), *Teaching English as a second or foreign language* (3rd ed., pp. 303–318). Boston: Heinle & Heinle.

Swain, M., & Johnson, R. K. (1997). Immersion education: A category within bilingual education. In R. K. Johnson & M. Swain (Eds.), *Immersion education: International perspectives* (pp. 1–16). New York: Cambridge University Press.

Tedick, D. J., Fortune, T., & Walker, C. L. (2003, May). *The complexity of integrating language in immersion teaching*. Paper presented at the Third International Conference on Language Teacher Education, Minneapolis, MN.

Tedick, D. J., & Walker, C. L. (1994). Second language teacher education: The problems that plague us. *Modern Language Journal, 78*, 300–312.

Tedick, D. J., Walker, C. L., Lange, D. L., Paige, M., & Jorstad, H. L. (1993). Second language education in tomorrow's schools. In G. Gunterman (Ed.), *Foreign Language Education Series: ACTFL Developing language teachers for a changing world* (pp. 43–75). Lincolnwood, IL: National Textbook Company.

Teachers of English to Speakers of Other Languages. (1997). *ESL standards for pre-K–12 students*. Alexandria, VA: Author.

Teachers of English to Speakers of Other Languages. (2003). *Standards for the accreditation of initial programs in P–12 ESL teacher education*. Alexandria, VA: Author.

Walker, C. L., & Stone, K. (2003, May). *Teaming up: How rethinking staff development might serve our second language students*. Paper presented at the annual Minnesota ESL and Bilingual Education Conference, St. Paul, Minnesota.

Walker, C. L., & Tedick, D. J. (2000). The complexity of immersion education: Teachers address the issues. *Modern Language Journal, 84*, 5–27.

Chapter 18

Preparing Preservice Teachers for English Language Learners: A Content-Based Approach

Constance L. Walker
Susan Ranney
Tara W. Fortune
University of Minnesota

INTRODUCTION

Preparing teachers for an ever-changing world in education is an ongoing task. In second language teacher education in the United States, the four arenas in which we work—bilingual education, English as a second language (ESL), immersion education, and foreign languages—present a dizzying array of settings, practices, and challenges. Until recently, the majority of our professional development efforts focused on the needs of preservice and inservice second language teachers. As a result of changing demographics, we now face the task of moving beyond preparing second language teachers to preparing all teachers to address the language needs of their learners. The purpose of this chapter is to describe the evolution of a course designed to address this new teacher audience—a small course tailored to introduce preservice classroom teachers to language-sensitive instructional practices for English language learners in the Kindergarten through 12th grade (K–12) context. At the University of Minnesota, preservice teacher education is at the postbaccalaureate level and involves full-time study over a 15-month period. Teachers are prepared in specific content cohorts: elementary education and separate content areas (e.g., English literature and language arts, math, social studies) at the secondary level.[1] Second-language education is K–12 for those individuals planning to teach a foreign language and/or ESL (for a description of this preservice program, see Bigelow and Tedick, chap. 17, this volume).

Specifically, we examine the need for this introductory course both on a national and local level and its unique evolution as a cohort-based program in our institutional context. We conclude by examining what we have learned in the process of developing and teaching these courses, together with the institutional challenges inherent in making change in teacher education curriculum.

NEED FOR THE COURSE

Individuals in teacher preparation programs today will join a teaching force that finds its students to be substantially changed from years past. The single largest increasing student population in the United States is students for whom English is a second language—or, as they are sometimes called, English language learners or language minority students. Immigration continues to add to the number of American citizens whose children enter school in need of specialized English language services, and the last two decades have seen a substantial change in the populations of American classrooms in urban, suburban, and rural communities. It is estimated that 4.6 million English language learners were enrolled in school during the 2000 through 2001 school year, 9.6% of the total public school enrollment (Kindler, 2002). Growth in this population is expected to continue. These students are eligible according to law for access to English academic instruction that meets their language needs.

Yet the teaching population serving such children has often not been prepared to see themselves as responsible for nonnative English speak-

[1]The College of Education and Human Development at the University of Minnesota has a large number of preservice teacher preparation programs, most at the postbaccalaureate level. The Department of Curriculum and Instruction houses the largest number of preservice programs of any department in the college. Beginning teachers are prepared in elementary education, art, English literature/language arts, math, science, social studies, and second-language education. All of the program areas in the department (except second-language education) require this 1-credit course for their licensure candidates; however, this chapter includes discussion of a sample of them, namely, elementary education, English, math, and social studies.

ers in the classroom and thus have not been sufficiently attuned to the need to serve their language or their academic needs (Clair, 1995). Traditionally, U.S. schools have charged specialists with the task of dealing with learners who have special educational needs. These specialists work in a range of program models depending on their local context (Genesee, 1999). In a few communities, bilingual teachers or paraprofessionals provide the bridge between the home and school culture. Alternatively, ESL is offered by specially licensed individuals in the many schools with significant numbers of bilingual/ESL learners from a wide range of linguistic and cultural backgrounds. Other bilingual learners are served through federally funded programs such as Title I and Migrant Education, some inappropriately through special education programs. Although it is illegal to ignore their needs, many school districts today do not serve the full number of language minority students identified.

Given the increase in numbers of school-age children needing access to English and the dearth of teachers available to meet both their first language and second language-specific instructional needs, grade level teachers at the elementary level and content-area teachers at the secondary level are those individuals who inevitably have the greatest impact on the schooling outcomes faced by second language learners. Despite any type of program that may provide supplementary English language assistance, it is the classroom teacher who provides instruction in the students' regular school program and spends the greatest proportion of instructional time with them. In addition, grade-level and content-area teachers have come to the place where their responsibilities for ESL students are not only clearly necessary but endorsed by federal and state mandates for monitoring achievement and accountability. Finally, and most significantly, second language learners are not succeeding at school. Decades of data document school failure with language minority students (e.g., Manuel, 1930; National Center for Education Statistics, 1982, 1993; U.S. Commission on Civil Rights, 1974).

Preservice teacher education programs have on occasion addressed the needs of bilingual learners, primarily in geographic areas where population demanded such attention. In areas where language minority students have not made up a substantial portion of the total school population, such efforts have been slow to develop and have largely been left to inservice efforts at the local level.

HOW THIS COURSE EVOLVED

At the University of Minnesota during the past 20 years, little attention has been paid to ensuring that preservice teacher development included understanding of the unique challenges faced by second-language learners at school. Over the years, an occasional elementary education teacher development course might ask for a "guest speaker" to address those needs in a limited session. It was not until 2000 that the National Council for the Accreditation of Teacher Education began to press for inclusion of second language learner issues in the curriculum of teacher licensure programs. As a result, these issues might begin to appear in a text chosen for preparing for teaching reading, for example, or a small chapter in a special education unit within a foundations course would address the nature of language learning for bilingual students or the particular strategies teachers might use to help with newcomers to the classroom who knew no English.

There seemed to be a belief that such information was not necessary for all teachers but rather simply for those who might teach in urban populations and who could learn "on the job." There is also an ongoing consensus that there is no "room" in an already crowded teacher development curriculum for any additional coursework and/or content. It is important to note that the tradition of change in teacher education in Minnesota (and nationally, there are many similar stories) is one of responding to reform efforts and legislative mandates by simply adding another piece to the tail of the dog. For example, as drug and alcohol awareness and instruction was mandated, a small course was added. Federal Law 94–142 (1975), Education for All Students With Disabilities Act, brought the addition of the special education piece. In fact, two systematic restructurings of the foundations courses in the College of Education and Human Development at University of Minnesota between the years 1985 and 1995 did not result in a corresponding recognition that the needs of second language learners would play a significant role in the teaching lives of Minnesota teachers despite national predictions to the contrary and record numbers of new immigrants to the state during the 1990s.

The College has had a traditionally strong Second Languages and Cultures (SLC) area within Curriculum and Instruction that has prepared teachers for second language teaching settings (both preservice and inservice education), and the staff has had extensive experience working with elementary teachers. This program, in fact, has been recognized as distinct in its structure and efforts to prepare educators for diverse student populations (Gonzalez & Darling-Hammond, 1997). Yet not until 2000 did the College approach SLC staff about the possibility of instituting a small course for preservice teachers addressing the needs of ESL learners. Prior to this, various attempts to argue for need and centrality of this issue in preservice K–12 teacher education were rebuffed. Ultimately, it was the preservice teachers themselves who repeatedly expressed frustration about their lack of preparedness for this growing student audience that got the attention of teacher education faculty. Even so, the College's Council on Teacher Education voted not to require a special course for all preservice teachers, with council members arguing that the curriculum lacked room for such an addition, that any available credits might better be used in other ways "foundational," and that an occasional chapter in a foundations course taught by a nonexpert in second-language issues would suffice. Nevertheless, teacher educators in Curriculum and Instruction, where most of the primary content areas of public school curriculum are housed (see endnote 1), decided to require such a course for their preservice teachers.

Hamayan (1990) called for the curriculum of teacher development programs to include one course in the education of linguistically diverse students and argued that the entire preservice curriculum should be addressed, even if briefly, to attend to the needs of second language learners likely to be found in the schools. "Teachers in training would not only focus on these issues in a special course but would have the opportunity to reflect on how to handle linguistically or culturally diverse students within the framework of mainstream education" (Hamayan, 1990, p. 4). In response, the SLC staff developed a course for one semester credit that would address the specific needs of preservice K–12 teachers.

Clearly, the strength of the Department of Curriculum and Instruction as a whole is its organization around content disciplines and the belief that they have their own structure, genre, and strategies for successful teaching and learning. Building on that strength, we designed a cohort model to reflect the unique needs of the various disciplines. This choice was congruent with our own philosophy that builds on the research support for linking content and language to sustain effective language development. For students whose academic success is dependent on the development not only of English but academic content knowledge at the same time, this link becomes not only effective but imperative.

Although the institutional expectation was that we would be able to create a one-size-fits-all minicourse and in large-group lecture format transmit the necessary information, we felt it essential to design this course to reflect research-based best practice and to capitalize on the department's cohort-based model tailoring both instruction and scheduling to the unique needs of each program area.

THE STRUCTURE OF THE COURSE ACROSS DISCIPLINES

Given the increased pressure for accountability for the achievement of all students including second language learners, research in second-language education, and a pressing need to assist K–12 teachers in responding to changing demographics, we began with our fundamental premise that the best teaching where second-language learners are concerned requires an effective integration of language and content. Will classroom teachers buy into this premise that they are, in fact, language teachers as well as content teachers? How can we open the door to this understanding? This was our task.

Cohort-General Course Design

As we developed the course, we focused on some basic understandings that we believe that all teachers need to work effectively with students learning in and through a second language.[2] An exploration of the following questions forms the structure of what we call the minimal elemental information necessary for introducing preservice teachers to the issues. What we wish to stress here is that these basic questions, encompassing very fundamental concepts in second language education, must be addressed within the context of particular grade levels (elementary vs. secondary) and disciplines:

1. Who are the learners (characteristics, definitions, demographics)?
2. What misconceptions might a teacher carry concerning second language learners, their language needs, and their academic growth as they learn through English?
3. What is involved in learning a second language, learning through a second language?
4. What is an optimum classroom climate and what are effective curricular and instructional practices for second language learners?

To address these broad questions, each 1-credit course contains the following:

1. Demographic information about the numbers and origins of English language learners in the United States as a whole as well as in our local area.

[2]Reference texts that inform our practice in teacher preparation for working with students learning ESL include August and Hakuta (1998); California State Department of Education (1981); Carrasquillo and Rodriguez (1996); Chamot and O'Malley (1994); Cummins (2000); Echevarria, Vogt, and Short (1999); García (1994); Richard-Amato and Snow (1992); Samway and McKeon (1999); and Snow and Brinton (1997).

2. A shock language experience in which students are asked to listen to and respond to information given in a language which few of them speak.
3. Instruction in the underlying theoretical principles related to the instruction of English language learners such as the four-quadrant model provided by Cummins (1984).[3]
4. A task comparing myths and realities surrounding immigrants in the United States.
5. Some basic cultural information about immigrant groups that teachers are likely to encounter in the area.
6. Readings on the characteristics of English language learners and best practices in instruction with them.[4]
7. A demonstration of the use of learning strategies and guidelines for instruction on learning strategies.
8. A course project that requires in-school experiences working with or observing English language learners.[5]

Whereas these areas were common across cohorts, other aspects of the course were tailored to each cohort as described following.

Cohort-Specific Course Design

Elementary Education. Elementary education teachers' experiences with ESL learners are shaped by the fact that they work with a given group of learners for all academic subjects throughout the day. Unlike secondary teachers who may work in parallel with ESL teachers, elementary teachers more often must coordinate their efforts with the ESL teacher either in pull-out models in which teachers must agree on when students will be taken out of their class for ESL services or in inclusion models in which teachers work together in the grade-level classroom (see Dubetz, chap. 13, this volume, for other descriptions of inclusion). These models

---

[3]Cummins (1984) is well known for this model, which identifies the range of contextual support and degree of cognitive involvement in communicative activities. It uses two intersecting continua to illustrate the ranges (context embedded vs. context reduced instructional situations; cognitively undemanding vs. cognitively demanding language use and instruction). The model has appeared in numerous Cummins' publications including Cummins (1982, 1984).

[4]The basic texts were divided by elementary and secondary levels: Stephen Cary's (2000) *Working With Second Language Learners: Answers to Teachers' Top Ten Questions* was used for the elementary level and Aida Walqui's (2000) *Access and Engagement: Program Design and Instructional Approaches for Immigrant Students in Secondary School* for the secondary levels.

[5]The secondary-level students are required to do 4 to 5 hr of tutoring an ESL student, whereas the elementary education students can elect to tutor a student or observe in an elementary classroom and interview a grade-level teacher about working with English language learners.

depend for their success on the collaboration between the grade-level teacher and the ESL teacher, making it very important for elementary teachers to understand and support ESL services.

Another factor shaping the elementary teacher's experience is the responsibility for all subject area instruction and especially for developing children's literacy skills. Literacy development is a special challenge for ESL learners whose progress is affected not only by their overall proficiency in the English language but also by the amount of formal schooling and initial literacy development in the native language (Collier & Thomas, 1989; Cummins, 1991).

A third consideration that makes the elementary setting unique is its emphasis on whole child development—the integration of social-emotional, linguistic, and cognitive academic learning. One teacher over the course of the academic year is responsible for the successful learning experiences of each individual learner.

With these needs in mind, we designed the elementary education sections of the course to emphasize issues related to the development of literacy in a second language, with readings, videos, and discussions geared to considering challenges and strategies for the instruction of reading and writing. The course also presents ways of enhancing instruction in general to support ESL students' success and to help develop their oral language skills. In addition, students read about and discuss different models of ESL services.

One of the major issues that concerns the elementary education students is the question of models of ESL services and how the particular model used in their school will affect them as classroom teachers. They are concerned about the limitations of pullout ESL instruction, both in terms of academic success for their students and in terms of the impact on their instructional schedules. We discuss alternative models and the importance of cooperation between the grade-level and ESL teachers. Given their exposure to research findings on the value of bilingual education (Thomas & Collier, 2002) combined with their own lack of knowledge of the languages of the major immigrant groups they are likely to teach, the elementary education cohort also expresses anxiety about their ability to provide quality education to bilingual children. To respond to this need, class discussions and handouts emphasize the importance of supporting the native language by steps such as encouraging parents to use the native language at home and finding native language books and other resources for the classroom.

Secondary Level Teachers

Secondary teachers interact with ESL students and professionals from another perspective in that their work generally runs parallel to that of

ESL teachers. As single-subject specialists, they set high priority on the content knowledge and processes of their particular discipline. They are concerned about the need to deliver effective instruction in that area, particularly with the pressure to demonstrate student performance on established subject area and graduation standards. Because of their high student load and the particular organization of most secondary schools, they may be unaware of which students in their classes that are receiving ESL services. As the needs of the language minority students become visible within secondary schools, more content teachers are enlisted to adapt their instruction to this particular population by teaching "sheltered" content courses. A sheltered learning environment allows for a group of students learning ESL to develop their content skills with additional attention paid to their language needs. This underscores the need for all content area teachers to have expertise in adapting their instruction for second language learners.

Mathematics. Given the assumption shared by math teachers as well as others that math is a language unto itself, it is often assumed that the English language proficiency of students is not as important to their success in math. Hence, even low-proficiency ESL students are often mainstreamed in math classes. Teachers need to be prepared to work with these students and they also need to understand how English language proficiency affects a student's ability to attend to the complexity of mathematical concepts and processes and complete the required work, for example, reporting on the problem-solving process and understanding story problems. With new standards for mathematics achievement, the curriculum now demands greater skill in the use of English to both comprehend and express mathematical meaning. It is no longer the case that mathematics "transcends" a need for language.

In response to these needs, preservice mathematics teachers devote a considerable amount of time examining the integrated math curriculum practiced in many schools. They also analyze math textbooks, and the instructor guides them to look for vocabulary and syntax that can be challenging to English language learners, such as passives, certain verb forms, and unusual word orders. Cultural information that is assumed but that may be new to students who are recent immigrants is focused on as well. As students examine story problems, they began to see that some background information that is essential to the problems, such as knowledge about sports that are popular in the United States, is culture specific and can pose problems to new immigrant students.

Through these activities, the math cohort begins to move away from their original belief that issues of reading and vocabulary are not in their domain. Using readings and discussion, it becomes clear that English language and literacy skills have an impact on students' ability to connect with and process new mathematical understandings and that specific attention to math vocabulary and reading strategies can benefit their ESL students. Preservice teachers are also asked to develop concrete ideas for illustrating cultural concepts that appear in particular lessons. For example, in exploring probability, many instructors use the context of basketball free throws, which might not be familiar to ESL students.

Social Studies. As a language-intense subject, social studies assumes high levels of reading and writing skills, which are not always developed in English language learners. It also depends heavily on prior knowledge, which is often highly culture specific, such as knowledge of American history and government systems. Because social studies is a core area in the secondary curriculum, social studies teachers often have students at low levels of English proficiency. Thus the gap between the language competence necessary for success in a social studies classroom and the language skills brought by ESL students can be significant.

The reading and writing demands of social studies form a focus for much of the readings and discussions in the course for the social studies cohort. In particular, the course focuses on the use of graphic organizers, prereading strategies, and ways of responding to language needs and errors in writing. The course also examines specific social studies textbooks for their linguistic and cultural challenges. Social studies assignments and assessments are examined with a view to possible modifications teachers can make to adapt them for English language learners. These principles are modeled through the use of video clips of sheltered social studies classes.

The social studies students come to the course already aware of the challenges posed by their discipline for ESL students; they identify challenges such as the comprehension of abstract concepts, the need for learning new vocabulary, the reading/writing intensive nature of the discipline, the cultural assumptions of the field, the wide variety of content, and the need for advanced oral skills in class discussions. They are very receptive to learning about strategies for facilitating the comprehension and participation of ESL students in their classes.

English Literature/Language Arts. English is in a unique position in that ESL students generally do not take English language arts until after they have exited from ESL services. For this reason, lower proficiency level students are not likely to be enrolled in the standard English curriculum until they have achieved higher levels of English proficiency. This distinguishes it from the other content areas. However, given the haste with which students are "exited" from ESL programs and the length of time it takes to develop academic literacy (Collier, 1989), most students' language needs remain significant. The challenge in working with students who no longer qualify for ESL services is that they still require a great deal of support in developing their language and literacy skills to a level at which they can participate in advanced study commensurate with their peers. Unlike other teachers who may be able to make a distinction between content knowledge and language skills, English teachers deal with language and literacy skills as their content. Given that English language study, critical analysis, literature, and writing skill development are the core of the English curriculum, it makes it impossible to, in effect, claim, "English language teaching is not my job," a refrain more likely to be heard from a math or science teacher, for example. Thus, although the level of English proficiency of English language learners in their classrooms may be higher when compared with other subject areas, the demands of English language arts in terms of language skills are also higher.

Aside from the core topics for the course, the section for English language arts majors draws heavily on texts and information used for preparing ESL teachers on the assumption that much of what they need is preparation for working on language and literacy skills. The readings and discussions focus on teaching through literature, developing vocabulary in a second language, and teaching writing as process. To introduce the types of grammatical explanations that can help English language learners edit their writing, four common error types are presented, with students asked to identify the grammatical structures involved using ESL textbooks as a resource. This reflects best practice in the preparation of teachers for meeting the needs of second language learners. As Wong-Fillmore and Snow (2000) and others suggest, teachers need to directly attend to language in their instruction, not to expect that such skill will evolve incidentally from the use of the language. The course also provides resources including references to works of literature that represent different cultures and that have been found to be powerful tools within the English classroom for both native and nonnative speaking students.

The aspect of the course that proves to be the most urgent as well as somewhat unsettling for preservice English teachers is the explanation of common ESL grammatical errors. Whereas English teachers assume that they are experts in the language and can teach writing, these preservice teachers have no background to equip them to explain many of the grammatical errors that are common to English language learners and instead are only able to identify common errors as being "awkward." Based on their preparation for working with native English speakers, they do not expect to use any explicit explanations of grammar in their teaching of writing. The course challenges this view by presenting samples of the writing of advanced ESL students with many errors to illustrate the importance of effective and focused error correction. Guidelines presented for error correction emphasize that teachers need to be selective rather than correcting all errors in any given piece of writing. These prospective teachers understand the importance of multicultural literature. After discussion of the value of specific grammatical instruction, they see the benefit of asking ESL students to focus and attend to particular aspects of the language. In reflection papers that were submitted in the course, some students express the idea that they have shifted their views from feeling that they could simply expose students to standard English and expect them to master it to understanding that the acquisition of language proficiency involves more than exposure. This is an important concept for teachers to internalize given that the research in second language education is now showing that failure to attend to the "details" of the English language results in atrophy in overall language development (Gibbons, 2002; Wong-Fillmore & Snow, 2000).

WHAT HAVE WE LEARNED?

Benefits and Limitations of the Cohort Design

Benefits. The cohort and content-area specific design described previously has many benefits, among them the following:

1. Students consistently request that the course provide practical strategies that they can use in their teaching. Although some general strategies are applicable to all levels and subjects, specific tools depend on the demands of the subject and the age of the student. Because we divide the group into subject-specific cohorts, we are able to address those needs.
2. We are able to assign readings that are directly relevant to students' needs. The general text used for the secondary-level groups is written for that level, whereas the text used for the elementary education students focuses on classroom examples at the elementary level. Supplemental articles for each cohort focus specifically on the needs of each subject area and level.
3. We are able to choose video segments that directly relate to the students' teaching areas. If the course were to include mixed cohorts, we would need to omit the video clips or we would be unable to show clips that correspond to their specific teaching context.

4. We utilize specific materials from actual classrooms. The math, science, and social studies classes use samples from textbooks in those fields, permitting us to cite specific examples of language structure and use within the discipline.

5. Because students know their classmates and share common goals and experiences, class discussions can comfortably explore more content-specific issues than would be possible in a large class of heterogeneous students.

Limitations. In addition to the benefits, a number of limitations arise from the cohort, content-area specific design:

1. One credit does not allow for the time or investment to go into any of these topics in detail. Although we are able to give background and cover a wide range of strategies for instruction that have been determined to be "best practice," the time limitation simply prevents the kind of exploration that the discipline requires. (Indeed, within a year-long second languages teacher development program, we lament the lack of time necessary to understand the complexity of both theory and practice—a mere 1-credit course begins to tap this field.) Areas that need more attention include assessment, cultural issues, working with parents and the community, advocacy, and collaboration.

2. The development of separate courses for particular content areas is a formidable task.

3. The course is added on to an already crowded schedule, and students are sometimes tired and resentful about spending more time in classes. Furthermore, some students resent the imposition of perceived extra demands on their future jobs so as to accommodate English language learners in their classes.

4. Students bring along the class dynamics and subcultures of their areas. As a cohort, they have had months of exposure to each other as peers—the instructor is the newcomer bringing challenging (and sometimes unwelcome) information about yet another new dimension of teaching. Some do not welcome any direct instruction; some receive instruction with a critical posture. Any general strategies we present for teaching English language learners that are similar to those used with native speakers are sometimes seen as information that they have already been exposed to.

Institutional Barriers

No matter the national or local need for teachers to understand the needs of their students learning ESL it is no simple matter to move in that direction in a teacher development program. Even given experienced faculty specifically knowledgeable in this area there is no guarantee that the institution will open itself to the conceptual restructuring necessary to carry out such a task. There are several reasons for this situation.

The Conflicted Social Context of Race, Language, and Culture. Were it a simple matter of recognizing that teachers need particular new skills at the preservice level, curriculum change might well occur through the natural course of evolution toward what is termed to be best practice in preparing teachers for particular fields. As research in education has illuminated the intricacy of learning particular content, such information, we would hope, finds its way to the preparation of teachers. For example, we would be hard pressed to find teacher development programs that do not touch on the importance of inquiry learning or cooperative group structures for science. Yet concerning students acquiring English at school, it has been particularly difficult for the field of second language education to convey to our colleagues in other educational fields the importance of meeting these learners where they are. Seventy years of data on the dropout rates of Latino students and decades of reports of school failure have seemingly not made the case for an improvement in the preparation of all teachers. The difficulties of addressing ethnicity, language, and culture at school have long been part of American educational history. Today, preparing individuals to teach in schools with diverse student populations is a pressing concern in education, and given the quantity of volumes on the topic produced by major publishers, it does not lack for immediacy or impact. Still, the underlying cultural predisposition to argue for assimilation for ethnic and linguistically diverse groups often produces the following question: "Is this really necessary?"

The "Special Needs" Umbrella. As the terms *diversity, diverse student population*, and *at risk* have come to be part of the educational lexicon, they have included English language learners under that rubric. Lumped with learners having special needs, second language learners have in many cases been seen as needing special education to remediate their language difficulties. This unfortunate situation has confused language difference with language disability (Fradd & Larrinaga-McGhee, 1994; Hamayan & Damico, 1991), resulted in countless examples of misplacement and misunderstanding of learner strengths and needs, and created the assumption that what serves as best practice for one field is automatically the case for the other. It categorizes second language learners as special education students, confusing unique characteristics of language acquisition with a range and variety of "disabilities." With this as a background, it is no wonder that any attempt to focus the attention of preservice teachers on bilingual learners is met with resistance.

The Economy of Scale. The transmission model of education extends to practice in teacher development when the need to address second language learners' issues is seen as necessitating nothing more than a lecture session or two with readings to accompany them. Given the institutional interest in maximizing efficiency, larger groupings for this purpose make sense in terms of resources. We have found that the smaller the conversation group around issues of ESL students, the more successful the teacher preparation will be. Time for an interactive presentation style together with small group activities and small group question and answer sessions produces a climate for addressing both the underlying social and political issues at work in schools as well as the unique needs of second language learners. Most important, such a structure supports what we know to be effective in professional teacher development (Darling-Hammond, 1994).

The Difficulties of a Short-Term Class Structure. The limitations of time plague us all. However, when the need for preservice teachers to understand concepts of second language acquisition and apply such information to their own practice is so great, the limitations of a minicourse are apparent. Simply put, a 1-credit course is a low status piece. When such a course addresses those sensitive issues that at their root have to do with identity, language, immigration, and race relations, the ground is fertile for skepticism that such information is necessary for effective teaching. When the principles and strategies of best practice for second language learners are major objectives, the limited time period often precludes addressing the full range of both. In addition, the combination of lack of time and large cohorts prevents the development of a rapport between instructors and the preservice teachers.

We notice that once we begin to address those practices specific to literacy instruction or the social studies classroom, for example, preservice teachers will sometimes argue that they have "already done that." The resistance to revisit a strategy with a particular focus on the ESL learner reflects students' unwillingness to critically reexamine their teaching with a different lens and from a different vantage point.

In fact, it is reflective of a "coverage model" within education itself—"we've already been there, done that. On to the next topic."

Given the time for development and preparation for the elementary and secondary content-specific areas, the issues of economy of scale and the short-term nature of the class combine to create yet another difficulty—the lack of recognition that each separate area requires unique readings, content, and orientation to the specific content-area groups. For administrative purposes, a course bearing the same course number yet multiple sections directed toward different teaching areas is still one course—three such sections combine to form a standard course (regardless of their different audiences and content material). Given that there are no institutional incentives for collaboration to create content-specific courses, the tendency of teacher education programs to consider a generic offering with respect to ESL students is understandable.

WHAT KEY INSIGHTS DO WE FEEL MAKE A DIFFERENCE?

During the course of teaching multiple four-session sections of the class to the elementary education cohorts, a few essential awakenings in the students' understanding of English language learners and their issues repeatedly surface as key to improving teacher practice. Because of the relatively short amount of instructional time, the course designers elect to focus efforts on dispelling potential myths and misconceptions and providing these preservice teachers with a number of research-based principles from which to make decisions once they are actually in the classroom. It has been a learning experience for both teacher educators and teachers to find that certain insights and understandings are perceived to be particularly powerful: for example, (a) research findings on the time it takes before an English language learner is capable of demonstrating academic achievement on standardized assessments; and (b) the difference between being conversationally proficient in informal, linguistically undemanding situations versus being academically literate and able to function in more formal, linguistically demanding settings. These are key concepts that are new to these preservice teachers and that we might expect to be unfamiliar to them.

Others insights have surprised us. For example, often these preservice teachers begin the sessions expressing concern and frustration regarding their need to adapt their instruction for yet another learner group with unique and special educational needs. Over the course of the four sessions, however, they come to understand that most instructional modifications for English language learners serve to enrich the learning environment for all students. In other words, teaching and learning is not a zero-sum game. It is not a matter of attending to one group of learners at the expense of another. Believing that making changes to one's instructional practices will benefit the whole group enables the teachers to view English language learners in their classrooms as assets, not detriments to the teaching and learning they are committed to facilitating. On several occasions the teachers have commented that many of the strategies modeled in the instructional videos and discussed in the readings seem to reflect best practice generally. Differentiating between good teaching and good teaching for students learning through a second language is difficult at times. It is important, however, to call attention to the reality that although good teaching is always preferred practice regardless of the learner's linguistic and cultural background, good teaching is a sine qua non for the educational success of students learning through a second language.

Another one of the more surprising insights into effective practices for English language learners is an understanding that use of a students' first language both at home and at school can actually serve as an important bridge to the acquisition of English. Initially the majority of these preservice elementary teachers assume that the quicker a child uses English exclusively the better. Research that points to the positive effect of schooling in one's first language and the importance of native language literacy development raises many questions about the current state of educational practice in the United States. Inevitably, several of the course participants ask, "If research has clearly demonstrated the difference this makes, why are so few educational resources allocated to implementing programs that do this?" (A good question, indeed!) This question requires discussing social perceptions of language in the United States and perspectives on bilingualism. After we discuss various obstacles such as finding licensed teachers and appropriate materials and resources in all the different languages U.S. schools encounter, we follow up with a rich discussion and brainstorming session devoted to how teachers can proactively support their English language learners' use of their first language within and outside of the classroom. Suggestions include helping parents understand their role in maintaining and developing their child's thinking skills in their first language and allowing peers with similar language backgrounds to work together and use their first language as needed to develop conceptual understandings of the topic at hand as well as to support comprehension of instructional tasks and procedures. Conscious fostering of a child's first language use as an important vehicle to accessing academic success in the second language seems counterintuitive. Moving these predominantly monolingual preservice teachers to appreciate the role of first-language development in second-language acquisition and academic success is a significant step.

Often the participants express genuine fears about not being able to understand or communicate with their students. These fears appear to fuel a perception that a language other than English in our English-medium schools is the problem. To address the language-as-problem perception, schools frequently pull those who have this "problem" out of the classroom and place them in a separate environment that is focused primarily on fixing their language problem. They do this by providing the students with English language development support with the aim of moving students from their first language to English as quickly as possible. Helping these teachers understand that language is not a problem but rather can be considered a resource they can use to support the educational success of their students is both new and exciting. The need for educators to consider language as a resource rather than a problem has long been heralded in literature on bilingualism and bilingual education (e.g., Anderson & Boyer, 1970; Ruíz, 1984), yet both institutionally as well as within classrooms, "problematization" still remains the single most formidable obstacle to optimal instruction for bilingual learners.

Another important awareness for these teachers is how easy it is to mistake communicative fluency and well-developed word-calling skills for academic literacy and solid concept comprehension skills. Participants are provided with a couple of language shock experiences in which they are exposed to oral and written activities carried out in a second language. These experiences lay the foundation for understanding how easy it can sometimes be to participate in a group activity by taking your cues from your peers even though you understand little to nothing of what is being said. Likewise, proficient decoders are able to "read" text and even answer a series of simple text comprehension questions without drawing any real meaning whatsoever. On the heels of observing an English language learner in an elementary setting, the students reflect on how easy it is to assume that the child is lazy or lacking in motivation because he or she is oftentimes more than capable of using English with his or her friends and seems able to communicate his or her needs with ease. Understanding the key difference between social and academic literacies as well as decoding versus reading comprehension makes an impact.

Hamayan (1990) identifies the role of the K–12 teacher as significant in multiple ways. The two most important among them include serving as a mediating agent of content as well as a facilitator of English language development. Have preservice teachers been prepared to assume these dual roles? If content is the ideal medium for teaching language in a language classroom, then elementary and secondary content teachers are an untapped language teaching resource in our schools. Thus, in addition to preparing teachers in our own fields for this endeavor, it seems increasingly important to embrace the task of making sure that school staff K–12 have the necessary background to work with second language learners in their classrooms.

The issues are indeed complex and comprehensive. How can we prepare teachers to meet the needs of so many young people who yearn to learn and learn English in our public schools? Our attempt to begin this process with our own teacher education candidates has been a learning experience for all. In attempting to utilize best practice in our own teaching while at the same time encourage best practice for work with second language learners and respect the unique nature of teacher preparation within a cohort model, we have encountered a significant challenge. The critical academic needs of literally millions of our nation's children make it imperative that we try our best. We hope that sharing one program's struggle through the process of addressing this need will be of value to teacher educators who face a similar need to respond to this call.

REFERENCES

Anderson, T., & Boyer, M. (1970). *Bilingual schooling in the United States.* Washington, DC: U.S. Government Printing Office.

August, D., & Hakuta, K. (Eds.). (1998). *Educating language minority children.* Washington, DC: National Academy Press.

California State Department of Education. (1981). *Schooling and language minority students: A theoretical framework.* Los Angeles: Evaluation, Dissemination and Assessment Center, California State University, Los Angeles.

Carrasquillo, A. L., & Rodriguez, V. (1996). *Language minority students in the mainstream classroom.* Clevedon, England: Multilingual Matters.

Cary, S. (2000). *Working with second language learners: Answers to teachers' top ten questions.* Portsmouth, NH: Heinemann.

Chamot, A., & O'Malley, J. M. (1994). *The CALLA handbook. Implementing the cognitive academic language learning approach.* Reading, MA: Addison-Wesley.

Clair, N. (1995). Mainstream teachers and ESL students. *TESOL Quarterly, 29,* 189–196.

Collier, V. P. (1989). Age and rate of acquisition of second language for academic purposes. *TESOL Quarterly, 21,* 617–641.

Collier, V. P., & Thomas, W. P. (1989). How quickly can immigrants become proficient in school English? *Journal of Educational Issues of Language Minority Students, 5,* 26–38.

Cummins, J. (1982, February). Tests, achievement, and bilingual students. *FOCUS, 9,* 1–7.

Cummins, J. (1984). *Bilingualism and special education: Issues in assessment and pedagogy.* San Diego: College-Hill.

Cummins, J. (1991). Interdependence of first- and second-language proficiency in bilingual children. In E. Bialystok (Ed.), *Language processing in bilingual children* (pp. 70–89). Cambridge, England: Cambridge University Press.

Cummins, J. (2000). *Language, power and pedagogy: Bilingual children in the crossfire*. Clevedon, England: Multilingual Matters.

Darling-Hammond, L. (Ed.). (1994). *Professional development schools: Schools for developing a profession*. New York: Teachers College Press.

Echevarria, J., Vogt, M., & Short, D. (1999). *Making content comprehensible to English language learners: The SIOP Model*. Needham Heights, MA: Allyn & Bacon.

Fradd, S. H., & Larrinaga-McGee, P. (1994). *Instructional assessment: An integrative approach to evaluating student performance*. Reading, MA: Addison-Wesley.

García, E. (1994). *Understanding and meeting the challenge of student diversity*. Boston: Houghton Mifflin.

Genesee, F. (Ed.). (1999). Program alternatives for linguistically diverse students (Educational Practice Rep. No. 1). Santa Cruz, CA: Center for Research on Education, Diversity & Excellence.

Gibbons, P. (2002). *Scaffolding language, scaffolding learning: Teaching second language learners in the mainstream classroom*. Portsmouth, NH: Heinemann.

Gonzalez, J. M., & Darling-Hammond, L. (1997). *New concepts for new challenges: Professional development for immigrant youth*. McHenry, IL, and Washington, DC: Center for Applied Linguistics.

Hamayan, E. V. (1990). *Preparing mainstream classroom teachers to teach potentially English proficient students*. Proceedings of the First Research Symposium on Limited English Proficient Student Issues, Office of Bilingual Education and Minority Langauge Affairs, U. S. Department of Education. Retrieved August 2, 2003, from http://www.ncela.gwu.edu/ncbepubs/symposia/first/preparing.htm

Hamayan, E. V., & Damico, J. S. (1991). *Limiting bias in the assessment of bilingual students*. Austin, TX: PRO-ED.

Kindler, A. (2002). Survey of the states' limited English proficient students and available educational programs and services 2000–2001 summary report. Retrieved October 11, 2003 from National Clearinghouse for English Language Acquisition http://www.ncela.gwu.edu/ncbepubs/reports/index.htm

Manuel, H. T. (1930). *The education of Spanish speaking children in Texas*. Austin: University of Texas Press.

National Center for Education Statistics. (1982). *Hispanic students in American high schools: Background characteristics and achievement*. Washington, DC: US Department of Health, Education, and Welfare.

National Center for Education Statistics. (1993). *The condition of education*. Washington, DC: US Department of Health, Education, and Welfare. NCES Number: 93290.

Public Law 94-142: The Education of All Handicapped Children Act (1975). Section 612(5)B.

Richard-Amato, P., & Snow, M. (1992). Strategies for content-area teachers. In P. Richard-Amato & M. Snow (Eds.), *The multicultural classroom: Readings for content-area teachers* (pp. 300–315). Reading, MA: Addison-Wesley.

Ruíz, R. (1984). Orientations in language planning. *NABE Journal 8*(2), 15–34.

Samway, K. D., & McKeon, D. (1999). *Myths and realities: Best practices for language minority students*. Portsmouth, NH: Heinemann.

Snow, M. A., & Brinton, D. M. (Eds.). (1997). *The content-based classroom: Perspectives on integrating language and content*. White Plains, NY: Longman.

Thomas, W., & Collier, V. (2002). A national study of school effectiveness for language minority students' long-term academic achievement. Retrieved February 13, 2000 from Center for Research on Education, Diversity & Excellence Web site: http://www.crede. ucsc.edu/research/llaa/1.1_final.html

U. S. Commission on Civil Rights. (1974). *Toward quality education for Mexican Americans. Report VI: Mexican American education study.* Washington, DC: Author.

Walqui, A. (2000). *Access and engagement: Program design and instructional approaches for immigrant students in secondary school.* McHenry, IL: Center for Applied Linguistics and Delta Systems.

Wong-Fillmore, L., & Snow, C. (2000). *What teachers need to know about language.* ERIC Clearinghouse on Languages and Linguistics, Special Report. Washington, DC: Center for Applied Linguistics. Retrieved June 13, 2003 from http://www.cal.org/resources/teachers/teachers.pdf

Author Index

Subject Index

A

B

C

P

R

S

U

V

W